ADVANCED OPTIONS TRADING

The Analysis and Evaluation of Trading Strategies, Hedging Tactics and Pricing Models

Robert T. Daigler

McGraw-Hill

New York San Francisco Washington, D.C. Auckland Bogotá
Caracas Lisbon London Madrid Mexico City Milan
Montreal New Delhi San Juan Singapore
Sydney Tokyo Toronto

McGraw-Hill

A Division of The **McGraw·Hill** *Companies*

ISBN 1-55738-552-1

Printed in the United States of America

BB

5 6 7 8 9 0

DEDICATION

To my family and friends
Especially to my daughters Wendy and Shaina
And to my wife Joyce

IN MEMORIUM

To Charles Ascencio
An Honest Person, a Patriot,
A Unique Individual who was enthusiastic about life
Why do the good ones die young?

Contents

4 Option Pricing Sensitivities and Pricing Evidence 117

5 Option Strategies: Speculating and Spreading   159

6 Hedging with Options   207

7   Options on Futures   237

8   Currency Options   259

9   Financial Engineering: Synthetic Instruments and Exotic Options   283

Preface

Unfortunately, there is no magic way to earn a million dollars in options markets without knowledge of what will happen to the underlying asset. However, this book shows how these markets are best used when the speculator has information (or strong beliefs) about the security or index being priced by the options contract. Perhaps more important, this book examines how to manage risk by using options contracts. A speculator is willing to increase risk in order to obtain a higher return. A pension fund or company treasurer often wants to decrease risk by hedging. Investment managers are willing to take risk-free profits above the T-bill interest rate by engaging in arbitrage transactions. Therefore, risk management becomes a key focus in the use of options contracts.

Today's option trader must be able to use all of the tools available to obtain the desired risk and reward combination consistent with the needs of the trader/hedger. This book is written to provide the tools necessary for successful trading and hedging in options markets. The goals of this book are:

- To provide a thorough, informative, and accurate guide to the concepts, empirical evidence and applications of financial futures markets.

- To show how options markets are employed to adjust the risk and return characteristics of a portfolio.

The topics in this book examine the important aspects of the financial futures markets, including speculative and hedging strategies, the pricing of options, the option sensitivities, and how options are traded on the option trading floor (arbitrage). The orientation employed here is geared toward *understanding* how these markets work and how they can be used.

In addition to the readability and thorough presentation of the material (including numerous examples, exhibits, and tables), this book has three unique characteristics:

- Two and three-dimensional graphs provide insights into how options relationships work, especially the option sensitivities.

- Discussion of PC computer programs for options show a trader or hedger how to best use a PC in conjunction with trading.

- Discussion of empirical evidence shows which strategies have been successful in the past and which have not, as well as the accuracy of option pricing models.

Those wanting basic PC programs for option pricing and options sensitivities can contact the author for information on these programs. Additional information is provided in a full page description of these models elsewhere in this book.

Acknowledgements

The quality of the options material in this book has been improved immeasurably by the generosity of Mark Rubinstein. When I was a Visiting Scholar at Stanford, Mark Rubinstein graciously allowed me to attend his graduate class offered by The University of California, Berkeley. His insights into the options markets helped me to solidify my presentation of options markets. In addition, his organization of the material and presentation of notes to the class ranks him as the best instructor I know. These notes are the source of many of the option tables on prices used here. Mark also provided me with a beta version of his PC software "Options and Futures Simulator" to create the three-dimensional graphs, many of the two-dimensional options graphs, and printouts of screens in the program. All of this material is referenced in the book. This material has allowed me to bring two tools to the study of options: three-dimensional surface graphs to help explain complicated relationships and sophisticated PC programs that bring reality to the finance topics. I greatly appreciate Mark's generosity.

There are many other individuals who have helped improve the quality, readability, and completeness of this book. Reviewers of this book noted important areas for improvement and clarification. Officials at the exchanges and financial institutions graciously provided information and ideas concerning the markets that helped to make this book more relevant to the users. Finally, my experiences as a Visiting Scholar at the Graduate School of Business at Stanford allowed me to clarify issues related to options markets and how models are employed on Wall Street. The gracious hospitality provided by the faculty at Stanford is appreciated and will remain a fond memory. I thank all of the above individuals, but retain the responsibility for the mistakes contained here.

My contacts and the exchanges and institutions who helped me in many respects to find important information are:

Patrick Catania	The Chicago Board of Trade
Ted Doukas	The Chicago Board of Trade
Ira Kawaller	The Chicago Mercantile Exchange

William Mullen	Loomis-Sayles, Inc.
Todd Petzel	The Chicago Mercantile Exchange
Mark Powers	Powers Research Inc. and *The Journal of Futures Markets*
Juliet Reinert	The Chicago Board of Trade
Joseph Sweeney	The Chicago Board of Trade

Those who read this book and provided helpful advice are:

Amy Adams	Templeton Worldwide Inc.
Robert E. Brooks	The University of Alabama
Anthony F. Herbst	The University of Texas, El Paso
Avraham Kamara	The University of Washington
Rohinton M. Karanjia	Fordham University
George W. Kutner	Marquette University
Renee Schwartz	previously, American Express
Joseph D. Vu	DePaul University

There are many individuals at Stanford University to whom I owe a debt of gratitude and thanks. All of the faculty and staff were very kind to me during my stay at Stanford as a Visiting Scholar. In particular, I would like to thank the following: Darrell Duffie, Allan Kleidon, Anne Peck, Paul Pfleiderer, and Kenneth Singleton.

Last, but certainly not least, are those who helped me obtain information, prepare the manuscript, and make typing corrections. Many student assistants worked long and hard for slave wages, while Ruth Chapman helped to make corrections.

Finally, I would like to thank my family for enduring yet another book. Shaina, my lovable seven-year-old, had a particularly difficult time understanding why her dad was always at the computer.

Robert T. Daigler
Miami, Florida

Quotations and Characteristics of Stock Options | 1

Options contracts possess characteristics that are beneficial to both specula-tors and hedgers. A major advantage of options is that they alter the risk-return characteristics of a portfolio. Thus, speculators who buy options obtain substantial leverage with a minimal cash investment while having a maximum potential loss equal to the cost of the option. Hedgers reduce the risk of owning a cash instrument by using options, or they can increase their total portfolio returns by selling options. In general, options provide profit distributions different from those obtained by either owning stocks or trading in futures contracts.

A call option gives the buyer the *right* to purchase a stock at a fixed price for a specific period of time. Speculators who purchase call options typically expect that the price of the underlying stock will increase. A put option gives the buyer the right to *sell* the stock at a fixed price for a specific period of time. The buyer of the put typically expects that the stock price will decline.

The profits or losses a speculator obtains from buying and holding an option until it expires depend on the fixed ("exercise") price of the option, the stock price, and the cost of the option. Payoff diagrams help illustrate the relationships among these variables.

Another form of a stock option is a stock index option, which is an option on a popular portfolio of stocks, such as the S&P 100 Index. Index options are equivalent to individual stock options, except that index options are settled in cash at the expiration date, while stock options are settled by delivering the stock.

OPTIONS MARKETS AND CONTRACTS

Why Do Options Markets Exist?

Option contracts exist because they provide unique risk-return choices for speculators and hedgers. In particular, options markets are employed:

- To adjust the risk and return of a position at a minimum cost.

- To hedge both price and quantity risk—that is, options are preferable to futures markets when the quantity one wishes to hedge is uncertain.

Speculators often prefer options to other speculative instruments because options provide large returns when the forecast of asset movements is correct, while limiting the loss to the cost of the option when the forecast is incorrect. In addition, the cost of "playing the game" is often only a few hundred dollars. Hedgers like options because the cost of the hedge is known when the hedge is initiated, and no additional funds are needed throughout the hedge.

The consequence of having an options market is that speculators accept risk for the chance for a large profit, while hedgers reduce their risk to obtain a more stable return on assets. This *risk transfer* has made options markets popular for both individuals and financial institutions. In addition, the options markets provide *price discovery* for the underlying asset, since the liquidity and low cost of many options cause traders to enter the options market before trading in the underlying asset.[1] Unlike futures markets, options also provide price discovery for *volatility*. Options include a time value in their cost that reflects the volatility of the asset. Thus, when expectations concerning a change in volatility occur, the price of the option changes. All of these factors make options an important and interesting market.

History of Options Markets

Option trading can be traced back to the 1600s, when the Dutch traded options on tulips. Tulip bulbs were traded as a speculative commodity by many of the Dutch, with prices reaching 1,000 times their true value. Tulip growers sold options which allowed the buyers to profit if prices declined. When prices did fall, the growers went bankrupt without fulfilling the option contracts, giving options a bad name. In the 1900s, overseas traders reintroduced put and call options, but they manipulated their prices based on placing rumors. Trading in options was banned in England, especially in the 1930s and from World War II until 1956. In the United States, options traded in the streets of Chicago on an illegal basis. In 1934, the Options Dealers Association was established, although trading volume was thin and options cost 30% more than their fair value.

Modern Options Markets

Stock options, as we know them today, started to trade in April 1973 on the Chicago Board Options Exchange (CBOE). Prior to that time, options were created by option dealers. These pre-1973 "Over-the-Counter" (OTC) options were very expensive, almost impossible to resell before they expired, and usually structured to take advantage of the six-month capital gains tax laws. CBOE-traded options possess several important advantages over the OTC options. In particular,

- The CBOE options have *standardized* characteristics regarding their **expiration** date (when the option stops trading) and **exercise price** (the purchase price of the stock or asset).

- The standardized characteristics cause like options to be *interchangeable*—that is, they can be traded before the option expires.

- The tradeability of the options provides significant **liquidity** for these options, which in turn creates lower option prices and lower commissions.

- The existence of the options exchanges provides traders with added safeguards against trading abuses.

The CBOE traded 16 stocks when the exchange opened in 1973. In 1975-76 the American, Philadelphia, and Pacific Exchanges began to trade stock options. Later, the New York Exchange added options. By the early 1980s the volume on the options exchanges exceeded the stock volume on the New York and American stock exchanges. After the 1987 stock market crash, option volume decreased substantially. Current option volume is over 1 million contracts per day (each for 100 shares of stock), while NYSE stock volume is typically 200 to 300 million shares per day. Currently, options on over 700 stocks trade on the options exchanges.

Options on stock indexes started trading in 1983, and by 1985 these indexes made up over 30% of total option volume. Current index option volume is approximately 350,000 contracts per day, which is about 25% of total stock option volume. Exchange-traded options on foreign exchange (currencies) and options on futures contracts also exist. Furthermore, most specialized options on various assets and interest rate securities trade on an over-the-counter basis. Here we concentrate on the popular stock options. Later we examine the other option contracts. Figure 1–1 shows the growth of exchange-traded stock and non-stock options since 1980. Notice the drop in equity options after the crash of 1987.

Calls and Puts

The two basic types of options are **call options** and **put options**. A call option for a stock gives the buyer the *right* to purchase the stock at a fixed price for a specific period of time. The term "option" reflects the concept that

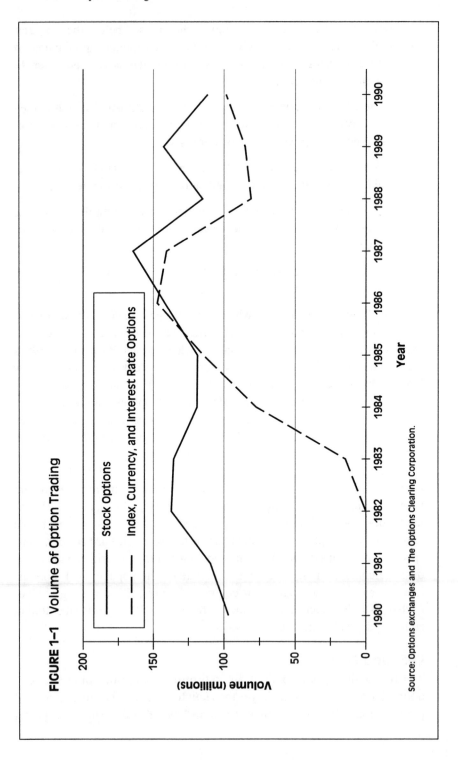

FIGURE 1–1 Volume of Option Trading

Source: Options exchanges and The Options Clearing Corporation.

the call buyer has the right, *but not the obligation,* to purchase the stock. This means that the maximum amount of money the buyer can lose is the initial cost of the option. If the stock price *increases* sufficiently, the call buyer profits. A put option for a stock gives the buyer the right to *sell* the stock at a fixed price for a specific period of time. The put buyer has the right, *but not the obligation,* to sell the stock. If the stock price *declines* sufficiently, the put buyer profits.

The seller of an option is often called the **writer** of the option. Buyers of call options are typically speculators, while the buyers of puts and the writers of call and put options can be either speculators or hedgers, depending on the strategy involved. Strategies for call and put options are discussed in Chapters 5 and 6. Options are often called **derivative assets**, since the dollar payoffs of an option are completely determined by the price of the underlying asset of the option.[2]

The "fixed price" of an option is typically called the **strike price** or exercise price. The strike price for a call option is the price the buyer pays for the stock, if and when the right to purchase the stock is exercised. The put strike price is the price the buyer *sells* the stock for, if and when the put option is exercised. The "specific period of time" until the expiration of the option states the amount of time remaining before the option ceases to exist. Once the option expires, the buyer *no longer* has the right to buy/sell the stock at the exercise price. An "American" option can be exercised any trading day on or *before* the expiration date. A "European" option can be exercised only *at* its expiration. Stock options traded in the United States are American-type options. Exhibit 1–1 summarizes what buyers of options *can* do and what sellers are *obligated* to do.

STOCK CALL OPTION QUOTATIONS AND PRICING RELATIONSHIPS

The price of the option is negotiated between the buyer and the seller. Each option on an individual stock is for 100 shares of the stock, although the option quotations illustrate the option price per *one* share of the stock. Therefore, one must multiply the option price by 100 to obtain the total dollar price for an option contract representing 100 shares of stock.

Call Option Quotations

The vast majority of the option quotations encountered in the newspaper are for individual stocks. Each line in Exhibit 1–2 shows a different option. Options differ in terms of the underlying stock, whether they are a call or a put option, their strike price, and/or the expiration date. Financial newspa-

---

EXHIBIT 1–1 Option Decisions for Buyers and Sellers

Buying options

- **Call**: can *purchase* the stock at the strike price.
- **Put**: can *sell* the stock at the strike price.

Selling options

- **Call**: obligated to *sell* the stock at the strike price (the buyer chooses if and when to exercise the option).
- **Put**: obligated to *buy* the stock at the strike price (the buyer chooses if and when to exercise the option).

---

pers such as *The Wall Street Journal* provide a full page showing the 1400 most active individual stock options. The volume shows the number of option contracts traded, with each contract representing 100 stock shares. The **open interest** is the number of contracts outstanding with both a long and short position. Current stock option open interest exceeds 15 million contracts, representing 1.5 billion shares of stock, while stock index options add another 2 million contracts to open interest. Exhibit 1–3 presents selected call option quotations for a hypothetical stock called ABC Corporation. These call prices are listed in table format in order to better compare option prices with different characteristics.

The quotes in Exhibit 1–3 illustrate the meaning of call option quotations and describe various concepts relating to options. The hypothetical ABC stock price on the day in question closed at 100 per share. The strike prices listed for ABC in the exhibit range from 90 to 110.[3] The ABC options listed here expire during the third week of the expiration month in January, February, and March; other expiration months also exist. The next option to expire is called the **nearby option.** Later expirations are called **deferred options.**[4]

Notation. Symbols and equations will be simplified wherever possible. The P_S is the price of the stock and P_C is the price of the option. Many books use the symbol $P_C(P_S, t, K, \sigma, E)$, or something similar, to refer to the call price. The symbols within the parentheses are the factors affecting the call—i.e., P_S = the stock price, t = the time until the option expires, K = the strike price, σ = the volatility of the stock, and E = a European option. American options are designated by A. For simplicity, we will place these factors in parentheses only when it is necessary to distinguish between options with different strike prices or other variables.

EXHIBIT 1–2   Stock Option Quotations

MOST ACTIVE CONTRACTS

Option/Strike			Vol	Exch	Net Last	Chg	Stock Close	Open Int
GM	May	40	5,090	CB	$1\frac{1}{2}$ +	$^{13}/_{16}$	$40\frac{1}{2}$	9,713
IBM	May	50	3,152	CB	$^{11}/_{16}$ –	$\frac{1}{8}$	$47\frac{3}{4}$	21,264
Intel	May	105	2,961	AM	$^{13}/_{16}$ –	$\frac{1}{2}$	$92\frac{3}{4}$	7,876
Marriot	May	$22\frac{1}{2}$ p	2,925	PB	$^{1}/_{16}$ +	$^{1}/_{16}$	$25\frac{1}{8}$	...
Chryslr	May	40	2,471	CB	$1\frac{1}{2}$ +	$^{5}/_{16}$	$39\frac{5}{8}$	9,489
Intel	May	100	2,467	AM	$1^{11}/_{16}$ –	$^{15}/_{16}$	$92\frac{3}{4}$	8,059
Intel	May	95	2,444	AM	$3\frac{3}{8}$ –	$1\frac{1}{2}$	$92\frac{3}{4}$	979
Amgen	Jul	45	2,304	AM	$1\frac{3}{4}$ +	$\frac{1}{8}$	$39\frac{3}{4}$	2,912
ASA	May	40	2,186	AM	$3\frac{1}{8}$ +	$1\frac{1}{8}$	$43\frac{1}{8}$	4,477
GM	May	35	2,143	CB	$5\frac{5}{8}$ +	$1\frac{3}{8}$	$40\frac{1}{2}$	2,741
Intel	May	90	2,025	AM	$3\frac{1}{8}$ +	$1\frac{3}{8}$	$92\frac{3}{4}$	2,234

EQUITY OPTIONS
-A-B-C-

Option/Strike				Vol	Exch	Net Last	Chg	Stock Close	Open Int
A Hess	May	50		160	PB	$2^{15}/_{16}$ –	$^{13}/_{16}$	53	634
A Hess	Jun	55		53	PB	$1\frac{1}{8}$ –	$^{1}/_{16}$	53	42
AMD	May	25		1,111	PC	$5\frac{1}{2}$ –	$\frac{5}{8}$	$30\frac{1}{2}$	3,223
AMD	May	25	p	917	PC	$\frac{1}{4}$ +	$^{1}/_{16}$	$30\frac{1}{2}$	1,115
AMD	Jun	25	p	115	PC	$\frac{5}{8}$ +	$^{3}/_{16}$	$30\frac{1}{2}$	466
AMD	Jul	25		115	PC	$6\frac{1}{4}$ –	$\frac{1}{2}$	$30\frac{1}{2}$	2,546
AMD	Jul	25	p	251	PC	$\frac{3}{4}$	...	$30\frac{1}{2}$	829
AMD	May	30		1,312	PC	$1\frac{7}{8}$ –	$\frac{1}{2}$	$30\frac{1}{2}$	2,484
AMD	May	30	p	1,446	PC	$1\frac{3}{8}$ +	$\frac{1}{8}$	$30\frac{1}{2}$	1,475
AMD	Jun	30		216	PC	$2\frac{5}{8}$ –	$\frac{3}{8}$	$30\frac{1}{2}$	1,061
AMD	Jun	30	p	262	PC	$2\frac{1}{8}$ +	$\frac{1}{8}$	$30\frac{1}{2}$	443
AMD	Jul	30		635	PC	$3\frac{1}{8}$ –	$\frac{3}{8}$	$30\frac{1}{2}$	1,942
AMD	Jul	30	p	67	PC	$2^{13}/_{16}$ +	$\frac{5}{8}$	$30\frac{1}{2}$	289
AMD	Oct	30		830	PC	$4\frac{1}{2}$	...	$30\frac{1}{2}$	1,290

EQUITY OPTIONS
-A-B-C-

Option/Strike				Vol	Exch	Net Last	Chg	Stock Close	Open Int
AMD	Oct	30	p	153	PC	$3\frac{1}{2}$	...	$30\frac{1}{2}$	396
AMR	May	65		321	AM	$4\frac{7}{8}$ –	$1\frac{5}{8}$	$69\frac{3}{8}$	6,642
AMR	May	65	p	171	AM	$^{11}/_{16}$ +	$^{5}/_{16}$	$69\frac{3}{8}$	3,563
AMR	May	70		76	AM	$1\frac{7}{8}$ –	$\frac{5}{8}$	$69\frac{3}{8}$	2,563
AMR	May	70	p	456	AM	$2\frac{1}{8}$ +	$^{1}/_{16}$	$69\frac{3}{8}$	2,092
AMR	Jun	70		81	AM	$2^{13}/_{16}$ –	$^{13}/_{16}$	$69\frac{3}{8}$	353
AMR	May	75		127	AM	$^{7}/_{16}$ –	$\frac{1}{4}$	$69\frac{3}{8}$	1,168
AMR	Jun	75		186	AM	1 –	$\frac{3}{8}$	$69\frac{3}{8}$	243
AMR	Aug	75		80	AM	$2\frac{1}{8}$ –	$\frac{1}{2}$	$69\frac{3}{8}$	2,672
AT&T	May	55		306	CB	$2\frac{1}{4}$ –	$\frac{3}{4}$	56	1,323
AT&T	May	55	p	1,005	CB	$\frac{3}{4}$ +	$\frac{1}{4}$	56	5,224
AT&T	Jun	55	p	642	CB	$1\frac{1}{4}$ +	$^{5}/_{16}$	56	355
AT&T	May	60		159	CB	$^{7}/_{16}$ –	$^{1}/_{16}$	56	2,102
AT&T	May	60	p	60	CB	$3\frac{5}{8}$ +	$\frac{7}{8}$	56	366
AT&T	Jun	60		103	CB	$\frac{5}{8}$ –	$\frac{3}{8}$	56	348
AT&T	Jul	60		404	CB	$^{15}/_{16}$ –	$^{5}/_{16}$	56	7,324
AT&T	Oct	60		418	CB	$1\frac{7}{8}$ –	$\frac{1}{8}$	56	2,847
Abbt L	May	25		53	PB	$1\frac{1}{2}$	...	$25\frac{3}{4}$	3,453
Abbt L	May	25	p	64	PB	$^{9}/_{16}$ –	$^{1}/_{16}$	$25\frac{3}{4}$	2,737
Abbt L	Jun	25		255	PB	2	...	$25\frac{3}{4}$	324
Abbt L	Jun	25	p	160	PB	$^{15}/_{16}$	...	$25\frac{3}{4}$	174
AmExp	May	25		85	AM	$4\frac{1}{4}$ +	$\frac{7}{8}$	$29\frac{1}{4}$	1,112
AmExp	May	25	p	70	AM	$^{1}/_{16}$ –	$\frac{1}{8}$	$29\frac{1}{4}$	1,814
AmExp	Jul	25	p	150	AM	$\frac{3}{8}$ –	$^{1}/_{16}$	$29\frac{1}{4}$	2,653
AmExp	May	30		642	AM	$\frac{1}{2}$ +	$^{3}/_{16}$	$29\frac{1}{4}$	3,133
AmExp	May	30	p	109	AM	$1\frac{3}{8}$ –	$\frac{3}{8}$	$29\frac{1}{4}$	291
AmExp	Jun	30		99	AM	1 +	$\frac{3}{8}$	$29\frac{1}{4}$	319
AmExp	Jun	30	p	456	AM	$1\frac{5}{8}$ –	$\frac{3}{4}$	$29\frac{1}{4}$	227
AmExp	Jul	30		97	AM	$1^{3}/_{16}$ +	$^{7}/_{16}$	$29\frac{1}{4}$	10,727
AmExp	Oct	30		74	AM	$1\frac{3}{4}$ +	$^{5}/_{16}$	$29\frac{1}{4}$	1,912

c = call
p = put
CB = Chicago Board Options Exchange
AM = American Stock Exchange

PB = Philadelphia Stock Exchange
PC = Pacific Stock Exchange
NY = New York Stock Exchange

Source: Options Exchanges, April 23.

In-the-Money and Out-of-the-Money Call Options. Let us first examine the prices of the ABC call options with a strike price of 95. For example, the Feb 95 call price is 7, or $700 for a 100-share call option. The ABC 95 call options are **in-the-money** calls—that is, the stock price is greater than the strike price. In-the-money call options have *positive* **intrinsic values**, with the Feb 95 call having an intrinsic value of 5: the 100 stock price less the 95 strike price. In general, the intrinsic value is described by Pricing Relationship #1 and Equation (1–1).

EXHIBIT 1–3   Call Option Quotations

Company	Stock Price	Strike Price	Calls		
			Jan	Feb	March
ABC	100	90	10 $^1/_8$	11	11 $^3/_4$
	100	95	5 $^1/_2$	7	8
	100	100	2 $^1/_8$	4	5
	100	105	$^1/_2$	2	3
	100	110	$^1/_{16}$	$^7/_8$	1 $^5/_8$

Current date: January 1
Expiration dates: January 16; February 20; March 20
Volatility = 25%
Interest rate = 4%
Dividend = $0.00

Pricing Relationship #1: The intrinsic value of a call option is either the stock price less the strike price, or zero, whichever is greater.

$$IV_C = Max\ [P_S - K,\ 0] \qquad\qquad (1\text{-}1)$$

where IV_C = intrinsic value of the call option C
$\quad\ P_S$ = the price of the stock
$\quad\ K$ = the strike price of the option

The value of the call option when the option *expires* is the call's intrinsic value at that time.

The ABC 100 call options are known as **near-the-money** or **at-the-money** options. For "near-the-money" options, the current stock price and the strike price are approximately the same. An "at-the-money" option exists when the stock price equals the strike price. The February 100 at-the-money option sells for 4, or $400. The ABC February 105 call is an **out-of-the-money** option. An "out-of-the-money" call option exists when the stock price is less than the strike price. The February 105 option trades for 2, or $200, for a 100-share option on ABC stock. Since the stock price is less than the strike price, we say that the intrinsic value for this option is equal to zero. At option expiration there is no reason to exercise an out-of-the-money option to purchase ABC stock at 105, since one can buy the stock in the open market for 100. The stock must increase in value (above 105) before an out-of-the-money option is worth exercising.

The Effect of Time. Exhibit 1–3 shows that the prices of the March calls are greater than the February call prices. For example, the March 95 sells for 8, while the February 95 sells for 7. Comparing the other expiration dates (of equivalent strike prices) shows that the price of the option increases as the time until expiration increases. This **time to expiration factor** means that the buyer of the call option must pay in order to "purchase" more time for the stock price to increase. Conversely, as the time to expiration declines, the option price decreases (if all other factors remain constant).

The difference between the option *price* for the February 95 call of 7 and the *intrinsic value* of 5 for this option is called the **time value**. The size of this time value is determined by the time until option expiration, the difference between the stock price and strike price, and the volatility of the stock. The time value is defined as:

$$TV_C = P_C - IV_C \qquad \text{(1-2)}$$

where TV_C = the time value for the call
$ P_C$ = the current price of the call option

Equations (1–1) and (1–2) provide us with our second pricing relationship:[5]

Pricing Relationship #2: An option before expiration sells for at least its intrinsic value; that is:

$$P_C \geq \text{Max} \, [P_S - K, 0] \qquad \text{(1-3)}$$

Equation (1–3) is known as a boundary condition; that is, the lower bound for the price of a call option cannot be less than the "boundary" represented by whichever is the maximum: zero or P_S − K. If a boundary condition is violated, risk-free profits (**arbitrage**) are possible.[6] Exhibit 1–4 provides a summary of the above relationships.

Strike Price Relationships. Exhibit 1–3 shows that the option prices constantly decrease (for the same expiration month) moving from the 90 strikes to the 110 strikes. Thus, in-the-money options are worth more than out-of-the-money options (when they have the same time to expiration). For example, the March 90 strike price has a call value of 11 ³/₄, while the higher 105 strike only has a value of 3. This pattern for the call option prices is due to the combination of the intrinsic value and time value relationships given in Equations (1–1) and (1–2). This can be formalized into the following pricing relationship:

Pricing Relationship #3: Call options with a lower exercise price are worth at least as much as call options with a higher exercise price—that is:

$$P_C(K_1) \geq P_C(K_2) \qquad \text{(1-4)}$$

where $K_1 < K_2$

EXHIBIT 1–4   Call Option Relationships

The price of a call can be broken down into two basic components:

Price	Intrinsic Value	+	Time Value
P_C =	Max $[P_S - K, 0]$	+	$P_C - $ Max $[P_S - K, 0]$

If:	The Call Is:
$P_S > K$	In-the-money
$P_S = K$	At-the-money
$P_S < K$	Out-of-the-money

Profits at Call Option Expiration and Payoff Diagrams

Figure 1–2 illustrates the payoff diagram for purchasing and keeping a call option until its expiration. The call buyer has a maximum loss equal to the cost of the option. The loss on the option is reduced if the stock price at option expiration trades between the strike price and the break-even point. Above the break-even point, the speculator profits from buying the call option. The stock price break-even point for the purchase of a call option is calculated by:

$$BE_C = K + P_C \qquad\qquad \textbf{(1-5)}$$

where BE_C = the break-even price for the stock (the stock price at which the original cost of the call option is recovered).

The dashed line in the graph represents the profit/loss from a stock-only position. The stock position provides a profit/loss in dollars that is superior to the option profit/loss as long as the stock price is greater than the strike price minus the cost of the option—that is, when $P_S > K - P_C$. When the stock price is below $K - P_C$, the option position generates a smaller dollar loss than the stock position. On the other hand, options provide *larger percentage* changes than the stock position. Hence, the stock position can generate larger dollar profits, but the option provides greater **leverage** plus a limited loss feature.[7]

Figure 1–3 illustrates the payoff diagrams at option expiration for buying the Feb 95 and Feb 100 ABC call options. The profit (loss) from these option positions depends on the option purchase price and the stock price at option expiration. The figure shows that if the stock is priced below 100 when the Feb 100 option expires, then the entire $400 cost of the option is lost. In other

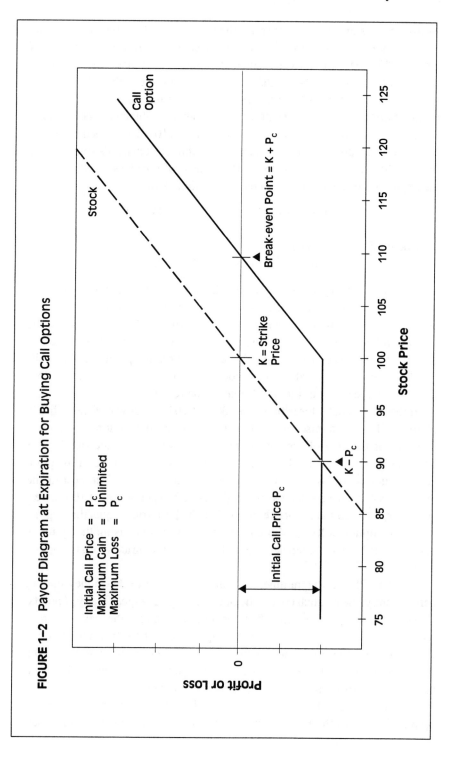

FIGURE 1-2 Payoff Diagram at Expiration for Buying Call Options

words, there is no reason to exercise the right to purchase the stock at 100, since the stock price is below the exercise price. If the stock trades above 104 when the Feb 100 option expires, then the option buyer makes money, since a stock price above 104 means that the cost of the Feb 100 option is recovered and a profit is received. For example, if the stock trades at 110 at option expiration, then a net profit of 6 points is obtained: the 10-point intrinsic value profit from exercising the option (110 – 100) less the original option cost of 4 points. Notice that the size of the profit depends solely on the price of the ABC stock being above 104.[8] The profit (or loss) relationship at the expiration of the option is stated in Equation (1-6):

$$\text{Profit} = \text{Max } [P_s - K, 0] - P_c = IV_c - P_c \qquad (1\text{-}6)$$

where IV_c = the intrinsic value at option expiration
P_c = the original cost of the call option

Thus, the profit on a call option position that is kept until the expiration of the option is the price of the stock less the strike price less the original option price. If the call option at expiration has an intrinsic value of zero, then the loss is limited to the original cost of the option. Example 1–1 illustrates important concepts concerning buying a call option: the potential profitability, the leverage, the small initial amount of funds needed, the limited loss feature, and the effect of the time value on the results.

If the ABC stock closes between 100 and 104, the buyer of the Feb 100 option will still exercise the option. In this case, the option buyer loses money, but the size of the loss is reduced by exercising the option. For example, if ABC closes at 102, then the intrinsic value of the Feb 100 option is 2 points (the 102 stock price less the 100 strike price). The cost of the option was 4, creating a net loss of 2 points, or $200 per option of 100 shares. However, if the option is *not* exercised, then the loss would equal the original cost of the option: $400, or 4 points. Consequently, exercising the option is beneficial as long as the stock price is above the strike price when the option expires.

The Feb 95 call diagrammed in Figure 1–2 is an in-the-money option; consequently, the original cost of the option is higher—specifically, 7 points. If the stock falls below 95 when the option expires, the call option is worthless and the call buyer loses the original cost of $700. If the option is exercised when the stock trades between 95 and 102 (the strike price plus the option price), then the option buyer's losses are reduced. Above 102 ³/₈ the option buyer profits, since the original cost of the option is covered.

Figure 1–3 also shows the *relationship* between the payoffs of the two options. The 95 in-the-money option is profitable at a lower stock price than

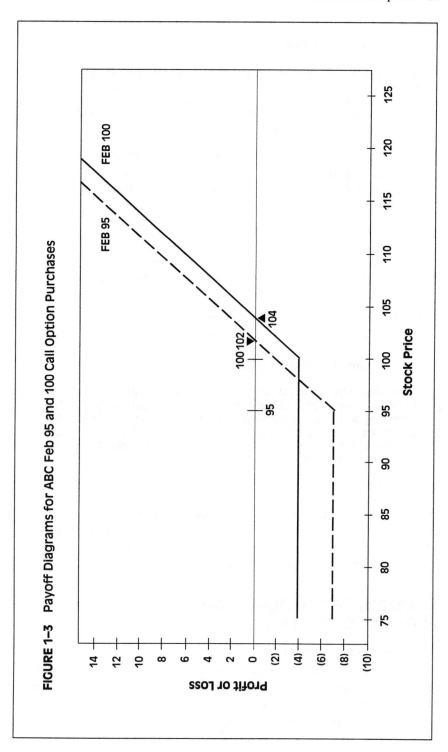

FIGURE 1–3 Payoff Diagrams for ABC Feb 95 and 100 Call Option Purchases

---

EXAMPLE 1–1   Buying a Call Stock Option

Motorola stock sold for 65 1/2 in early April. During the following 10 days Motorola stock increased, based on a strong earnings report and the anticipated announcement of a new computer chip to rival Intel's Pentium chip. The stock and options prices on April 5 and April 16 (the expiration date of the options) are:

	April 5	April 16
Motorola stock	65 1/2	73
April 65 call	2 1/8	8
April 70 call	7/16	3

The profits on these positions are:

Option profit = $IV_c - P_c$
April 65 profit = 8 − 2 1/8 = 5 7/8 or $587.50 per contract
April 70 profit = 3 − 7/16 = 2 9/16 or $256.25 per contract
Motorola stock = 73 − 65 1/2 = 7 1/2 or $750 per 100 shares

The rates of return on the options and stock are:

April 65 = $578.50/$212.50 = 276.5%
April 70 = $256.25/$43.75 = 585.7%
Motorola stock = $750/$6500 = 11.5%

A correct forecast of Motorola's price increase translates into a large percentage gain on the options (leverage). The April 65 (originally) near-the-money option has a greater dollar profit, but the out-of-the-money April 70 option has a larger percentage return (given its low initial price and smaller time value). While the stock has a larger dollar profit, the options possess significantly greater leverage.

---

the 100 option, but it costs more and hence loses more if the stock price declines below 98. The 100 at-the-money call is less profitable than the 95 option at any stock price above 98 (the difference in the option prices of 7 − 4 plus the 95 strike price), but it costs less.

STOCK PUT OPTION QUOTATIONS AND PRICING RELATIONSHIPS

Put Option Quotations

Exhibit 1–5 provides sample hypothetical quotations for puts. Previously, Exhibit 1–2 showed the newspaper presentation of put options. A put option provides the buyer with the right, but not the obligation, to *sell* the stock at a fixed price for a specific period of time. Thus, a put buyer profits when the price of the stock *declines* sufficiently. Put options are often considered mirror images of call options. The prices for the ABC put options in Exhibit 1–5 illustrate the "mirror-image" concept: put option prices are higher for larger strike prices, while call option prices are lower for smaller strike prices.

Out-of-the-Money and In-the-Money Put Options. Out-of-the-money put options exist when the stock price is *above* the strike price (since no put option buyer would want to *sell* stock at the strike price when it is possible to sell at a higher price in the open market). Therefore, the 1 ½ price for the Feb 95 out-of-the-money put is entirely a time value. Only if the stock falls to below the strike price of 95 will the put option have a positive intrinsic value. In-the-money puts occur when the stock price is *below* the strike price. The price of 6 ³/₈ for the Feb 105 in-the-money put includes an intrinsic value of 5 and a time value of 1 ³/₈ points. The intrinsic value of 5 exists because the buyer of the put option can *sell* the stock at the strike price of 105, while simultaneously buying the stock in the open market at 100. An additional one point is the difference between the option price and the intrinsic value. In general, the put intrinsic value is described by Pricing Relationship #4 and Equation (1–7). The put time value is defined by Equation (1–8).

Pricing Relationship #4: The intrinsic value of a put option is either the strike price less the stock price, or zero, whichever is greater.

$$IV_P = Max \: [K - P_S, \: 0] \qquad\qquad \textbf{(1-7)}$$

and

$$TV_P = P_P - IV_P \qquad\qquad \textbf{(1-8)}$$

EXHIBIT 1–5   Put Option Quotations

Company	Stock Price	Strike Price	Calls		
			Jan	Feb	March
ABC	100	90	0	¹/₂	¹⁵/₁₆
	100	95	³/₈	1 ¹/₂	2 ¹/₈
	100	100	2	3 ³/₈	4 ¹/₈
	100	105	5 ⁷/₈	6 ³/₈	7
	100	110	10	10 ¹/₄	10 ⁵/₈

Current date: January 1
Expiration dates: January 16; February 20; March 20
Volatility = 25%

Interest rate = 4%
Dividend = $0.00

where IV_p = the intrinsic value of the put
$\quad\quad\ P_p$ = the current price of the put
$\quad\quad TV_p$ = the time value for the put

The price of the put at option expiration is the put's intrinsic value. Exhibit 1–6 provides a summary of the relationships given above. As with a call, the lower boundary condition for a put option before expiration is that a put sells for at least its intrinsic value.[9]

Time and Strike Price Relationships. The time factor relationships for put options parallel those for call options. Put options with a longer time to expiration are worth more, although Exhibits 1–3 and 1–5 show that the differences in put prices from one expiration to another (for equivalent strike prices) are smaller than they are for the associated call options. As with call options, relative put option prices are directly related to strike prices for equivalent expiration months. Exhibit 1–5 shows that put option prices are higher for larger strike prices. This pattern is based on a combination of the intrinsic value and time value relationships in Equations (1–7) and (1–8). These patterns and boundary conditions are formalized as follows:

> *Pricing Relationship #5:* Put options with a higher strike price are worth at least as much as put options with a lower strike price, or:

$$P_P(K_2) \geq P_P(K_1) \tag{1-9}$$

Profits at Put Option Expiration and Payoff Diagrams
Figure 1–4 illustrates the payoff diagram at option expiration for purchasing a put option. A put buyer purchases the right to *sell* the stock at the relevant

---

EXHIBIT 1–6 Put Option Relationships

The price of a put can be broken down into two basic components:

Price	Intrinsic Value	+	Time Value
P_p =	Max $[K - P_s, 0]$	+	P_p – Max $[K - P_s, 0]$

If:	The Call Is:
$P_s > K$	In-the-money
$P_s = K$	At-the-money
$P_s < K$	Out-of-the-money

strike price. If the stock price is above the put strike price at option expiration, then the buyer of the put loses the original cost of the put (the maximum loss). Any gain from buying a put depends on how much the stock price declines. The break-even point is the strike price less the cost of the put:

$$BE_P = K - P_P \qquad \text{(1-10)}$$

where BE_P = break-even point for the stock price (the stock price at which the original cost of the put option is recovered).

If the stock price declines to a point significantly below the strike price, the put option buyer obtains a large profit on a small initial investment. The dashed line in the figure represents a **short sale** on the underlying stock. A short sale produces a larger profit than the put option when the stock price is below the strike price, but the maximum loss on the put is limited to the cost of the put. In addition, the put has more leverage than a short sale.

Figure 1–5 shows the payoff diagrams for the Feb 95 and Feb 100 put options at option expiration (see Exhibit 1–5 for the original cost information for the puts). The figure illustrates that if the stock is priced at or above 95 when the 95 put option expires, there is no reason to exercise the right to sell the stock at 95. In this case, the buyer of the put option loses the original cost of the option of $150 (1 $\frac{1}{2}$ points). The break-even point for the Feb 95 put is 93 $\frac{1}{2}$; that is, the strike price of 95 less the original cost of 1 $\frac{1}{2}$ = 93 $\frac{1}{2}$. If the stock trades below 124 $\frac{1}{4}$ when the put option expires, the buyer of the put profits. For example, if ABC stock closes at 90 on the expiration day, a trader could buy the stock in the open market at 90 and then exercise the put option to sell the stock at the strike price of 95. This transaction would generate a gross profit (intrinsic value) of 5 points. After considering the original cost of the put option of 1 $\frac{1}{2}$, the trader would net a profit of 3 $\frac{1}{2}$ points, or $350, for a 100-share option. The lower the price of the stock at option expiration, the larger the profits for the put buyer. The net profit (loss) for the buyer of a put option when the option is exercised *at expiration* is determined as follows:

$$\text{Profit} = \text{Max}\,[K - P_S, 0] - P_P = IV_P - P_P \qquad \text{(1-11)}$$

where IV_P = the intrinsic value of the put at option expiration
P_P = the original cost of the put option

Thus, the profit on a put option position that is kept until the expiration of the option is the strike price less the stock price less the original cost of the put. The put buyer exercises the put option as long as the stock trades below 95 at the expiration of the option. Between 95 and 93 $\frac{1}{2}$, the put buyer loses money; however, exercising the option reduces the size of the loss. If the put

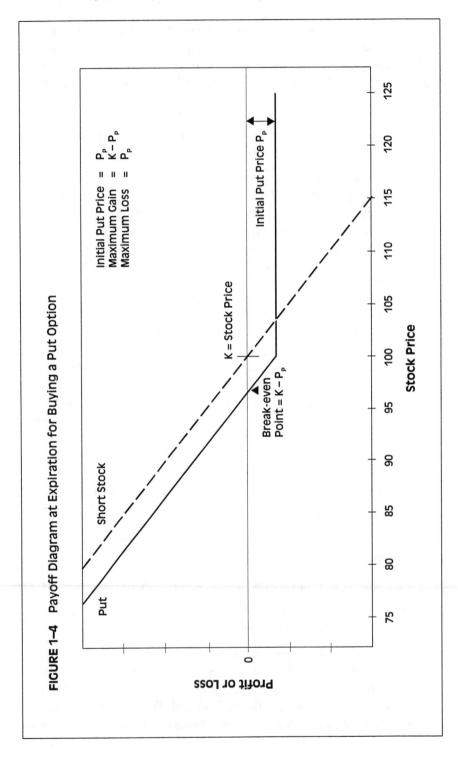

FIGURE 1–4 Payoff Diagram at Expiration for Buying a Put Option

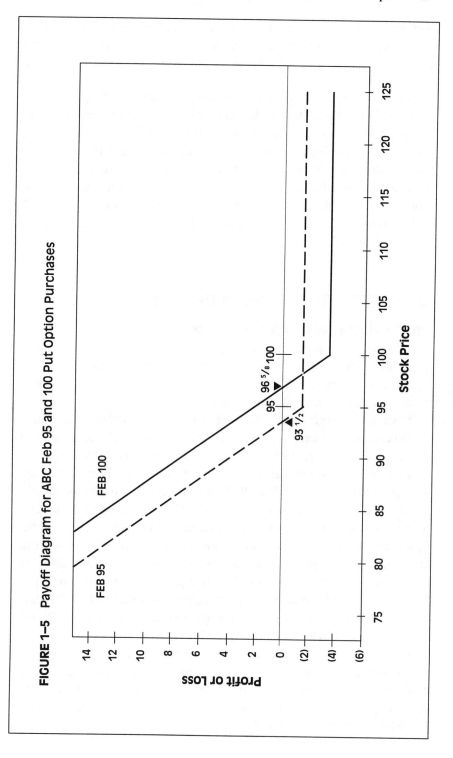

FIGURE 1-5   Payoff Diagram for ABC Feb 95 and 100 Put Option Purchases

option has an intrinsic value of zero at expiration, then the maximum loss on the put is the cost of the option. (Example 1–2 shows how a speculator would profit if he or she purchased a put option on Intel before adverse news was made public.)

The Feb 100 put option is an at-the-money option. The 100 put provides a net profit as long as the stock trades below 96 at the expiration of the option—that is, the strike price of 100 less the cost of 3 $^3/_8$. If the stock trades above 100, the put expires worthless. Comparing the 95 and 100 puts shows that the 100 option is profitable below 96 $^5/_8$. However, the 100 put costs more and therefore loses more money if the stock price trades above the 100 strike price. The 100 put is a better choice than the 95 put as long as the stock trades below 98 $^1/_2$ (the strike price of 100 less the difference in the option prices of 3 $^3/_8$ – 1 $^1/_2$).

CHARACTERISTICS OF STOCK OPTIONS

Option Classes and Expiration Dates

An **option class** is a designation for all of the options on the same stock. Thus, all of the calls and puts (all strikes and expiration dates) on IBM represent an option class. An **option series** is a particular option with a specific strike price and expiration date.

Stock option expirations follow one of the January, February, or March **option cycles**. The January cycle consists of the option expiration months of January, April, July, and October. Similarly, the February and March cycles vary by three-month intervals (thus, the February cycle is February, May, August, and November). Before 1987, only the next three expiration months in the stock option cycle were traded. As of 1987, almost all of the options follow the procedure that the current calendar month, the next calendar month, and the next two monthly expirations in the option cycle of the stock are traded. Thus, a stock in the January cycle would trade the following options on February 1: February, March, April, and July. On March 1, a January cycle stock would trade March, April, July, and October. *The Wall Street Journal* lists only the most active options on a particular stock. Quotes for other expirations are available from a broker.[10]

Options expire on the Saturday following the third Friday of the expiration month. The last day of trading for the option is the third Friday of the expiration month; delivery is on the following Monday. The next relevant option expiration is listed on the option exchange the Monday following the expiration of the previously traded option.

EXAMPLE 1–2   Buying a Put Stock Option

As the premier PC chip maker, Intel's sales and profits rose dramatically due to the 386 and 486 PC chips. Over a period of one year, the stock price rose from 46 to over 121. However, the loss of a court case which allowed rival Advanced Micro Devices to sell a competing chip caused Intel's stock to drop 12 $1/4$ points in one day on volume of over 17 million shares. Over a period of one week, the stock fell 17 $1/4$ points on nearly 45 million shares traded. The following Monday, Intel dropped another 5 $3/8$ on news from Motorola that it was going to sell a chip to compete with Intel's Pentium (a "586" chip). A speculator who bought a put on Intel before the major decline started and kept the put until expiration, profited as follows:

	April 18	May 14
Intel stock	110	87 $3/8$
May 115 put	7 $3/8$	27 $5/8$
May 105 put	2 $7/8$	17 $5/8$

The profits on the put and short sale positions are:

Option profit = $IV_p - P_p$

May 115 put profit = 27 $5/8$ – 7 $3/8$ = 20 $1/4$ or \$2025 per contract

May 105 put profit = 17 $5/8$ – 2 $7/8$ = 14 $3/4$ or \$1475 per contract

Intel short sale = 110 – 87 $3/8$ = 22 $5/8$ or \$2262.50 per 100 shares

The rates of return are:

May 115 put = \$2025/\$737.50 = 274.6%

May 105 put = \$1475/\$287.50 = 513.0%

Intel short sale = \$2262.50/\$11,000 = 20.6%

Strike Prices, Stock Splits, and Position Limits

Strike prices are typically spaced at intervals of $2.50 when the underlying stock is priced below $25; at $5 when the stock is between $50 and $200; and at $10 when the stock is over $200. When a new option expiration month starts to trade, the two strike prices nearest the stock price are activated for trading purposes. A *new* option strike price is created when the stock price closes two days in a row closer to the potential new option strike price than to the currently traded strike prices. For example, if a stock option has strike prices of 35 and 40, and the stock closes above $42.50 for two days in a row, then a 45 strike price starts to trade.

The strike price of an option remains the same unless a **stock split or stock dividend** occurs for the stock. The strike price adjustment for a stock split or stock dividend reflects the relative change in the stock price resulting from the split or dividend.[11] Cash dividends paid by the corporation do *not* affect strike prices.

Position limits refer to the maximum number of option contracts a trader can hold at one time. An option trader can hold only 3000 to 8000 option contracts, with the size of the limit depending on the stock's volume and number of shares outstanding.

LEAPS

LEAPS are long-term options that expire up to three years in the future. Except for the expiration date difference, they have equivalent characteristics to other stock options. However, the market for LEAPS is less active than for shorter-term options, creating the possibility that these options will be mispriced relative to their value and that liquidity problems will occur.

STOCK INDEX OPTIONS

Characteristics of Index Options

A stock **index option** is an option on an index of common stocks, with the index representing a portfolio of stocks weighted by price or by total market value. The S&P 100 Index option, also known as the OEX, began to trade in March of 1983. The S&P 100 was the first stock index option and has been the most popular. This index is based on the largest 100 companies in terms of the Standard & Poor's criteria. Other active index options are the S&P 500, the S&P Midcap Index, Russell 2000, the Major Market Index (MMI), the Institutional Index, and the Japan Index.[12]

Delivery of all of the stocks represented in a stock index when an index option expires would be very difficult, especially since each stock has a different weight in the index. Consequently, index options are settled "in cash" at option expiration. **Cash settlement** means that when the option buyer exercises the option at expiration, the buyer receives from the seller the difference between the stock index value and the strike price of the option (multiplied by the size of the option contract). Most options, such as the S&P 100 options, are American options. The S&P 500 options are European options. The expiration of most index options occurs on the Saturday after the third Friday of the expiration month.[13] Many of the index options have expirations for the current month and the next three consecutive months. Other index options possess expirations during the current month and the following month, plus the next one or two expirations in one of the January, February, or March option cycles. The position limits for the S&P 100 and S&P 500 index options are 25,000 and 5000 contracts, respectively.

Flex options also are available for S&P 100 and S&P 500 options. These "flexible options" allow institutional investors to design their own positions by customizing options. Flex options allow customers to choose the strike prices, expiration date, type of exercise (e.g., American or European), and type of settlement procedure of the index options. The minimum face value of these flexible options is $10 million. So far, over $6 billion of face value of exchange-traded flex options has traded; over-the-counter flex options total over $50 billion per year. A major benefit of exchange-traded flex options compared to the over-the-counter version is that exchange-traded options eliminate the credit risk problem. In addition, these trades become public, providing price information to the market. Because of the success of these flex options, plans exist to trade flex options on the Russell 2000 small stock index, a mid-size stock index, and a Japanese stock index.

The popularity of index options is based on two factors: (1) the cash settlement feature avoids the necessity of delivery, and (2) options on "the market" provide trading and hedging opportunities not available with individual stock options. Specifically, index options allow a trader or hedger to concentrate on the risk of the market (**systematic risk**), ignoring the effects of company risk (**unsystematic risk**).[14,15]

Quoting Index Options

Exhibit 1–7 provides the quotes for the most popular index options. The S&P 100 options are by far the most active, with call and put volume totaling 300,000 contracts. The S&P 100 options also have a large open interest of 600,000 contracts. The S&P 500 options trade 70,000 contracts per day but possess a larger open interest than the S&P 100, with over 800,000 in total open interest. Total volume and open interest for stock index options are less than what existed before the stock market crash of October 1987.

The option prices for stock index options are on a per-unit basis. The total cost of the option is the per-unit price times the option's multiple. For example, the S&P 100 and S&P 500 Index options are multiplied by 100 to obtain the total cost. Similarly, the value of the option *at expiration* is determined by multiplying the *difference* between the value of the appropriate cash index and the strike price by $100. Thus, if the S&P 100 Index settles on the expiration day at 414, then a call option with a 400 strike price settles for 14 x $100 (with 414 – 400 = 14). The minimum price change for the stock index options is 1/8th for options priced above $3 and 1/16th for

EXHIBIT 1–7 Popular Stock Index Options

S&P 100 INDEX (OEX)

Strike		Vol.	Close	Net Chg.	Open Int.
May	405 c	16,627	5 3/8 –	1/2	12,705
May	405 p	29,040	5 3/4 +	1/2	29,549
Jun	405 c	1,031	7 7/8 –	7/8	692
Jun	405 p	2,834	8 3/8 +	3/4	4,894
Jul	405 c	129	10 –	2 3/4	36
Jul	405 p	115	10 1/4 +	2 2/8	553
May	410 c	33,597	3 1/8 –	1/4	39,100
May	410 p	18,726	8 1/2 +	3/4	39,185
Jun	410 c	1,435	5 3/8 –	5/8	9,317
Jun	410 p	983	10 7/8 +	3/4	8,729
Jul	410 c	140	7 1/8 –	7/8	2,057
Jul	410 p	17	12 1/4 +	1	1,897
Aug	410 c	45	9 1/4 –	3	879
Aug	410 p	23	13 3/4 +	3/4	481
May	415 c	27,124	1 1/2 –	3/16	45,578
May	415 p	5,708	11 7/8 +	1/2	27,131
Jun	415 c	2,251	3 3/8 –	3/8	4,130
Jun	415 p	535	14 1/8 +	3/4	1,861
Jul	415 c	67	5 –	2	74
Jul	415 p	19	15 1/8 +	1 7/8	74
May	420 c	10,505	5/8 –	1/16	36,285
May	420 p	821	16 1/4 +	1	5,414
Jun	420 c	2,963	2 –	5/16	7,964
Jun	420 p	140	18 +	2 1/8	1,079
Jul	420 c	929	3 3/8 –	7/8	1,286
Jul	420 p	16	18 1/2 +	3 1/4	263
Aug	420 c	265	4 3/4 –	1 3/4	601
Aug	420 p	15	19 1/2 +	2 3/4	62
May	425 c	4,572	1/4	...	27,278
May	425 p	33	20 1/2 +	2	423
Jun	425 c	1,586	1 1/16 –	1/4	3,788
Jun	425 p	3	22 1/2 +	7 1/2	74
Jul	425 c	428	2 1/8 –	3/8	1,580
Jul	425 p	5	23 1/2 +	6	5
May	430 c	588	1/8	...	25,050
Jun	430 c	652	9/16 –	1/16	12,224
Jun	430 p	6	25 1/4 +	5 1/4	94
Jul	430 c	4,100	1 3/16 –	5/16	6,536
Aug	430 c	2,694	2 1/4 –	7/16	5,458
Aug	430 p	14	28 +	4 3/4	21
May	435 c	358	1/16	...	21,112
Jun	435 c	287	5/16 –	1/8	9,094
May	440 c	10	1/16	...	16,484
Jun	440 c	9	3/16	...	1,882
Jul	440 c	25	1/2	...	1,349
Jul	440 p	1	35 1/2 +	5	5

Call vol. ....122,141 Open Int......315,423
Put vol. ....143,763 Open Int......303,616

S&P 500 INDEX-AM(SPX)

Strike		Vol.	Close	Net Chg.	Open Int.
May	440 c	3,089	4 1/8 –	3/4	9,643
May	440 p	1,688	7 3/8 +	1 1/4	8,144
Jun	440 c	196	6 7/8 –	3/4	6,578
Jun	440 p	2,989	10 1/8 +	1 1/8	5,841
Jul	440 c	78	9 1/2 +	9 1/2	...
Jul	440 p	155	12 +	3 7/8	382
May	445 c	4,168	2 1/4 –	1/2	12,399
May	445 p	1,576	10 1/4 +	1 1/4	10,186
Jun	445 c	564	4 3/4 –	1 1/8	8,252
Jun	445 p	713	12 1/2 +	1 1/2	7,258
May	450 c	1,806	1 –	1/2	13,719
May	450 p	3,318	14 3/8 +	1 5/8	14,258
Jun	450 c	3,055	3 –	1/2	30,580
Jun	450 p	305	16 +	2	27,739
Jul	450 c	250	4 3/4 –	2	3,000
Jul	450 p	50	16 1/2 +	4 3/8	53
May	455 c	447	1/2 –	1/4	7,513
May	455 p	97	18 1/2 +	3	1,060
Jun	455 c	735	1 13/16 –	7/16	3,468
Jun	455 p	42	19 3/4 +	5 3/8	818
Jul	455 c	13	3 1/4 –	1/4	1,375
May	460 c	4,425	1/4	...	12,091
Jun	460 c	2,831	1 3/16 –	1/8	15,148
Jun	460 c	3	23 +	6	186
Jul	460 p	3	24 +	3 3/4	7
May	465 c	1,732	1/8	...	13,621
May	465 p	5	27 5/8 +	3 3/8	36
Jul	465c	4	1 1/8 –	1	425
May	470 c	71	1/16	...	12,669
Jun	470 p	2	32 1/2 +	4 1/2	6,702
May	475 c	40	1/16 –	1/16	5,644
Jun	475 c	300	1/8 –	1/8	5,530
Jun	475 p	300	36 7/8 +	2 3/8	1,076

Call vol. .....29,791 Open Int......328,938
Put vol. .....38,891 Open Int......417,889

c = call
p = put

Source: Options Exchanges, April 23.

options below $3. Strike prices for the index options vary by units of five. Otherwise, the concepts for index options are identical to those described for individual stock options.[16]

LEAPS also exist on index options. The Amex has LT-20s, which are 1/20th of the MMI index. The CBOE has OEX leaps, which are 1/10th of the S&P 100 stock index. The total cost/value of each LEAP is $100 times the option price. Volume on these LEAPS tends to be low, but the open interest is relatively large.

Cash Settlement Versus Asset Settlement

Stock index options are settled in cash. Individual stock options are settled by exchanging the underlying asset (the stock).

The advantages of cash settlement relative to asset settlement are:

- Sellers of call or put options are not forced to sell the asset (for calls) or buy the asset (for puts).

- There is a potential reduction in transaction costs, since assets do not change hands.

The relative disadvantages of cash-settled options are:

- Cash-settled assets such as stock indexes are difficult to hedge, not because of cash settlement per se but because of the nature of the asset.

- There is a risk of becoming temporarily unhedged when the option is exercised because the option is transformed into cash based on the closing price, which removes the hedge until the seller learns of the exercise the next business day. Conversely, traders of asset-settled options exchange the asset, keeping the hedge in place.

- A wildcard characteristic exists in index option exercise, since the option is priced at 4:00 P.M. (Eastern time) but can be exercised until 4:10 P.M., providing a timing benefit to the option buyer. The seller does not learn of the exercise until the next business day.[17]

The disadvantages of cash-settled stock index options have not adversely affected trader interest; About one-third of total stock option volume is typically in index options.

MARKET ORGANIZATION

The Clearing Corporation

Options trades *appear to be* between the buyer and seller. However, technically each trade is with the Options Clearing Corporation. This arrangement is beneficial in two ways. First, when either the buyer or the seller wants to close his or her option position, this can be done on the exchange with *any willing trader,* rather than being restricted to the party who took the other side of the trade. Second, if a trader defaults, the clearing mechanism comes into play to guarantee the other side of the option contract.[18]

When an option buyer exercises an option, the Options Clearing Corporation randomly selects a member firm to be the deliverer of the stock.

Member firms then execute their own policy concerning who gets exercised. At the brokerage house level, the individual customer with the oldest short option position is often chosen as the designated seller of the stock. The Clearing Corporation automatically exercises stock options owned by individuals if the option is in-the-money by more than $3/4$ point at expiration. Index options are exercised if they are $1/4$ point in-the-money. Options owned by institutions are automatically exercised if a stock is in-the-money by $1/4$ point or an index is $1/100$ in-the-money.

Costs of Trading

Three types of costs exist when trading options:

- Commissions for trading the options.

- Stock commissions if the option is exercised and a stock is received or delivered.

- The bid-ask spread when the option is traded on the floor of the options exchange. For example, if the bid-ask spread is 3 to 3 $1/4$, then an individual buying an option pays the higher ask price of 3 $1/4$, while the bid price of 3 is received when selling an option.

Table 1–1 shows a representative commission schedule from a discount broker. Commissions from full-service brokers are higher.

Regulation

The regulation of options is split between two government agencies. Options on stocks, indexes, and foreign exchange are regulated by the Securities and Exchange Commission. Options on futures contracts are regulated by the Commodity Futures Trading Commission. These agencies monitor trading activity, make sure that all traders abide by exchange rules and trading laws,

---

TABLE 1–1   Commission Schedule for a Discount Broker

Dollar Amount of Trade	Commission*
< $2500	$20 + .02 of the dollar amount
$2500 to $10,000	$45 + .01 of the dollar amount
> $10,000	$120 + .0025 of the dollar amount

* The maximum commission is $30 per contract for the first five contracts plus $20 per contract for each additional contract. Minimum commission is $30 per contract for the first contract plus $2 per contract for each additional contract.

and make sure that no illegal insider trading occurs. Rutz (1988) gives a thorough overview of the clearance, payment, and settlement systems of options and futures exchanges.

SUMMARY AND LOOKING AHEAD

This chapter provides an overview of the quotations, basic concepts, and basic pricing relationships for individual stock options and index options. Call and put options are defined and the characteristics associated with these options are explained. Chapters 2 and 3 discuss the pricing of options. The Black-Scholes option pricing model is the focus of this discussion, but other approaches to pricing are relevant as well, such as put-call parity and the binomial model. The inputs and outputs of the pricing models are discussed in order to determine how such models can help an option trader to determine whether an option is under- or overpriced.

END NOTES

[1] Options on the S&P 100 Index and other indexes provide price discovery, because some of the stocks in the index may not have traded recently, making the index "old." Options do not have this problem.

[2] A "contingent claim" is a class of assets whose payoffs are completely determined by a predefined set of underlying variables. For example, an inflation futures contract whose payoff depends on the Consumer Price Index (CPI) is a contingent claim but not a derivative asset, since the CPI is not an asset. Contingent claims include derivative assets such as stock options.

[3] Other strike prices often exist for a given stock option. However, limited trading occurs for options when the strike price varies substantially from the current stock price.

[4] Option expiration dates and the option expiration cycle are discussed later in this chapter.

[5] Jarrow and Rudd (1983) prove these pricing relationships. Merton (1973) provides an extensive discussion of, and is the original source for, these option pricing relationships. Since these pricing relationships are intuitive, they do not need to be proved here.

[6] More formally, the lower bound of a call is $P_C(E) \geq \text{Max} [0, P_S - K(1 + r)^{-t}]$, where r is the risk-free interest rate. Due to the possibility of early exercise for an American call (when dividends exist), $P_C(A) \geq P_C(E)$. The upper bound on a call is $P_C \leq P_S$.

[7] Here we assume the initial stock price equals the strike price, but differing initial stock prices are easily implemented into the graph. Unless otherwise noted, the graphs and strategies ignore dividends, taxes, transactions costs, and the time value of money. Dividends are easily added but serve only to unnecessarily complicate the graphs and strategies. Taxes and transactions costs increase the cost of the position, but do not add to the analysis.

[8] Pricing relationships among the stock price, strike price, and option price, as well as speculative strategies for options, are examined in later chapters.

[9] More formally, the lower bound for an American put is $P_p(E) \geq Max\ [0,\ K(1 + r)^{-t} - P_s]$. The lower bound for a European put is $P_p(E) = Max\ [0,\ K - P_s]$. Also, $P_p(A) \geq P_p(E)$ due to the possibility of early exercise for the American put. The upper boundary condition is $P_p(E) \leq K\ (1 + r)^{-t}$. Also, $P_p(A) \leq K$.

[10] Newspapers listing quotations in the table format given in Exhibit 1–3 show options that do not trade on a particular day with the notation "r." The symbol "s" means that this particular option has never traded.

[11] When the stock split is an integer multiple such as a 2-1 split, then the strike price is divided by the integer split; thus a $60 strike price would be reduced to $30 for a 2-1 stock split and a second option contract would be issued. For a non-integer split, both the strike price and the number of shares are adjusted. Hence, for a 3-2 or, equivalently, a 1.5-1 split, the strike price is divided by 1.5 and the number of shares for an option is multiplied by 1.5. A stock dividend of 10% means that an option is based on 110 shares and the strike price is adjusted to $1/1.10 = .90909$ (rounded to the nearest 1/8) of its former price.

[12] The S&P Midcap Index is an index of midsize companies that are smaller than S&P 500 firms. Options on the NYSE, Value Line, utility, Japan, and gold/silver indexes also exist, although the volume for these industry index options is relatively small. Options on the S&P 500 Index, the Institutional Index, and the Financial News Composite Index are European options. The other options are American. The NSX option also differs from the S&P 500 option in that the former's final settlement price is based on the *opening* price of these stocks in the index on the third Friday rather than on the closing price, thereby escaping any volatility created by the expirations of stock options, index options, and futures contracts.

[13] Starting with the June 1987 contract, *some* option indexes are valued on the *open* of this third Friday, with trading in the option ceasing on the previous day. The S&P 100 option, the most popular stock index option, still expires on the close of the third Friday of the expiration month. The change in expiration dates for some index options was initiated because the concurrent expirations of individual stock options, index options, and futures contracts on stock indexes sometimes created volatile markets due to unusual supply and demand factors. The simultaneous expiration of these contracts became known as the "triple witching hour."

[14] One problem does exist with the cash-settlement feature of index options that are valued at the next day's open after the last trading day. This problem is called "exercise risk." If an option buyer exercises an in-the-money option early on the final trading day, only to have that option become an *out*-of-the-money option when the next day's opening price is used for pricing purposes, then the *buyer* of the option must *pay* the seller the difference between the index value and the option strike price. Thus, a trader should wait as long as possible on the final trading day before exercising an index option that is valued on the next day's open.

[15] Other problems exist for those who *sell* index options. If the option seller is using the sale of options to hedge a portfolio of stocks, two difficulties arise. First, the stock portfolio typically does not exactly match the index represented by the option. This is called "basis risk." Second, if the stocks are sold to pay off the option, a "timing risk" can exist—that is, if the sale of the stocks is made at a different time from the opening of the option on expiration day, then pricing differences exist.

[16] Newspapers listing option quotations in the table format show " . . . " for index options that did not trade on the day in question. *The Wall Street Journal* also provides a listing of the most active index options.

[17] While an option buyer does not officially have to provide notification of exercise until 4:10 P.M., some brokerage houses require notification by 12 P.M. Option writers who are not notified until late the next day lose their hedge position, since they end up selling their stocks one day after the option is officially exercised.

[18] During the 1987 stock market crash, the Clearing Corporation did have a default. When a trader defaults, the brokerage firm must pay; if the brokerage house goes bankrupt, the clearing member of the exchange must pay. If the clearing member goes bankrupt, the Clearing Corporation covers the default.

Principles of Option Pricing and the Binomial Model | **2**

The change in the option price *before option expiration* is a more complicated issue than the value of an option at expiration. Factors such as the change in the stock price, how close the stock price is to the exercise price, the time before option expiration, the volatility of the stock, and the level of interest rates all affect option price changes. The "Pricing Relationships" discussed below help to define how the option price changes as these factors change. Additional conditions for option prices also are developed.

From our general discussion of pricing relationships, we can proceed to a more concrete relationship between option prices. Specifically, put-call parity shows that a call option plus a risk-free instrument must equal a put option plus the underlying stock. If one combination is priced lower than the other, then arbitrage profits are possible. Thus, put-call parity is our first model of option prices.

The simple two-event binomial option model is then used as a tool to help explain the important aspects of an option pricing model. In particular, the binomial model shows how to construct a hedge between the option and the stock in order to eliminate risk. In fact, if the option is mispriced, such a hedge will earn a return in excess of the risk-free rate. When a large number of time periods are employed, the binomial model is equivalent to the Black-Scholes model discussed in Chapter 3. Binomial models are also useful in valuing certain types of options discussed in later chapters, such as options on debt.

CALL OPTION PRICE CHANGES BEFORE EXPIRATION

Boundary Conditions

Boundary conditions were introduced in Chapter 1. Boundary conditions provide specific quantitative relationships for option prices, specifying the upper and lower limits that options can trade without violating an arbitrage boundary. This chapter provides more specific boundary conditions in relation to time and the difference between strike prices via equations. Recall the symbols for our equations: t = the time until option expiration, K = the strike price (with K_1 representing a lower strike price), E = a European option, and A = an American option. Commission costs and taxes are ignored in these relationships. The discussion in this chapter examines the behavior of option prices before expiration. After discussing option relationships and boundary conditions, we will examine a relative pricing relationship between calls, puts, and the stock. This will be followed by exact option pricing models. Table 2–1 summarizes all of the boundary conditions from this and the previous chapter.

Trading Options and Pricing Factors

Unlike the over-the-counter options exclusively traded before 1973, exchange-traded options can be bought or sold at any time prior to option expiration. This liquidity allows traders to take their profits or cut their losses at any time. Trading options eliminates the disadvantages of exercising the option, including paying for and taking possession of the common stock when a call option is exercised. Trading options before expiration also increases the benefits of accurate forecasting and timing, since the trader can cover the option position before the entire time value is eliminated. Since

TABLE 2–1 Summary of the Option Boundary Conditions

	European Calls	American Calls	European Puts	American Puts
Lower bound:				
Approximation	Max $[P_s-K,0]$	Max $[P_s-K,0]$	Max $[K-P_s,0]$	Max $[K-P_s,0]$
Exact	Max $[P_s-K(1+r)^{-t},0]$	Max $[P_s-K(1+r)^{-t},0]$	Max $[K(1+r)^{-t}-P_s,0]$	Max $[K-P_s,0]$
Upper bound	P_s	P_s	$K(1+r)^{-t}$	K
Effect of time	$P_c(t_2) \geq P_c(t_1)$	$P_c(t_2) \geq P_c(t_1)$	$P_p(t_2) \geq P_p(t_1)$	$P_p(t_2) \geq P_p(t_1)$
Effect of strike	$P_c(K_1) \geq P_c(K_2)$	$P_c(K_1) \geq P_c(K_2)$	$P_p(K_2) \geq P_p(K_1)$	$P_p(K_2) \geq P_p(K_1)$
Maximum difference between strikes	$(K_2-K_1)(1+r)^{-t}$	K_2-K_1	$(K_2-K_1)(1+r)^{-t}$	K_2-K_1
Other relationships:				
American vs. European	$P_c(A) \geq P_c(E)$		$P_p(A) \geq P_p(E)$	

option prices before expiration typically include a time value, it is usually unwise to *exercise* options much before the expiration date.

The option profit obtainable from advantageous changes in the stock price is the most important reason most naive speculators purchase options. Therefore, a naive speculator's decision to purchase an option depends on the speculator's forecast concerning the stock price, even though the *actual price of an option* does *not* depend on the *expected* future stock price change (this is discussed in detail later).

Well-informed speculators also consider other factors that affect the option price and time value—namely, the time to expiration of the option, the volatility of the underlying stock price, the level of interest rates, and the difference between the stock and strike price. Thus, a speculator must determine if the price of the option in the market is fair, given the characteristics of the stock and the option. The relationships between these factors and option prices are examined next.[1]

Pricing Relationships

A rule of thumb is that at-the-money options change in price by about 50% of the change of the underlying stock price.[2] Deep in-the-money options (where the stock price is substantially above the strike price) change in price almost point for point with the stock price change. On the other hand, deep out-of-the-money options change very little as the stock price changes since the probability that this strike price will become an in-the-money option is minimal.[3]

Pricing Relationship #6: Options change less in absolute price than the associated stock price does.

Pricing Relationship #7: The percentage price change for options is greater than the percentage price change for the underlying stock.

Pricing Relationship #8: Near-the-money options change less in price than in-the-money options for a given stock price change, but near-the-money options have greater leverage (the %Δ in price is greater for near-the-money options).

Pricing Relationship #9: The absolute price change for deep in-the-money options is almost as large as the associated stock price change.

Pricing Relationship #10: The price of deep out-of-the-money options changes only minimally as the associated stock price changes.

Boundary conditions for strike prices can also be obtained. For call options, the relevant boundary condition is:

$$K_2 - K_1 \geq P_c(K_1) - P_c(K_2) \qquad \text{(2-1)}$$

Call Prices Before Expiration

Figure 2–1 illustrates the effect of changing stock prices on the value of an option *before* the option expires. The line labeled T(0) in Figure 2–1 has the same shape as our original option valuation graph at expiration, as given in Figure 1–1. T(1) illustrates how the option price varies *before* expiration, as the stock price changes.

Another way to view pricing relationships is to examine the intrinsic values and time values for the call options (as originally defined in Equations (1–1) and (1–2)). Each statement below is illustrated by using Figure 2–1:

- The intrinsic value of a call option decreases as the stock price declines (assuming the call option is in-the-money; thus an in-the-money call option declines in value as stock prices decline).

- The time value decreases as the stock price moves away from the strike price.

- As the intrinsic value increases, the time value decreases.

- The option buyer typically avoids purchasing options with a large amount of intrinsic value, because the cost is high and there is less leverage.

- As the underlying stock price moves toward the strike price, the time value for an out-of-the-money option increases.

Example 2–1 illustrates the profit, return, and leverage for an option before expiration.

The Time to Expiration

Time to expiration is an important factor affecting the price of the option. The shorter the time to expiration, the smaller the option price and the smaller the time value. This relationship between time and option price is related to the *probability* of the option buyer obtaining profits (or increasing profits) from a change in the stock price. The less time remaining, the smaller the probability of profiting from holding an option.

Time values across option months can be illustrated by finding the *differences* between option prices for the same strike price but different expiration months. The differences between the Feb and March ABC call option prices in Exhibit 1–3 are 1 for the 95, 100, and 105 strike prices, and 3/4 for the 90 and 110 strikes. The differences between the January and February call prices range from $^{13}/_{16}$ to $1\ ^{7}/_{8}$. These differences illustrate the effect of time on the option price. If the stock price remains stable, then option prices will decrease as the time to expiration decreases. Conse-

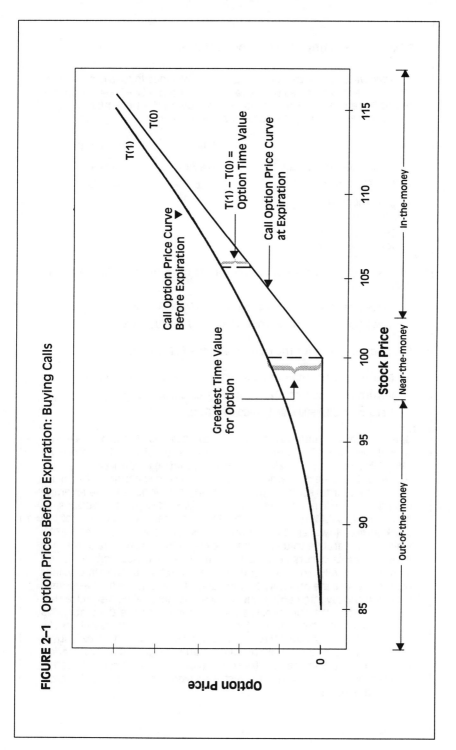

FIGURE 2–1 Option Prices Before Expiration: Buying Calls

EXAMPLE 2–1   Buying a Call Index Option

The following states the values for the Dow Jones Industrials, the S&P 500 Index, and the values of the call options on the S&P 500 for October 15 and December 10. The profitability of buying the December 410 and 425 call options on the S&P 500 is then determined.

	October 15	December 10
Dow Jones Industrials	3174.68	3323.81
S&P 500 Index	409.61	435.65
December 410 call (near-the-money)	10 $7/8$	27
December 425 call (out-of-the-money)	3 $3/4$	10 $3/4$

Profit from buying the call options on October 15 and selling them on December 10:

December 410 option profit = (27 – 10 $7/8$) 100 = $1612.50

December 425 option profit = (10 $3/4$ – 3 $3/4$) 100 = $700

The rates of return for the options and the S&P 500 are:

Return on December 410 option = $1612.50/$1087.50 = 103.4%

Return on December 425 option = $700/$375= 186.7%

Return on S&P 500 = 26.04/409.61 = 6.4%

One could even annualize the returns to obtain 674% and 1217%)! (The annualized rate of return is obtained by multiplying the return by 365/56. However, annualizing the return would be very unrealistic, since this would assume the same return for each 56-day period of the year.)

The most interesting aspect of buying call options is the leverage obtained: a return of 103.4% and 186.7% in 56 days on the options, as compared to a 6.4% return if the trader purchases the equivalent of the stock index. However, the option profits are only $1612.50 and $700, while a comparative value for the index is a $2604 profit. The difference in dollar profits occurs because the time value declines from 10 $7/8$ and 3 $3/4$, respectively, to 1.35 and 0.10. The reduction in the time values occurs because the options go from out-of-the-money to in-the-money, reducing the leverage effect and, hence, the time value. Also note that the December 410 option earns more money than the December 425 option, but the latter earns a larger percentage return based on the original cost. A critical factor in this example is that the call buyer forecasted the direction of the market *and* the timing of the market move correctly. Such perfect forecasting can be exploited by the use of options; however, less than perfect forecasting provides smaller profits, or even losses.

quently, one can say that purchasers of call options buy time—time for the stock price to increase so that the call option will be profitable. If the stock price does not increase, then the call option buyer forfeits the time value. On the other hand, part of this time value is retained if the option is sold before expiration.

Pricing Relationship #11: An option with a longer time to expiration is worth at least as much as an option with a shorter time to expiration (if the options have the same strike price).

This boundary condition in equation terms is:

$$P_c(t_2) \geq P_c(t_1) \qquad (2\text{-}2)$$

Pricing Relationship #12: Time values decrease as the time to expiration decreases (when other factors are kept constant).

Pricing Relationship #13: A call option is worth more "alive" than "dead"—that is, it is better to sell a call option before the expiration date than to exercise it.[4]

Figure 2–2 compares various times to option expiration, with T(1) having a shorter time to expiration than T(2), and so on. The differences in the option values for T(1), T(2), and T(3) are due to the change in the time value over time. Figure 2–2 shows that the largest time values occur near the exercise price for any given time to expiration, with the size of these values decreasing for deep in-the-money and deep out-of-the-money options. Pricing Relationships #11 and #13 are also verified by Figure 2–2.

Since the time to expiration of an option is an important factor affecting the price of the option, a speculator must determine whether a particular option expiration month provides sufficient time for the stock price to change substantially. Moreover, since an option is a "wasting asset"—that is, its value decreases over time (after stock price movements have been taken into account)—a speculator must determine whether the price paid for "time" is appropriate when compared to the estimated probability of making money from the forecasted stock price change.

The relationship between time to expiration and price is curvilinear, since a greater proportion of the time value is lost during the last few weeks of an option's life. This curvilinear relationship is shown in Figure 2–3. The curvilinear association is more difficult to recognize when option prices are examined on a daily or weekly basis, since changes in the stock price also alter the size of the time value.

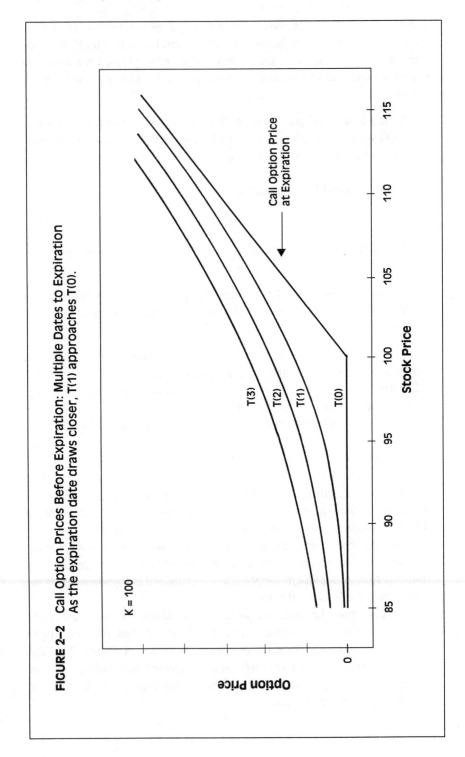

FIGURE 2–2 Call Option Prices Before Expiration: Multiple Dates to Expiration As the expiration date draws closer, T(1) approaches T(0).

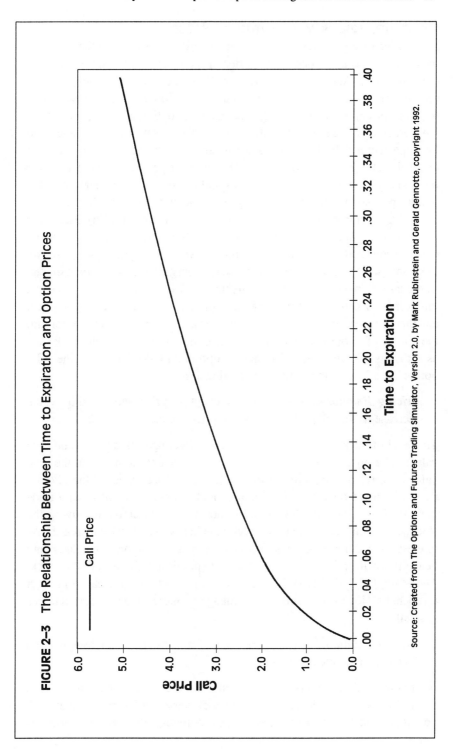

FIGURE 2-3   The Relationship Between Time to Expiration and Option Prices

Source: Created from The Options and Futures Trading Simulator, Version 2.0, by Mark Rubinstein and Gerald Gennotte, copyright 1992.

Leverage, Volatility, and Interest Rates

Stock price changes have immediate and significant effects on the prices of the associated call options. As the price of the stock increases, the prices of the call options increase. Similarly, as the stock price decreases, the call options prices decrease. Just as important, the option price changes *less* than the stock price, but the percentage change in the option price is *greater* than the percentage change in the stock price. This relationship is called the leverage factor. The leverage factor means that the rate of return on the original cost is greater for options, but the absolute price change is greater for the underlying stock. Examples in this and the previous chapter show that options possess much greater leverage than the underlying stock.

A third factor affecting the price of an option is the **volatility factor** for the underlying stock. The greater the volatility of the stock, the larger the option price and the time value. Exhibit 1–2 (the stock option quotes) shows that some stocks have options which possess larger time values than others. These larger time values are due to greater stock volatilities. Because a stock that is more volatile has a greater chance of increasing significantly in price, and thereby creating a larger profit, option traders incorporate this factor into the pricing of an option. Consequently, an option on a more stable stock such as ATT has a lower time value than an option on IBM. However, the ATT option has a lower probability of obtaining a *large* profit.

> *Pricing Relationship #14:* Both the option price and the time value increase as the volatility of the stock price increases.

The level of interest rates is the final factor affecting option prices and time values. The higher the interest rate, the larger the option price and the time value. The relative importance of this factor is determined by the alternative investment opportunities available and the costs for those who trade options. Thus, one can view a call option as an alternative to buying the stock, at least in terms of obtaining future gains as a stock price increases. As interest rates increase, the cost of financing a stock purchase increases, and hence the call option becomes a more favorable purchase than the stock. Therefore, the option price increases when interest rates increase to reflect this benefit. However, the effect of a change of interest rates on option prices is small.

> *Pricing Relationship #15:* The price of a call option increases with an increase in the interest rate.

In summary, four factors affect the size of the time value: the time to expiration factor, the leverage factor (stock versus strike price), the stock volatility, and the level of interest rates. Although this chapter describes these factors as if they affected the time value as independent forces, in reality they act on an interrelated basis to determine the time value and the option price. These relationships are considered in the pricing equations for options given in Chapter 3.

PUT OPTION PRICE CHANGES BEFORE EXPIRATION

In a manner essentially equivalent to call options, put options change price as stock prices change. However, put options change in the *opposite* direction of the stock price. As stock prices decline, put prices increase, and vice versa. As with calls, in-the-money put options can be exercised before expiration in order to obtain the intrinsic value of the option. However, since options sell for a price above their intrinsic value prior to expiration, put options are typically exercised prior to expiration only in specific situations. Thus, options are usually worth more "alive than dead." The associated boundary condition relating to time to expiration for puts is:

$$P_P(t_2, A) \geq P_P(t_1, A) \tag{2-3}$$

The time to expiration boundary condition for European puts is more complex, as two competing factors affect the price of the put. Buying a put is like deferring selling the stock at the strike price K. Thus, (1) to gain a longer time until expiration, one has to wait longer until receiving the sales price K (it is worth less now due to present value consideration); and (2) a longer time can generate greater profits if prices fall. The second factor tends to dominate in most cases. The boundary condition for the difference in two strike prices is as follows:

$$K_2 - K_1 \geq P_P(K_2) - P_P(K_1) \tag{2-4}$$

Example 2–2 illustrates the profit, return, and leverage factors for a put option before expiration.

Leverage

Put option prices change by a smaller dollar amount than the change in the stock price, while the percentage change in put prices is greater than the percentage change in stock prices, as is the case for call options. Thus, put options possess leverage. In general, the effects of the leverage factor and the associated pricing relationships for puts are equivalent to those previously discussed for call options. The statements concerning the intrinsic value of a call option and the call time value are also relevant for put options, with the exception of the first intrinsic value relationship for call options:

EXAMPLE 2–2 Example of Buying a Put Option:
The Market Crash of 1987

How did speculators who were lucky enough to hold a put option when the market crashed fare? On Thursday, October 13, 1987, the Dow Jones Industrials dropped over 90 points. On the following day, the market fell more than 100 points. On Monday, October 19, 1987, the Dow Jones Index took a free-fall of over 500 points!

The following illustrates the profits available to a speculator who purchased a put on Tuesday, October 13, and sold it at the end of the day on October 19. The S&P 100 put options are used for this example.

	Tuesday October 13	Monday October 19*
S&P 100 Index	307.36	216.31
S&P 100 Nov 305 put	7 1/8	118

Option profit = (118 – 7 1/8) 100 = $11,087.50
Return on option = $11,087.50/$712.50 = 1557%
Return on short sale of index = 91.05/307.36 = 29.6%

The profit on the put option was $11,087.50 per contract, for a period of one week! This created a return on the put of 1557%, while the cash index declined by 29.6%. In fact, the time value *increased* on the put, causing a *larger* dollar change in the option than in the cash index. This increase was due to the significant increase in market volatility.

* The index and option prices for October 19 may not be end-of-the-day prices since *The Wall Street Journal* had incomplete data for that day.

- The intrinsic value of a put decreases as stock prices increase (assuming the put is in-the-money).

Time to Expiration, Volatility, and Interest Rates

The other factors affecting put option prices and their associated pricing relationships are similar to the equivalent factors for call options.[5] In particular,

- **The time to expiration factor:** The longer the time to expiration, the larger the put option price and the put time value. As with calls, the time value decreases as the option approaches the expiration date.

- **The volatility factor**: The more volatile the underlying stock, the larger the put option price and the time value.

- **The interest rate**: The higher the interest rate, the *smaller* the put option price and the time value. This relationship is opposite that

EXHIBIT 2–1   Effects of Changes in Factors on Option Prices

Factor	Effects of Increase in Factors	
	Call Prices	Put Prices
Stock price	Increase	Decrease
Strike price	Decrease	Increase
Time to expiration	Increase	Increase
Volatility of stock	Increase	Increase
Interest rates	Increase	Decrease
Cash dividends on stock	Decrease	Increase

discussed for call options, since a put effectively mimics the profitability of a short sale when the stock price declines below the strike price.[6]

Pricing Relationship #16: The price of a put option decreases with an increase in the interest rate.

Exhibit 2-1 provides a summary of the effects of the various factors on option prices/time values.

DYNAMICALLY REPLICATING OPTIONS

The payoffs from an option contract can be *duplicated* simply by changing the number of shares of stock owned. A trader would increase the number of shares when stock prices increase and decrease the number of shares when stock prices decrease. A replicating portfolio changes the stock position on a dynamic basis as the stock price changes. Owning the proper number of shares at all times (plus cash) creates the same payoff diagram as buying a call option. The number of shares needed is determined by the "hedge ratio" obtained from an option pricing model such as the one developed below or the model examined in Chapter 3. Option pricing models find and use hedge ratios, also called deltas (δ). The replicating portfolio determines the call value as: call value = $P_S \, \delta$ – borrowing. Figure 2-4 illustrates the initial setup of a replicating portfolio.

An alternative way to look at traded options in relation to dynamically replicated option portfolios is to realize that traded options are equivalent to a *prepackaged* dynamic strategy. Thus, the option trader does not need to constantly change the stock/cash portfolio to obtain the option payoff. Moreover, traded options adequately reflect jumps in stock prices, while a

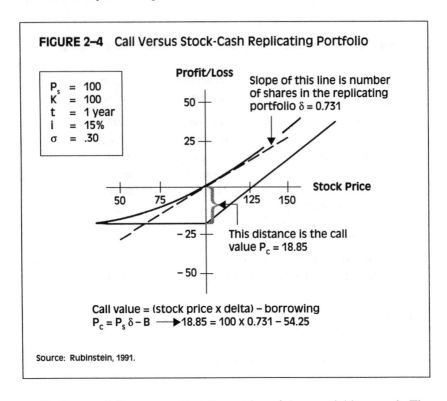

FIGURE 2–4 Call Versus Stock-Cash Replicating Portfolio

P_s = 100
K = 100
t = 1 year
i = 15%
σ = .30

Profit/Loss

Slope of this line is number of shares in the replicating portfolio δ = 0.731

50

25

Stock Price

50   75   125   150

– 25   This distance is the call value P_c = 18.85

– 50

Call value = (stock price x delta) – borrowing
$P_c = P_s \delta - B$ ——▶ 18.85 = 100 x 0.731 – 54.25

Source: Rubinstein, 1991.

replicating portfolio cannot adjust the number of shares quickly enough. The best-known application of replicating portfolios is a strategy called "portfolio insurance," which is discussed in a later chapter.

A dynamic replicating portfolio also is useful to Wall Street for other reasons. When options do not exist, Wall Street firms can "create" options by dynamically trading the asset and cash (or bonds). The firms can then sell these new options to customers.

PUT-CALL PARITY

Put-call parity equates buying a call (plus placing the present value of the strike price into a risk-free instrument) to buying a put and buying the stock. Figure 2–5(A) illustrates the payoff diagrams of buying a call, investing in a risk-free instrument, and their combination. Figure 2–5(B) shows the payoff diagrams of buying a put, buying stock, and their combination. Comparing Figures 2–5(A) and 2–5(B) shows that these two strategies are equivalent. Alternatively, Exhibit 2–2 uses cash flows to show how these two strategies are equivalent, as well as proving Equation (2–5):[7]

$$P_c + K e^{-rt} = P_p + P_s \qquad (2\text{--}5)$$

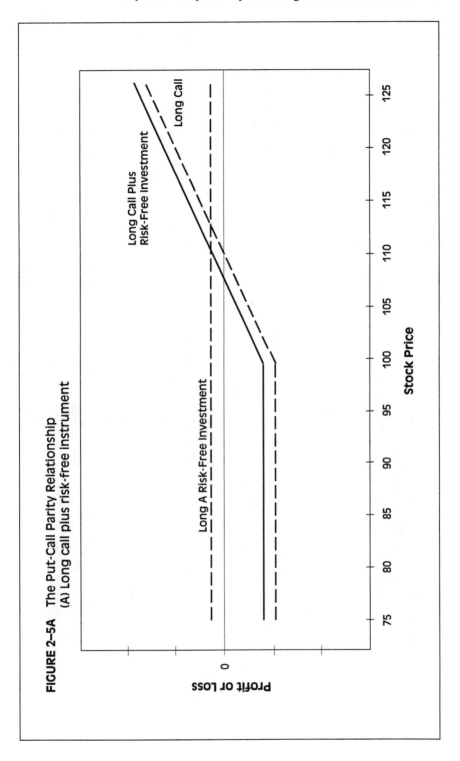

FIGURE 2–5A   The Put-Call Parity Relationship
(A) Long call plus risk-free instrument

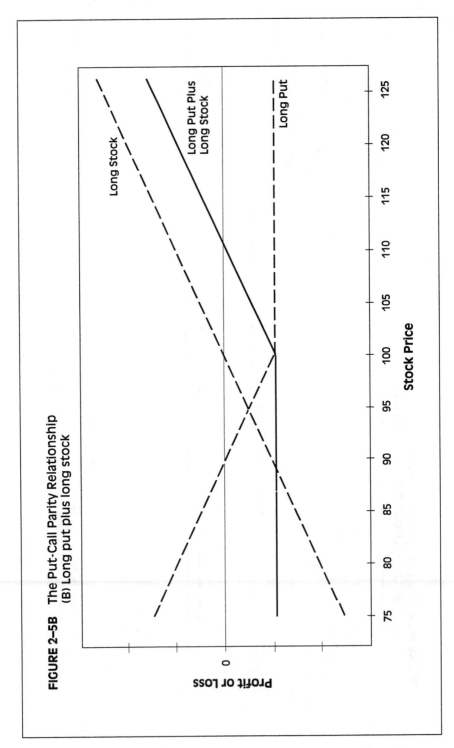

FIGURE 2–5B The Put-Call Parity Relationship
(B) Long put plus long stock

The initial significance of put-call parity is that it represents an arbitrage relationship between calls, puts, and the underlying asset. If either the call or the put price becomes mispriced relative to the other instruments (by more than the transactions costs), an arbitrageur can profit by buying the lower-priced combination and selling the higher-priced combination. Hence, put-call parity is a pricing and arbitrage relationship.

THE BINOMIAL OPTION PRICING MODEL

While the discussion and graphs above provide insights as to the effect of stock prices, time, volatility, and interest rates on the option price, a model is needed that considers all of these factors simultaneously. The Black-Scholes option model, covered in Chapter 3, considers all four of the input factors listed above to determine a fair price for a call option. Before turning to the Black-Scholes model, we examine what is known as the **binomial option pricing model**, developed by Cox, Ross, and Rubinstein (1979). The binomial model determines the fair value for an option based on *discrete* changes for the stock price. While the binomial model is not typically used to calculate stock option prices, it is a simple and intuitive model that illustrates the concept of a **hedge ratio**. A hedge ratio is the proportion of asset shares to option shares that creates a risk-free combination when the asset changes in price. Therefore, understanding the binomial model provides a foundation for a better understanding of the Black-Scholes pricing model. In addition, the binomial model is used to price debt options and other types of options.

Two States of Nature

The binomial option pricing model involves two possible outcomes, or "states of nature." Restricting the number of outcomes to two allows us to examine how a basic call option pricing model works before discussing the more complicated Black-Scholes model. The two stock prices associated with the two states of nature are designated as P_s^+ and P_s^-. These two possibilities are an increase (+) and a decrease (–) from the current stock price to the hypothetical stock price at the expiration of the option. Both price changes occur one time period from now. Similarly, the corresponding option prices for these two states of nature are designated as P_c^+ and P_c^-. Note the two simplifications from reality: (1) only two ending prices are possible, and (2) there is only one time period in which a price change can occur. Our example is based on the assumption that the current stock price is $100 and the two possible outcomes are a stock price of either $95 or $105 at the expiration of the option, which is one time period from now. The strike price of the call option is $100, and the risk-free interest rate for invested

---

EXHIBIT 2-2   Justifying the Put-Call Parity Relationship

Justifying the validity of the put-call parity relationship is straightforward. We examine two equivalent alternatives for investing funds in stocks, while protecting against downward movements in the stock price. Then we set the two alternatives equal to each other and solve for the put-call parity equation.

1. Buy a call option at P_C and invest the present value of the strike price ($K\,e^{-rt}$) in a risk-free instrument.

2. Buy a put option at P_P and buy the stock at P_s, with the put providing downside protection against losses in the stock.

The payoff table below shows how these alternatives are equivalent at option expiration if the put and call have the same strike price and the same expiration date. Equating the two alternatives generates Equation (2–5):

$$P_C + K\,e^{-rt} = P_P + P_s \qquad\qquad (2\text{-}5)$$

	Cash Flows		
	Current Date	At Expiration	
Strategy		$P_s \le K$	$P_s > K$
(1) Buy call	$-P_C$	0	$P_{S,E} - K$
Invest present value of the strike price	$-K e^{-rt}$	K	K
Total of (1)	$-(P_C + K e^{-rt})$	K	$P_{S,E}$
(2) Buy put	$-P_P$	$K - P_{S,E}$	0
Buy stock	$-P_s$	$P_{S,E}$	$P_{S,E}$
Total of (2)	$-(P_P + P_s)$	K	$P_{S,E}$

$P_{S,E}$ = the stock price at option expiration

---

funds over the time period in question is 0.5%—that is, 1/2 of 1% per month, or 6% per year.

Given the above information, we can determine the value of the current option price that is consistent with the two possible future stock prices. We begin by finding the option value expiration under each state of nature. Thus, if the stock price decreases to $95 when the strike price is $100, the option is out-of-the-money and expires worthless. If the stock price increases to $105, then the option is worth $5. These relationships are shown in Figure 2–6(A). Figure 2–6(B) plots these two states of nature, with the stock price being on

---

FOCUS 2–1   OptionVue: What Is It?

OptionVue is a commercial PC program providing option pricing models (such as the binomial model and models found in Chapter 3) and trading selection screens to help traders best implement their strategies in the options market. The base OptionVue package sells for less than $900; additional modules for record keeping and real-time quotations cost $300 and $500, respectively. (Call 800-733-6610 for more information; a trial package is available for under $50.)

The following provides an overview to the functions and uses of OptionVue. Various tables, exhibits, and graphs throughout the options chapters are created using OptionVue, as indicated in the source notes to the tables, exhibits, and figures.

- The fair values of options on stock, stock indexes, futures, and currency are determined based on the binomial, Black-Scholes (see Chapter 3), or a proprietary model. Values of the option "sensitivities" are also calculated (see Chapter 4).

- Option strategies discussed in this chapter and in Chapters 5 and 6 can be evaluated in terms of risk and return using current option prices. Various criteria can be chosen to evaluate the options in relation to the goals of the trader. The program even ranks the best option positions according to the criteria given. Graphs can be produced showing the potential profitability based on expected asset movements.

- A monthly database can be purchased that provides stock tickers, dividend information, current strike prices, and historical volatilities of all stocks and other assets that have exchange-listed options.

- A record-keeping function provides a summary of portfolio activity, including information on commissions, cash available, and margins.

- OptionVue can be hooked up to on-line quotation feeds in order to input up-to-the-minute option prices for analysis of the best options to trade.

---

the X-axis and the option price plotted on the Y-axis. Joining the two points representing the two possible outcomes for the stock and option prices at option expiration generates the straight line shown in Figure 2-6(B). The slope of a line is simply $\Delta Y/\Delta X$, or in this case a difference of $5 for the two possible option prices divided by a difference of $10 for the two stock prices. The resultant slope of this line is .5. The slope of this option/stock price line is called a hedge ratio; we will use this value to eliminate (hedge) the risk of the position.

FIGURE 2–6   The Binomial Option Pricing Concept

(A) Stock and option prices with two states of nature:

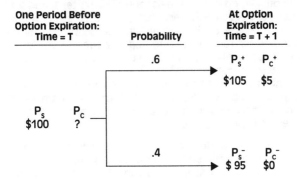

(B) Plotting the stock and option prices at option expiration:

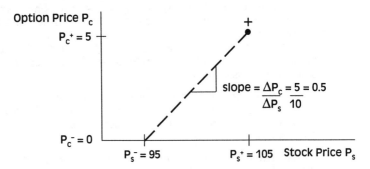

Note: Only two states of nature exist, namely a + to a stock price of 105 and a – to a stock price of 95. Other stock prices are not relevant for this example. The slope between these two points is drawn simply to illustrate the hedge ratio.

Eliminating Risk: The Hedge Ratio

In order to eliminate all of the risk of a position by option hedging, one must obtain a combination of call options and stock that results in identical ending values for the two states of nature. The hedge ratio for this example is 0.5; this means that the appropriate combination of the stock shares and option shares is a ratio of 1 to 2, or 0.5. For each share of stock, the hedger needs to *sell* two shares of the option—an opposite position is taken in the option to offset the stock price change. This hedge ratio is determined by the relationship between the option price difference of $5 between the two states of nature and the stock price difference of $10, as shown in Figure 2–6.

How does one use the knowledge of the hedge ratio to guarantee a perfect hedge? Multiplying the stock and option price changes by the number of stock and option shares determined by the hedge ratio results in the following:

$$\text{Total stock price change} = \text{Total option price change}$$

$$\Delta P_S\, N_S = \Delta P_C\, N_C \qquad\qquad \textbf{(2-6)}$$

where ΔP_S, ΔP_C = the change in prices for the stock and the call option
$\quad\quad\;\; N_S$, N_C = the number of shares for the stock and the call option

For our example, we show that a 2 to 1 hedge ratio creates a perfect hedge:

$$(\$10)\,(1) = (\$5)\,(2)$$

Thus, the stock and option total dollar changes offset each other.[8] Therefore, the ratio of the stock to option shares is directly linked to the ratio of price changes between the option and stock. Alternatively, solving Equation (2–6) for the ratio between the stock and the option shares determines the hedge ratio in terms of the changes in price:

$$\frac{N_S}{N_C} = \frac{\Delta P_C}{\Delta P_S} \qquad\qquad \textbf{(2-7)}$$

Equivalently, one can calculate the hedge ratio for a binomial model from the following formula:

$$h = \frac{P_C{}^+ - P_C{}^-}{P_S{}^+ - P_S{}^-} \qquad\qquad \textbf{(2-8)}$$

Exhibit 2–3(A) also shows that the ending portfolio value is the same ($95), regardless of which state of nature occurs. As above, this example sells two options per share of stock purchased, designated as $P_S - 2P_C$ in Exhibit 2–3(A). Only one additional step remains to complete our discussion of the binomial model: to obtain a value for the call option one period before option expiration.[9]

The Value of the Option

Recall that the risk-free interest rate over the time period in question is 0.5% per month. Since our hedge procedure creates a risk-free situation—that is, the ending value of the stock/option position is known with certainty—the

EXHIBIT 2-3   Hedge Ratios and Option Prices

One Period Before Option Expiration	State (1): Stock Price Increase	State (2): Stock Price Decrease

(A) $P_s = \$100$
     $P_c = ?$

	State (1): Stock Price Increase	State (2): Stock Price Decrease
	$P_s^+ = \$105$	$P_s^- = \$95$
	$P_c^+ = \$5$	$P_c^- = \$0$
	$P_s^+ - 2 P_c^+ = \$95$	$P_s^- - 2 P_c^- = \$95$

(B) $P_s = \$100$
     $P_c = \$2.736$ (from Example 2-3)

Investment:	$P_s - 2 P_c = \$94.528$	$P_s - 2 P_c = \$94.528$
Ending Value:	$P_s^+ - 2 P_c^+ = \$95.00$	$P_s^- - 2 P_c^- = \$95.00$
Rate of Return:	($95.00 - $94.528)/$94.528	($95.00 - $94.528)/$94.528
	$0.472/$94.528 = 0.5\%	$0.472/$94.528 = 0.5\%

(C) **Option Overpriced**

$P_s = \$100$
$P_c = \$2.85$

Investment:	$P_s - 2 P_c = \$94.30$	$P_s - 2 P_c = \$94.30$
Ending Value:	$P_s^+ - 2 P_c^+ = \$95.00$	$P_s^- - 2 P_c^- = \$95.00$
Rate of Return:	($95.00 - $94.30)/$94.30	($95.00 - $94.30)/$94.30
	$0.70/$94.30 = 0.74\%	$0.70/$94.30 = 0.74\%

(D) **Option Underpriced: Naive Hedger**

$P_s = \$100$
$P_c = \$2.60$

Investment:	$P_s - 2 P_c = \$94.80$	$P_s - 2 P_c = \$94.80$
Ending Value:	$P_s^+ - 2 P_c^+ = \$95.00$	$P_s^- - 2 P_c^- = \$95.00$
Rate of Return:	($95.00 - $94.80)/$94.80	($95.00 - $94.80)/$94.80
	$0.20/$94.80 = 0.21\%	$0.20/$94.80 = 0.21\%

(E) **Option Underpriced: Reverse Hedge**
    (short stock and receive funds, buy options, invest funds from short sale)*

$P_s = \$100$
$P_c = \$2.60$

Investment:	$+2 P_c = \$5.20$	$+2 P_c = \$5.20$
Ending Value:	$-P_s^+ + 2 P_c^+ + P_s(1 + R_f) =$	$-P_s^- + 2 P_c^- + P_s(1 + R_f) =$
	$-\$105 + 2(\$5) + \$100(1.005)$	$-\$95 + 2(\$0) + \$100(1.005)$
	$= \$5.50$	$= \$5.50$
Rate of Return:	($5.50 - $5.20)/$5.20	($5.50 - $5.20)/$5.20
	$0.30/$5.20 = 5.8\%	$0.30/$5.20 = 5.8\%

* (E) assumes the short seller has access to all of the funds generated from the short sale. Actually, active option traders receive only 85% or less of these funds, while individuals often must put up additional funds to cover a short sale.

return earned on this stock/option position should equal the risk-free rate. Therefore, the original investment, compounded at the risk-free rate, must equal the ending stock/option position value ($95 in this case):

$$I(1 + R_f) = V \qquad (2\text{–}9)$$

where I = the original *net* investment one period before option expiration

R_f = the risk-free interest rate

V = the value of the combined stock/option position at option expiration

Moreover, the original net investment, I, is based on the cost of the stock *less* the amount received from selling the call options:

$$I = N_S P_S - N_C P_C \qquad (2\text{–}10)$$

Example 2-3 shows how these equations are employed for the case at hand.

Mispriced Binomial Options

Example 2–3 determines the fair value of the option one period before expiration, when two possible states of nature exist for the stock price. What if the price of the option differs from its fair value? For example, what if the option sells for either $2.85 or $2.60—that is, it sells for $1/8$ of a point higher or lower than its fair value?

If the option is overpriced—that is, it is selling for $2.85 one period before expiration—then the hedger receives more than the fair value of the option. This reduces the net investment needed and increases the rate of return to 0.74%, which is above the 0.5% return available from other risk-free investments. This situation is illustrated in Exhibit 2–3(C). When traders realize that a higher (risk-free) return is available by hedging in options rather than by investing in other risk-free investments, they will construct the stock/option hedge with the appropriate hedge ratio of 0.5. This activity of selling the options drives down the option price until the return on the hedge equals the risk-free rate of 0.5% available from other investments.

If the option is underpriced—that is, it is selling for $2.60—then two situations could occur. One possibility is that naive hedgers who are unaware of the fair value of the option would execute the same type of hedge as shown above: for each share of stock purchased, the hedger sells two option shares. Exhibit 2–3(D) shows that selling the underpriced option results in a return on investment of 0.21%, which is *less* than can be obtained by putting the equivalent funds in other risk-free investments earning 0.5%.

EXAMPLE 2-3   Solving for the Binomial Option Value

Using the data from Exhibit 2–3 plus Equation (2–10), we have:

$$I = N_s P_s - N_c P_c \qquad\qquad (2\text{–}10)$$

$$I = (1)\ (\$100) - (2)\ P_c$$

Substituting I from Equation (2–10) into (2–9) and using our values for R_f = 0.005 and V = \$95, we have:

$$I\ (1 + R_f) = V \qquad\qquad (2\text{–}9)$$

$$(\$100 - 2\ P_c)\ (1 + 0.005) = \$95$$

Solving for the value of the option one period before expiration, P_c, we find:

$$-2\ P_c = (\$95/1.005) - \$100 = -\$5.47$$

$$P_c = \$2.736$$

Thus, the fair value of the call option one period prior to expiration is \$2.736. This is verified by the following:

a. The original investment of buying the stock and selling two call options (where the hedge receives the price of these options) is:

$$I = \$100\ - 2\ (\$2.736) = \$94.528$$

b. Investing this original amount at 0.5 % equals the final value of the stock/option position:

$$\$94.528\ (1.005) = \$95$$

These relationships are summarized in Exhibit 2–2(B).

A second possibility is that a sophisticated hedger realizes that a higher return can be obtained by *buying* the option and *selling* the stock short. This strategy is called a **reverse hedge**. In this case, the hedger sells the stock short, deposits the \$100 received from the short sale into an interest-bearing account, and buys the option. Exhibit 2–3(E) shows that this alternative provides a return of 5.8% on the hedger's funds, which is much higher than the return available from other risk-free investments.

The above examples show that if an option is mispriced, an arbitrageur can step in and buy the underpriced and/or sell the overpriced instrument to earn a higher return than is available from other risk-free investments. These actions cause the price of the option to revert to its appropriate fair price. An alternative approach for potential arbitrage situations with mispriced options is to borrow funds at the risk-free interest rate in order to cover the cost of the investment. Thus, an arbitrageur would buy stock, sell options, and finance the net cost with borrowed funds. When an option is mispriced, the profit earned on the arbitrage is greater than the interest on the borrowed funds. Therefore, risk-free profits are obtained without any net investment on the part of the arbitrageur.

Call Prices and a Binomial Example

The procedure developed above shows how a hedge ratio and a call option price are determined based on a two-state model of stock prices for one period in the future. The equation for the value of a call option in a two-state world is:

$$P_C = \frac{P_S (1 + R_f) (P_C^+ - P_C^-) - P_S^- P_C^+ + P_S^+ P_C^-}{(P_S^+ - P_S^-) (1 + R_f)}$$ (2-11)

Example 2–4 demonstrates how to find the hedge ratio and the value of the call option for a two-state situation.

Extending the Model and a Summary

The above discussion of the binomial model is restrictive in that only two possible states of nature and one time period are examined. However, this simple binomial model is important for understanding the concepts of option pricing and introducing the option models discussed below. The binomial model also can be extended to a number of time periods and states of nature. For example, Figure 2–7 shows a three-state, two-period model extension of our original example. In this situation, the stock price increases or decreases 5% each period in relation to the previous period's binomial value. The value of the call option and the associated hedge ratio can be determined for each step in the binomial process. In particular, note that the hedge ratio *changes* from period T to period T + 1. Thus, when multiple periods are used in the binomial model, the hedge ratio must be dynamically altered for each time period. This binomial process can be extended to a large number of periods and to smaller stock price changes. When a large number of time periods are used, the resultant call values are equivalent to the prices obtained from the Black-Scholes model developed later. Table 2–2 shows the call option values derived from the binomial model with 5, 25, and 150 time periods. As the number of periods increases, the accuracy of the model increases. Appendix 2B extends the binomial model to *n* periods. For a rigorous derivation of the binomial approach for many time periods, see Ritchken (1987, ch. 9) or Jarrow and Rudd (1983, ch. 13).

EXAMPLE 2–4 The Binomial Option Model: An Example

The current stock price is 50, with the two possible outcomes for the stock price one period from now being 56 and 46. The risk-free rate for the next period is 1%. Thus, $P_s = 50$, $P_s^+ = 56$, $P_s^- = 46$, and $R_f = 0.01$. To determine the appropriate hedge ratio and the current value for a call option with a strike price of 50, employ the following equation:

$$h = \frac{P_c^+ - P_c^-}{P_s^+ - P_s^-} = \frac{\Delta P_c}{\Delta P_s} \qquad (2\text{–}8)$$

$$= (6 - 0)/(56 - 46)$$
$$= 6/10 = 0.6$$

The hedge ratio of 0.6 means that the appropriate ratio of shares of stock to option shares is 0.6, or $N_s/N_c = 0.6$. In other words, for every 6 shares of stock, the hedger needs 10 option shares. The equation for determining the value of the call option one period before expiration is:

$$P_c = \frac{P_s (1 + R_f)(P_c^+ - P_c^-) - P_s^- P_c^+ + P_s^+ P_c^-}{(P_s^+ - P_s^-)(1 + R_f)} \qquad (2\text{–}11)$$

$$= \frac{50(1.01)(6 - 0) - 46(6) + 56(0)}{(56 - 46)(1.01)}$$
$$= 2.673$$

The call option is worth $2.673.

The binomial option model provides several insights into the pricing of call options. Recall that a hedge ratio is calculated based on knowledge of the two possible values of the stock price one period in the future, at option expiration. A properly constructed hedge ratio eliminates all risk—that is, the value of the combined stock and option position one period later will be the same, *regardless* of whether the stock price increases or decreases. The fair return on such a risk-free stock/option position is the risk-free interest rate. Knowledge of this risk-free interest rate on other instruments allows us to determine the appropriate value of the call option one period before expiration of the option. If the option is mispriced, returns above the risk-free rate are available.

Finally, note that nowhere in our calculation of the hedge ratio or the value of the binomial option do the probabilities relating to the stock price change affect the results. While these probabilities would affect any calculations of the stock value, they do *not* affect the option value or the hedge ratio. This allows for the development of an option pricing model that is independent of the unknown stock price expectations. Since the option model does not need a forecast of the stock price, the resulting option equation is a very useful and powerful financial tool.

EMPIRICAL EVIDENCE

Empirical studies have examined whether option prices violate the boundary conditions or put-call parity. Such studies on past data provide evidence on whether the options markets are priced properly or whether arbitrage opportunities exist.

Option Boundary Tests

Bhattacharya (1983) employs transaction data for ten months on 58 stocks to test for violations of the option pricing relationships. The first test examines whether option prices trade below the intrinsic value of the option. He finds that only 1.3% of over 86,000 transactions violate this pricing relationship, with the average size of these violations being $12 per contract. For 29% of the violations, this opportunity is eliminated by the next trade. A test on the lower bound for the option price finds violations 7.5% of the time, with an average value of $7.

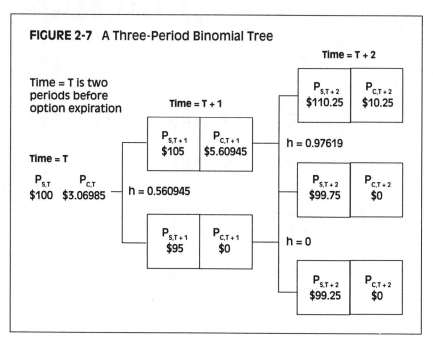

FIGURE 2-7 A Three-Period Binomial Tree

TABLE 2–2 Call Values Determined from the Binomial Method

$P_s = 100 \qquad I = .10$

months to expiration

σ	K	n=5				n=25				n=150			
		1	3	6	12	1	3	6	12	1	3	6	12
.2	85	15.67	17.10	19.38	23.64	15.67	17.11	19.35	23.57	15.67	17.11	19.34	23.54
	90	10.76	12.61	15.19	19.54	10.76	12.55	15.14	19.68	10.76	12.55	15.12	19.68
	95	6.25	8.41	11.29	16.23	6.20	8.51	11.38	16.12	6.20	8.50	11.34	16.15
	100	2.82	5.41	8.37	13.25	2.73	5.27	8.19	13.04	2.71	5.22	8.13	12.98
	105	.89	2.73	5.46	10.27	.84	2.92	5.62	10.23	.83	2.89	5.58	10.27
	110	.15	1.53	3.67	7.48	.17	1.42	3.65	7.99	.17	1.44	3.65	7.95
	115	.00	.46	2.38	6.07	.02	.60	2.22	6.06	.02	.65	2.28	6.07
.3	85	15.74	17.78	20.70	25.40	15.74	17.70	20.60	25.56	15.75	17.70	20.57	25.57
	90	11.06	13.70	16.68	22.17	11.09	13.64	16.92	22.31	11.08	13.64	16.88	22.24
	95	6.97	10.06	13.79	19.57	6.96	10.13	13.59	19.17	6.99	10.08	13.63	19.21
	100	4.02	7.45	11.17	16.97	3.88	7.22	10.86	16.59	3.84	7.15	10.77	16.47
	105	1.77	4.83	8.55	14.38	1.81	4.91	8.35	14.01	1.83	4.86	8.41	14.04
	110	.78	3.19	5.94	11.78	.74	3.15	6.49	11.98	.74	3.18	6.43	11.91
	115	.22	2.15	4.88	9.38	.26	1.99	4.82	10.12	.26	2.00	4.83	10.05
.4	85	15.91	18.89	22.23	27.83	15.98	18.76	22.27	28.29	16.00	18.71	22.33	28.20
	90	11.76	14.89	18.87	25.48	11.66	15.06	19.10	25.24	11.66	15.05	19.03	25.27
	95	7.73	11.97	16.43	23.13	7.96	11.82	16.01	22.58	7.93	11.84	16.07	22.56
	100	5.22	9.49	13.99	20.78	5.04	9.18	13.57	20.23	4.98	9.09	13.45	20.07
	105	2.72	7.01	11.55	18.43	2.95	6.84	11.13	17.89	2.91	6.88	11.18	17.88
	110	1.68	4.73	9.12	16.08	1.59	5.12	9.32	15.78	1.56	5.07	9.23	15.87
	115	.74	3.79	7.13	13.74	.79	3.90	7.63	14.15	.78	3.69	7.56	14.03

Source: Rubinstein, (1991).

Put-Call Parity Tests

Klemkosky and Resnick (1979, 1980) employ transactions data to examine 600 put-call positions by using one trade day per month for one year in order to test the put-call parity relationship and the pricing of options. Possibilities of early exercise are removed from the data set since the put-call parity relationship assumes that no premium for early exercise is impounded into the put option price.

Violations of the put-call parity relationship are exploited by setting up a hedge between the put, call, and stock such that the underpriced option is purchased and the overpriced option is sold. Based on the put-call relationship, an arbitrageur can buy a put and sell the call (when the put is deemed to be underpriced relative to the call) by executing the following transactions: buy the stock, buy a put, sell a Treasury bill, and sell the call option. A similar position is initiated when the put is overpriced relative to the call option.

Klemkosky and Resnick determine that 27% of put underpricing situations are profitable after transaction costs, with most of these situations occurring soon after puts started to trade on the exchanges. Only 7% of the call underpricing situations are profitable. Klemkosky and Resnick then examine the effect of the delay time between recognizing the mispricing and acting on it. They determine that delay times of 5 to 15 minutes do not eliminate the mispricings; however, the bid-ask spread cost is not factored into their results. Klemkosky and Resnick state that this bid-ask cost would tend to eliminate most of these excess profits.

SUMMARY AND LOOKING AHEAD

This chapter explores basic pricing relationships for the call and put options before option expirations and the factors affecting option prices. The put-call parity and binomial pricing models are also examined. The binomial model provides an introduction to option pricing models. The next chapter discusses the Black-Scholes option pricing model.

END NOTES

[1] This section is discussed in terms of a speculator to promote simplicity and ease of exposition. Determination of a fair option price is also important to hedgers and arbitrageurs, as discussed later. The discussion of the pricing aspects of options later in this chapter and in Chapters 3 and 4 specifically describes how a "fair price" is determined for options and how various factors affect the pricing of an option. This chapter also provides an intuitive understanding of how call option prices change.

[2] This relationship is based on option pricing models discussed in this and the following chapter.

[3] At times, the prices listed for deep in-the-money and deep out-of-the-money options seem to violate logic (the intrinsic value appears to be larger than the option price). These circumstances arise because deep out-of-the-money options do not trade often. Thus, the listed option could have traded hours before the close, causing the apparent mispricing when in fact the stock price changes later in the day without an option trade.

[4] This statement refers to an American option since European options can be exercised only at expiration. Moreover, this pricing relationship was developed for non-dividend-paying stocks. Ritchken (1987) proves that call options on dividend-paying stocks should sometimes be exercised early, and that an American call option on a dividend-paying stock can be worth more than a corresponding European option on the same stock.

[5] However, there are circumstances in which a put option is exercised prior to the expiration of the option, as discussed in Chapter 3. Also notice that the differences in prices between the two expirations are smaller for puts than for calls. These differences also relate to the pricing process.

[6] The trader who sells a put option can hedge this position with a short sale on the stock. The large short seller can receive the funds at the time of the short sale. If interest rates increase, the interest proceeds from investing these funds increase as well; therefore, put time values decrease.

[7] Alternative approaches achieving the same result:

- Buying a call is equivalent to a portfolio of buying a put, buying stock, and borrowing the present value of the strike price.

- Buying a put is equivalent to a portfolio of buying a call, selling the stock short, and investing the present value of the strike price (investing proceeds of the short sale).

Technically, put-call parity does not *strictly* hold when early exercise of the options is possible.

[8] The concept of having a hedge ratio that eliminates risk is similar to having a correlation of -1 between two assets in portfolio analysis: The price change in one asset exactly offsets the change in the other asset.

[9] The general equation for the hedge ratio for a two-state option model given in Equation (2-8) is developed from what is known about the stock and option prices at option expiration. Thus, the value, V, of the combined stock/option position at option expiration is defined as follows, with (+) indicating an increase in the stock price and (−) indicating a decrease:

$$V^+ = N_s\, P_s^+ - N_c\, P_c^+$$
$$V^- = N_s\, P_s^- - N_c\, P_c^-$$

We want to determine the hedge ratio $h = N_s/N_c$ such that the position is risk-free—that is, where $V^+ = V^-$. Thus, we set these two equations equal to each other and substitute $h = N_s/N_c$:

$$h\, P_s^+ - P_c^+ = h,\ P_s^- - P_c^-$$

Solving for h we obtain Equation (2–8).

APPENDIX 2A
COMPARING OPTIONS TO FORWARD AND FUTURES CONTRACTS

The discussion of option contracts in this chapter emphasizes the payoffs of options and their risk and return characteristics. However, recognizing that a proper combination of options contracts is equivalent to a forward contract helps one understand the relationships between options and forward/futures contracts. Exhibit 2A–1 shows the funds flow and profits for buying a forward contract in comparison to buying a call and simultaneously selling a put option. (Selling a put means the option trader is obligated to receive stock at the stock price *if and when* the owner of the put exercises the option to sell the stock.) The first column of the payoff table shows the cash outlay at the present date (when the option and forward transactions are initiated). At the present date the forward contract does not require an investment, while buying a call and selling a put requires a cash outlay of $P_P - P_C$. The second column shows the value of the two positions when the forward contract and options expire. At option expiration, the forward contract and the option strategy provide the *same* payoff, regardless of whether the stock price is above or below the strike price at that time. Since the two positions provide the same ending value, buying a forward contract is equivalent to buying a call and selling a put. This relationship shows that options can be valued in relation to other contracts.

EXHIBIT 2A–1   Payoff Table for Options Versus Forward Contracts

	Present Date	Expiration Date	
		$P_{S,E} \leq K$	$K < P_{S,E}$
Buy Forward Contract Based on an asset price of K	0	$P_{S,E} - K$	$P_{S,E} - K$
Buy Call (Strike Price = K)	$-P_C$	0	$P_{S,E} - K$
Sell Put (Strike Price = K)	P_P	$P_{S,E} - K$	0
Total Option Value	$P_P - P_C$	$P_{S,E} - K$	$P_{S,E} - K$

K = The strike price and the forward contract asset price
P_C = Price of a call option
P_P = Price of a put option

A forward contract is equivalent to a portfolio consisting of one purchased call option on the underlying asset and one written put option on the underlying asset, both with a common expiration date equal to the delivery date, and both with a common strike price equal to the forward price.

Source: Rubinstein, 1991.

APPENDIX 2B
The Multiperiod Binomial Model

The chapter discusses the binomial model for the one-period and two-period cases, which is useful as an introduction to option pricing models. However, the binomial model can also be employed to obtain a fair value for options. This is especially useful for situations in which the option can be exercised early, or for options on assets for which the Black-Scholes model is inappropriate—for example, options on debt instruments. Since the binomial model is explained for n-periods below, the symbols are changed for ease of use. In particular, here u and d stand for an increase and decrease of the underlying asset price.

The value of an option using the Cox-Ross-Rubinstein binomial model for a large number of periods is determined as follows:

$$P_C = \frac{1}{(1+r)^n} \left[\sum_{i=0}^{n} \frac{n!}{i!\,(n-i)!}\, p^i(1-p)^{n-i}\, \text{Max}\, [0,\, P_S\, u^i\, d^{n-i} - K] \right] \quad \text{(2B–1)}$$

$$P_P = \frac{1}{(1+r)^n} \left[\sum_{i=0}^{n} \frac{n!}{i!\,(n-i)!}\, p^i(1-p)^{n-i}\, \text{Max}\, [0,\, K - P_S\, u^i\, d^{n-i}] \right] \quad \text{(2B–2)}$$

where r = non-annualized per-period interest rate
      n = the number of binomial periods
      p = the subjective probability of an increase in the asset price
      u = 1 plus the asset rate of return if the asset increases (up)
      d = 1 plus the asset rate of return if the asset decreases (down)
where u and d are determined by:
      $u = e^{\sigma_s \sqrt{t/n}}$
      $d = 1/u = e^{-\sigma_s \sqrt{t/n}}$

To prevent simple arbitrage: $u > r > d$
For an option on a stock:

$$p = \frac{(1+r)^n - d}{u - d} \quad \text{(2B–3)}$$

For an option on futures (see Chapter 7 for a discussion of futures options):

$$p = \frac{1-d}{u-d} \quad \text{(2B–4)}$$

While the binomial equations seem complicated, they simply find the value of an option as an average of all the possible call values at period n. Of course, those situations in which the option expires worthless are set equal to 0 (as designated in the equation). The factorial designation determines the number of paths generating the same ending value, so that each equivalent ending call value does not have to be calculated separately.

If the intermediate call values in the binomial tree are desired, then one must first find the ending call values for the individual cells for the ending time period. These are determined by finding the value of the option at that time by using the equation:

$$\text{call: Max } [0, P_s \, u^j \, d^{n-j} - K] \qquad \text{put: Max } [0, K - P_s \, u^j \, d^{n-j}] \qquad \textbf{(2B–5)}$$

where j = the number of periods the stock increased for the path in question

Then the recursive formula to calculate the call prices for individual cells at time period $T - 1$ is used:

$$P_{C,T-1} = [p \, P_{C,T}(u) + (1 - p) \, P_{C,T}(d)]/(1 + r) \qquad \textbf{(2B–6)}$$

where $P_{C,T}(u)$ = the up value of the call for period T

$P_{C,T}(d)$ = the down value of the call for period T

Example 2B–1 provides a multiperiod binomial tree with the individual call option values.

EXAMPLE 2B–1   A Multiperiod Binomial Example

A.   Input Values
$P_s = 100$ $K = 100$ $\sigma_s = 0.30$ $t = 0.25$
Annual $r = 10\%$ per period r: $1/(1 = r)^{t/n} = 1.00478$
$n = 5$ $u \equiv e^{\sigma_s \sqrt{t/n}} = 1.06938$
$d \equiv e^{-\sigma_s \sqrt{t/n}} = 0.935118$ $p = 0.518814$ $1 - p = 0.481186$

B.   Underlying Asset Binomial Tree

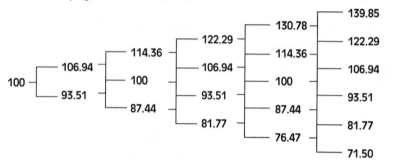

C.   Standard European Call Binomial Tree

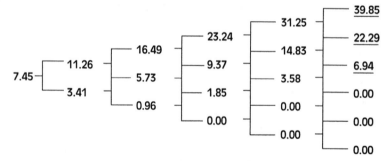

Note: Underlined option values should be exercised.

Cells where the value of the call expires worthless are shown as .00. Ending values for the last time period are determined by Max $[0, P_s\, u^j\, d^{n-j} - K]$.

The recursive rule is:

$$P_{C,\,T-1} = [pP_{C,T}(u) + (1-p)\,P_{C,T}(d)] \,/(1 + r)^{t/n}$$

Source: Rubinstein, 1991.

Option pricing models are the basis of a number of strategies for trading options. The strength of the Black-Scholes option model is that it provides both a theoretically sound and relatively simple equation for valuing options.

The Black-Scholes model provides both a value for the option and the appropriate hedge ratio between the stock and option positions. Alternatively, one can solve the option model to determine the implied volatility of the stock returns based on the current option price. Comparing this implied volatility to the past stock volatility provides information on the consensus of the market concerning future stock variability. Put options are priced by using either the Black-Scholes model or the put-call parity relationship. Call options paying dividends and put options have the potential of early exercise.

Floor traders use the models and strategies developed here to profit from mispricings in options. These traders use the option models, put-call parity, and combinations of options and stocks to initiate arbitrage transactions. The operations of the trading floor and how option prices behave within the trading day are other important issues that traders should understand.

Appendix 3A presents the assumptions of the Black-Scholes model. Each assumption is discussed in terms of its validity and how violations of the assumption can affect the option pricing results. Violations of the assumptions of the model may be the reason mispricings exist. Appendix 3B derives the Black-Scholes model.

BASIC PROPERTIES OF OPTION PRICING

Use of Option Models

The pricing of options is a cornerstone of Finance. Early models for option pricing in the 1960s became the building blocks for the **Black-Scholes option pricing model** of the early 1970s (1972, 1973).[1] The Black-Scholes model coincided with the initiation of exchange-traded options on the CBOE in 1973. Since then, the Black-Scholes model has become an important part of both financial theory and practice. The importance of this model lies in the fact that it is both conceptually sound *and* useful for practitioners.

Since its inception, the Black-Scholes model and similar models have been extended to price many types of option-like contracts, including options embedded in other financial instruments—for example, the delivery options for Treasury bond futures contracts. Option models have even been employed to value corporations. While many recent applications of option pricing involve complicated mathematics, the beauty of the basic Black-Scholes stock option pricing model is that it is solvable with a programmable calculator. In fact, many option traders on the floor of the exchange use calculators with a version of the Black-Scholes option model to determine the appropriate value of a given stock option.

The Fair Value of an Option

The purpose of an option model is to provide an estimate of the **fair value** of an option based on the inputs to the model. A fair value for an option exists when the option price provides an *expected* profit of zero to both the buyer and seller of the option. Chapter 1 concentrates on the value of an option at its expiration, which simply determines the intrinsic value of the option. Chapter 2 examines option prices before expiration in terms of the factors that affect the fair value of an option:

- The stock price in relation to the strike price (which affects the leverage of the option)

- The time until the expiration of the option

- The volatility of the stock returns

- The level of interest rates[2]

Finally, Chapters 1 and 2 present a number of "Pricing Relationships" that state how the above factors individually affect the price of an option. However, these pricing relationships do *not* integrate all of the individual factors, nor do they provide a precise value for an option. This chapter shows how the Black-Scholes option pricing model achieves these objectives.

BLACK-SCHOLES OPTION PRICING

An Overview of the Model

The binomial option pricing model can be extended to a large number of periods, as shown by Cox, Ross, and Rubinstein (1979). For an infinite number of periods, the binomial model is equivalent to the Black-Scholes model for European options. The derivation of the Black-Scholes model

(1973) is considered to be one of the most important developments in Finance. This derivation uses a branch of mathematics called "stochastic calculus" rather than the binomial model. A simplified derivation of the Black-Scholes model is given in Appendix 3B.

The foundation of the Black-Scholes option model is that arbitrage profits are *not* possible when the appropriate **hedge ratio** is generated between the stock and associated option. Thus, a long stock position and a short option position (as well as a short stock and a long option position) will earn the risk-free rate when the appropriate hedge ratio of stock to options is undertaken *and* the option has a fair price. If the option is either underpriced or overpriced, a return in excess of the risk-free rate is available to the arbitrageur. Arbitrageurs exploit any excess returns that exist, forcing the option back to its fair value.

One important aspect of the Black-Scholes formulation is that it does *not* depend on either the expected future stock price or investors' attitudes toward risk. Consequently, in addition to having a solid theoretical foundation, the Black-Scholes option model is easily calculated. The inputs to the model are the *current* stock price, the option exercise price, the time to expiration of the option, the volatility of the underlying stock, and the risk-free interest rate. Adjustments to the model, such as adding dividends, are considered later in this chapter.

Valuing a Call Option: The Black-Scholes Equation

The Black-Scholes option pricing model for valuing a European call option is:

$$P_C = P_S N(d_1) - K e^{-rt} N(d_2) \qquad (3\text{--}1)$$

where

$$d_1 = \frac{\ln(P_S/K) + [r + 0.5 \, \sigma_S^2]t}{\sigma_S \sqrt{t}} \qquad (3\text{--}2)$$

$$d_2 = d_1 - \sigma_S \sqrt{t} \qquad (3\text{--}3)$$

$N(d_1), N(d_2)$ = cumulative normal probabilities: the probability that the observation is to the left of "d," based on a normal distribution with a mean of zero and a standard deviation of one

$\ln$ = the natural logarithm[3] (of P_S/K)

P_C = the current fair value of the option

P_S = the current price of the stock

K = the exercise (strike) price of the option

$$e = 2.71828$$

r = the risk-free rate of interest (continuously compounded)

t = the time remaining before option expiration, as a proportion of a year

σ_S = the annualized standard deviation of the continuously compounded stock return

Appendix A (at the end of the book) provides values for the normal distribution N(d) to use in calculating the value of options. The value e^{-rt} stands for the continuous discounting function of the risk-free rate over time t; in other words, e^{-rt} calculates the interest factor for the present-value calculation needed in the Black-Scholes equation. Appendix B (at the end of the book) provides values of the natural logarithm ln. One must take care that the natural logarithm of P_S/K is calculated rather than log to the base 10. Using $\log_{10}$ will result in incorrect answers. Example 3–1 uses the Black-Scholes model given in Equation (3–1) and the values from Appendices A and B to calculate the value of a call option.

Finding the Value of the Normal Distribution Function

To calculate the Black-Scholes value of a call option, one must determine the value of the normal distribution function for $N(d_1)$ and $N(d_2)$. One method for finding N(d) is to use a normal distribution table, as found in Appendix A. In this case, one must interpolate if the exact value of N(d) is not in the table. Example 3–2 illustrates how to interpolate from a table.

An alternative method for determining the value of N(d), especially if one wishes to use a programmable calculator or a spreadsheet, is to obtain an accurate estimate of N(d) by an approximation equation. Exhibit 3–1 shows how to approximate the normal distribution function. Example 3–3 shows how to use this approximation formula.

The Black-Scholes equation uses the natural logarithm (P_S/K) in d_1. Combined with the normal distribution of d_1, $N(d_1)$, we have the lognormal distribution for stock prices. Using the lognormal distribution is equivalent to assuming that the *continuously compounded* rate of return on the stock is normally distributed. The significance of the lognormal distribution compared to the normal distribution is that the lognormal cannot have a return less than –100% (unlike the normal), and the lognormal is more skewed to the right to allow for larger positive returns. Thus, the lognormal is a more realistic distribution. Other distributions are possible, but they require other option models. Figure 3–1 compares the normal and lognormal distributions.

EXAMPLE 3–1 Black-Scholes Call Option Value

Equation (3–1) presents the Black-Scholes option pricing model. In this formula, Equations (3–2) and (3–3) define d_1 and d_2.

$$P_c = P_s \, N(d_1) - K \, e^{-rt} \, N(d_2) \qquad (3\text{–}1)$$

where

$$d_1 = \frac{\ln(P_s / K) + [r + .5 \, \sigma_s^2]t}{\sigma_s \sqrt{t}} \qquad (3\text{-}2)$$

$$d_2 = d_1 - \sigma_s \sqrt{t} \qquad (3\text{-}3)$$

Based on the following information, we calculate the fair value for the call option:

P_s = $98 (the current stock price)
K = $100 (the strike price)
r = .05 (the continuously compounded annual risk-free rate)
t = .25 (one-quarter of a year)
σ_s^2 = .25 (the continuously compounded variance of the stock returns)
σ_s = .5 (the standard deviation of the stock returns)

The values of d_1 and d_2 for the data given above are:

$$d_1 = \frac{\ln(98/100) + [.05 + .5 \, (.25)].25}{.5 \sqrt{.25}}$$

$$= \frac{-.02020 + [.175].25}{.5 \, (.5)}$$

$$= +.02355/.25 = .0942$$

$$d_2 = .0942 - (.5) \sqrt{.25}$$

$$= -.1558$$

The value of the natural logarithm ln(98/100) is found by using the table in Appendix B. The normal probabilities associated with d_1 and d_2, as determined from the interpolation shown in Example 3–2, are:

$N(d_1)$ = $N(+.0942) = .5375$
$N(d_2)$ = $N(-.1558) = .4381$

The value of the option is:

$$P_c = 98 \, (.5375) - 100 \, e^{-.05(.25)} \, (.4381)$$

Note that $e^{-.05(.25)} = 1/e^{.05(.25)} = 1/e^{.0125}$. Since e = 2.71828, $e^{.0125} = 1.0126$ and 1/1.0126 = .9876. Thus,

$$P_c = 98 \, (.5375) - 100 \, (.9876) \, (.4381)$$
$$= 52.675 - 43.267$$
$$= \$ 9.41$$

EXAMPLE 3–2 Interpolating from a Table

The values of $N(d_1)$ and $N(d_2)$ from Example 3–1 are:

$N(d_1)= N(+.0942)$
$N(d_2)= N(-.1558)$

The normal distribution table in Appendix A provides only two decimal places for d: the integer and first decimal are in the left column and the second decimal is in the top row, with the resultant value of N(d) appearing within the table. To obtain the resultant value of N(d) to four decimal places, as recommended for accurate Black-Scholes calculations, one must interpolate.
From Appendix A:

$N(.09)= .5359$
$N(.10)= .5398$

Since N(.0942) is 42/100 between N(.09) and N(.10), we calculate the following:

$$\begin{aligned} N(.0942) &= N(.09) + (42/100) \, [N(.10) - N(.09)] \\ &= .5359 + (42/100) \, (.5398 - .5359) \\ &= .5359 + (42/100) \, (.0039) \\ &= .5359 + .0016 \\ &= .5375 \end{aligned}$$

Similarly, since $N(-d) = 1 - N(d)$:

$$\begin{aligned} N(-.15) &= 1 - N(.15) &= 1 - .5596 &= .4404 \\ N(-.16) &= 1 - N(.16) &= 1 - .5636 &= .4364 \end{aligned}$$

$$\begin{aligned} N(-.1558) &= N(-.15) + (58/100) \, [N(-.16) - N(-.15)] \\ &= .4404 + (58/100) \, (.4364 - .4404) \\ &= .4404 + (58/100) \, (-.0040) \\ &= .4404 - .0023 \\ &= .4381 \end{aligned}$$

Interpreting the Black-Scholes Model

A close examination of Equation (3–1) provides some insights into the value of a call option:

- If the exercise of the call option is certain, then both d_1 and d_2 approach infinity and $N(d_1) = N(d_2) = 1$. Thus, $P_C = P_S - K\,e^{-rt}$.

- If it is certain that exercise of the option will *not* take place, then d_1 and d_2 approach negative infinity and $N(d_1) = N(d_2) = 0$. Thus, $P_C = 0$.

- The current value of a call option is the *weighted* difference of the present value of its potential benefit (P_S) and the present value of its potential costs ($K\,e^{-rt}$), where the weights $N(d_1)$ and $N(d_2)$ are between zero and one.

**EXHIBIT 3–1   The Approximation Formula for a
Normal Distribution**

To approximate the value of the normal distribution function N(d) at a
specific value d > 0, one can use the following formula:

$$N(d) = 1 - N'(d) \, [b_1k + b_2k^2 + b_3k^3 + b_4k^4 + b_5k^5 + \ldots]$$

where $N'(d) = (1/\sqrt{2\pi}) \, e^{-d^2/2}$

$$k = 1/(1 + \alpha d)$$

To achieve an accuracy within .00002, use three terms in the approximation equation, with:

$\alpha = .33267$
$b_1 = .4361836$
$b_2 = -.1201676$
$b_3 = .9372980$

To achieve an accuracy within .00000015, use five terms in the approximation equation, with:

$\alpha = .2316419$
$b_1 = .319381530$
$b_2 = -.356563782$
$b_3 = 1.781477937$
$b_4 = -1.821255978$
$b_5 = 1.330274429$

In addition:

If d = 0, then N(d) = .50
If d < 0, then find N[| - d |], and then calculate N(d) = 1 - N[| - d |]

Source: M. Abramowitz and I. Stegen (1970). *Handbook of Mathematical Functions.* Washington,
D.C., United States Department of Commerce, p. 932.

- The call price can also be interpreted as follows:

$$P_C = P_S \, N(d_1) + \text{Borrowing} \tag{3-4}$$

where $N(d_1) = $ the hedge ratio
   Borrowing $= -K \, e^{-rt} \, N(d_2)$

The hedge ratio is an important element of the Black-Scholes pricing model.
It is discussed below and used both here and in Chapter 4.

The Hedge Ratio

The Concept. The basic concept of a hedge ratio for the Black-Scholes
option model is equivalent to a hedge ratio for the binomial model: The

EXAMPLE 3–3   Using the Approximation Formula for the Normal Distribution

In order to find the Black-Scholes option value, one must calculate $N(d_1)$ and $N(d_2)$. Example 3–2 shows how to use the normal distribution table and interpolate. An alternative method, which is useful for computers, is the approximation method.

From Example 3–1, we have $N(d_1) = N(.0942)$. Based on the formula in Exhibit 3–1 we have:

$$N(d) = 1 - N'(d) [b_1 k + b_2 k^2 + b_3 k^3 + b_4 k^4 + b_5 k^5 + \ldots]$$
$$\text{where } N'(d) = (1/\sqrt{2\pi}) e^{-d^2/2}$$
$$k = 1/(1 + \alpha d)$$

For our example,

$$
\begin{aligned}
N'(d_1) &= (1/\sqrt{2\pi})e^{-(.0942)^2/2} \\
&= [1/\sqrt{2(3.14159)}]\, e^{-.044368} \\
&= (.398942)\,(.995573) \\
&= .397176 \\
k &= 1/[1 + (.33267)\,(.0942)] \\
&= 1/1.031338 = .969614 \\
N(d) &= 1 - (.397176)\,[(.4361836)\,(.969614) - .1201676\,(.969614)^2 \\
&\quad + .9372980\,(.969614)^3] \\
&= 1 - (.397176)\,[.4229297 - .1129757 + .8544257] \\
&= 1 - (.397176)\,[1.1643797] \\
&= 1 - .46246 \\
&= .5375
\end{aligned}
$$

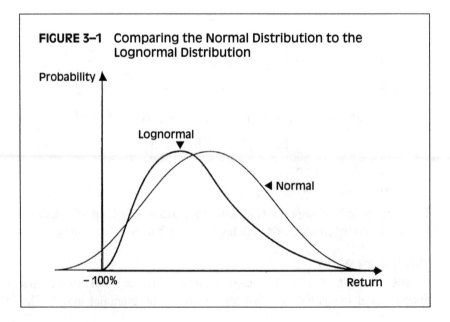

FIGURE 3–1   Comparing the Normal Distribution to the Lognormal Distribution

FOCUS 3–1   The Option Simulator: What Is It?

The Options and Futures Simulator is a unique and useful PC computer program that allows the user to practice trading options and futures by using actual intraday historical prices. The program also determines the option value and other factors affecting call and put pricing (we will examine these factors in Chapter 4). Option prices can be determined for many types of options, as well as for different option pricing models. Moreover, all of the three-dimensional graphs presented later in this book were developed using the Simulator, as well as many of the two-dimensional options graphs.

A brief look at the Option Simulator shows some of its power.

- The PC trader can buy and/or sell any combination of S&P 500 calls and puts, the S&P 500 Index, and index futures to create a portfolio. Prices used by the program are actual five-minute prices for these securities. Prices are updated either by the user or automatically to show the wisdom of the trader's choices. The status and history of the trader's account is one of the alternative choices in the program. News events for the period show at the bottom of the screen and historical news summaries can be accessed.

- The values of the various options and the "sensitivities" of the options (see Chapter 4) are available, as calculated by the Black-Scholes, binomial, jump process, and constant elasticity option pricing models. The extended binomial trees can be shown on the screen. The values of alternative options (see Chapter 9) are also available in either table or graph form.

- Two-dimensional graphs on the payoffs of current or anticipated positions are available, as well as graphs on the option "sensitivities." Three-dimensional graphs (two inputs and one output) are available for the different option pricing models and the alternative options discussed in Chapter 9 (and their sensitivities), for a total of 32 different models/options. Graphs and actual Monte Carlo simulations on various dynamic replication strategies are also available.

- Tables on the option models and types of options noted above also can be generated (for an example, see Table 3–1). All tables and graphs provide alternatives that allow the user to change the value of the inputs.

- Historical data on 5- and 30-minute and one- and two-day volatilities are available in table form. Daily historical data on stock index, futures, and options, in addition to monthly data on bonds, are available for a number of years. Tables and graphs on implied volatility can also be generated.

(continued)

FOCUS 3–1 (continued)

The Simulator is a very powerful and interesting program. It will be useful to provide hands-on experience to current and future traders, as well as knowledge of what affects option prices. There is also potential for research into how option prices react in certain circumstances. The Options and Futures Simulator's anticipated availability is late 1994, with an expected price of $5,000 to universities for a site license. Prices and availability for commercial use have not yet been determined.

The initial market screen of the Options Simulator is shown below. The market screen provides price quotations, time of the quotations, last trade price, and time of the trade. This screen also shows several hypothetical trades.

Market Screen

							4/07/86		11:05
Sn	Security	Bid	Ask	QTime	Trade	TTime	Volume	Held	Open
1	SP500 Index	227.73	227.73	11:05	227.73	11:05			
2	F/ /Jun86				228.20	11:05			
3	F/ /Sep86		230.85	11:05	231.10	11:05			
4	F/ /Dec86		234.10	11:05	234.00	8:35			
5	F/ /Mar87		236.90	11:05	239.00	4/04			
9	C/230/Apr86	2.06	2.25	11:00	2.63	4/04	5		
10	C/235/Apr86	0.88	1.00	11:00	1.13	4/04	20		
11	C/240/Apr86	0.31	0.38	10:55	0.44	10:20	10		
12	C/245/Apr86	0.13	0.19	9:30	0.19	10:25	50		
18	C/245/May86	1.19	1.31	11:00					
109	P/235/Apr86	8.38	8.63	11:05					

Created from The Options and Futures Trading Simulator, Version 2.0, by Mark Rubinstein and Gerald Gennotte, copyright 1992.

---

hedge ratio is the ratio of stock shares to option shares that keeps the combined portfolio value the same for a given small change in the stock price. The hedge ratio does *not* keep the portfolio value the same for larger stock price changes unless the hedge ratio is altered accordingly. Equations (2–2) and (2–3) show the relevance of a hedge ratio.

Figure 3–2 shows the relationship between the option value and stock prices before the expiration of the option. The *slope* of the option value line *at the current stock price* represents the Black-Scholes hedge ratio. This hedge ratio is conceptually equivalent to Figure 2–2 for the binomial model, where the slope of the line for the two possible stock prices in the binomial case equals the hedge ratio. However, the Black-Scholes model allows a continuous stock price distribution to occur, not just the two stock prices used in the one-period binomial model. Therefore, one interprets the Black-Scholes hedge ratio in terms of a small **instantaneous** (immediate) price change for the stock.[4]

FIGURE 3–2 Black-Scholes Hedge Ratio

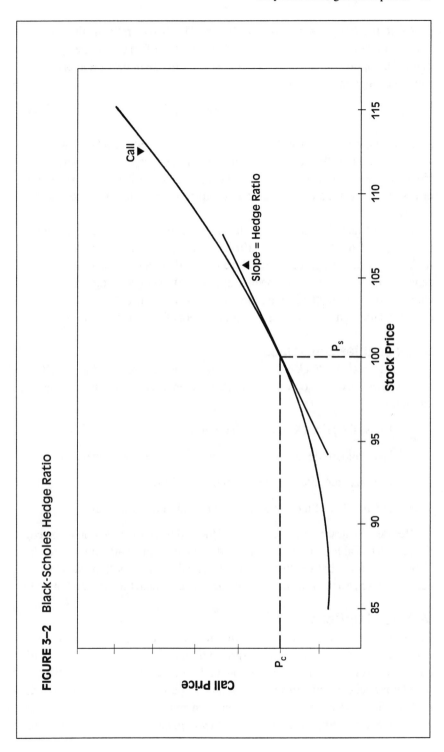

Defining Delta as the Hedge Ratio. The hedge ratio in the Black-Scholes model is equivalent to $N(d_1)$. This value is often called the option's **delta**. The option's delta states the (expected) change in the option price for a given change in the stock price:

$$\text{Delta} = \Delta P_C / \Delta P_S = N(d_1) \qquad (3\text{--}5)$$

A rule of thumb is that an at-the-money option has a delta of 0.5—that is, for a change of $1 in the stock price, the option changes by $0.50. The delta ranges from 0 to 1, which confirms the statement in Chapter 2 that option prices move less than stock prices. Chapter 4 examines how to use an option's delta.

For the Black-Scholes model, the slope of the line at the current stock price *differs* from the slope at a different stock price. This is the reason for referring to the hedge ratio as relevant for a "small instantaneous price change." In other words, the hedge ratio (delta) *changes* as the stock price changes. In addition, the hedge ratio changes as the time to option expiration changes, although small changes in time do not affect the hedge ratio.

Black-Scholes Call Values

Table 3–1 presents Black-Scholes call values for a stock priced at 100. The table shows how the option value changes in relation to the following variables:

- The strike price (K in the left column)

- The standard deviation of the stock (σ in the left column)

- The risk-free interest rate (r in the second row)

- The number of months to option expiration (the third row)

Besides illustrating the sensitivity of the call price to the variables listed, the results in Table 3–1, when compared to the binomial call values given in Table 2–2, show that the two models value call options within one cent of each other when 150 time intervals are used to calculate the binomial model.

Mispriced Options

One objective of floor traders is to find mispriced options—that is, to buy underpriced options and to sell overpriced options, or, equivalently, to *avoid* buying overpriced options or selling underpriced options. If the Black-Scholes model correctly prices options, and if a particular option is mispriced, then a ratio between the stock and option shares can be created in order to exploit the mispricing. Such a transaction would earn a return that is greater

TABLE 3–1 Call Values Using the Black-Scholes Model

$P_s = 100$

		i = .05				i = .10				i = .15			
							months to expiration						
σ	K	1	3	6	12	1	3	6	12	1	3	6	12
.2	85	15.35	16.18	17.61	20.39	15.67	17.11	19.34	23.54	15.99	18.00	21.00	26.58
	90	10.43	11.65	13.46	16.62	10.76	12.55	15.12	19.67	11.09	13.43	16.74	22.68
	95	5.89	7.69	9.83	13.27	6.20	8.50	11.34	16.14	6.49	9.29	12.86	19.03
	100	2.51	4.60	6.86	10.39	2.71	5.23	8.14	12.99	2.92	5.87	9.47	15.71
	105	.74	2.47	4.56	7.97	.83	2.90	5.58	10.27	.92	3.36	6.68	12.74
	110	.15	1.18	2.89	5.99	.17	1.44	3.66	7.97	.20	1.73	4.51	10.16
	115	.02	.51	1.75	4.43	.02	.65	2.29	6.07	.03	.80	2.92	7.97
.3	85	15.43	16.86	19.05	22.85	15.75	17.70	20.57	25.56	16.05	18.51	22.04	28.19
	90	10.77	12.84	15.45	19.63	11.08	13.63	16.89	22.24	11.38	14.40	18.30	24.81
	95	6.72	9.38	12.29	16.74	6.99	10.09	13.62	19.22	7.25	10.78	14.93	21.69
	100	3.65	6.57	9.61	14.17	3.85	7.16	10.78	16.49	4.04	7.75	11.97	18.84
	105	1.71	4.41	7.37	11.92	1.83	4.87	8.40	14.06	1.95	5.35	9.44	16.27
	110	.68	2.84	5.57	9.97	.74	3.18	6.43	11.92	.80	3.54	7.33	13.97
	115	.23	1.75	4.14	8.29	.26	2.00	4.85	10.05	.28	2.26	5.60	11.92
.4	85	15.70	17.96	20.96	25.79	16.00	18.72	22.32	28.18	16.29	19.46	23.63	30.50
	90	11.37	14.33	17.73	22.93	11.65	15.04	19.02	25.25	11.93	15.74	20.28	27.52
	95	7.68	11.18	14.86	20.32	7.92	11.83	16.07	22.56	8.16	12.46	17.26	24.76
	100	4.80	8.54	12.36	17.97	4.99	9.10	13.47	20.10	5.18	9.66	14.57	22.22
	105	2.77	6.39	10.19	15.85	2.91	6.86	11.20	17.87	3.04	7.34	12.20	19.90
	110	1.48	4.68	8.35	13.96	1.56	5.08	9.24	15.85	1.65	5.47	10.15	17.78
	115	.73	3.37	6.79	12.27	.78	3.68	7.58	14.04	.83	4.00	8.39	15.85

Source: Rubinstein (1991).

than the risk-free interest rate. In fact, arbitrageurs on the floor of the option exchange execute such transactions daily. They find risk-free arbitrage situations in which they can sell overpriced call options (buying the stock and selling options in the proportion dictated by the relevant hedge ratio) or they can buy underpriced options (selling stock and buying options in relation to the appropriate hedge ratio). Similar transactions can be executed for put options. As discussed below, these arbitrageurs must adjust their hedge ratios as conditions warrant, and such trades must be virtually free of commission charges.

Option traders off the exchange floor can also use the Black-Scholes model for mispricings, although such traders execute different strategies from those of arbitrageurs. Brokerage houses and other services create lists of the "most underpriced" and "most overpriced" options on a daily basis. However, care must be taken in using such lists, since timing differences between the stock price and option price can account for specific options making this mispricing list. The traders on the floor of the exchange also generate such lists; consequently, these mispricing opportunities often disappear early on the following trading day because of transactions made by these floor traders as soon as the option exchanges open. Chapter 5 discusses strategies for off-the-floor traders to benefit from mispricings of options.

A more general approach to using an option model and benefiting from any potential mispricing of the options is to employ the pricing sensitivities to determine the appropriate option strategy. The pricing sensitivities are the hedge ratio, time to expiration, volatility, the option leverage, and the change in the hedge ratio. Chapter 4 examines how to use these sensitivities to determine appropriate trading strategies.

Basic Assumptions of the Black-Scholes Model

Hedge ratios can be examined by comparing the binomial model to the Black-Scholes model. The hedge ratio for the one-period binomial model shown in Figure 2–7 is relevant for the *two* possible future stock prices, which in turn creates a position with no risk. Consequently, the return from the hedge between the option and the stock with a binomial model earns the risk-free rate. Figure 2–7 shows how the hedge ratio *changes* from time period T to T + 1 if the upper stock price of $105 occurs at T + 1. Similarly, as the stock price or time to expiration changes, the hedge ratio for the Black-Scholes model also changes. Hence, both the binomial and Black-Scholes models are based on the assumption that arbitrageurs periodically adjust their hedge positions as the hedge ratio changes. If the hedge position is not adjusted, then the stock/option position is no longer risk-free. The conclusion that arbitrageurs can adjust their hedge position and that the hedge ratio provides a risk-free position is based on the following assumptions:

- There are no transaction costs. Thus, an arbitrageur can adjust the hedge ratio almost continuously without cost.

- Only small changes in the stock price occur within a short time period. Therefore, the arbitrageur has sufficient time to alter the hedge ratio before a large stock price change occurs.

The first assumption is true for arbitrageurs on the floor of the options exchange, but not for others who have to pay commissions each time they trade. This means that off-the-floor traders must rely on arbitrageurs who are on the floor of the exchange to keep the prices of options "fair." Consequently, only floor arbitrageurs have the opportunity to profit when option prices differ from their fair value. Moreover, to profit from arbitrage opportunities, the floor trader must take a position with the appropriate hedge ratio and be able to change this hedge ratio as stock prices change.

The second assumption, which relates to the existence of small price changes, is typically valid in normal markets. However, when a chaotic market exists (such as the October 1987 market crash), or when a takeover bid for a stock is announced, prices "jump." When prices do *not* change smoothly, arbitrageurs cannot adjust their hedge ratios quickly enough. In these circumstances, floor traders often go bankrupt. This "jump" factor also is used as a justification for pricing call options higher than the value calculated by the Black-Scholes model—that is, the unpredictable risk from jumps may create an additional premium in the call price.[5]

The Black-Scholes model is *not* a good model for valuing long-term options since Black-Scholes assumes that volatility increases *exponentially* as time increases. Therefore, LEAPs and other long-term options need a more realistic volatility process. One such process is a mean reverting volatility assumption.

While the above discussion suggests that an option pricing model that is superior to the Black-Scholes model may exist (in fact, researchers have developed more sophisticated models), the Black-Scholes model is still considered the most important model for option traders for two reasons. First, actual option prices tend toward the Black-Scholes price because of arbitrage, since jumps in price are infrequent and predictable. Second, major brokerage houses and many traders use some form of the Black-Scholes or binomial models to generate their estimates of a fair option price. Further discussion of the assumptions of the Black-Scholes model and alternative models is presented in Appendix 3A.

CALCULATING THE INPUTS

The inputs to Equation (3–1) are the current stock price, the strike price, the time to expiration of the option, the risk-free interest rate, and the volatility of the stock returns. The strike price of the option is a known value that does not have to be calculated. The other variables need some explanation.

Current Stock Price

If the stock has traded within the last few minutes, then the last stock price is a valid value for the current stock price. However, if the stock has not traded for hours, then the last trade may be an inappropriate value to use in the Black-Scholes model. In addition, stock index options suffer from the fact that stocks trade at different times, causing the index to be "old." There is no widely accepted method for dealing with old prices in the option model.

Time to Expiration

The time until option expiration in Equation (3–1) is input as a fraction of a year. Hence, an option with 90 days left until expiration has a value of $t = 90/365 = 0.2466$. The number of decimal places employed for the calculation depends on the accuracy desired. Four decimal places provide sufficient accuracy to obtain a call value that is accurate to within one cent. Traders using the Black-Scholes model use the actual number of days until expiration when trading within the day. However, near the end of the day these traders start to use the *following* trading day's time to expiration in order to price the option. Thus, near the end of a Friday session, traders use the value of t for the following Monday in the Black-Scholes calculations.

The number of trading days appears in the option pricing equation in two places. The first place is in the discounting function for the exercise price, or, e^{-rt} in Equation (3–1). Here the number of days used should equal the actual number of days until option expiration, since interest is earned/paid on a calendar-day basis. The second place time appears is in adjusting the variability of the stock price in Equations (3–2) and (3–3). For this situation, some researchers argue that t needs to be adjusted to reflect the nonconstant variability of stock prices over time. In particular, stock prices vary less over the nontrading time periods of weekends, as compared to when the market is open during the week. A rule of thumb is to equate three nontrading days to one actual trading day in order to make the variability more consistent. However, in our examples we will assume constant variability across time for simplicity.

The Risk-Free Rate

Typically, the Treasury bill interest rate is employed to calculate the risk-free rate. T-bills do not have default risk and are very liquid. The average of the bid and ask discount interest rates often is employed to obtain a *simple* T-bill risk-free discount interest rate. The next step is to determine the risk-free discount price as a percentage of the par value:

$$P_{RF} = 100 - i_d \, (M/360) \qquad (3-6)$$

where P_{RF} = the risk-free discount price as a percentage of the par value
$\quad\quad\ \ i_d$ = the discount interest rate, typically as an average of the bid and ask discount rates
$\quad\quad\ \ M$ = the number of *days* until maturity of the T-bill (the maturity matches the option expiration)

Note that M in Equation (3–6) refers to a number of days, while t in Equations (3–1) through (3–3) refers to a portion of the year. Also, the discount price in (3–6) is based on a 360-day year, which is based on historical convention. The simple *yield* for this risk-free instrument is determined by:

$$R_f = [100/P_{RF}]^{365/M} - 1 \qquad (3-7)$$

The Black-Scholes model uses the continuously compounded risk-free interest rate to determine the value of a call option. The simple rate calculated above employs *annual* compounding. An interest rate that is *continuously* compounded uses the exponential function "e" to calculate the effect of compounding (see Equation [3–1]). A simple interest rate is converted to a continuously compounded rate by using the natural logarithmic function, which is the inverse of the exponential function:[6]

$$r = \ln(1 + R_f) \qquad (3-8)$$

where r = the continuously compounded risk-free interest rate
$\quad\quad\ \ \ln$ = the natural logarithm
$\quad\quad\ \ R_f$ = the simple risk-free interest rate

An example of how to implement the above equations is given later in this chapter.[7]

Volatility

The Black-Scholes option model employs the volatility of the underlying stock returns as part of the option valuation equation. Volatility is an important variable, since option prices are sensitive to small changes in volatility.

Volatility typically is determined by calculating the historical variance of the returns—that is, the standard deviation of the returns squared.[8] Both the variance and the standard deviation of returns are used in Equations (3–2) and (3–3) to calculate the option value. Daily, weekly, bimonthly, monthly, or similar data can be employed to determine the historical volatility.[9] As with the risk-free rate, the variance of the returns is defined in terms of continuously compounded returns. Thus, the return for each period used to calculate the variance needs to be converted to a continuous return. Per-period returns below 0.05 are not affected significantly by the conversion from simple returns to continuously compounded returns. Therefore, the difference between simple and continuous returns is noticeable only in the third or fourth decimal place. However, returns above 0.05 are affected more noticeably by the conversion.

A full-function calculator or a spreadsheet easily and automatically makes the conversion from simple returns to continuously compounded returns. Determining the variance of returns is a four-step process:

1. Calculate the rate of return for each time period:

$$R_{S,T} = (P_{S,T} - P_{S,T-1})/P_{S,T-1} \qquad (3\text{-}9)$$

where $R_{S,T}$ = the simple rate of return for the stock during time period T
$P_{S,T}$ = the price of the stock at time T

2. Convert the simple returns to continuously compounded returns:

$$r_{S,T} = \ln(1 + R_{S,T}) \qquad (3\text{-}10)$$

where $r_{S,T}$ = the continuously compounded return on the stock during time period T

3. Determine the variance of the continuously compounded returns:

$$\sigma_{S,T}^2 = \frac{\sum_{t=1}^{N} (r_{S,T} - \bar{r}_S)^2}{N-1} \qquad (3\text{-}11)$$

where $\sigma_{S,T}^2$ = the variance on the stock returns using daily, weekly, monthly, etc., intervals
$\bar{r}_S$ = the average return on the stock over the period in question
N = the number of observations used in the calculation

4. Annualize the variance [the variance calculated in Equation (3–11) is based on the time intervals used. For example, weekly time periods provide a weekly variance]:

$$\sigma_S^2 = \sigma_{S,T}^2 N_T \qquad (3\text{-}12)$$

where σ_S^2 = the annualized continuously compounded variance for the stock

N_T = the number of time intervals in a year; for example, for weekly time intervals $N_T = 52$, for monthly intervals $N_T = 12$

The standard deviation, σ_S, is then computed by taking the square root of the annualized variance.[10]

The volatility value determined by the above calculations is based on historical information. The appropriate value for the variance in the Black-Scholes option model is the volatility *during* the time period when the option is being traded. The difference between the historical volatility and the market's estimate of future volatility is examined shortly.

Dividends on Stocks

The Black-Scholes option model as discussed so far ignores the effects of dividends—that is, the model is based on a non-dividend-paying stock. However, dividends are added to the model with a relatively minor adjustment. Cash dividends tend to reduce the value of a call option, since the strike price is *not* adjusted for cash dividends but the stock price does decline when a stock goes ex-dividend. The adjustment procedure used here quantifies the appropriate reduction in the price of the call option, given the size and timing of the cash dividends on the stock.

The most popular adjustment for dividends is to subtract the present value of the cash dividends from the stock price, using the resultant adjusted stock price in the Black-Scholes model. Using the continuously discounted interest rate for the present value adjustment, we have:

$$P_S' = P_S - D_T\, e^{-r\tau} \qquad (3\text{-}13)$$

where P_S' = the stock price adjusted for dividends (this value then is used in the Black-Scholes model)

D_T = the dollar dividend paid at time T

$e^{-r\tau}$ = the continuously discounted risk-free rate r, discounted over time period τ

τ = the proportion of the year from the present time until the ex-dividend date for the stock

Note that τ differs from t, where t is the expiration of the option. P_s' must adjust for *each* cash dividend expected before option expiration.[11]

Call options are sometimes exercised early in order to obtain the cash dividends on a stock about to go ex-dividend. If there is a short time before option expiration, this is a rational strategy, since the stock prices are adjusted downward on the ex-dividend day by the size of the dividend, while strike prices are *not* adjusted. At times, call options are exercised a significant time before the expiration date. However, such exercises are generally irrational decisions on the part of the call option buyer, since the call option could be sold for a greater profit than generated from exercising the option.[12] Other things being equal, the optimal early exercise of an American call is more appropriate the higher the stock price, the lower the strike price, the shorter the time to option expiration, and the higher the cash dividends yet to be paid. Table 3–2 shows the effect of different dividend payments on call option values.

Since the existence of dividends creates the possibility of early exercise for an American call option, one can now recognize the difference between American and European options. While the dividend adjustment to the European Black-Scholes model provides a credible adjusted call option value, some traders prefer using the binomial model that directly shows each cell when the call should be exercised.

Dividends on an Index

The above procedure is based on a discrete dividend payment made at a specific time. Such a procedure is very cumbersome to use for index options, since a large number of dividends are paid on the individual stocks that make up the index. An alternative procedure is to use the dividend yield for the stock index. Such yields for the major stock indexes are found in *Value Line Options*. The appropriate adjustment to the stock index price is:

$$P_s' = P_s\, e^{-d\tau} \qquad\qquad (3\text{–}14)$$

where d = the dividend yield on the index

This procedure is based on the assumption that dividends are paid continuously. While this assumption is not strictly true for an index of stocks, it creates only a minor adverse effect on the estimate of the fair price of the option. More important, the continuous dividend adjustment reduces the complexity of calculating the effect of individual dividends on the index option. Equation (3–14) also can be employed for individual stocks, but the resultant call option value is too large.[13]

Calculating Inputs. Examples 3–4 and 3–5 illustrate how to calculate the inputs to the Black-Scholes option model. The calculations for the

TABLE 3–2 Call Values for Different Dividend Payments

$P_s = 100$ $I = .10$

		Div = 5%				Div = 10%				Div = 15%			
						months to expiration							
σ	K	1	3	6	12	1	3	6	12	1	3	6	12
.2	85	15.27	15.94	17.10	19.27	14.89	14.84	15.07	15.60	14.52	13.82	13.24	12.49
	90	10.37	11.46	13.05	15.69	9.99	10.46	11.22	12.35	9.64	9.54	9.61	9.60
	95	5.85	7.56	9.53	12.51	5.53	6.73	7.96	9.56	5.24	5.98	6.63	7.20
	100	2.49	4.51	6.63	9.78	2.28	3.89	5.37	7.24	2.10	3.36	4.33	5.28
	105	.73	2.42	4.40	7.49	.65	2.02	3.45	5.37	.58	1.68	2.69	3.79
	110	.15	1.16	2.78	5.62	.12	.93	2.11	3.90	.11	.75	1.59	2.66
	115	.02	.50	1.68	4.15	.02	.39	1.23	2.78	.01	.30	.89	1.84
.3	85	15.35	16.61	18.52	21.64	14.97	15.60	16.67	18.27	14.62	14.66	15.01	15.37
	90	10.71	12.64	15.01	18.58	10.36	11.74	13.34	15.47	10.04	10.91	11.85	12.84
	95	6.68	9.23	11.94	15.83	6.39	8.46	10.46	12.99	6.12	7.76	9.17	10.63
	100	3.63	6.46	9.32	13.39	3.43	5.84	8.05	10.84	3.24	5.28	6.96	8.74
	105	1.69	4.33	7.15	11.26	1.57	3.86	6.09	8.98	1.47	3.44	5.19	7.14
	110	.68	2.79	5.39	9.41	.62	2.44	4.52	7.40	.57	2.14	3.80	5.80
	115	.23	1.72	4.00	7.82	.21	1.49	3.31	6.06	.19	1.28	2.74	4.69
.4	85	15.62	17.70	20.39	24.45	15.26	16.76	18.65	21.22	14.92	15.88	17.08	18.41
	90	11.31	14.12	17.24	21.73	10.99	13.27	15.65	18.70	10.68	12.49	14.22	16.10
	95	7.63	11.01	14.45	19.25	7.37	10.27	13.01	16.44	7.11	9.59	11.73	14.04
	100	4.77	8.41	12.01	17.02	4.57	7.78	10.72	14.41	4.38	7.21	9.59	12.21
	105	2.75	6.29	9.90	15.01	2.61	5.77	8.77	12.61	2.48	5.30	7.78	10.59
	110	1.47	4.61	8.10	13.21	1.38	4.19	7.12	11.01	1.30	3.82	6.27	9.18
	115	.72	3.31	6.59	11.60	.67	2.99	5.74	9.60	.63	2.70	5.02	7.94

Source: Rubinstein (1991).

volatility of the stock shown in Example 3–5 typically are completed with a spreadsheet in order to reduce calculation time and avoid errors.

VOLATILITY AND OPTIONS

Implied Volatility

The only input to the Black-Scholes option model that is not known with certainty when one calculates the value of a call option is the volatility of the underlying stock. This is because σ_S and σ_S^2 in Equations (3–2) and (3–3) represent the volatility of the stock *over the life of the option*. Since no one knows with certainty what this *future* volatility will be, traders typically use historical variance as an appropriate estimate of future volatility. Some traders then adjust the historical volatility based on their forecast of the relevant current factors affecting this stock or index.

The price of the option includes the consensus opinion of the market participants concerning the future volatility of the stock. This estimate of the future volatility is determined by solving the Black-Scholes option equation for the **implied volatility**—that is, the volatility implied by the current option price. Thus, Equations (3–1) to (3–3) are solved for the standard deviation of the stock returns, with the current call option price as an input to the equation. In other words, the implied volatility is the standard deviation and variance in Equations (3–2) and (3–3), which makes the call option price from the Black-Scholes *model* equal to the current *market* price for the call option. Since volatility appears in several places in Equations (3–2) and (3–3), solving for volatility is not a simple undertaking; in fact, it requires a computer. Typically, as shown initially by Latane and Rendleman (1976), implied volatility is obtained by a trial-and-error procedure in which various values of the standard deviation and associated variance are input into Equations (3–2) and (3–3) until the market and model option prices are equal. For example, if the stock price and strike price are 40, t = 0.333, the risk-free interest rate is 5%, and the market call price is 3.07, one calculates an implied volatility of 0.3.[14]

Implied volatility is an important concept for option pricing. It determines the market's estimate of the future volatility of the stock. This estimate is then compared to the stock's historical volatility to determine the market's opinion on the potential change in volatility. A difference between the option value calculated from historical data and the market call option price is typically due to the difference between the implied and historical volatility values.

If the Black-Scholes model is a perfect model, then options on the same stock that have the *same maturity* should have the same implied volatility. In

EXAMPLE 3–4   Calculating the Inputs to the
Black-Scholes Model

A. Basic Information

Stock: J Enterprises P_s = 127.375   K = 125   Annual Dividend = $4.40

Current date = July 23   Dividend date = August 4

B. Time Until Option Expiration

time until expiration: 90 days = M (October 21)

t = 90/365 = 0.2466

C. The Risk-Free Interest Rate

P_{RF} = 100 – i_d (M/360)

i_d = 8.50

P_{RF} = 100 – 8.5 (90/360)

P_{RF} = 97.875

R_f = $[100/P_{RF}]^{365/M}$ – 1

R_f = $[100/97.875]^{365/90}$ – 1

R_f = 0.091

r = ln(1 + R_f)

r = ln(1 + 0.091)

r = 0.087

D. Dividend Effect

P_s' = P_s – D_T e^{-rt}

P_s' = 127.375 – 1.10 $e^{-(0.087)(11/365)}$

P_s' = 126.28

E. Option Price

Using the inputs calculated above and in Example 3–5, and the Black-Scholes equations (3–1), (3–2), and (3–3), the value of the call option for the October 125 strike price is 7 $7/8$.

EXAMPLE 3–5 Calculating the Volatility of a Stock

Date	Close	$R_{s,T}$	$r_{s,T}$	$(r - \bar{r})^2$
JAN 8	114.875			
15	119.000	0.0359	0.0353	0.0010
22	110.500	– 0.0714	– 0.0741	0.0061
29	112.375	0.0170	0.0168	0.0002
FEB 5	108.000	– 0.0389	– 0.0397	0.0019
12	112.000	0.0370	0.0364	0.0010
19	113.375	0.0123	0.0122	0.0001
26	115.750	0.0209	0.0207	0.0003
MAR 4	116.875	0.0097	0.0097	0.0000
11	115.500	– 0.0118	– 0.0118	0.0003
18	114.250	– 0.0108	– 0.0109	0.0002
25	107.000	– 0.0635	– 0.0656	0.0049
31	107.625	0.0058	0.0058	0.0000
APR 8	111.625	0.0372	0.0365	0.0010
15	114.125	0.0224	0.0221	0.0003
22	113.750	– 0.0033	– 0.0033	0.0001
29	113.375	– 0.0033	– 0.0033	0.0001
MAY 6	110.500	– 0.0254	– 0.0257	0.0009
13	110.375	– 0.0011	– 0.0011	0.0000
20	109.375	– 0.0091	– 0.0091	0.0002
27	108.000	– 0.0126	– 0.0127	0.0003
JUN 3	113.250	0.0486	0.0475	0.0019
10	116.000	0.0243	0.0240	0.0004
17	117.500	0.0129	0.0128	0.0001
24	125.125	0.0649	0.0629	0.0035
30	127.375	0.0180	0.0178	0.0002
TOTALS			0.1033	0.0248

$\bar{r}$ = 0.1033/25 = 0.0041
σ^2 = 0.0248/24 = 0.0010
Annualized σ^2 = 0.001(52) = 0.0520
Annualized σ = $\sqrt{0.052}$ = 0.2280

practice, different options on the same stock have different implied volatilities. Table 3–3 shows the implied volatilities for IBM.

While many traders use the near-to-the-money option's implied volatility, one also can calculate an average implied volatility estimate by using most of the traded options that have the same maturity by:[15]

$$\sigma^* = \Sigma \, (w_j / \Sigma w_j) \, \sigma_j^* \qquad (3\text{-}15)$$

TABLE 3–3 IBM Implied Volatilities

Strike Price	Time to Expiration			
	1 month	2 months	3 months	6 months
50	31.9%	31.3%	35.2%	34.7%
55	35.1%	33.9%	34.9%	33.6%
60	NA	NA	33.9%	33.8%

Source: Calculated using IBM option prices with OptionVue.

where σ^* = the estimate of the implied volatility of the stock
w_j = the weight for the jth option's implied volatility
σ_j^* = the implied volatility for the jth option

The weights are determined by the trader, with the largest weight typically being assigned to the near-to-the-money option.[16] In addition, Brenner and Subrahmanyam (1988) determined that an at-the-money call price can be approximated by the equation:

$$P_C \approx .398\, P_S\, \sigma_S\, \sqrt{t} \qquad\qquad (3\text{–}16)$$

Thus, solving for the implied volatility, we have:

$$\sigma_S = P_C\, /\, .398\, P_S\, \sqrt{t} \qquad\qquad (3\text{–}17)$$

Large differences in implied volatilities should be investigated to determine whether mispricing exists. Such an investigation should include whether all of the different option strikes traded at the same time of the day, since consistency in the use of the correct stock-option price combination is critical in determining if mispricing exists.

Beckers (1981) compares the implied volatility calculated from the Black-Scholes option model to the historical volatility from the stock in order to determine which measure provides a superior prediction of the actual future volatility. Beckers finds that the implied volatility is the superior predictor. Moreover, the implied volatility for the near-to-the-money strike price is a better predictor of future volatility than the average of the implied volatilities for all of the strike prices of the option, perhaps because the nearby option trades more frequently. Harvey and Whaley (1992) find that S&P 100 options transactions prices can forecast future market volatility. However, a trading model cannot provide excess returns based on this information.

Later we examine how a trader's volatility estimates that differ from the market's estimate of future volatility are used to create trading strategies. In other words, a trader can determine that an option is under- or overpriced based on comparing these two values for the volatility of the stock, and then exploit this mispricing. Figure 3–3 shows the historical and implied volatilities for Eastman Kodak. Figure 3–4 illustrates the volatilities for the S&P 100 Index. These figures show that historical and implied volatilities often differ and that both measures of volatility change over time. In fact, the assumption that volatility remains constant usually is not valid.

Forecasting Volatility and GARCH

Since the future volatility of the stock is the only unknown variable in the option pricing equation, an accurate forecast of volatility is a critical factor in trading options. In fact, many option traders concentrate on volatility to make their speculative decisions. Moreover, traders predict that options whose prices are quoted in terms of volatility will trade within five years.

Methods of forecasting volatility include economic, fundamental, and technical procedures. One statistical method that has received attention in the financial community is called GARCH. GARCH stands for "generalized autoregressive conditional heteroscedasticity." Basically the GARCH methodology uses past data to find patterns in changing volatility over time. These patterns are expressed in equation form so that an estimate of future volatility can be made based on the changing structure of the most recent volatility and past patterns. Of course, this procedure is based on the assumption that future volatility can be forecasted from past changes in volatility. Recent work on different financial time series shows that volatility has a significant predictable component. In fact, O'Conner Associates, a large options trading firm, successfully uses GARCH models to trade options.

Volatility and Stock Indexes

Using the standard deviation with historical data creates a downward bias for the measure of volatility for stock indexes. In other words, the measured standard deviation is smaller than the true standard deviation. The reason for this is the illiquidity of some stocks in the index. Since all stocks do not trade at or near the close, using daily index values creates a smaller volatility measure than if true closing prices were available. Another way to state this price relationship is to realize that stock index changes have a positive and significant correlation from one day to the next which reflects the movement of information and volatility from one day to the next. This bias needs to be eliminated before the Black-Scholes model can be used effectively to value stock index options.

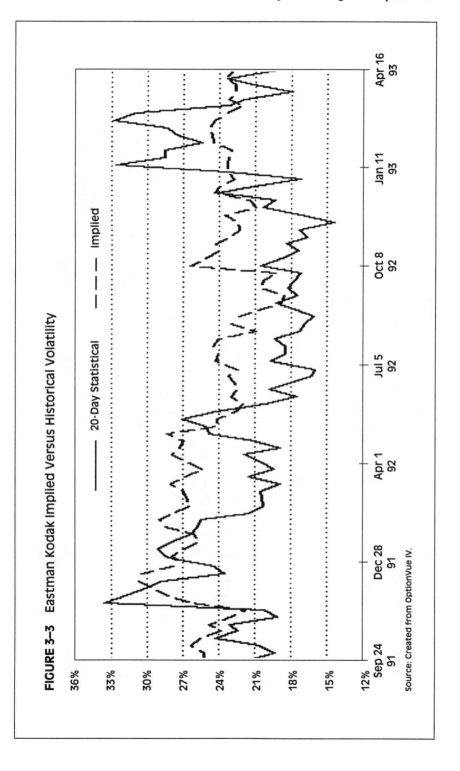

FIGURE 3-3 Eastman Kodak Implied Versus Historical Volatility

Source: Created from OptionVue IV.

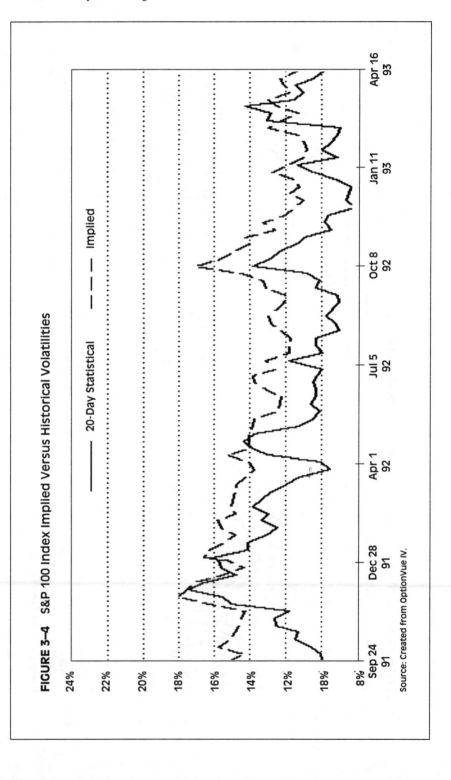

FIGURE 3–4 S&P 100 Index Implied Versus Historical Volatilities

Source: Created from OptionVue IV.

FOCUS 3–2   OptionVue and Volatilities

One of the interesting features of the OptionVue historical database is that it provides information on the short-term and long-term statistical volatilities (S.V.), as well as the corresponding implied volatilities (I.V.). As an example, the following shows the S.V. and I.V. values for the most recent time and the long term for stock index options, ranked by option volume. One also can rank the results by other variables, such as volatilities or the ratio of I.V. to S.V. The ranking feature is even more useful for stock options, given the large number of stocks that trade options. Of course, one benefit of the ranking feature is the ability to determine which options have the highest/lowest volatility (if the trader has a belief about the direction of the market) or which options possess the largest difference between implied and historical volatility. The term R.D.V.O. in the table stands for the "relative dollar volume of options trading."

OPTIONVUE IV DATA BASE SURVEY

Report Based on Data as of Apr 16, 1993
List the best 10 indexes in terms of options trading volume

	Symbol	Type	R.D.V.O.	/--- Current ---\ S.V.	I.V.	V-- Historical --\ S.V.	I.V.
1.	OEX	Index	35970	9.8%	11.2%	11.4%	13.5%
2.	NSX	Index	5965	8.9%	10.6%	10.0%	11.2%
3.	SPX	Index	5965	8.8%	10.8%	10.6%	13.1%
4.	SP	Index	4344	8.9%	10.7%	11.7%	13.3%
5.	XMI	Index	400	10.8%	11.0%	12.1%	13.3%
6.	MID	Index	326	9.4%	12.3%	10.2%	14.8%
7.	JPN	Index	205	15.5%	24.2%	12.9%	28.4%
8.	VLE	Index	166	6.0%	10.9%	7.1%	10.8%
9.	XOC	Index	103	16.5%	18.3%	18.1%	19.6%
10.	XII	Index	92	11.0%	10.3%	11.9%	13.2%

The symbols stand for the following indexes:
OEX = S&P 100; NSX = New York Stock Exchange; SPX = S&P 500 (cash); SP = S&P 500 (futures); XMI = Major Market; MID = S&P Midcap; JPN = Japan; VLE = Value Line; XOC = National OTC; XII = Institutional.

Source: Created from OptionVue IV.

Volatility Quoted Options

GLOBEX (a computer trading system that operates when the U.S. exchanges are closed) trades options on T-bond and T-note futures in terms of *volatility*. Thus, instead of the price being quoted in dollars, it is quoted in terms of the (implied) volatility of the underlying asset. Such volatility quoted options are common on the over-the-counter options market and are being considered by the CBOE for potential future listing. Volatility-quoted options are purchased when an increase in volatility is anticipated, while options are sold when a decrease in volatility is expected. An exchange option model converts the volatility quote to a price paid by the option buyer. The interest rate for the model is determined by the nearby Eurodollar futures rate. In addition, the trade is set up on GLOBEX to create a delta-neutral position by trading both the option and the underlying futures contract at the same time. Volatility-quoted options could become a major trading vehicle within the next few years.

PUT OPTION PRICING

Black-Scholes and Put-Call Parity Put Pricing

Black and Scholes (1973) also present a model to value puts:

$$P_P = -P_S N(-d_1) + K e^{-rt} N(-d_2) \qquad (3\text{--}18)$$

where d_1 and d_2 are defined in Equations (3–2) and (3–3) in conjunction with the call option formula, and the symbols here are equivalent to those of the call formula of Equation (3–1). Note the similarity between this put formula and the formula to value call options. In addition, put prices can be adjusted for dividends in the same manner as call options. Example (3–6) shows how to calculate the Black-Scholes put value.

An alternative method often used to calculate the value of a put option is known as **put-call parity**, as explained in Chapter 2. Put-call parity creates the equivalent of a put option with a call option, stock, and invested funds. Such a transaction is called a **synthetic put**. The resultant put price based on put-call parity is given in Equation (3–19), which is simply a rearrangement of Equation (2–5):

$$P_P = P_C - P_S + K e^{-rt} \qquad (3\text{--}19)$$

The put priced in (3–19) must have the same strike price and expiration as the call option. If we substitute the Black-Scholes value for a call option from Equation (3–1) into Equation (3–19), we obtain the Black-Scholes put equation given in (3–18).[17] Example 3–7 shows how to determine a put value based on the put-call parity equation.

Dividends are added to the put valuation equation without creating any significant problems. A put for a stock that pays dividends is valued as follows:

$$P_P = P_C - P_S + K e^{-rt} + D e^{-r\tau} \qquad (3\text{-}20)$$

where τ = the time period until the ex-dividend date for the stock.

EXAMPLE 3–6 Black-Scholes Put Value

Equation (3–18) defines the Black-Scholes put option value as:

$$P_p = - P_s\, N(-d_1) + K\, e^{-rt}\, N(-d_2) \qquad\qquad (3\text{–}18)$$

where d_1 and d_2 are defined in conjunction with call options (see Equations (3–2) and (3–3)).

Using the same input information as in Example 3–1, we have:

$d_1 = 0.0942$
$d_2 = -0.1558$

Then (from Appendix A and interpolating):

$N(-d_1) = N(-0.0942) = 1 - N(0.0942) = 1 - 0.5375 = 0.4625$
$N(-d_2) = N(+0.1558) = .5619$

Since $e^{-0.05(0.25)} = 0.9876$

$P_p = -98(0.4625) + 100\,(0.9876)(0.5619)$
$\quad = -45.325 + 55.493$
$\quad = \$10.17$

The value of the put is larger than the call value in Example 3–1 because the put is in-the-money while the call is out-of-the-money.

EXAMPLE 3–7 Put Prices in Terms of Put-Call Parity

The value of a put based on the put-call parity relationship is:

$$P_p = P_c - P_s + K\, e^{-rt} \qquad\qquad (3\text{–}19)$$

Based on the information in Example 3–1, we have:

$P_p = 9.41 - 98 + 100\, e^{-0.05(0.25)}$
$\quad = 9.41 - 98 + 100\,(0.9876)$
$\quad = \$10.17$

This is equivalent to the put value found with the Black-Scholes formula in Example 3–6.

Early Put Exercise and the Resultant Put Models

The Black-Scholes formulation for the value of a put is based on a European-style option in that the exercise can occur only at the expiration of the option. However, the American-style put stock options that trade in the United States are often exercised early (unless large dividends are yet to be paid), while American *call* options are exercised early only if a dividend occurs near the expiration date. An early exercise for a put option on a non-dividend-paying stock occurs when a large stock price decrease makes it more profitable to exercise the put than to wait until its expiration date. This situation occurs if the price of the American put loses all of its time value.

An extreme example shows why puts are exercised early. Suppose a trader purchases a put with a strike price of $100 when the associated stock is selling for $100. Subsequently, the stock declines to $5, causing the put to have an intrinsic value of $95. If the put option still has one year before expiration, and the current interest rate is 10%, then it is more profitable to exercise the put and invest the profits from the put at 10% than to keep the put for a maximum additional gain of $5. Similarly, when a put loses all of its time value, exercising the put and investing the funds in a risk-free instrument provides a higher risk-adjusted return than the expected value of holding the put option.

The effect of stock dividends on puts is to decrease the probability of early exercise. Thus, the early exercise feature of American puts is worth less when the stock pays dividends, especially when ex-dividend dates exist near the expiration of the option. The put should be exercised only after the dividend is paid and the stock price is adjusted downward. Other things being equal, early exercise for an American put is more appropriate the lower the stock price, the higher the strike price, the shorter the time to expiration, and the lower the cash dividends yet to be paid.

Unfortunately, including the likelihood of early exercise in the put valuation equation creates complex problems. In fact, the resulting pricing models are not closed-form equations; they generally cannot be solved by a calculator. Several American put models have been developed; some are approximation methods, while others are exact pricing models. The approximation methods are simpler and typically only vary from the true value by several cents. The most popular methods for pricing puts with early exercise are by Parkinson (1977); Brennan and Schwartz (1977); Cox, Ross, and Rubinstein (1979); and Geske and Johnson (1984). The exact models involve complex computer calculations. Binomial models also can be used to solve for the American put value.

TRADING ON THE OPTION FLOOR

The Trading Floor
Traders on the floor of the options exchanges must know the last price of the stock underlying the option being traded, as well as the bid, ask, and most recent trades for the various strike prices and expirations of the associated

EXHIBIT 3–2   Computer Screen on the Options Floor

POLAR		CLOSE	LAST	B-BID A-ASK	SIZE	MKT-QUOTE
A	Jan 30	8 1/2	7 5/8	7 3/8 - 7 3/4	2 X 5	7 1/2 - 7 3/4
B	Jan 35	3 3/4	2 13+	2 3/4 - 3	1 X 2	2 13+ - 2 15+
C	Jan 40	11+	7+	3/8 - 1/2	3 X 2	3/8 - 1/2
D	Jan 45	1+		- 3+	X 2	- 1+
E	Apr 35	5 1/2	4 3/4	4 1/2 - 5	3 X 6	4 5/8 - 4 3/4
F	Apr 40	2 11+	2 1/4	2 1/8 - 2 7+	1 X 2	2 3+ - 2 5+
G	Apr 45	1 1/8	3/4	1/2 - 1 1+	3 X 2	3/4 - 7/8
H	Jul 35	6 1/2	5 7/8	5 1/4 - 6	1 X 1	5 5/8 - 5 7/8
I	Jul 40	4	3 1/4	3 - 3 5/8	2 X 2	3 1/4 - 3 3/8
J						
K						
L						
M						
N						
O						
P						

PRD 37 1/2 - 1   B 37 3/8   A 37 5/8   O 38 3/8   H 38 1/2   L 37 1/2   V 96,000 at 1:12
PRD 37 5/8   PRD 2s 37 1/2   PRD 800s 37 1/2

Note: A "+" refers to 1/16 of a point.
Bid and Ask prices are the best prices in the limit order book.
"Size" (2 X 5) is the number to buy (2) and the number to sell (5) in the
limit order book.

Source: Rubinstein (1991).

options. All of this information appears on the large screens in front of the trading area, as illustrated in Exhibit 3–2. The floor trader buys options at the lower bid price and sells at the ask price. Floor traders use hand signals and shout their bid and ask quotes to show their willingness to trade a specific option (hand signals are not officially recognized by the exchange for trading purposes). Only large stocks, such as IBM and General Motors, have options that trade frequently; most of the trading areas have options on ten to fifteen stocks.

Exhibit 3–3 illustrates how trading on the option floor is conducted. Two aspects of the trading procedure are particularly important. First, note that options start trading *after* the initial stock trade on that option. Subsequently, each option on that stock is opened sequentially to find the equilibrium price for trading that option. This procedure is called the option rotation. Second, orders to buy/sell options are offered to the option floor for bids/asks. On the day of the market crash in 1987, it took two hours to go through the entire option rotation. Due to this extensive delay, the exchange then went through *another* rotation. No wonder traders lost substantial amounts of money given such a delay!

EXHIBIT 3–3 Trading Options on the Floor

7:00 A.M.* Exchange floor quiet.

7:00   Members and trade checkers arrive to rectify clerical errors from the previous day.**

8:25   Floor is crowded with hundreds of market makers, floor brokers, order book officials, and employees of the exchange and member firms.

8:30   New York and American stock exchanges open. Options trading at each post awaits the first print of the underlying stock.

8:35   Stock prints. Officer opens each associated option series, one at a
•   time, calls before puts, by calling for bid and ask quotes from the
•   trading crowd.
•

2:09 P.M. A *limit* order to sell 5 PRD/JUL/40 calls at 3 3/8, initiated off the floor, reaches one of the communication booths lining the perimeter of the floor. Order is imprinted by a teletype machine on an order card.

2:10   Runner delivers order to a floor broker standing at the Polaroid post. The book bid-ask is 3-3 5/8. The floor broker calls for a market and is quoted 3 1/4 - 3 3/8 by the trading crowd. To afford his customer priority, he "books" the order.

2:12   A *market* order to sell 5 PRD/JUL/40 calls is delivered to the floor broker and he calls for a market. He is again quoted 3 1/4 - 3 3/8 by the trading crowd—"1/4-1/2" by one market maker and "1/8-3/8" by another. He offers to sell at 3/8 but the crowd shows no interest. He then turns to the market maker quoting "1/4-1/2" and says, "sold at 1/4; I have five." The market maker says "done."

2:13   The floor broker fills out a sell ticket and the market maker fills out a buy ticket. The floor broker time stamps the sell ticket and places it in a conveyer belt in front of the post.

2:14   The sell ticket is automatically conveyed to a small bin at one end of the post. The PRTO key punches the trade information into the exchange computer system. The price and volume of the trade appear in brokerage houses across the country.

3:00   New York and American stock exchanges close.

3:10   Chicago Board Options Exchange closes.

* All times are Central time.
** Out trades occur when only one side of a trade is reported.
Source: Rubinstein, 1991.

Trades are made by the floor broker or market maker. A floor broker executes trades that come from the public "at the best possible price," earning a fee for each trade. Market makers trade for their own accounts, profiting from their trading skills. Market maker strategies are discussed shortly.[18] A third type of floor trader at the CBOE is the order book official (OBO), who puts unfilled limit orders into the computer and later executes the orders if the prices specified are reached. Limit orders have priority over all other orders at the specific price of the limit order. Orders for 10 contracts or less on the S&P 100 option (OEX) are executed via the automatic execution system called "RAYS." The cost of a seat on an exchange that allows one to trade on the floor is typically over $200,000. Two-thirds of the floor traders make over $75,000 per year.

Floor Trading

The methods employed by option floor traders to profit from trading in options and their associated stocks are listed here. Subsequent sections discuss these methods in more detail. The trading methods are as follows:

- Heavily traded options are bought at the bid and sold at the ask, generating a bid-ask profit for the market maker.

- Black-Scholes hedge ratios between the stock and option are created when options are mispriced.

- **Ratio spreads** between two options for the same stock also are initiated when option mispricing exists. Ratio spreads use Black-Scholes hedge ratios to determine the number of options to trade and which option should be purchased/sold.

- Traders execute **box spreads**, consisting of two call options with different strike prices and two put options with strike prices equivalent to the calls.[19] Box spreads are executed when the options become mispriced on a *relative* basis.

- Put-call parity identifies mispriced relationships between the call, put, and stock. If the call is overpriced relative to the put, then the put is purchased and a **synthetic put**, made up of a short call and long stock, is sold (this strategy is called a **conversion**).[20] If the call is underpriced relative to the put, then the call is purchased and a short **synthetic call**, made up of a short put and short stock, is sold (called a **reverse conversion**).

Except for the market maker's bid-ask spread, the other strategies given above are arbitrage transactions. However, strategies based on the Black-

Scholes model require dynamic changes in the hedge ratio as the input variables change. Consequently, the possible existence of jumps in the asset price creates a risk for the floor trader using Black-Scholes strategies. The other strategies do not require dynamic adjustments and therefore are truly risk-free strategies.

The Market Maker as Scalper

When a market maker buys at the bid and sells at the ask price, he/she is called a **scalper**. Market makers can trade the same option on a bid-ask basis when sufficient liquidity exists, which typically occurs for nearby, near-the-money options. Exchange-imposed limits exist for the bid-ask spread, as shown below:

Bid Price	Maximum Bid-Ask Spread
< 2	1/4
≥ 2 and ≤ 5	3/8
> 5 and ≤ 10	1/2
>10 and ≤ 20	3/4
> 20	1

Using Black-Scholes and Ratio Spread Strategies

Both the Black-Scholes and ratio hedge strategies require an accurate estimate of the option's fair price. Hence, traders using these methods carry hand-held programmable calculators to determine the option's fair value. The option valuation equation is programmed into the calculator; then the trader inputs the current stock price, the option's time to expiration, and the strike price (interest rates and stock volatility are input in the morning, since these factors do not change frequently). Traders previously employed some version of the Black-Scholes model in their calculators. More recently, the binomial model has become the popular option valuation model.

Ratio spreads are employed by floor traders in order to profit from options mispriced on a relative basis. The number of option contracts traded is based on their relative hedge ratios from the Black-Scholes model. Thus, if option A is underpriced and has a Black-Scholes hedge ratio of 0.25, and option B for the same stock is overpriced and has a hedge ratio of 0.5, then the trader would initiate a ratio spread where A is purchased and B is sold in the combination of 0.5/0.25 = 2.0 to 1.0 of the A to B options. The relationship between the number of option contracts is as follows:

$$\frac{\text{Purchase A shares}}{\text{Sell B shares}} = \frac{HR_B}{HR_A} \qquad (3\text{-}21)$$

The ratio spreader profits when the option mispricing corrects itself, while avoiding the risk from option price changes caused by stock price changes (since these option price changes offset each other). For our example, the hedge ratio of 0.25 for A means that stock A will change by $0.25 for a $1 change in the asset. Consequently, purchasing 50 shares of A and selling 25 shares of B [as determined by Equation (3–21)] results in the following situation when the stock changes by $1:

$$\begin{aligned} \text{Buy A } (\Delta P_A) &= \text{Sell B } (\Delta P_B) \\ 50 \, (\$0.25) &= 25 \, (\$0.50) \\ \$12.50 &= \$12.50 \end{aligned} \qquad \text{(3-22)}$$

Thus, the risk caused by small stock price changes is eliminated, while the eventual realignment of the mispriced option prices will generate a profit.

Floor traders prefer ratio spreads to regular Black-Scholes stock/option hedges, since the amount of investment is substantially less and the options are traded by the floor trader directly, without going to the stock exchange to buy or sell stocks. However, as with Black-Scholes hedges, using ratio spreads does require dynamic management of the ratio spread position. Since the Black-Scholes hedge changes as the stock price and other input variables change, the ratio between the option hedge ratios often changes as well. Consequently, large stock price jumps could create difficulties for managing the ratio spread. Moreover, off-the-floor traders cannot use ratio spreads effectively in most circumstances because of the costs of managing the position and the need to change the ratio on short notice.

Box Spreads and Conversions

Box spreads and conversions do not require the dynamic management of the hedge ratios needed for Black-Scholes hedges and ratio spreads. Thus, box spreads and conversions are a less risky form of option arbitrage.

The advantage of box spreads over conversions is that only options are involved; the option floor trader does not need to go to the NYSE to trade stocks as part of the arbitrage strategy. In addition, all of the options in a box spread should have the same implied volatility—and hence the same price response to a change in the stock price—since all the options have the same expiration date. In other words, the price risk of the call spread is offset by the opposite position in the put spread, leaving only the profit from the mispricings of the options. However, the profit opportunities for a box spread are available only to floor traders who instantly recognize the relative mispricing among the options. Delays in executing a box spread result in other floor traders implementing the same strategy, which causes prices to realign to their relative fair values.[21]

Conversions and reverse conversions involve calls, puts, and the underlying stock. Exhibit 2–2 showed that buying a call plus investing the present value of the strike price was equivalent to buying a put and buying stock. Using the same logic, we find that:

- If a trader can *buy* an underpriced put and *sell* an overpriced or fairly priced synthetic put (a short call and long stock position), then a profit is achieved from this conversion, because *net cash flows* are positive:

$$- P_P + P_C + (K - P_S) - (P_S + P_P - P_C) (e^{rt} - 1) > 0 \qquad \text{(3–22)}$$

The positive signs before a position show a positive cash flow, while negative signs show a negative cash flow. For a conversion, funds must be borrowed to finance the purchase of the stock so that the trader does not need to use his or her own funds for the conversion. The last term in Equation (3–22) calculates the interest paid on the net borrowings. Notice that $K - P_S$ is relevant whether stock prices decline and the long put is executed at K, or stock prices increase and the stock is called away via the short call at K.

- If a trader can buy an underpriced call and *sell* an overpriced or fairly priced synthetic call (a short put and short stock), a profit is achieved from a reverse conversion because of the *positive cash flows:*

$$- P_C + P_P + (P_S - K) + (P_S + P_P - P_C) (e^{rt} - 1) > 0 \qquad \text{(3–23)}$$

For a reverse conversion, the funds *received* from selling short the stock are placed in a risk-free investment that earns interest. The last term in Equation (3–23) calculates this interest received. The value of $P_S - K$ occurs whether the call is executed to buy stock at K, or the stock is put to the trader at K via the execution of the short put. Again, the trader's funds are not needed for this reverse conversion. One difficulty in executing reverse conversions is that the trader typically does not receive all of the funds from a short sale.

Conversions and reverse conversions are pure, risk-free transactions, since the price change on the option purchased is offset from the sale of the synthetic option (the payoff diagrams are equivalent). Consequently, only the option mispricing should affect the transaction's profits.

The most profitable transactions for market makers are trading deep-in-the-money calls and puts, since these trades create large bid-ask spreads. For example, if an individual wants to sell a deep-in-the-money call with a bid-ask spread of 8 1/2 to 9 (due to the lack of liquidity on these options), then the market maker creates a reverse conversion with a short synthetic call to offset the call purchased by the market maker. While a trade of 8 $\frac{7}{8}$ could be a fair price, the market maker buys the call for 8 $\frac{1}{2}$ and locks in a $\frac{3}{8}$ profit by creating a short synthetic call at the 8 $\frac{7}{8}$ fair price. Of course, this assumes the put is fairly priced. Moreover, risks do exist for this trade. First, the stock price could change in the following one or two minutes, before the stock trade is executed. Second, the short uptick rule on stocks could keep the market maker from shorting the stock at the needed price. Example 3-8 shows that the above reverse conversion generates a profit. However, if the market maker receives only 85% of the proceeds from the short stock sale, these profits disappear at current interest rate levels. In this case, the broker keeps the remaining 15% of the short sale funds, often called a "haircut."

A total of four synthetic positions are possible with calls and puts:

Conversion positions:

- short synthetic put (equals a short call and long stock), which offsets a long put

- long synthetic call (equals a long put and long stock), which offsets a short call

---

EXAMPLE 3–8   Reverse Conversion

The premise of a reverse conversion is that the market maker can buy an underpriced call and sell a synthetic call (a short put and short stock). The cash flows on a reverse conversion are:

$$- P_c + P_p + (P_s - K) + (P_s + P_p - P_c)\, (e^{rt} - 1) > 0 \qquad (3\text{–}24)$$

The following prices exist in the market:

$P_c = 8\,\frac{1}{2}$ $P_c\text{(fair)} = 8\,\frac{7}{8}$ $P_s = 100$ $t = 0.5$ year $r = 0.05$

Therefore, based on Equation (3–24):

$- 8.50 + 6.375 + (100 - 100) + (100 + 6.375 - 8.50)\, (e^{(0.05)(0.5)} - 1)$
$= - 2.125 + 97.875\, (1.025315 - 1)$
$= - 2.125 + 2.478$
$= \$0.35$

Thus, the trader makes \$0.35 per share on the reverse conversion (with no funds invested). If the current price of the call is 8 $\frac{3}{4}$, the profit declines to \$0.096. If the market maker has access to only 85% of the short sale funds (with a call price of 8 $\frac{1}{2}$), then a *loss* of \$0.03 would occur. Thus, the amount of funds available, the level of interest rates, and the difference between the market and fair option prices are all important factors for a profitable reverse conversion.

Reverse conversion positions:

- short synthetic call (equals a short put and short stock), which offsets a long call

- long synthetic put (equals a long call and short stock), which offsets a short put

While the two new synthetic positions listed here are simply rearrangements of the previously discussed synthetic positions, they provide important opportunities for market makers. Since most individuals want to buy call and put options, market makers typically take a short position in these options—at least until someone else wants a short call or short put. Consequently, the market maker can generate a long synthetic call or long synthetic put to offset selling calls or puts to individuals. Market makers profit from these transactions when they earn the bid-ask spread or when demand causes call and/or put prices to rise above their fair values.

MARKET MICROSTRUCTURE IN THE OPTIONS MARKET

Intraday Options Pricing Behavior

Market microstructure is the study of price behavior within the day. Interest in intraday pricing has increased substantially since transactions price data on stock, futures, and options markets have become available in the past few years. Such intraday data is particularly important for studying options markets, since the pricing of options relies critically on the price of the underlying asset. Using end-of-day options and stock prices creates problems due to timing differences between when the options and stocks last traded. Chapter 4 will examine studies of the Black-Scholes and alternative option pricing models, many of which use intraday data. Here we look at the price behavior of option prices within the day.

Stephan and Whaley (1990) show that stock prices and volume *lead* individual option price movements and volume by 15 to 20 minutes, which contradicts previous studies showing that the options markets lead the stock market. Stephan and Whaley also show that option trading activity is at a maximum 45 minutes into the day, while the maximum stock activity occurs at the open and the close.

Abnormal Pricing Behavior and Bid-Ask Spreads

Kumar, Sarin, and Shastri (1992) show that options exhibit abnormal price behavior starting 30 minutes before a block trade is executed and ending one hour after the block trade. In comparison, the stock itself has abnormal pricing behavior for 15 minutes *after* the trade and *no* abnormal behavior before the blocks when the stock increases in price; stocks that decrease after the block trade have abnormal behavior both 15 minutes before and 15 minutes after the block trade. The authors attribute the more extensive option abnormal price behavior to traders using the options market before the stock market in what is known as "frontrunning."

Jameson and Wilhelm (1992) determine that option market makers have unique risks in managing their option inventory. In particular, the risks involved in the discrete rebalancing of their option position and the uncertainty of the stock's future volatility account for an important part of the option's bid-ask spreads. However, Dawson and Gemmill (1990) claim that these risks do not adversely affect the market maker's profit. In particular, they find that market makers on the London index option market could average over $700,000 per year, based on the authors' trading strategy and actual transactions prices.

The existence of options also affects the bid-ask spreads on the underlying stock. Fedenia and Grammatikos (1992) show that after the initial listing of options contracts on a stock, the spread decreases for less liquid stocks but *increases* for highly liquid stocks.

SUMMARY AND LOOKING AHEAD

This chapter examines option pricing using the Black-Scholes option pricing model. Both the Black-Scholes option model itself and calculating the inputs to the model are important concepts for understanding what influences option prices. The inputs to and output from the model also are discussed, including the importance of implied volatility. Put pricing follows directly from call option pricing. Finally, how option trading is executed on the floor of the exchange is discussed. Chapter 4 examines option pricing in greater detail, including the option sensitivities and empirical evidence concerning option models.

END NOTES

[1] Black and Scholes (1972, 1973) derive their option pricing model in the 1973 article and test the model on over-the-counter options in their 1972 article.

[2] The current option price is *independent* of the expected future stock price.

[3] The natural logarithm is used for two purposes: first, it improves the computational properties of the stock distribution, and second, the value is converted to a continuously compounded return.

[4] The slope to a curvilinear line at a particular point is the derivative of the line at that point. The concept of an instantaneous change is directly related to the derivative.

[5] Any pricing model is based on certain assumptions that are used to derive the final result of the model (in this case, the option price). For example, one criticism concerning

the input factors of the Black-Scholes model is that stock price changes do *not* follow a normal distribution (which includes possible jumps in prices). If the actual option price in the market deviates from the price estimated by the model, either the actual option price is mispriced (providing profit opportunities), the assumptions of the model are incorrect, or the model is missing one or more important input factors. Chapter 4 investigates how well the Black-Scholes model estimates the true market option prices. While some deviations do exist, overall the Black-Scholes model provides very accurate estimates of actual option prices.

[6] R_f and $r = \ln(1 + R_f)$ create the same ending value for \$1 invested for a particular length of time. However, the continuous compounding nature of r allows this ending value to occur with a value of r, which is less than the corresponding value for R_f.

[7] Chapter 2 states that a change in the risk-free interest rate does not significantly affect the value of the call option. Therefore, one might be tempted to use the simple R_f rate rather than calculate the continuously compounded rate r. Whether a trader employs such a substitution depends on the accuracy desired for the analysis. The use of R_f determines a value for the call option that is about 0.2% too high. Similarly, the use of an interest rate that does not exactly correspond to the actual expiration of the option has only a minor effect on the calculated value of the option.

Some traders and researchers state that the certificate of deposit rate or the broker call rate (the rate of interest charged to investors for loans on margin accounts) is more appropriate than the T-bill rate. Their reasoning is that the T-bill rate is below the borrowing rate for funds. The T-bill rate is still justifiable if marginal investors obtain funds from their cash management account, which is invested in T-bills. Moreover, the call price is not very sensitive to varying interest rates.

[8] An alternative to using the historical volatility is for the analyst to devise a probability distribution of *expected* outcomes, determining the variance of that probability distribution.

[9] The reliability of the historical volatility estimate can be improved by using the open, high, low, and close of whatever measurement interval is chosen. For example, if daily data are employed, then the daily open, high, low, and close prices can be used to improve the estimate of volatility by a factor of eight. See Garman and Klass (1980).

[10] The calculation of the variance in Equation (3–10) involves dividing by N–1. Subtracting 1 from N is required when a sample is used for the calculation, as in this case. If a spreadsheet is used to determine the relevant volatility values, an adjustment must often be made for the variance, since most spreadsheets use N in the divisor. The relevant adjustment is to multiply the results by N/(N–1).

[11] The stock owner does not receive the dividends until four to six weeks after the ex-dividend date. However, the ex-dividend date is when the stock price is adjusted downward and, therefore, when the call option price is adversely affected.

[12] Exercising an option entails a commission on the stock, even though the stock is not purchased on the exchange. Thus, an option exercise does not avoid this cost.

[13] Using a continuously accrued dividend yield avoids potential problems relating to known discrete dividends. A dividend yield is a known percentage of the index value or stock price. As stock price levels change, the *dollar* value of the dividends changes under the procedure of a constant *yield*. This assumption is more realistic than taking a specific known dollar dividend, especially for stock indexes. An in-depth development and proof of the various dividend adjustments to the option model is found in Jarrow and Rudd (1983, ch. 9).

[14] While finding implied volatility is a trial-and-error procedure, the Newton-Raphson search technique provides a very rapid procedure for finding the implied volatility. However, the difficulty of the technique and the speed of modern PCs make such a search process less important. Alternatively, one can use the approximation equation for the normal distribution given in Exhibit 3–1 to solve the option equation for volatility by trial and error.

[15] Typically, deep-in- and deep-out-of-the-money options are not considered when calculating the weighted implied volatility, since small changes in the option price have significant effects on the implied volatility, *and* because these options are often mispriced or have not traded recently.

[16] Technically, the largest weight should be the call with the largest $\partial C_j / \partial \sigma_j^*$, which is usually the near-to-the-money call.

[17] Jarrow and Rudd (1983) prove a number of relationships associated with different forms of the put-call parity theorem.

[18] The CBOE and Pacific Exchanges use competing market makers. The American and Philadelphia Exchanges use one specialist per option, with the specialist being responsible for "making a market to the public." The American and Philadelphia Exchanges also have Registered Option Traders who buy and sell options for their own account. The CBOE does use a "designated market maker" for new stocks. The designated market makers act like specialists in that they are allowed to see the *entire* limit order book rather than only the best bid and ask limit orders. This special designation is intended to provide liquidity for new issues.

[19] This combination is called a box spread because the options traded form the four corners of a box when the call and put option prices from Exhibits 1–3 and 1–5 are placed next to each other.

[20] Exchanges could not list puts during the mid 1970s. Market makers and others sold "a put" to those institutions wanting to hedge with a long put. The "short put" on the market maker's books was offset by a synthetic long put, created by buying a call and selling short stock.

[21] Box spreads are very sensitive to any transaction costs. In addition, box spread profits often rely on buying at the bid and selling at the ask price.

APPENDIX 3A
Assumptions of the Black-Scholes Option Model

The Black-Scholes option model is based on several assumptions concerning the input data. All financial models are based on assumptions, with the validity of the assumptions being a major factor in determining whether a particular model is useful in explaining the financial variable of interest. The assumptions associated with the Black-Scholes model are given below, along with a discussion concerning their importance for the accurate pricing of options. These assumptions are as follows:

- The variance of the stock returns is constant over the life of the option.

- The interest rate is constant over the life of the option.

- A continuous stock price occurs—that is, no "jumps" in price exist.

- Stock returns are described by a lognormal distribution.

- No transaction costs exist.

- No dividends are paid on the stock, and the option can be exercised only at expiration.

Constant Variance and Interest Rates

Perhaps the most important assumption of the Black-Scholes model is that the stock variance is constant. A major problem with a nonconstant variance is that the hedge ratio breaks down—that is, the hedge ratio does *not* provide a risk-free hedge. However, this problem is not severe for short time periods when the hedge is constantly revised. Also, if the variance changes in a predictable pattern, then the *average variance* over the remaining life of the option can be used in the Black-Scholes model as an estimate for the variance, since the spirit of the model remains the same. An exact option model cannot be obtained for a nonconstant variance which does *not* have a predictable pattern over time, although the value for such an option can be estimated with computerized numerical techniques. In practice, this assumption of constant variance may seem unimportant, since no one knows ahead of time the true future variance of the stock over the life of the option. However, a nonconstant variance reduces the accuracy of the pricing model even *if* the true *average* future variance is known. Cox (1975) developed a "constant elasticity of variance diffusion" option model in which the variance of the stock increases as the stock price falls. Jarrow and Rudd (1983) derive this model. MacBeth and Merville (1980) and Rubinstein (1985) test the model against the Black-Scholes model. MacBeth and Merville find the Cox model to provide somewhat better estimates of actual option prices than the Black-Scholes model, but Rubinstein does not find this dominance.

The effect of an unknown and nonconstant interest rate over the life of the option is similar to a nonconstant variance, except that changing interest rates have less of an effect on the hedge ratio and the option price. To incorporate predictable nonconstant interest rates into the model, one replaces the interest rate in the formula with the product of the interest rates over each remaining subperiod before option expiration. In general, the effect of different levels of interest rates is shown in Chapter 4. Those results illustrate the relatively minor effect of interest rates on option prices. One important effect of using nonconstant, but predictable, variances and interest rates is that options with different maturities can/should use different volatilities and interest rates for their inputs to the model.

Continuous Stock Price and Lognormal Distribution

A continuous stock price is needed so that hedgers can adjust their hedge ratios whenever stock prices change in order to keep a risk-free hedge. Large jumps in stock prices make this needed revision in the hedge ratio impossible to achieve. While Merton (1976) and Cox and Ross (1976) develop a model to consider such jumps, the lack of data makes such a model difficult to test. Jarrow and Rudd (1983) develop Merton's model mathematically. Some researchers believe that the existence of jumps in stock prices is one reason for some mispricings by the Black-Scholes model, since jumps are equivalent to saying that the true distribution of returns has fatter tails than assumed by the lognormal distribution.[1]

Using the variance of the continuously discounted stock returns means that the distribution of these returns must follow a lognormal distribution. However, a significant amount of empirical evidence on stock returns suggests that there are more large price changes than warranted by a lognormal distribution. In essence, this means that the true variability of the stock is not measured accurately by the variance of the returns, creating a bias in the model. This bias is more severe as the stock price moves away from the strike price.[2]

Transaction Costs, Dividends, and Exercise

The assumption of no transaction costs is needed to insure that a hedge ratio can be revised often in order to keep the position risk-free. The existence of transaction costs for off-the-floor traders means that such traders are precluded from initiating an arbitrage transaction. While floor traders do have small transaction costs, these costs do not severely hamper the traders' ability to perform arbitrage, although the existence of these costs probably does reduce the accuracy of the pure Black-Scholes model slightly.

The dividend and exercise assumptions were discussed previously. Dividends are added to the model with a simple adjustment. The effect of early exercise on call options is typically minimal, except when a dividend occurs near expiration. The effect of early exercise on puts is more severe, but American models that consider this early exercise feature generally do not perform any better than the European Black-Scholes model. Tables 3A–1 and 3A–2 compare American and European call and put option values for various strike prices, volatilities, and months-to-expiration.

Index Options and Assumptions of the Model

Combining stocks into a portfolio could create price effects for the resultant cash index that differ from the behavior of individual stocks. In addition, other characteristics of the cash index and index options should be investigated for their effect on pricing. The following lists these factors.

- **Index lognormality**

  Stock indexes are closer to lognormality than individual stocks. Therefore, this factor does not adversely affect the model. Moreover, stock indexes have greater stability of volatility and fewer effects due to jumps in prices than individual stocks.

- **Wildcard option on cash-settled options**

  Index options are settled in cash. The option buyer can exercise up until 4:10 P.M., with the index value based on a 4:00 P.M. stock market close. This causes index options to be worth more than their Black-Scholes values.

- **Artificial serial correlation of the cash index**

  Serial correlation is prevalent in the cash index due to the nontrading of smaller stocks making up the index. Thus, the actual volatility in the index is higher than the observed volatility.[3]

- **Dividends are paid daily with seasonal spikes**

  Dividends with spikes are not adequately treated in the Black-Scholes model.

In addition, arbitrageurs typically use stock index *futures* rather than cash stocks when executing put-call parity trades, even for the S&P 100 Index options. Therefore, the options may seem to be mispriced if the *cash index* is

TABLE 3A–1   European Versus American Call Option Values

$P_s = 100$ $I = .10$ Div = 15%

| | | European | | | | American (n = 500) | | | |
| | | months to expiration | | | | | | | |
σ	K	1	3	6	12	1	3	6	12
.2	85	14.52	13.82	13.24	12.49	<u>15.00</u>	<u>15.00</u>	<u>15.00</u>	15.19
	90	9.64	9.54	9.61	9.60	<u>10.00</u>	10.16	10.60	11.31
	95	5.24	5.98	6.63	7.20	5.36	6.26	7.16	8.27
	100	2.10	3.36	4.33	5.28	2.13	3.48	4.61	5.94
	105	.58	1.68	2.69	3.79	.58	1.73	2.83	4.20
	110	.11	.75	1.59	2.66	.11	.77	1.66	2.91
	115	.01	.30	.89	1.84	.01	.30	.93	1.99
.3	85	14.62	14.66	15.01	15.37	<u>15.00</u>	15.33	16.09	17.33
	90	10.04	10.91	11.85	12.84	10.22	11.30	12.58	14.27
	95	6.12	7.76	9.17	10.63	6.20	7.99	9.65	11.68
	100	3.24	5.28	6.96	8.74	3.27	5.41	7.27	9.51
	105	1.47	3.44	5.19	7.14	1.48	3.51	5.39	7.71
	110	.57	2.14	3.80	5.80	.57	2.18	3.93	6.23
	115	.19	1.28	2.74	4.69	.19	1.30	2.83	5.00
.4	85	14.92	15.88	17.08	18.41	15.16	16.36	17.96	20.18
	90	10.68	12.49	14.22	16.10	10.81	12.81	14.86	17.50
	95	7.11	9.59	11.73	14.04	7.18	9.80	12.20	15.15
	100	4.38	7.21	9.59	12.21	4.41	7.34	9.93	13.09
	105	2.48	5.30	7.78	10.59	2.50	5.39	8.03	11.31
	110	1.38	3.82	6.27	9.18	1.31	3.88	6.45	9.76
	115	.63	2.70	5.02	7.94	.63	2.74	5.15	8.40

American options with underlined values should be exercised immediately.

Source: Rubinstein (1991).

TABLE 3A–2 European Versus American Put Option Value

$P_s = 100$ $\qquad$ $I = .10$ $\qquad$ $Div = .15$

American options with underlined values should be exercised immediately.

		European				American (n = 500)			
		months to expiration							
σ	K	1	3	6	12	1	3	6	12
.2	85	.00	.15	.56	1.31	.00	.15	.57	1.39
	90	.06	.56	1.28	2.27	.06	.57	1.33	2.45
	95	.51	1.54	2.52	3.64	.51	1.58	2.64	3.98
	100	2.10	3.37	4.39	5.45	2.13	3.48	4.64	6.03
	105	5.31	6.16	6.92	7.70	5.43	6.42	7.42	8.66
	110	9.68	9.78	10.08	10.39	<u>10.00</u>	10.32	10.94	11.88
	115	14.52	14.00	13.74	13.46	<u>15.00</u>	<u>15.00</u>	15.17	15.69
.3	85	.08	.82	1.97	3.67	.08	.83	2.03	3.86
	90	.40	1.74	3.23	5.16	.41	1.76	3.33	5.45
	95	1.33	3.21	4.93	6.96	1.34	3.27	5.09	7.40
	100	3.24	5.32	7.08	9.07	3.27	5.43	7.34	9.70
	105	6.27	8.07	9.67	11.48	6.35	8.28	10.09	12.37
	110	10.21	11.41	12.68	14.17	10.37	11.75	13.30	15.40
	115	14.73	15.23	16.06	17.13	15.03	15.76	16.95	18.75
.4	85	.35	1.91	3.84	6.48	.36	1.93	3.93	6.77
	90	1.00	3.21	5.46	8.31	1.01	3.25	5.59	8.70
	95	2.29	4.99	7.44	10.38	2.30	5.06	7.63	10.92
	100	4.39	7.27	9.76	12.69	4.41	7.38	10.04	13.39
	105	7.33	10.03	12.42	15.22	7.39	10.21	12.82	16.14
	110	11.00	13.23	15.40	17.97	11.11	13.51	15.94	19.13
	115	15.22	16.82	18.65	20.91	15.41	17.21	19.37	22.35

Source: Rubinstein (1991).

used in the put-call parity equation, but not when the futures price index is employed. If the futures are mispriced relative to the options, then an arbitrage trade is executed.

END NOTES FOR APPENDIX 3A

[1] Both the Black-Scholes model and the Cox-Ross jump model can be derived from the binomial model. Differing definitions of the binomial terms generate the two option models.

[2] Ritchken (1987, ch. 6) discusses the distribution of returns in more detail. Cox and Rubinstein (1985) have an excellent bibliography on research articles concerned with stock return distributions.

[3] Rubinstein (1991) estimates the daily serial correlation of the S&P 500 Index at .168 and the NYSE Composite Index at .218.

APPENDIX 3B
Derivation of the Black-Scholes Model

To obtain the Black-Scholes option pricing model, one must first make an assumption concerning the stochastic process dictating the movement of asset prices. The typical process employed is known as an Ito process, which has an instantaneous expected mean return of $\mu_s\, P_s$ and an instantaneous variance rate of $\sigma_s^2\, P_s^2$. Thus, in derivative terms, the change in the asset price is:

$$dP_s = \mu_s P_s\, dt + \sigma_s\, P_s\, dz \qquad \text{(3B-1)}$$

In discrete terms, $dt = \Delta t$, which refers to the change in time, and $dz = \varepsilon\, \sqrt{\Delta t}$ (where ε is a random drawing from a standard normal distribution).

A call or put option must be a function of P_s and t. Using Ito's lemma on (3B–1) provides:

$$dP_c = \left[\frac{\partial P_c}{\partial P_s}\, \mu_s\, P_s + \frac{\partial P_c}{\partial t} + \frac{1}{2}\, \frac{\partial^2 P_c}{\partial P_s^2}\, \sigma_s^2\, P_s^2 \right] dt + \frac{\partial P_c}{\partial P_s}\, \sigma_s\, P_s\, dz \qquad \text{(3B-2)}$$

Note that a put can be represented in Equation (3B–2) by substituting P_p for P_c. Later we will distinguish a call equation from a put equation.

The objective of the Black-Scholes model is to eliminate risk with an appropriate combination of long $\partial P_c / \partial P_s$ shares of stock and short one option. Defining V as the value of the portfolio:

$$V = -P_c + \frac{\partial P_c}{\partial P_s}\, P_s \qquad \text{(3B-3)}$$

The change in the value becomes:

$$\partial V = -dP_c + \frac{\partial P_s}{\partial P_s}\, dP_s \qquad \text{(3B-4)}$$

Substituting (3B–1) and (3B–2) into (3B–4) and simplifying, one obtains:

$$dV = \left[-\frac{\partial P_c}{\partial t} - \frac{1}{2}\, \frac{\partial^2 P_c}{\partial P_s^2}\, \sigma_s^2\, P_s^2 \right] dt \qquad \text{(3B-5)}$$

Equation (3B–5) does not include dz; thus it is risk-free over dt. Since the portfolio represented by V is risk-free:

$$dV = r\, V\, dt \qquad \text{(3B-6)}$$

with r = risk-free interest rate

Substituting the term in parentheses from Equation (3B–5) for dV/dt in (3B–6), and Equation (3B–3) for V on the right side of (3B–6), and multiplying both sides by –1, we have:

$$\left[\frac{\partial P_c}{\partial t} + \frac{1}{2} \frac{\partial^2 P_c}{\partial P_s^2} \sigma_s^2 P_s^2 \right] = r \left[P_c - \frac{\partial P_c}{\partial P_s} P_s \right] \qquad \text{(3B–7)}$$

Rearranging:

$$\frac{\partial P_c}{\partial t} + r P_s \frac{\partial P_c}{\partial P_s} + \frac{1}{2} \sigma_s^2 P_s^2 \frac{\partial^2 P_c}{\partial P_s^2} = r P_c \qquad \text{(3B–8)}$$

Equation (3B–8) is called the Black-Scholes differential equation. The final equation to evaluate P_c is found by using the boundary condition at option expiration for the asset in question.

$$\text{For calls: } P_c = \text{Max } [P_s - K, 0]$$
$$\text{For puts: } P_p = \text{Max } [K - P_s, 0] \qquad \text{(3B–9)}$$

Recall that the hedge ratio changes as P_s or t changes. This is why calculus is used to derive the equation. See Jarrow and Rudd (1983), Kutner (1988), and Ritchken (1987) for additional details related to this proof.

Option Pricing Sensitivities and Pricing Evidence | **4**

Option pricing sensitivities derived from the option formula are key factors in controlling the risk of an option position. These sensitivities are the hedge ratio (the change in the option price for a given change in the stock price), the sensitivity of the hedge ratio (the change in the hedge ratio for a given change in the stock price), leverage (the percentage change in the option price for a given percentage change in the stock price), the time factor (the change in the option price for a given change in the time to option expiration), and the volatility (the change in the option price for a given change in the stock volatility). These sensitivities are examined quantitatively, graphically, and descriptively.

The empirical evidence concerning the Black-Scholes model provides two basic conclusions: First, in general, this model generates very accurate estimates of actual option prices; second, the model has certain systematic biases. These biases relate to high- and low-volatility stocks and to away-from-the-money options. More sophisticated option models do not seem to provide substantially better results than the Black-Scholes model, at least on a consistent basis. Another finding of the empirical studies is that actual market-generated option prices tend to be slightly mispriced. Floor traders can capitalize on these mispricings by using ratio hedges to obtain returns above the risk-free interest rate.

THE PRICING SENSITIVITIES

What Are Pricing Sensitivities?
Pricing sensitivities represent the key relationships between the individual characteristics of the option and the option price. These sensitivities are the change in the stock price, the change in the hedge ratio, a change due to **leverage**, changes in the time until the expiration of the option, and changes in the volatility of the stock. The purpose of examining the effect of these sensitivities on option prices is twofold: First, it helps us to understand what

causes option prices to change, and second, it provides insights for specific option strategies.

The pricing sensitivities are **derivatives** of the option price in relation to each of the individual factors. The derivative calculates the change in the option price in relation to the change in the factor. For example, Chapter 3 defines delta as the hedge ratio: the change in the option price for a given change in the stock price. A delta of 0.5 indicates that the option price changes by $0.50 for a change of $1 in the stock price. The Greek names for the pricing sensitivities and the relationships measured by these sensitivities are:

- **Delta**: the change in the option price for a given change in the stock price—that is, the hedge ratio.

- **Lambda,** or leverage: the percentage change in the option price for a given percentage change in the stock price.

- **Gamma**: the change in the delta for a given change in the stock price.

- **Theta**: the change in the option price given a change in the time until option expiration.

- **Vega**: the change in the option price for a given change in the volatility of the stock (also known as kappa).

- **Rho**: the change in the option price for a given change in the risk-free interest rate.

The risk exposure of any option position is explained via the sensitivities defined above. For example, arbitrageurs on the option trading floor are particularly concerned about their risk exposure; consequently, they monitor each of the above sensitivities carefully. Other option traders can also better understand the types and extent of their risk exposure from a particular option strategy by computing the values of the pricing sensitivities. The discussion in this chapter of the pricing sensitivities and the associated equations emphasizes call options; however, these pricing sensitivities also are relevant for put options and other strategies covered in later chapters. Appendix 4A provides the partial derivatives of the Black-Scholes option model, which are the pricing sensitivities when derivatives are employed. Option sensitivities for puts are obtained by substituting P_P for P_C in all of the sensitivity equations given below. These call and put pricing sensitivities are important measures of options that are applied in certain circumstances to the option trading and hedging strategies covered in the following chapters.

Delta

The Concept. Delta represents the hedge ratio for the option model, which is also the ratio of the change in the option price for a given change in the stock price:

$$\text{Delta} = \delta = \frac{d(\text{option price})}{d(\text{stock price})} = \frac{\Delta P_c}{\Delta P_s} \qquad (4\text{-}1)$$

where $d(\bullet)$ = the (partial) derivative, which is the (**instantaneous**) small change in the variable; $d(\bullet) = \Delta$ when discrete (interval) changes are used.

Graphically, the hedge ratio is represented as the slope of the option pricing line at the current stock price, as shown previously in Figure 3–2. The instantaneous hedge ratio also can be found by solving the Black-Scholes option formula. The deltas for different option and stock positions are:

Long Position	Delta	Short Position	Delta
Long call	0 to +1	Short call	-1 to 0
Long put	-1 to 0	Short put	0 to +1
Long stock	+1	Short stock	-1

Long put options possess negative deltas, because the put price declines as the stock price increases. Similarly, short positions have deltas that are opposite long positions, as the values of long and short positions go in opposite directions.

Delta measures the option price's sensitivity to changes in the stock price. A near-the-money call option typically has a delta near .5—that is, the option price changes by one-half of the stock price change. In fact, notice that a slight rearrangement of Equation (4–1) provides the *expected* change in the option price for a given stock price change:

$$\Delta P_c = \delta \Delta P_s \qquad (4\text{-}2)$$

Delta and Pricing Relationships. Delta is associated with the pricing relationships discussed in Chapter 2. One function of these relationships is to indicate how option prices change for in-the-money and out-of-the-money options. For example, delta increases as the option goes in-the-money, showing the increased price appreciation as the stock price increases. Deep-in-the-money options change almost point for point with the stock price change (the delta is near one). Delta declines as the option goes out-of-the-money, which shows the decreased exposure of the option price to stock price declines. Delta quantifies these pricing relationships between the stock and option prices, as shown in Equation (4–2). Figure 4–1 shows how both the call price and delta change as the stock price changes, with delta measuring the slope to the call price line at the relevant stock price. Table 4–1 provides call deltas for a stock price of 100 and volatilities of 15% and 25%. Figure 4–2 illustrates how delta changes in terms of the stock price for three different volatilities. Figure 4–3 shows delta as a function of both the stock value and the strike price.

Risk Exposure and Position Delta. Intuitively, a trader who buys one call option position with a $\delta = .6$, and *sells* a different call option position with a $\delta = .4$, has a net $\delta = .6 - .4 = .2$. Thus, a $1 change in the stock price creates a $+.20 increase in the combined option position. Similarly, if a hedger is long stock ($\delta = 1$) and short one call option with a $\delta = .55$, then the delta of the combined position is $1 - .55 = .45$. However, a method is needed to evaluate more complicated portfolios of several option/stock positions or portfolios with an unequal number of shares among the different positions. Besides showing how the option price reacts to stock price changes, delta is used to find the net dollar exposure of combined positions to stock price changes. The position delta measures the risk of a portfolio of option-stock positions:

$$\text{Position delta} = \Sigma \, n_i \, \delta_i \qquad (4\text{-}3)$$

where n_i = the number of option or stock shares in a position
δ_i = the delta of the position

Recall that each option is equivalent to 100 shares. One interprets the position delta in terms of the dollar change in the position per a $1 change in the stock price. Therefore, a position delta of 45 means that the value of the position will change by $45 for a $1 per share stock price change. Example 4–1 provides an example of position delta.[1]

Position delta measures both the direction and extent of the risk exposure of the multiple option or the option-stock position when the stock price changes. The direction is associated with the positive or negative sign of the position delta:

Position Delta	Profitable Stock Direction
Positive	Bullish (price increases beneficial)
Zero	Neutral
Negative	Bearish (price decreases beneficial)

The extent of the risk exposure is measured by the size of the position delta. The position delta approach works equally well for individual options,

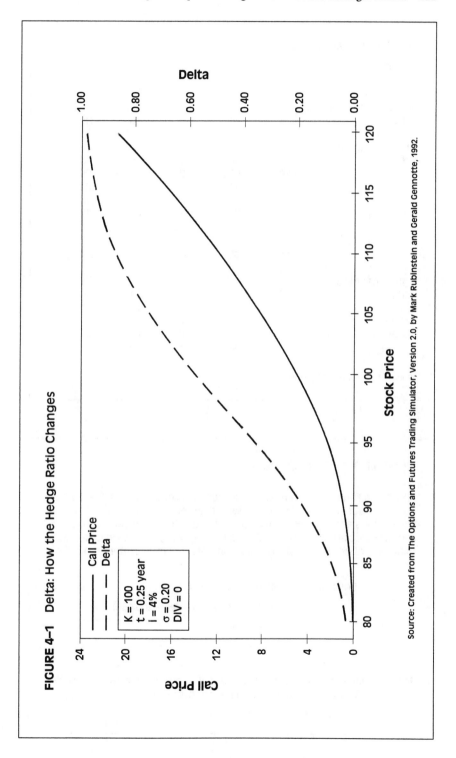

FIGURE 4–1 Delta: How the Hedge Ratio Changes

Source: Created from The Options and Futures Trading Simulator, Version 2.0, by Mark Rubinstein and Gerald Gennotte, 1992.

TABLE 4–1   Call Deltas

$P_s = 100.00$
$r = 5\%$

Panel A: Volatility = 15%

Strike:	90	95	100	105	110
Time remaining:					
1 day	1.00	1.00	.51	.00	.00
1 week	1.00	.99	.52	.01	.00
1 month	.99	.90	.55	.16	.02
3 months	.95	.81	.58	.33	.14
6 months	.90	.78	.61	.43	.27

Panel B: Volatility = 25%

Strike:	90	95	100	105	110
Time remaining:					
1 day	1.00	1.00	.51	.01	.00
1 week	1.00	.94	.52	.07	.04
1 month	.94	.79	.54	.28	.11
3 months	.84	.72	.56	.41	.27
6 months	.80	.70	.59	.48	.38

Source: Created from OptionVue IV.

EXAMPLE 4–1   Position Delta

An option trader buys a near-the-money call option with a $\delta = .55$ and buys two out-of-the-money puts with each put having a $\delta = -.35$. Later, the trader's account executive convinces the trader to sell two out-of-the-money calls, each with a $\delta = .30$ (selling an option is recorded as a minus number of shares). The position delta for the combined position is:

$$\text{Position delta} = n_1\delta_1 + n_2\delta_2 + n_3\delta_3 \qquad (4\text{-}3)$$

$$= 100\,(.55) + 200\,(-.35) - 200\,(.30)$$

$$= 55 - 70 - 60$$

$$= -75$$

For a $1 *increase* in the stock price, this combined option position *declines* $75. Thus, the trader has a net *short* position.

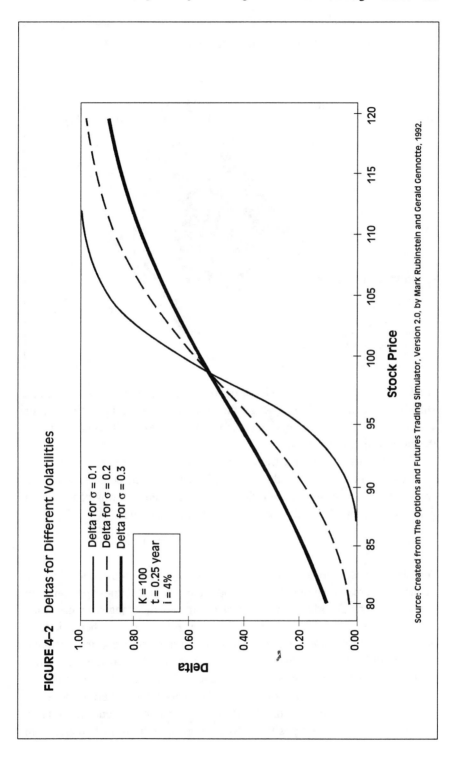

FIGURE 4-2   Deltas for Different Volatilities

Source: Created from The Options and Futures Trading Simulator, Version 2.0, by Mark Rubinstein and Gerald Gennotte, 1992.

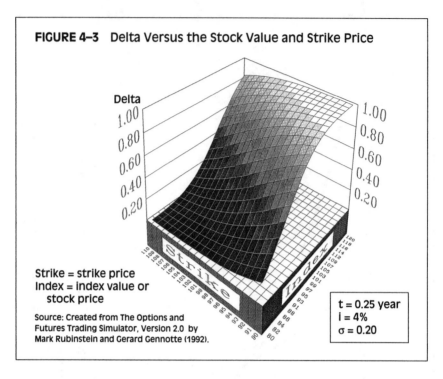

FIGURE 4–3 Delta Versus the Stock Value and Strike Price

Strike = strike price
Index = index value or
stock price

Source: Created from The Options and
Futures Trading Simulator, Version 2.0 by
Mark Rubinstein and Gerard Gennotte (1992).

t = 0.25 year
i = 4%
σ = 0.20

combinations of stock and options, or for a combination of calls and puts. However, recall that δ *changes* as the stock price, time to expiration, or volatility of the stock changes; hence, the same value of delta is not valid for the entire life of the option.

Hedgers and Delta. If a trader wants a position delta of zero when using two stock-option positions, then setting Equation (4–3) equal to zero and solving for δ_2/δ_1 provides the ratio of shares needed in terms of the given deltas of positions 1 and 2 in order to obtain a delta of zero:

$$n_1\,\delta_1 + n_2\,\delta_2 \;=\; 0 \longleftrightarrow n_1/n_2 \;=\; \delta_2/\delta_1 \qquad \textbf{(4-4)}$$

A trader who uses the hedge ratio (delta) to set up a risk-free hedge when the delta is zero creates a combined stock-option position that does *not* change in value as the stock price changes (at least for small changes in the stock price). In other words, the delta for a risk-free hedge is zero. When a delta of zero is created for a stock-option position (or with multiple option positions), *and* a return above the risk-free rate is guaranteed, then the trader has generated an arbitrage transaction. Example 4–2 illustrates Equation (4–4).

The above discussion shows that delta is useful in determining a net measure of risk (the position delta). In fact, hedgers often use delta to measure the net risk of a position. Even margins on options often are set in

EXAMPLE 4–2   Delta and Risk-Free Hedges

A floor trader is short 20 call options with a $\delta = 0.6$. To set up a risk-free hedge with the underlying stock, the trader uses Equation (4–4) as follows:

$$n_1/n_2 = \delta_2/\delta_1 \qquad (4\text{-}4)$$

Defining the call option delta as δ_1 we have:

$$2000/n_2 \; = \; 1/-0.6$$
$$n_2 \; = \; 2000 \, (-0.6)$$
$$n_2 \; = \; -1200 \text{ stock shares (short)}$$

An increase in the stock price causes the delta to increase to 0.7. To keep the risk-free hedge the stock position now changes to:

$$n_2 \; = \; 2000 \, (-.7)$$
$$n_2 \; = \; -1400 \text{ stock shares (short)}$$

terms of the delta of an option position. Consequently, delta is the most significant option factor used in connection with option positions.

Elasticity (Lambda)

Elasticity refers to the leverage of the option position. Elasticity measures the percentage change in the option price for a 1% change in the stock price:

$$\text{Elasticity} \; = \; \text{lambda} \; = \; \lambda \; = \; \frac{\%\Delta P_C}{\%\Delta P_S} \qquad (4\text{-}5)$$

A lambda of 8 means that a 1% increase in the price of the stock causes an 8% increase in the price of the option. Typical elasticity values are 8 to 10. Leverage is an important characteristic of options that attracts speculators. Also note that Equation (4–5) is equivalent to the following:[2]

$$\lambda = \delta \, (P_S/P_C) \qquad (4\text{-}6)$$

Figure 4–4 illustrates how lambda changes as the stock price changes. This graph shows that the leverage is very high when the option is deep out-of-the-money and relatively low when the option is deep in-the-money. While the *delta* of an option decreases significantly when the option goes out-of-the-money (Figure 4–1), the lambda increases for out-of-the-money options. Consequently, many speculators prefer buying out-of-the-money options.

A more encompassing illustration of leverage is shown by Table 4–2. The effect of leverage is shown by comparing the call option prices when the stock is at 100 and 105. While the stock price change from 100 to 105 is not a major one, Table 4–2 shows that leverage has a major effect on the associated option prices. For example, the one-month 95 call increases from 6 1/4 to 10 5/8, a 70% increase. The corresponding stock increased by only 5%. Similarly, the one-month 105 option increased 170% and the other options also obtained large percentage increases.

A similar leverage effect exists for puts. Table 4–3 shows that the decline in the price for the stock creates large percentage changes for the put options.

TABLE 4–2   The Leverage Factor for Calls

$P_s = 100$ $\sigma_s = 0.25$ risk–free rate = 5%   No dividends

	Call Prices					
	Stock = 100			Stock = 105		
Strike Price	1 month	2 months	3 months	1 month	2 months	3 months
95	6 1/4	7 3/8	8 1/2	10 5/8	11 1/2	12 3/8
100	3 1/8	4 3/8	5 5/8	6 1/2	7 5/8	8 3/4
105	1 1/4	2 3/8	3 3/8	3 1/4	4 5/8	5 7/8

Source: Developed using OptionVue IV.

TABLE 4–3   The Leverage Factor for Puts

$P_s = 100$ $\sigma_s = 0.25$ risk–free rate = 5%   No dividends

	Put Prices					
	Stock = 100			Stock = 95		
Strike Price	1 month	3 months	6 months	1 month	3 months	6 months
95	15/16	1 5/8	2 3/8	2 1/2	3 3/8	4 1/8
100	2 3/4	3 5/8	4 3/8	5 5/8	6 3/8	6 7/8
105	5 3/4	6 1/2	7 1/8	10	10 1/8	10 1/2

Source: Developed using OptionVue IV.

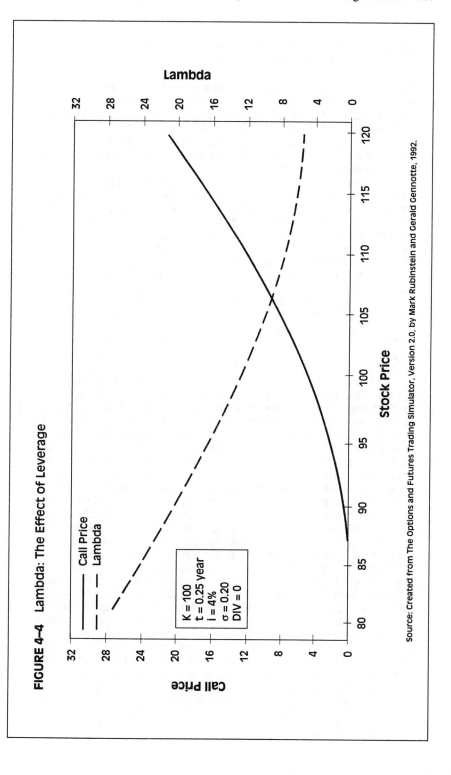

FIGURE 4–4 Lambda: The Effect of Leverage

Lambda

Call Price

Stock Price

Call Price
Lambda

K = 100
t = 0.25 year
i = 4%
σ = 0.20
DIV = 0

Source: Created from The Options and Futures Trading Simulator, Version 2.0, by Mark Rubinstein and Gerald Gennotte, 1992.

FOCUS 4–1   The Behind-the-Scenes Story on the
Black-Scholes Model

The Black-Scholes option pricing model is widely known in finance circles because it has an elegant proof, it is easy to use, and it provides an answer to an important question (the value of an option). When Fischer Black went to Japan to give a talk on the Black-Scholes model, over 10,000 people showed up! (They were surprised to find out that his name was Fischer Black rather than Black-Scholes; they thought only one person developed the model.)

The Black-Scholes model did not come about by accident. Myron Scholes met Fischer Black when Scholes was teaching at MIT and Black was a consultant at Arthur D. Little in Boston. Black was interested in the interrelationships between security prices and risk, the structure and combination of assets, and substituting one security for another (which we call arbitrage). Scholes was interested in empirical research and how new ideas related to the financial literature.

While Scholes was a "pure academic" who had recently received a Ph.D. from the University of Chicago (a university that produced many of the initial wave of financial theorists), Black had wandered among many fields before settling on Finance. Black went to Harvard mainly because of its glee club. At various times he majored in French, psychology, social relations, anthropology, mathematics, chemistry, and physics (the latter being his undergraduate major). In graduate school he started in physics and then switched to applied mathematics (computers).

Black and Scholes started by writing papers on the relationships between risk and return. They began to talk about options and warrants in the spring of 1969 (remember, there was no formal options exchange at the time). They then started working on the pricing of options, including ideas related to arbitrage. The basic approach was to determine a formula that included all the factors affecting a change in the option price, while at the same time determining how many options would have the same total price change as the underlying stock. Thus, in today's terms they wanted to create an arbitrage, or hedged position. Since the hedged position would essentially be risk-free, the return on the position should be the risk-free interest rate. The Capital Asset Pricing Model was applied to every moment in an option's life (how the discount rate for the option varies with time and the stock price). This resulted in a specific differential equation known as the "heat equation."

Robert Merton (also known for his work on options), Black, and Scholes had long discussions about how to best show the relationships between the stock and the option. They had difficulty obtaining a solution at first, but when they found the result they wanted, Black and Scholes tried to have the paper published. An early version of the paper was submitted in the summer of 1970, but both the *Journal of Political Economy* and the *Review of Economics and Statistics* rejected the paper—perhaps because the ideas were so new and/or because Black was not an academic. After revising the approach and receiving encouragement from University of Chicago professors Merton Miller and Eugene Fama, an article testing the model empirically was published in 1972 in

The Journal of Finance. The proof of the model was published in 1973 in the *Journal of Political Economy* (published by The University of Chicago). In 1972, the Chicago Board Options Exchange started to trade options.

Black and Scholes looked for a way to test their model on real securities. They found a warrant on National General that seemed to be substantially underpriced. Soon American Financial announced a tender offer for National General, an offer whose terms were disadvantageous for those holding the warrants. Thus, the first caveat of the option model was discovered: If the market knows something not considered by the formula, then the model will not work well.

The Black-Scholes model was put into use immediately by market makers on the floor of the CBOE and investment houses in New York, which surprised both Black and Scholes. Since then, the model has become a staple of finance courses and is used to price almost all types of securities. It led to the development of the binomial option model, which is used to price securities not well-fitted for the Black-Scholes model. And it is directly related to the development of dynamic trading strategies, such as portfolio insurance (and therefore indirectly associated with events such as the market crash in October 1987). The only thing left now is the Nobel prize!

Source: This focus is based on information in Szala (1988) and Black (1989).

For example, the one-month in-the-money put increases from 5 $^3/_4$ to 10 as the stock price declines, a 74% increase in value, while the stock itself changes by only 5%.

Gamma

The Concept. Gamma measures the change in the delta for a given change in the stock price:

$$\text{Gamma} = \gamma = \frac{d(\text{delta})}{d(\text{stock price})} = \frac{\Delta \delta}{\Delta P_s} \qquad (4\text{--}7)$$

The gamma shows the *risk* inherent in delta—that is, the change in delta as caused by a change in the stock price. If gamma is small, delta is not sensitive to changes in the stock price. If gamma is large, delta *is* sensitive to stock price changes.[3] Gamma measures the amount of *curvature* in the call price curve. Thus, while delta measures the slope of the line at a particular point on the call price curve, gamma measures the *change* in the delta (i.e., when the stock price changes, the slope measured by delta changes). Equivalently, gamma is the slope of the *delta* curve at a particular point: When the *slope of the delta line* is the greatest, the gamma is the largest; when the slope of the delta is small, the gamma is near zero.[4] These relationships are shown in Figure 4–5.

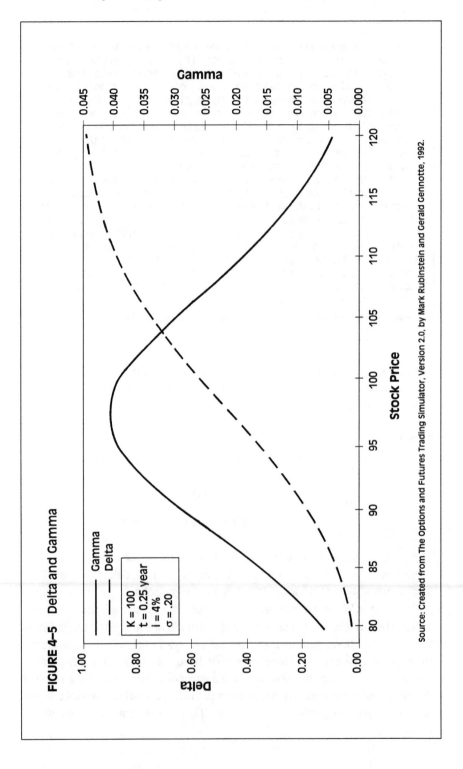

FIGURE 4–5   Delta and Gamma

Source: Created from The Options and Futures Trading Simulator, Version 2.0, by Mark Rubinstein and Gerald Gennotte, 1992.

Both long call and long put positions have positive gammas; a stock has a $\gamma = 0$. Gamma is one measure of the effect of instability on the option position. The other measure is volatility (vega). Gamma is interpreted as follows:

γ (gamma)	P_s	δ
> 0	increases	increases
	decreases	decreases
< 0	increases	decreases
	decreases	increases

In other words, if γ is positive, delta changes in the *same* direction as the stock price. If γ is negative, delta changes in the *opposite* direction of the stock price. If gamma is .10 and the current delta is 0, then an increase in the stock price of $1 causes the delta to increase from 0 to .10. The new delta of .10 means that an increase in the stock price of $1 will now increase the option price by $.10. If the trader wants a delta neutral position ($\delta = 0$), the number of stock shares will need to be rebalanced, as noted in the discussion of delta. Figure 4–6 shows how gamma changes as the stock price changes, by illustrating gammas for three different standard deviations (volatilities).

In terms of volatility, gamma shows the sensitivity of the option to changes in the underlying stock's volatility:

Gamma	Volatility
Positive	Bullish (volatility increases beneficial)
Zero	Neutral
Negative	Bearish (volatility decreases beneficial)

Hence, a positive gamma means a position will benefit from an increase in volatility, while a negative gamma will benefit from a decrease in volatility. Figure 4–7 illustrates how gamma changes as the volatility changes.

Position Gamma. Position gamma allows the trader to determine the effect of a $1 change in stock price on the position delta. Position gamma is calculated by:

$$\text{Position gamma} = \Sigma \, n_i \, \gamma_i \qquad \text{(4-8)}$$

where γ_i = the gamma of position i

The absolute size of the position gamma, when calculated at the target delta, shows how quickly changes in the stock price will force the trader to revise the position delta to keep it constant. Example 4–3 illustrates the position gamma.[5]

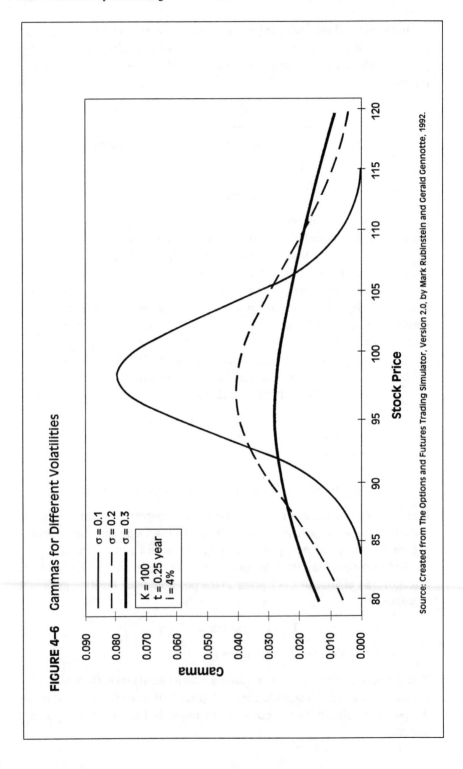

FIGURE 4–6 Gammas for Different Volatilities

σ = 0.1
σ = 0.2
σ = 0.3

K = 100
t = 0.25 year
i = 4%

Stock Price

Gamma

Source: Created from The Options and Futures Trading Simulator, Version 2.0, by Mark Rubinstein and Gerald Gennotte, 1992.

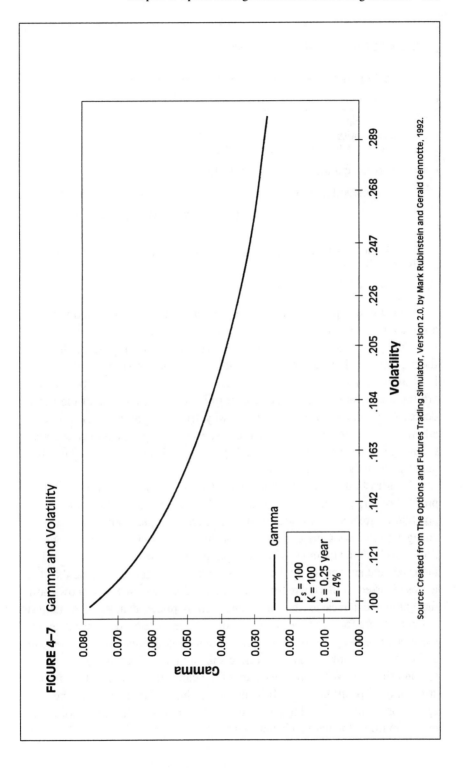

FIGURE 4–7   Gamma and Volatility

Source: Created from The Options and Futures Trading Simulator, Version 2.0, by Mark Rubinstein and Gerald Gennotte, 1992.

EXAMPLE 4–3 Position Gamma

The position held in Example 4–1 possesses the following gammas:

Position	δ	γ
long 1 call	0.55	0.052
long 2 puts	–0.35	0.0455
short 2 calls	0.30	0.045

The position gamma for this portfolio is:

$$\text{Position gamma} = \Sigma n_i \gamma_i \qquad \qquad (4\text{-}8)$$

$$= 100\,(0.052) + 200\,(0.0455) - 200\,(0.045)$$

$$= 5.2 + 9.1 - 9 = 5.3$$

For a $1 increase in the stock price, the *position delta* of this position will increase by 5.3.

Revising the position delta, and therefore gamma, is important for arbitrageurs who set up risk-free hedges. In particular, arbitrageurs want to know the price effect of a *change in the hedge ratio* (δ) or position delta on the net stock/option position *as the stock price changes.* If the position delta is continuously revised to minimize risk, then the maximum profit for the arbitrage is achieved. If the delta is not revised, then the size of the profit decreases as the stock price moves away from the initial stock price. In addition, the *size* of the position gamma shows the arbitrageur how sensitive the hedge is to changes in the stock price, which also suggests how frequently the hedge ratio needs to be revised.[6]

Changing Gammas. Another characteristic of a positive gamma is that profits are larger than losses; thus, a profitable change in the value of the position is greater than a loss in the position for equal (but opposite) size changes in the stock price. This relationship is shown in Figure 4–8, which illustrates both the gamma and the call price. The positive gamma at $P_S = 100$ indicates that an increase in the stock price to 110 is more profitable than the losses incurred from a decrease in the stock to 90. Figure 4-8 also shows how the gamma changes as the stock and option prices change. The largest gamma occurs for an at-the-money option. As the option becomes deep in-the-money or deep out-of-the-money, the gamma declines to near zero. In addition, notice how the gamma reflects the amount of curvature of the call option price line. When the curvature of the call price is the greatest, for the at-the-money position of $P_S = 100$, the gamma has its largest value. When the option price line is straight, for deep-in-the-money and deep-out-of-the-money options, the gamma is near zero.

FIGURE 4–8   Gamma and Call Option Prices

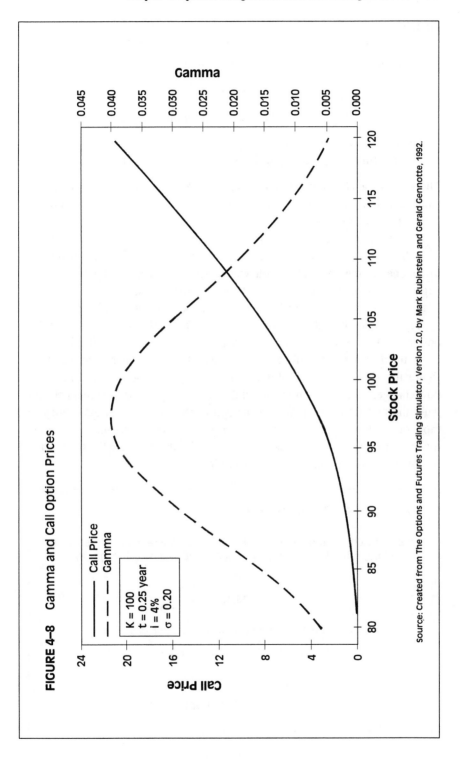

Source: Created from The Options and Futures Trading Simulator, Version 2.0, by Mark Rubinstein and Gerald Gennotte, 1992.

Theta

Interpreting Theta. Theta measures the change in the option value as the time until the expiration of the option declines:

$$\text{Theta} = \theta = \frac{d\,(\text{option price})}{d\,(\text{time to expiration})} = \frac{\Delta P_c}{\Delta t} \tag{4-9}$$

where θ is a negative number

t = the time to option expiration (in fractions of a year)

The greater the absolute value of theta, the larger the per-day *loss* in option value from holding a long option position due to the time decay of the option position. Equation (4–9) calculates an annualized theta value. However, many computer models treat theta as a per-day amount, rather than an annualized value. The negative theta illustrates the fact that option buyers lose money as the time value declines over time. Both call and put thetas are negative. Sellers of an option generate profits from a positive theta as a result of this time decay. Example 4–4 provides an example of calculating theta.

Figure 4–9 illustrates the time decay for an at-the-money call. As the option nears the expiration date, the theta declines rapidly (the absolute size of the theta increases rapidly during the last 30 days before expiration). This figure also shows the effect of theta on the call price. Figure 4–10 illustrates how changes in the stock price affect theta. The largest negative theta occurs when the stock is at-the-money. As an option becomes more in-the-money or more out-of-the-money—that is, as the time value declines—the theta tends toward zero. Figure 4–11 shows how theta varies in relation to the stock price for three different times to option expiration.

EXAMPLE 4–4   The Value of Theta

When stock price and stock volatility are held constant, one determines that a long call price declines by $3/8$ of a point over 17 calendar days:

$$\theta = \frac{-.375}{(17/365)} = -8.051$$

The annualized theta can be converted to a per-day value of:

Per-day loss = $-8.051/365$ = $\$ -.022$

or a three-month loss of:

$\$ -.022 \times 91$ = $\$1.99$ per option share

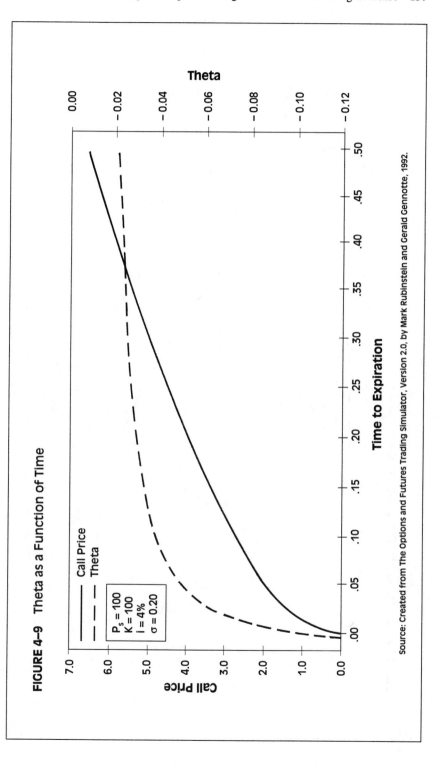

FIGURE 4-9   Theta as a Function of Time

Source: Created from The Options and Futures Trading Simulator, Version 2.0, by Mark Rubinstein and Gerald Gennotte, 1992.

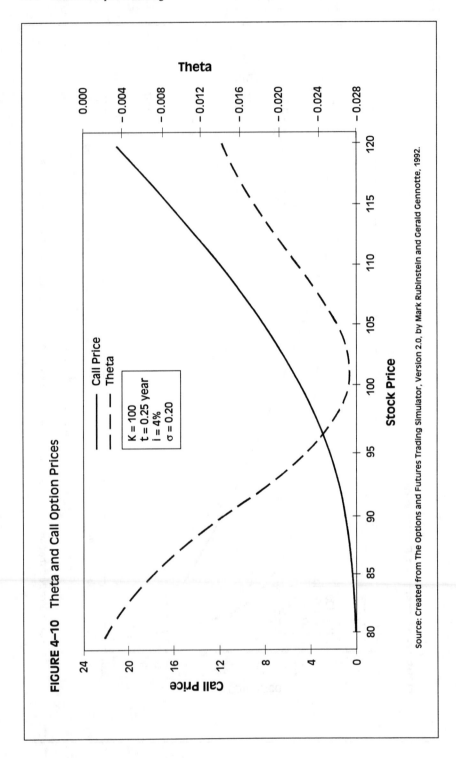

FIGURE 4–10   Theta and Call Option Prices

Source: Created from The Options and Futures Trading Simulator, Version 2.0, by Mark Rubinstein and Gerald Gennotte, 1992.

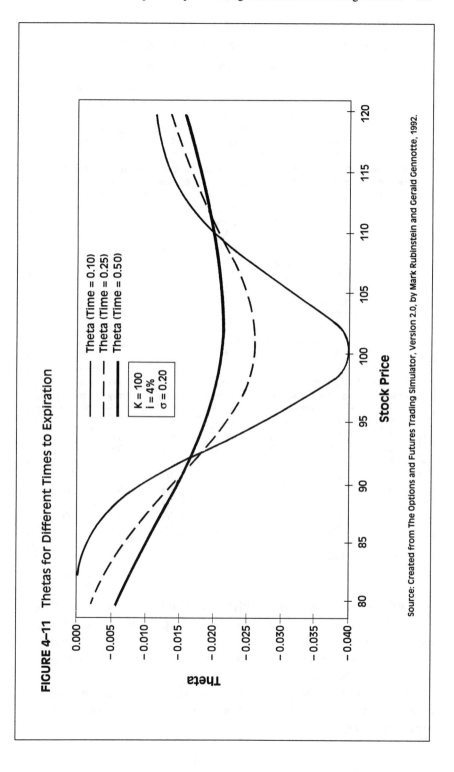

FIGURE 4–11   Thetas for Different Times to Expiration

Source: Created from The Options and Futures Trading Simulator, Version 2.0, by Mark Rubinstein and Gerald Gennotte, 1992.

TABLE 4–4   Time to Option Expiration and Option Prices

$P_s = 100$ $\sigma_s = 0.25$ Risk-free rate = 5%   No dividends

	Option Prices			Price Difference from Previous Month		
	Call option strikes:			Call option strikes:		
	95	100	105	95	100	105
Expiration month	In-the-money	At-the-money	Out-of-the-money	In-the-money	At-the-money	Out-of-the-money
1	6 1/4	3 1/8	1 1/4			
2	7 3/8	4 3/8	2 3/8	1 1/4	1 1/4	1 1/4
3	8 1/2	5 5/8	3 3/8	1 1/8	1 1/4	1
4	9 3/8	6 1/2	4 3/8	7/8	7/8	1
5	10 1/4	7 1/2	5 1/4	7/8	1	7/8
6	11	8 1/4	6	3/4	3/4	3/4
7	11 7/8	9	6 3/4	7/8	3/4	3/4
8	12 1/2	9 3/4	7 1/2	5/8	3/4	3/4
9	13 1/4	10 1/2	8 1/8	3/4	3/4	5/8

	Put option strikes:			Put option strikes:		
	95	100	105	95	100	105
Expiration month	Out-of-the-money	At-the-money	In-the money	Out-of-the-money	At-the-money	In-the money
1	15/16	2 3/4	5 3/4			
2	1 5/8	3 5/8	6 1/2	11/16	7/8	3/4
3	2 3/8	4 3/8	7 1/8	3/4	3/4	5/8
4	2 7/8	4 7/8	7 5/8	3/4	3/4	1/2
5	3 3/8	5 3/8	8	1/8	1/2	3/8
6	3 3/4	5 3/4	8 3/8	3/8	3/8	3/8
7	4 1/8	6 1/8	8 3/4	3/8	3/8	3/8
8	4 3/8	6 1/8	9	1/4	3/8	1/4
9	4 3/4	6 3/4	9 1/4	3/8	1/4	1/4

Source: Developed using OptionVue IV.

Table 4–4 keeps the other sensitivities constant so that the effect of time can be analyzed. The table shows that the option price differences from one expiration month to another are larger for the nearby months as compared to the more distant months.[7] In addition, the call option price differences are larger than the put differences.

Position Theta. The position theta measures how much a position decreases in value as the time to expiration decreases (when the stock price remains unchanged).

$$\text{Position theta} = \Sigma n_i \theta_i \qquad \textbf{(4-10)}$$

where θ_i = the theta of position i

The effects of position theta values are:

Position theta	Effect
Positive	Profits from positive time decay
Zero	Neutral time effect
Negative	Losses from negative time decay

Example 4–5 shows how to calculate and interpret the position theta.

Theta and Gamma. The relationship between theta and gamma is also important. Theta and gamma generate tradeoffs: When theta is at its lowest point, gamma is at its highest, and vice versa. This tradeoff between the time factor and price variability is shown in Figure 4–12. A positive gamma strategy benefits from a large change in the stock price, while the associated negative theta shows that the longer it takes to generate such a large price

---

EXAMPLE 4–5   Position Theta

Extending the position delta and position gamma examples to position theta, we have:

Position	δ	γ	Per day θ
long 1 call	.55	.052	– .17
long 2 puts	– .35	.0455	– .125
short 2 calls	.30	.045	– .14

Technically, the theta of the short two calls position is positive (one earns time value by selling calls). However, we will keep our previous convention of placing a negative in front of the number of shares of a short position, while reporting a negative theta for all calls and puts.

The position theta is:

$$\begin{aligned} \text{Position theta} &= \Sigma n_i \theta_i \qquad \textbf{(4-10)} \\ &= 100\,(-0.17) + 200\,(-0.125) - 200\,(-0.14) \\ &= -17 - 25 + 28 \\ &= -14 \end{aligned}$$

The option portfolio will *lose* $14 for each day it is held (the change in the option value for a one-day change in time).

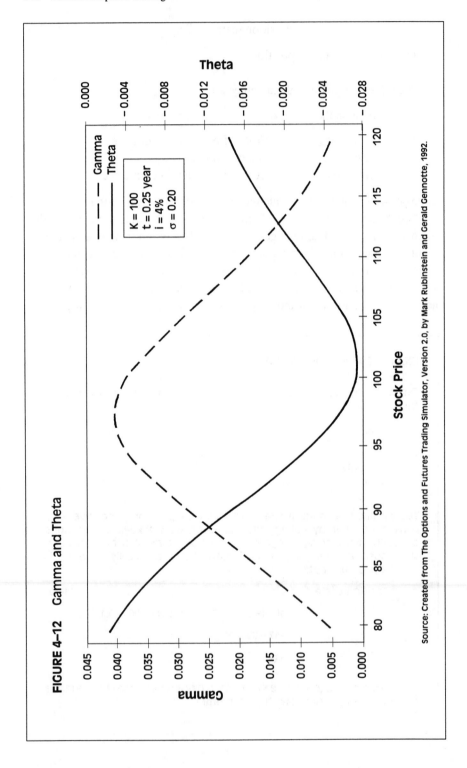

FIGURE 4–12   Gamma and Theta

Source: Created from The Options and Futures Trading Simulator, Version 2.0, by Mark Rubinstein and Gerald Gennotte, 1992.

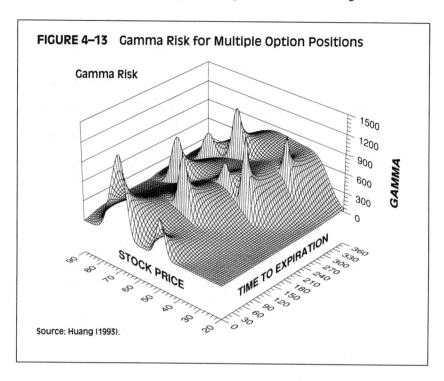

FIGURE 4–13   Gamma Risk for Multiple Option Positions

Source: Huang (1993).

change, the greater the loss of the time value. A trader must be aware of this tradeoff when initiating and maintaining a position. Conversely, a writer of such a strategy benefits from the time decay if the writer loses when the stock price changes significantly. Consequently, the key consideration for a theta-gamma tradeoff strategy is if the tradeoff is favorable to the trader. In fact, the relationships between gamma, theta, and the underlying stock price can be very complicated when dealing with multiple option positions. For example, Figure 4–13 shows the gamma for a portfolio of 10 options for varying times to expiration and stock prices.

Vega

Traders often attempt to determine which options are cheap or expensive in terms of volatility—that is, options whose implied volatility is less than or greater than what the trader believes is appropriate for the given stock. Moreover, recall the importance of volatility for option pricing, including the fact that option prices are usually sensitive to relatively small changes in volatility. Table 4–5 shows how a change in volatility affects option prices. In particular, a relatively small change in the annual standard deviation of returns causes a relatively large change in the option price, especially for the longer-term options. Volatility is the only input factor that is not directly

FOCUS 4–2 OptionVue: The Matrix of Prices and Sensitivities

An important screen in the OptionVue program is the "matrix" of prices and option sensitivities. This matrix is illustrated below using the OEX (S&P 100) options. The "Options" section of the matrix provides theoretical option prices, the percentage each option is over- or underpriced from the current option price, and a choice of 27 other possible variables. Here we have the implied volatility of each option, the delta, and the gamma. The position of each variable is defined below the matrix. The data represented here are actual OEX prices. The volatility input into the model prices is 11.4%, the long-term statistical volatility of the OEX. Therefore, the apparent mispricing of the options should be related to a change in the volatility.

The "Summary" section of the matrix provides the position delta, position gamma, position vega (discussed later), and per-day dollar theta. These values represent the portfolio of the following option positions (not shown in the matrix): long May and June 390 calls and short May and June 395 calls (note that the most overpriced options are sold and the least overpriced options are purchased). Thus, OptionVue provides the net portfolio position sensitivities for any (complicated) portfolio.

OPTIONVUE IV		MATRIX		S&P 100 Index			FRI APR 23	
ACTUALS								
	OEX	Inx						
	404.40	−1.89						

FUTURES	⊢——— MAY-(29) ———⊣			⊢——— JUN-(57) ———⊣			⊢——— JUL-(85) ———⊣	
CALLS	16 1/4	15	+8%	18 1/2	16 3/8	+13%	....	17 7/8	
390	16.0%	0.869	0.0164	15.7%	0.795	0.0157		0.759	0.0141
CALLS	12 1/2	10 7/8	+15%	14 3/4	12 3/4	+16%	....	14 3/8	
395	16.0%	0.766	0.0237	15.1%	0.706	0.0190		0.681	0.0162
CALLS	8 1/2	7 1/2	+13%	10 7/8	9 1/2	+14%	13	11 3/8	+14%
400	13.8%	0.631	0.0291	13.6%	0.603	0.0213	13.6%	0.596	0.0175
CALLS	5 3/8	4 3/4	+13%	7 7/8	6 7/8	+15%	10	8 3/4	+14%
405	12.8%	0.479	0.0308	12.9%	0.494	0.0220	13.1%	0.506	0.0181
CALLS	3 1/8	2 13/16	+11%	5 3/8	4 3/4	+13%	7 1/8	6 1/2	+10%
410	12.2%	0.332	0.0280	12.3%	0.387	0.0211	12.2%	0.418	0.0177

SUMMARY						
Orig.Reqmt:	(unknown)	Commis: _____	Delta:	+19.23	AvgMIV:	13.8%
Maint.Reqmt:	(unknown)		Gamma:	−1.06	Calls:	13.8%
Cash Flow:	(unknown)	Theta: +$2.48/day	Vega:	−20.2	Puts:	_____

[Fl] = Help ——————————————————————————————————————

The "Actuals" section numbers are:

1. last index price   2. change in price

The "Options" section numbers are:

1. last option price   2. model price   3. % over/underpriced

4. implied volatility   5. delta   6. gamma

Source: Developed using OptionVue IV.

TABLE 4-5   Volatility and Call Option Prices

$P_s = 100$ $K = 100$ Risk-free rate = 5%   No dividends

Annual Standard Deviation	At-the-Money Call Option		
	1 month	3 months	6 months
.10	1 ³/₈	2 ⁵/₈	4 ¹/₈
.15	2	3 ⁵/₈	5 ¹/₂
.20	2 ¹/₂	4 ⁵/₈	6 ⁷/₈
.25	3 ¹/₈	5 ⁵/₈	8 ¹/₄
.30	3 ³/₄	6 ¹/₂	9 ⁵/₈
.35	4 ¹/₄	7 ¹/₂	11
.40	4 ⁷/₈	8 ¹/₂	12 ¹/₂

Source: Developed using OptionVue IV.

observable when it is used in an option pricing model; that is, the market utilizes *estimates* of future volatility to value options. Therefore, changes in implied volatility have a major effect on option prices.

Vega measures the change in the option price per unit of change in the volatility of the stock:

$$\text{Vega} = \upsilon = \frac{d \text{ (option price)}}{d \text{ (volatility)}} = \frac{\Delta P_C}{\Delta \sigma_S} \tag{4-11}$$

where σ_S = the annualized standard deviation (volatility) of the stock.

Thus, if $\upsilon = 0.08$, then an increase in the annual standard deviation of the stock of 1% causes the option price to increase by 0.08 (1) = $0.08.

Vega is shown in Figure 4–14. Notice that vega has the same shape as gamma, although the specific values of vega differ from gamma. As with gamma, vega is largest for at-the-money options, and drops as the option becomes more in- or more out-of-the-money. Thus, deep-in-the-money or deep out-of-the-money options have less dollar sensitivity to changes in volatility than near-the-money options. Figure 4–15 illustrates vega in terms of the stock price and the time to option expiration. While vega is significantly reduced by stock price movements away from the strike price, vega is also affected by a declining time to option expiration.

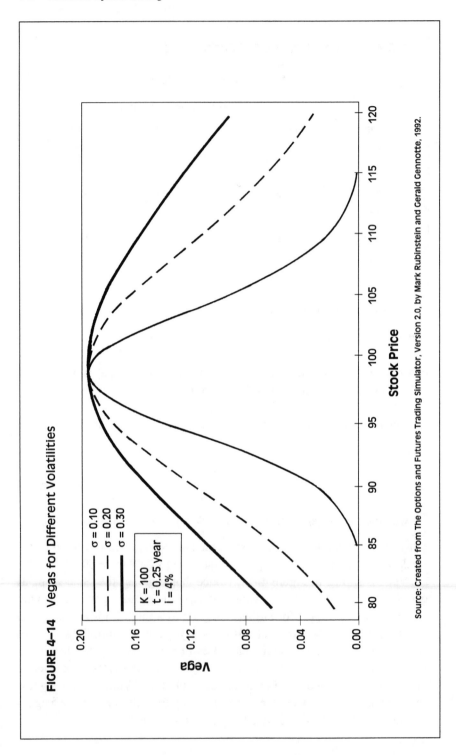

FIGURE 4–14 Vegas for Different Volatilities

Source: Created from The Options and Futures Trading Simulator, Version 2.0, by Mark Rubinstein and Gerald Gennotte, 1992.

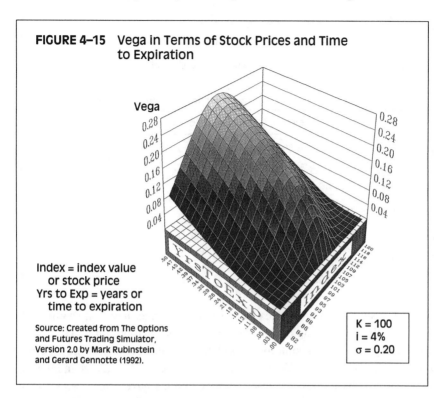

FIGURE 4–15   Vega in Terms of Stock Prices and Time to Expiration

Index = index value
   or stock price
Yrs to Exp = years or
   time to expiration

Source: Created from The Options
and Futures Trading Simulator,
Version 2.0 by Mark Rubinstein
and Gerard Gennotte (1992).

K = 100
i = 4%
σ = 0.20

Buying options creates a positive vega and a positive gamma, while selling options creates a negative vega and a negative gamma. Strategies with a positive vega are "long volatility"; thus, these strategies profit when volatility increases (assuming prices keep the same expected value). Strategies with a negative vega are "short volatility" and profit when volatility is stable. Hedgers who want to protect against volatility need to take a net position that creates a small vega.

Vega indicates the sensitivity of a given strategy or position to a change in the implied volatility of the stock, whether this change occurs because of a change in the traders' forecasts or because of a change in the volatility of the stock itself. On the other hand, gamma indicates the effect of the *current* level of volatility on the option price as the stock price changes.

Rho

Rho measures the change in the option price for a given change in the risk-free interest rate:

$$\text{Rho} = \frac{d \text{ (option price)}}{d \text{ (interest rate)}} = \frac{\Delta P_c}{\Delta r} \qquad (4\text{-}12)$$

TABLE 4–6 Interest Rates and Fair Call Option Prices

$P_s = 100$ $K = 100$ $\sigma(\text{returns}) = 0.25$ No dividends

Risk-Free Interest Rate	At-the-Money Call Options		
	1 month	3 months	6 months
4%	3 1/8	5 1/2	8
6%	3 1/8	5 3/4	8 1/2
8%	3 1/4	6	9
10%	3 3/8	6 1/4	9 1/2
12%	3 3/8	6 1/2	10 1/8

Source: Developed using OptionVue IV.

Table 4–6 shows that moderate changes in interest rates have only a minimal effect on the value of an option. The three-month call option in Table 4–6 changes by only 1/4 of a point for a 2% change in interest rates, while the one-month option changes by 1/8 of a point or less for each 2% change in interest rates. Out-of-the-money and in-the-money options have price changes that are similar to the at-the-money options presented in Table 4–6. Therefore, option traders have only a minor interest in rho during normal times.

Interactions and a Summary of the Pricing Sensitivities

The discussion of the pricing sensitivities shows the complexity of examining the characteristics of option strategies: The sensitivities are interrelated, and the relationships between the sensitivities and the option price are nonlinear as the stock price changes. Table 4–7 shows how the option sensitivities interact.

Considering the interactions of the pricing sensitivities can be complicated. Tables such as Table 4–7, created either from OptionVue or the Option Simulator, can provide a basis for analysis. In addition, three-dimensional graphs from the Option Simulator can provide a visual aid to understanding these interactions. Equation 4–13 provides another approach. Here gamma, theta, the change in the stock price, and the change in time are combined to estimate the change in the value of the portfolio for a position where $\delta = 0$:

$$\Delta\pi = \theta\,\Delta t + \gamma\,\Delta P_s^2/2 \qquad (4\text{-}13)$$

where $\Delta\pi$ = the change in price of the portfolio

TABLE 4–7   Option Sensitivity Values for Varying Strike Prices

$P_s = 100$ $\sigma_s = 0.25$ Risk-free rate = 5%   No dividends $t = 1/4$ year

Call Option						Put Option					
K	P_c	δ	γ	θ	υ	K	P_p	δ	γ	θ	υ
90	12 1/8	.84	.019	-.026	.120	90	1 1/8	-.16	.019	-.014	.12
95	8 1/2	.72	.027	-.032	.169	95	2 3/8	--.28	.027	-.019	.169
100	5 3/8	.56	.032	-.034	.197	100	4 3/8	-.44	.032	-.021	.197
105	3 3/8	.41	.031	-.032	.194	105	7 1/8	-.59	.031	-.018	.194
110	2		.27	.027	-.027	.166	110	10 5/8	-.73	.027	-.012	.166

Similar results are obtained if the strike price remains the same and the stock price varies.

Source: Developed using OptionVue IV.

The interactions of δ, γ, θ, and the current interest rate are shown via Equations (4–14) and (4–15):

For δ = 0: $P_C = [\theta + .5\,\sigma_s^2\,P_s^2\,\gamma]/r$ **(4–14)**

For δ ≠ 0 and a continuous dividend d is paid:

$$P_C = [\theta + (r - q)\,P_s\,\delta + .5\,\sigma_s^2\,P_s^2\,\gamma]/r \qquad \textbf{(4-15)}$$

Based on these equations, one can determine that when θ is large and negative, γ tends to be large and positive, and vice-versa. Thus, tradeoffs exist among the sensitivities.

The pricing sensitivities are summarized in Table 4–8. This table lists each sensitivity, its function, and under what circumstances a positive or negative sign to the sensitivity is beneficial. Table 4–9 lists the basic strategies discussed so far, stating the delta, gamma, and theta of these strategies. The strategies in this table also can be reversed; for example, the signs for the sensitivities when selling a call option are opposite the signs for buying a call.

TABLE 4–8   Summarizing the Effect of the Pricing Sensitivities

Sensitivity	Function of Sensitivity	Sign of the Sensitivity*	
		Positive	Negative
$\delta = \Delta P_c / \Delta P_s$	Hedge ratio; exposure to directional price change	Position benefits from price increase	Position benefits from price decrease
$\lambda = \%\Delta P_c / \%\Delta P_s$	Leverage; elasticity	Position benefits from price increase	Position benefits from price decrease
$\gamma = \Delta\delta / \Delta P_s$	Price instability	Position benefits from price instability	Position benefits from price stability
$\theta = \Delta P_c / \Delta T$	Effect of time decay	Position benefits from passage of time	Position declines in value with passage of time
$\upsilon = \Delta P_c / \Delta\sigma_s$	Effect of change in Volatility	Position benefits from volatility increase	Position benefits from volatility decrease
rho $= \Delta P_c / \Delta r$	Effect of change in interest rates	Position benefits from an increase in interest rates	Position benefits from a decrease in interest rates

* A zero value for a given pricing sensitivity means that the value of the position is not affected by a small change in the sensitivity. Puts have equivalent interpretations of their sensitivities.

TABLE 4–9   The Relationship Between Pricing Sensitivities and Basic Option Strategies

Strategy	Delta	Gamma	Theta
Buy a call	+	+	–
Buy a put	–	+	–
Put-call parity: buy stock, sell call, buy put	0	0	0

EVIDENCE ON OPTION PRICING

Empirical studies have examined how accurately the Black-Scholes model prices options and whether any systematic biases exist for the option pricing model. Violations of the pricing models provide possible arbitrage opportunities; if few violations exist, the option market is fairly priced.

The Black-Scholes Model

The Over-the-Counter Market. Black and Scholes (1972) test their call option pricing model on daily over-the-counter option prices. Since exchange-traded stock options only began trading in 1973, only over-the-counter prices were available for this initial test of the Black-Scholes model. For this test, data on 545 different stocks with 2039 different call options and 3052 call plus put contracts are tested. The volatility of the stock is estimated based on the daily returns over the previous year. Call options are priced by the Black-Scholes model as well as by market prices generated by actual trades. The availability of arbitrage profits using the option model hedge ratio to generate stock/option positions is tested; alternatively, the article tests the ability of the model to price over-the-counter market options correctly.

The conclusions of the Black-Scholes study are:

- On *average,* the model calculates prices that are neither too high nor too low when compared to market prices, although subperiods show mispricing.

- For 8 of the 10 subperiods, option sellers received too high a price (when the appropriate hedge ratios are employed); thus, option buyers paid too high a price for calls.

- When the model price is compared to the market price, significant positive excess returns are obtained when options that are underpriced via the model are purchased and overpriced options are sold. These transactions are initiated using the hedge ratio of the underlying stock to the option in order to generate a risk-free hedge.

- Profit opportunities exist for buying options on low-variance stocks and selling options on high-variance stocks using historical variance and the appropriate hedge ratio to create a risk-free hedge.[8]

- When the actual variance over the life of the option is employed, the model works well in pricing the options.

CBOE Tests. Galai (1977) performs tests similar to the Black and Scholes study, except the Galai data are for exchange-traded options. Galai examines daily prices for 152 trading days for 245 options on 32 stocks. The study uses T-bill and commercial paper interest rates and three estimates of the volatility of the stock to institute option/stock hedges based on the Black-Scholes option model. The conclusions from this study are:

- The model does a good job in differentiating between overpriced and underpriced options (an arbitrageur can profit even when hedge ratios are *not* readjusted).

- Adjusting the hedge ratios daily creates significantly higher profits than not adjusting the ratios, with an adjusted strategy earning an average return of $10 per contract per day, with one-third of the positions earning returns *significantly* greater than the risk-free interest rate.

- Different interest rates and volatility measures do not affect the conclusions of the tests.

- Including dividends increases the profits from $10 per contract to $15 per contract per day.

- When dividends are considered, low-dividend stocks provide superior profits relative to high-dividend stocks.

- When the profitable opportunities are delayed a day before a trade is executed, the majority of the profits disappear (note that a full day elapsed rather than using the next day's open).

Overall, Galai concludes that using the Black-Scholes model provides superior results relative to using the market option prices.

Biases in the Model. MacBeth and Merville (1979, 1980) examine possible systematic biases in the Black-Scholes option model. In their 1979 article, MacBeth and Merville employ the implied volatilities of the options for six actively traded stocks. They employ the average implied volatility calculated from the Black-Scholes model to price the options, using the assumption that at-the-money options with at least 90 days to expiration are priced correctly. Overall, the results show that the Black-Scholes model has a tendency to underprice in-the-money call options and to overprice out-of-the-money call options. Except for short-term out-of-the-money options, the extent of these mispricings increases when the options are deeper in-the-money or deeper out-of-the-money.[9] Moreover, on average, the mispricings increase as the time until expiration increases.

The extensive results by MacBeth and Merville do contradict (unsubstantiated) observations by others. Black (1975) states that deep in-the-money options are overpriced by the Black-Scholes model, while deep out-of-the-money options are underpriced by the model. Merton (1976) states that practitioners observe the Black-Scholes model underpricing both deep-in-the-money and deep-out-of-the-money options. In conclusion, it seems that the Black-Scholes model works better in some time periods and for some situations (at-the-money options) than for others. Moreover, the biases that do exist may change over time, causing the conflicting statements noted above. Alternatively, the Black-Scholes model may be incomplete; if this is the case, then a more sophisticated option pricing model should provide superior estimates for the option prices. Other models are briefly examined in the next section.

Market Efficiency Tests. Chiras and Manaster (1978) examine whether the Black-Scholes model is inaccurate or the option market is inefficient by buying options with low implied volatilities and selling options with high implied volatilities. This strategy obtained a profit of 10% per month, which suggests that the option market is inefficient and the Black-Scholes model is valid.

Index Options. Evnine and Rudd (1985) show that index options were substantially mispriced after one year of trading. Not only did mispricings exist relative to the binomial model, but option boundaries and put-call parity were also violated based on transactions data. Cootner and Horrell (1989) use daily closing prices to show that the Black-Scholes model over-prices calls, especially when historical rather than implied variance is used. This overpricing becomes larger as the time to expiration increases.

Sheikh (1991) uses transactions data on S&P 100 Index options to find that the market prices differ systematically from the Black-Scholes model prices. The biases created by the model are significant on both a statistical and an economic basis and are related to the changing volatility of the index. However, all of these efforts may be affected by the "old" cash index value and the difficulty in arbitraging an option on a portfolio of stocks. Moreover, Harvey and Whaley (1992) show that using a constant proportional dividend rate rather than the true discrete dividends for index options causes large pricing errors.

French and Maberly (1992) find that 28% of S&P 100 call index options are exercised early. They find this early exercise to be linked to the "wildcard" option that allows exercise until 4:10 P.M. Such early exercise near expiration could be associated with news after the 4:00 P.M. stock close or nontrading of some stocks in combination with a decline in the market.

Tests on Other Models

American Models. The Black-Scholes model is a European option model—that is, the option cannot be exercised until its expiration. An

American option can be exercised at any time. Roll (1977), Geske (1979), Geske and Johnson (1984), and Whaley (1981) all develop similar option models based on an American call option. Barone-Adesi and Whaley (1987) develop a method to approximate efficiently the price of an American option. Whaley (1982) and Sterk (1982, 1983a, 1983b) use daily data to compare the European and American versions of the call option models. They determine that the American call model is empirically superior to the European model. On the other hand, Blomeyer and Klemkosky (1983) use transaction prices to determine that the two models provide similar results. Blomeyer and Johnson (1988) examine the Geske-Johnson model for valuing puts, using transaction data. They find that the Geske-Johnson model is significantly closer to market prices than the Black-Scholes model, although both undervalue put options relative to market prices.

Other Alternative Models. Rubinstein (1985) compares the prices of several different option pricing models to actual market prices using transaction data and bid-ask quotes over a two-year period. He examines relationships and biases by determining the implied volatility on pairs of options differing by the strike price or time to expiration. Rubinstein concludes:

- Out-of-the-money options with a short time until expiration are relatively overpriced.

- Biases exist that relate to in-the-money and out-of-the-money options, but the direction of the bias changes with the time period.

- No model is consistently superior to the Black-Scholes model.

These results are consistent with the MacBeth and Merville study for the first period studied, but obtain results opposite to MacBeth and Merville for the second period. Rubinstein suggests that the strike price biases are related to macroeconomic factors such as the volatility of the market, interest rates, and the level of stock market prices.

A Summary of the Empirical Results

The empirical results emphasize one important fact: The Black-Scholes option model works extremely well, especially when pricing near-the-money options. In fact, the model does a good job of identifying mispriced options, although the mispricings are not large enough to be exploited by those who are off the exchange floor and, therefore, must pay commissions. However, delta arbitrageurs on the floor of the exchange can make returns above the risk-free rate by using the model to identify and then buy underpriced options and sell overpriced options, hedging their position in the underlying stock or in another option expiration or strike price. These hedges must be adjusted as the stock price or the time to expiration changes.

The Black-Scholes model often is less accurate when pricing stocks with very high or very low variances, when dividends are not properly considered in the model, and for deep-in-the-money and deep-out-of-the-money options. Specifically, the model tends to underprice in-the-money and overprice out-of-the-money options, with the extent of the mispricing increasing as the option becomes deeper in-the-money or deeper out-of-the-money and as the option has a longer time to expiration. However, the stability of these biases over different time periods has been questioned. The mispricing of in-the-money and out-of-the-money options also could be due to differences between the lognormal distribution used by Black-Scholes and the true empirical distribution. Other option models have characteristics that suggest they are superior to the Black-Scholes model, but empirical results to date show that none of the alternative models are consistently superior to the Black-Scholes model.

When examining empirical tests of pricing relationships for options, the following cautions must be observed:

- The option must have traded at the same time as the stock traded.

- The effect of the bid-ask spread needs to be considered.

- The procedure for estimating the future volatility of the stock must not impound biases into the results.

- Any test of options models is a joint test of both the validity of the model *and* whether the options markets are efficient. It is often difficult to determine whether the model is incorrect or the options are truly mispriced.

SUMMARY AND LOOKING AHEAD

This chapter examines the pricing sensitivities related to the option model and the empirical evidence concerning pricing models. The pricing sensitivities allow the option trader to determine the characteristics and risk of a particular strategy. The empirical evidence shows that the Black-Scholes model does an accurate job of predicting the market option price in general, although certain biases and mispricings do occur. The following chapter examines specific speculative strategies for options, while using the option sensitivities to enhance our knowledge of the characteristics of these strategies.

END NOTES

[1] Others refer to position delta as the "net share exposure." Hence, a position delta of 45 is equivalent to owning 45 shares of the underlying stock.

[2] Since $\%\Delta P_c / \%\Delta P_s = [\Delta P_c / P_c] / [\Delta P_s / P_s]$, a simple rearrangement creates $[\Delta P_c / \Delta P_s] [P_s / P_c] = \Delta (P_s / P_c)$.

[3] For stock-option hedgers, the absolute value of the gamma measures the extent to which a change in the stock price will force a revision in the hedge ratio.

[4] Since gamma is the derivative (slope) of the delta at each stock price, this explanation simply describes the calculation of the derivative.

[5] The position gamma can be used to indicate how sensitive the position is to changes in the stock's volatility when all of the options have the same expiration. For call options:

$$\Delta P_c / \Delta \sigma_c = \gamma P_s^2 t \sigma_s$$

[6] Since a two-asset zero delta position has $n_1 \delta_1 + n_2 \delta_2 = 0$, the position gamma for a zero delta position is:

$$\text{position gamma} = n_1 \Delta_1 [(\gamma_1 / \Delta_1) - (\gamma_2 / \Delta_2)]$$

[7] The fact that some later expiration months for the in-the-money calls and one out-of-the-money put possess larger differences than the nearby expiration is due to rounding of the option prices.

[8] Using historical stock data to estimate the stock variance causes the model to overprice options on high-variance stocks and underprice options on low-variance stocks. On the other hand, using market option prices to estimate the variance creates underpriced options on high-variance stocks and overpriced options on low-variance stocks.

[9] The biases found by MacBeth and Merville are opposite those determined by Black and Scholes (1972).

APPENDIX 4A
Derivatives of Option Inputs:
Option Value Sensitivities

The partial derivatives (∂) for each of the stock option sensitivities are given below. These derivatives use the Black-Scholes formulas for a call (P_C) and a put (P_P) developed in Chapter 3:

$$P_C = P_S N(d_1) - K e^{-rt} N(d_2) \tag{3-1}$$

where

$$d_1 = \frac{\ln(P_S/K) + [r + 0.5\,\sigma_S^2]t}{\sigma_S \sqrt{t}} \tag{3-2}$$

$$d_2 = d_1 - \sigma_S \sqrt{t} \tag{3-3}$$

In addition:

$$N(d_i) = \text{the cumulative normal distribution for } d_i$$

$$N'(d_i) = \partial N(d_i)/\partial d_i = \text{the normal density function}$$

$$= e^{-d_i^2/2} / \sqrt{2\pi}$$

Delta (δ)

$$\text{call } \partial P_C/\partial P_S = N(d_1) > 0 \tag{4A-1}$$

$$\text{put } \partial P_P/\partial P_S = N(d_1) - 1 < 0 \tag{4A-2}$$

$$\text{call on stock index } = e^{-dt} N(d_1) > 0 \tag{4A-3}$$

$$\text{put on stock index } = e^{-dt} [N(d_1) - 1] < 0 \tag{4A-4}$$

$$\text{for a continuous dividend d}$$

Gamma (γ)

$$\text{call } \partial\,\text{delta}/\partial P_S = \partial^2 P_C/\partial^2 P_S = N'(d_1)/P_S \sigma_S \sqrt{t} > 0 \tag{4A-5}$$

$$\text{put } \partial\,\text{delta}/\partial P_S = \partial^2 P_P/\partial^2 P_S = N'(d_1)/P_S \sigma_S \sqrt{t} > 0 \tag{4A-6}$$

Elasticity (leverage) (λ)

$$\text{call } = (P_S/P_C) N(d_1) \tag{4A-7}$$

$$\text{put } = (P_S/P_P) [N(d-1)] \tag{4A-8}$$

Theta (θ)

$$\text{call } \partial P_C / \partial t = -P_S\, \sigma_S\, N'(d_1)/2\sqrt{t}) - r\, K\, e^{-rt}\, N(d_2) < 0 \quad \textbf{(4A–9)}$$

$$\text{put } \partial P_P / \partial t = -P_S\, \sigma_S\, N'(d_1)/2\sqrt{t} + r\, K\, e^{-rt}\, N(-d_2) < 0 \quad \textbf{(4A–10)}$$

Vega (υ) (also called kappa)

$$\text{call } \partial P_C / \partial \sigma_S = P_S\, \sqrt{t}\, N'(d_1) > 0 \qquad \textbf{(4A–11)}$$

$$\text{put } \partial P_P / \partial \sigma_S = P_S\, \sqrt{t}\, N'(d_1) > 0 \qquad \textbf{(4A–12)}$$

Rho

$$\text{call } \partial P_C / \partial r = t\, K\, e^{-rt}\, N(d_2) > 0 \qquad \textbf{(4A–13)}$$

$$\text{put } \partial P_P / \partial r = t\, K\, e^{-rt}\, N(-d_2) > 0 \qquad \textbf{(4A–14)}$$

Strike price (relates to in-the-money versus out-of-the-money options)

$$\text{call } \partial P_C / \partial K = -e^{-rt}\, N(d_2) < 0 \qquad \textbf{(4A–15)}$$

$$\text{put } \partial P_P / K = e^{-rt}\, [1 - N(d_2)] > 0 \qquad \textbf{(4A–16)}$$

Option Strategies: 5
Speculating and Spreading

The three basic uses of options are speculating, spreading, and hedging. Each of these applications involves the management of risk, with each strategy changing risk in a different way. Speculators take on additional risk by trading options in order to obtain leverage. Spreaders want an option position that is less risky than a pure long or short option position. Hedgers reduce risk by offsetting some or most of the downside risk of their cash asset position with an option position. This chapter examines the strategies associated with speculating and spreading. The following chapter examines hedging.

The strategies examined here are illustrated with payoff diagrams and pricing sensitivity graphs. The payoff diagrams illustrate the relationship between the stock price and the profit for each strategy at the *expiration* of the related option. The payoff diagrams also provide basic information on the risk and return characteristics of the option position and the break-even point of the strategy. The sensitivity graphs show the relevant deltas, gammas, etc., so that informed decisions concerning risk and profitability characteristics can be made.

Speculative strategies include buying and selling call and put options. Buying an option creates large profits if the stock price changes significantly in the direction forecasted by the speculator. Otherwise, the speculator's loss is limited to the cost of the option. Selling options that are "uncovered" provides limited profits but potentially large losses.

Traders who use spreads and straddles want to reduce the risk of a pure option position. Spreaders buy one option and sell a different option in order to reduce risk. Straddles involve the purchase (or sale) of both a call and a put option.

Spreading strategies are segregated into calendar spreads, strike price spreads, and other spreads. A calendar spread occurs when an option with one expiration is purchased and another option expiration is sold. A strike price spread occurs when an option with one strike price is purchased while another strike price is sold. These strategies reduce the risk of a pure speculative position, but they also reduce the potential gain. In addition, commissions and mispricing often are important factors affecting the profitability of a spread strategy. Straddles offer other risk-return combinations not available when only a call (or a put) is used.

RISK MANAGEMENT WITH OPTIONS

Risk and Options

The principal benefit of options is that the user can employ them to alter the risk of a portfolio. The resulting amount of risk differs from the risk associated with other instruments, such as stocks or futures contracts. For example, as shown in Chapter 1, a speculator who purchases calls or puts benefits from an increase (call) or decrease (put) in the price of the underlying asset, while the potential loss from buying the option is limited to the cost of the option. Consequently, the typical view of risk used in Finance needs revision for option strategies. Risk typically is defined in terms of variability (standard deviation) for stock and bond portfolios. This proper use of the standard deviation is based on the assumption that a normal distribution exists. Option strategies alter the resulting profit distribution such that the distribution is no longer normal. For example, a speculator who purchases a call option has potential gains that are limited only by the price change of the stock, but the potential losses on the option are limited to the cost of the option. Thus, the speculator's potential distribution of profits and losses is truncated on the negative side of the distribution, as shown in Figure 5–1. Hence, a speculator in options should think of risk in terms of the *probability* and size of a loss, rather than the standard deviation of the profits.

Another way for a speculator to consider options is in terms of leverage and time. The leverage associated with the option allows the speculator to benefit from correctly forecasted stock price changes, with only a small cash investment in the option. The resultant *returns* from buying call options vary from a negative 100% (if the option expires worthless) to a positive return of several hundred percent (depending on the stock price change relative to the cost of the option and the strike price). The option also provides the buyer with *time* for the stock price to change before the option expires. In conclusion, the risks and rewards associated with option strategies must be examined in terms of the characteristics of these strategies, including the pricing sensitivities, rather than by the typical procedure of simply measuring the variability of their returns.

Strategies with Options

The success of speculative option strategies is based on appropriate forecasts of the direction, magnitude, and/or distribution of price changes of the

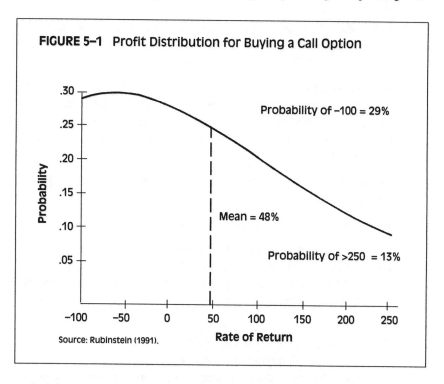

FIGURE 5-1   Profit Distribution for Buying a Call Option

Probability of -100 = 29%

Mean = 48%

Probability of >250 = 13%

Probability (y-axis): .30, .25, .20, .15, .10, .05

Rate of Return (x-axis): -100, -50, 0, 50, 100, 150, 200, 250

Source: Rubinstein (1991).

underlying asset, since a change in the asset price is the most important factor affecting the option price. Fundamental analysis and technical pricing forecasts are typical procedures used to determine whether and when to purchase or sell a particular option. Using option strategies assumes that such an analysis has already been completed. While such analyses are far from perfect, the evidence concerning speculating with options (discussed later) shows that the alternative of buying options at random often provides inferior results to simply investing in a Treasury bill.

The appropriate price for a particular option is another factor to consider for those who execute option strategies—that is, determining whether an option is over- or underpriced compared to its fair value. Pure speculative strategies are not dependent on the small deviations from an option's fair value that typically occur. However, strategies using combinations of options, discussed later in this chapter, often are sensitive to mispricings.

The Advantages and Disadvantages of Speculating with Options

Options possess characteristics that differ from other financial instruments. These characteristics provide the option buyer with certain advantages and disadvantages. The advantages of options for speculators are:

- **Leverage**   The percentage change in the option price is greater than the percentage change in the underlying stock. Thus, the rate of return on "invested" dollars is larger with options.

- **Small investment**   The cost of an option on 100 shares of stock is much less than the cost of the stock itself. This relatively small cost of an option is another aspect of leverage, but it is also a separate consideration for small speculators who are unwilling to risk large amounts of money.

- **Limited loss**   The maximum loss a speculator will endure is equal to the cost of the option.

Disadvantages of options for speculators are:

- **Time constraint**   An option is a wasting asset; that is, the price declines as the expiration date approaches. A speculator may forecast the direction of the underlying stock price correctly but misjudge the timing of the move, creating a loss in the option position due to the timing factor.

- **Time value**   The buyer of the option pays for "time" and "volatility." The cost of buying the time value can be larger than any beneficial change in the option price resulting from changes in the stock price.

SPECULATING WITH CALL OPTIONS

Buying Calls

The payoff diagrams and profits of buying a call option are examined in Chapters 1 and 2. Here we enhance the discussion of speculating with calls and then examine the pricing sensitivities of this strategy.

Those who purchase call options typically buy *slightly* out-of-the-money calls having a relatively short time remaining before expiration. These calls maximize the buyer's leverage and minimize the size of the time value. Call buyers are often small speculators who believe they can forecast the direction of the underlying stock or market. Thus, such speculators typically do *not* use option pricing models to determine whether a fair price exists for the option. In any case, these speculators are willing to pay an extra one-eight or one-fourth of a point above the fair value, due to their convictions concerning the direction of the stock price and the potential profitability of the option position.

The conventional wisdom on Wall Street is that 70% of those who buy options lose money. While this percentage seems large to an optimistic trader, the option buyer must overcome both the time value and the commission charges before obtaining a profit. Although the 70% value has not been verified by empirical results for an entire market cycle, Gombola, Roenfeldt and Cooley (1978) use three years of data to show that over 60% of individual long call positions held for the three months before expiration lost money. During the up market period of the study, 49% of the positions lost money, while 91% had negative returns during the down market period. The average return before commissions during this time period was – 0.4%, with an average return of 29.5% during the up market period and a –74% return during the down market period.[1]

Figure 5–2 shows the interrelationships between time to maturity and the asset value on the **delta** asset value and the time to expiration decrease. The figure shows the interaction of these factors on delta. The associated **gamma** is shown in Figure 5–3. The gamma is largest when the asset value is near the strike price *and* the time to expiration is short.

Figure 5–4 shows **theta** as a function of the strike price and asset value. In general, high and low asset values (for the same strike price) have smaller negative thetas (thetas nearer zero). Deep-in-the-money and deep-out-of-the-money options have the smallest negative theta. Figure 5–5 shows vega as a function of the asset value and volatility. Asset values near the strike price have the largest vega.

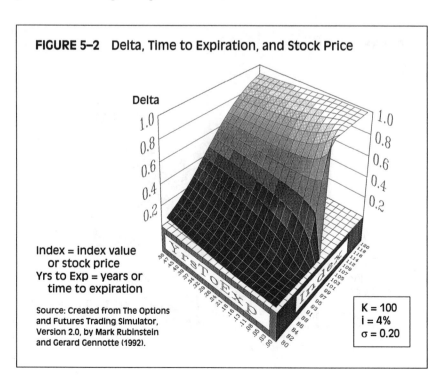

FIGURE 5–2   Delta, Time to Expiration, and Stock Price

Delta

Index = index value
   or stock price
Yrs to Exp = years or
   time to expiration

Source: Created from The Options
and Futures Trading Simulator,
Version 2.0, by Mark Rubinstein
and Gerard Gennotte (1992).

K = 100
i = 4%
σ = 0.20

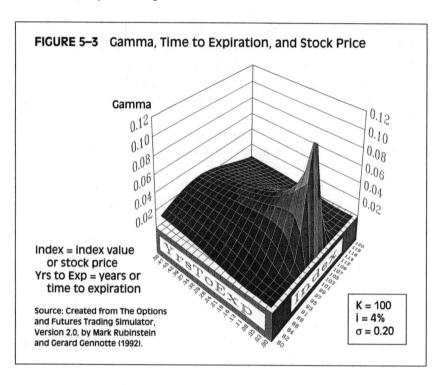

FIGURE 5–3 Gamma, Time to Expiration, and Stock Price

Index = index value or stock price
Yrs to Exp = years or time to expiration

Source: Created from The Options and Futures Trading Simulator, Version 2.0, by Mark Rubinstein and Gerard Gennotte (1992).

K = 100
i = 4%
σ = 0.20

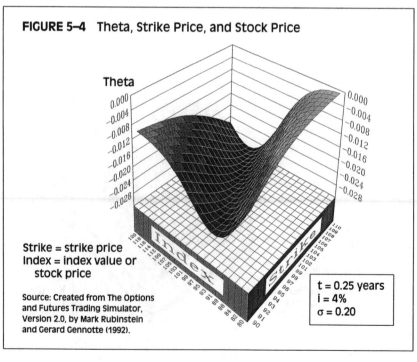

FIGURE 5–4 Theta, Strike Price, and Stock Price

Strike = strike price
Index = index value or stock price

Source: Created from The Options and Futures Trading Simulator, Version 2.0, by Mark Rubinstein and Gerard Gennotte (1992).

t = 0.25 years
i = 4%
σ = 0.20

FIGURE 5–5   Vega, Stock Price, and Volatility

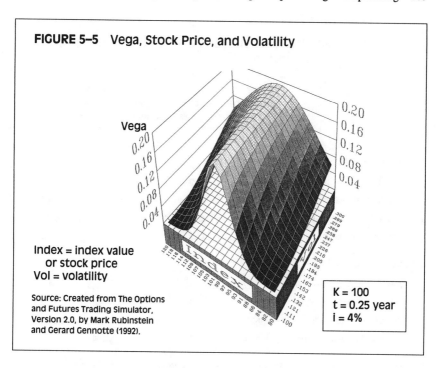

Index = index value
or stock price
Vol = volatility

Source: Created from The Options
and Futures Trading Simulator,
Version 2.0, by Mark Rubinstein
and Gerard Gennotte (1992).

K = 100
t = 0.25 year
i = 4%

Buying Calls Plus Investing in T-Bills

An alternative strategy to buying only a call is to buy the call *and* invest funds in a T-bill (or an alternative risk-free debt instrument). This alternative involves using the funds that one would have employed to purchase the stock. The purpose of this strategy is to benefit from upside gains in the stock while receiving downside protection from the limited loss feature of the call option. In addition, the interest from the debt instrument reduces the cost of buying the option. The resultant call plus T-bill strategy has the same payoff diagram as buying a call, but with a lower cost. Such a strategy is advocated by some for LEAPs (long-term options), since the trader gains if the stock increases, and the trader can purchase the stock at a lower cost if the stock declines significantly over the life of the option.

Merton, Scholes and Gladstein (1978) simulate the profitability of placing 10% of the total funds available into call options, while the remaining 90% of the funds are invested in commercial paper earning the market rate of interest. In-the-money, out-of-the-money, and at-the-money options are created by Merton, et al. in order to compare these different approaches to buying calls. Results are determined for both the Dow Jones Industrial stocks and a portfolio of 136 stocks. Return and risk measures are calculated for six-month option positions for a period of 12 1/2 years, with the call option price determined by calculating the Black-Scholes fair option price.[2]

TABLE 5–1 Simulated Results for a Call Option/Commercial Paper Strategy

	10% in-the-money	At-the-money	10% out-of-the-money	20% out-of-the-money	Stock
136-stock portfolio:					
Average rate of return (%)	6.3	8.2	11.1	16.2	7.9
Standard deviation (%)	7.8	10.6	15.7	27.2	16.6
Growth of $1,000 ($)	4370.	6372.	11,178.	25,670.	5043.
Standard deviation/Return	1.23	1.29	1.41	1.70	2.10
Dow Jones stocks:					
Average rate of return (%)	4.2	5.1	7.2	10.6	4.1
Standard deviation (%)	7.3	10.1	14.6	25.7	13.7
Growth of $1,000 ($)	2627.	3138.	4597.	7287.	2226.
Standard deviation/return	1.74	1.98	2.03	2.42	3.34

Source: Abstracted from Merton, Scholes, and Gladstein (1978).

Table 5–1 summarizes the results of the Merton et al. investigation. Specifically, Merton et al. find that buying call options and investing the remainder of the funds in commercial paper provides a superior (lower) risk/return ratio to investing in a stock-only portfolio. While this result suggests that speculating in options is profitable on average, Merton et al. correctly state that the results are sensitive to the time period studied. However, while the Merton et al. study is the most comprehensive examination of several important option strategies, criticisms of their results relating to the option pricing model cast doubt on the conclusion that the call option/commercial paper strategy will be profitable for traders.[3]

Selling Calls

Figure 5–6 shows the profit diagram for a speculator who *sells* a **naked call** option—that is, when a call is sold without holding the stock for protection against price increases. Selling a call option means that the seller is obligated to *deliver* 100 shares of the stock at the strike price to the buyer of the option (if the option is held to expiration). The option seller receives the original price of the option as compensation for the risk undertaken. Since selling a

FIGURE 5–6   Payoff Diagram at Expiration for Selling a Call Option Naked

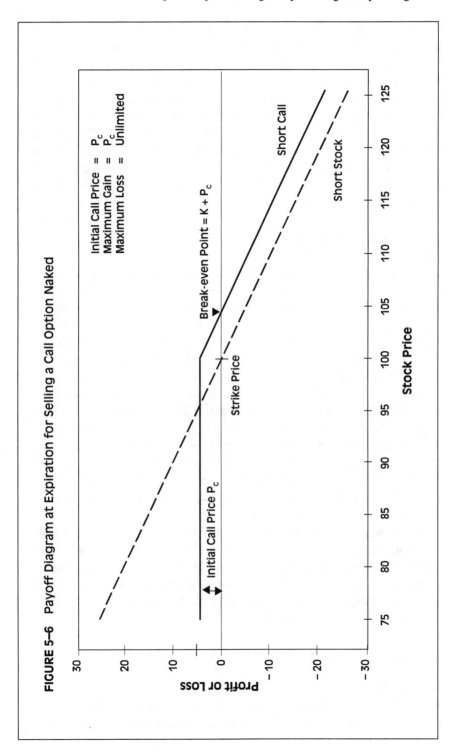

call "naked" means that the seller of the call does *not* own the stock, an in-the-money call at expiration forces the speculator to buy the stock in the open market and then deliver the stock to the option buyer, who pays the strike price. On the other hand, if the stock price is below the strike price at option expiration, the seller of the naked call keeps the entire original call option price.

Selling a naked call is the mirror image of buying a call option (the payoff diagrams are flipped vertically). The break-even point for selling a call naked is the strike price plus the cost of the option. The maximum gain is the price of the option, while the maximum loss is unlimited. For example, if a call option with a strike price of 100 is sold naked for 4 points when the stock price is 100, then the maximum profit is 4, but the possible loss depends only on how much the stock price increases. If the stock increases to 115, then the loss is 11 points (the stock price of 115 less the strike price of 100 less the option price received of 4).

The potential loss for selling a call naked is significantly greater than the potential maximum profit, as shown in the payoff diagram. The dashed line in the figure shows the payoff for a short sale of the stock. The short sale has a greater profit potential than selling a call naked, although more capital is required to initiate a short position. Since the potential loss on the sale of a naked call is much greater than the amount received from the option price, options exchanges and brokerage houses require the seller to put up additional funds to guarantee the fulfillment of the option contract. The margin for selling naked calls is the option price plus 20% of the stock value. If the call is out-of-the-money, the margin is reduced by the extent to which the call is out-of-the-money. The minimum margin is 10% of the stock value. For example, if a speculator sells a naked call option for $3 when the stock price is $27 and the strike price is $25, then the margin is 0.20 ($2700) + $300 = $840. If the stock price is $23 and the option price is $1, then the margin is 0.20 ($2300) + $100 − $200 = $360.

Those who do sell naked calls typically sell slightly in-the-money calls, since this maximizes the leverage of the position. However, if a speculator forecasts a significant drop in the stock price, then a sale of a deep-in-the-money option maximizes the total profits on the sale of the naked call, although this strategy also loses more money if the stock price increases (due to the small time value received).

SPECULATING WITH PUT OPTIONS

Buying Puts
Buying puts is covered in Chapters 1 and 2. The pricing sensitivities are equivalent or very similar to those presented for calls earlier in the chapter.

Therefore, we will concentrate here on the strategy of selling puts. First, however, Exhibit 5–1 shows the "Analysis" screen of the Option Simulator. This illustrates how one can obtain comparative option pricing sensitivities for different options to determine the best option for a given strategy. The exhibit shows the sensitivities for puts on the futures stock index. The "Analysis" Screen also allows users to examine the pricing sensitivities for any combination of options and/or the underlying asset. Two-dimensional graphs of these sensitivities can then be obtained for any chosen combination for any holding period.

Exhibit 5–2 shows how the "Value Sheet" function in OptionVue can be used to provide the theoretical option prices and pricing sensitivities for puts for different stock prices. The appropriate put (or other option or combination) can then be chosen from this list. Exhibit 5–3 shows the "Selection" function in OptionVue. This function provides recommended trades and expected profits (puts, in this case), based on price targets or ranges.

Selling Puts

Figure 5–7 shows the payoff diagram for selling a put option. The seller of the put *receives* the option price in exchange for the obligation to *accept* 100 shares of the stock at the strike price of the option, if and when the buyer of the put exercises the option to sell the stock. A profitable put sale provides a limited maximum gain equal to the put price. For example, if a put with a strike price of 100 is sold for 3, then the maximum gain is 3. The potential loss depends on the extent to which the stock price declines below the strike price. In our example, if the stock price falls to 93, the loss on the option equals 4 (the strike price of 100 less the stock price of 93 less the option price received of 3). The break-even point for the put is the strike price less the put option price. The break-even point is 97 for our example—that is, the strike price of 100 less the option price received of 3. The *maximum* loss occurs if the stock falls to zero, which equals the strike price less the price of the put option received. The margin rules for selling naked puts are equivalent to those for naked calls.

Those who sell puts often do so when they are willing to receive the stock at a price equal to the strike price less the option price received. Thus, those who sell puts often believe that the stock is a good buy at the strike price. On the other hand, some speculators sell out-of-the-money puts with the expectation that the put will *not* be exercised. In this case, the speculator earns the put price as the profit on the transaction. Of course, such a transaction is risky.[4]

EXHIBIT 5–1   Analysis Screen of the Option Simulator for Puts

Sn	Security	NPrice	Value	Delta	Gamma	Theta	Vega	Rho
1	SP500 Index	237.73	237.73	1.00				
2	F/ /Jun86	238.50	239.22	1.01		0.04		0.41
3	F/ /Sep86	241.31	241.45	1.03		0.04		0.98
4	F/ /Dec86	244.08	243.47	1.04		0.04		1.56
113	P/225/May86	1.14	0.85	−0.13	0.017	−0.04	0.15	−0.16
114	P/230/May86	2.28	1.82	−0.24	0.024	−0.05	0.22	−0.14
115	P/235/May86	4.00	3.44	−0.38	0.030	−0.06	0.27	−0.12
116	P/240/May86	6.37	5.82	−0.53	0.031	−0.06	0.28	−0.09
117	P/245/May86	9.56	8.95	−0.68	0.028	−0.05	0.25	−0.06
118	P/250/May86	13.43	12.73	−0.80	0.022	−0.03	0.20	−0.04
122	P/235/Jun86	5.79	5.52	−0.40	0.021	−0.04	0.39	−0.23
123	P/240/Jun86	8.22	7.89	−0.50	0.021	−0.04	0.40	−0.19
124	P/245/Jun86	11.21	10.77	−0.60	0.021	−0.04	0.39	−0.15
125	P/250/Jun86	14.59	14.13	−0.70	0.019	−0.03	0.35	−0.12
148	P/235/Sep86	8.67	8.70	−0.39	0.013	−0.03	0.59	−0.52
149	P/240/Sep86	11.22	10.99	−0.46	0.013	−0.02	0.61	−0.47
150	P/245/Sep86	13.54	13.62	−0.52	0.014	−0.02	0.62	−0.42
151	P/250/Sep86	16.45	16.55	−0.59	0.013	−0.02	0.60	−0.36
176	P/235/Dec86	10.18	11.16	−0.38	0.010	−0.02	0.74	−0.80
177	P/240/Dec86	12.22	13.42	−0.43	0.010	−0.02	0.76	−0.74
178	P/245/Dec86	14.26	15.92	−0.48	0.010	−0.02	0.77	−0.68

EXHIBIT 5–2   Value Sheet Function from Optionvue

SYMBOL : ABC	STRATEGY: Single options	EX-DIV : n/a
PR INTVALS : 5	CALL VLTY: 25.0	INTRST : 5.0%
	PUT VLTY: 25.0	

PARAMETER:	Call Th.Pr	PutTh.Pr,	PutDelta	PutTheta	PutVega	Call Th.Pr	PutTh.Pr,	PutDelta	PutTheta	PutVega
		FEB(31)					APR(90)			
ABC = 95										
90	6 1/4	13/16	(.20)	2.9	{ 7.8}	8 1/4	2 1/8	(.28)	1.8	{15.9}
95	3	2 1/2	(.46)	3.8	{11.0}	5 1/4	4 1/8	(.44)	2.0	{18.7}
100	1 1/8	5 5/8	(.73)	2.7	{ 9.2}	3 1/8	6 7/8	(.60)	1.7	{18.4}
105	5/16	10	(1.00)	0.0	{ 0.0}	1 3/4	10 1/2	(.74)	1.0	{15.4}
110	1/16	15	(1.00)	0.0	{ 0.0}	7/8	15	(1.00)	0.0	{ 0.0}
ABC = 100										
90	10 5/8	3/16	(.06)	1.3	{ 3.6}	12 1/8	1 1/8	(.16)	1.4	{12.0}
95	6 1/4	15/16	(.21)	3.1	{ 8.5}	8 1/2	2 3/8	(.28)	1.9	{16.9}
100	3 1/8	2 3/4	(.46)	4.0	{11.6}	5 5/8	4 3/8	(.44)	2.1	{19.7}
105	1 1/4	5 3/4	(.72)	2.9	{ 9.9}	3 3/8	7 1/8	(.59)	1.8	{19.4}
110	3/8	10	(1.00)	0.0	{ 0.0}	2	10 5/8	(.73)	1.2	{16.6}
ABC = 105										
90	15 3/8	1/16	(.01)	0.4	{ 1.1}	16 5/8	1/2	(.08)	1.0	{ 7.8}
95	10 5/8	1/4	(.07)	1.6	{ 4.2}	12 3/8	1/4	(.17)	1.6	{13.1}
100	6 1/2	1	(.22)	3.4	{ 9.1}	8 3/4	2 1/2	(.29)	2.0	{18.0}
105	3 1/4	2 7/8	(.46)	4.2	{12.2}	5 7/8	4 1/2	(.44)	2.2	{20.7}
110	1 3/8	5 7/8	(.71)	3.2	{10.6}	3 5/8	7 3/8	(.58)	1.9	{20.5}

Source: Developed from OptionVue IV.

EXHIBIT 5-3   Selection Function of OptionVue for Buying Puts

SYMBOL: ABC	DATE: JAN 01	VALUATION DATE: JAN 01

SYMBOL: ABC   DATE: JAN 01 VALUATION DATE: JAN 01
CAPITAL: $1,000   PRICE: 100   CALL VLTY: 25.0
STRATEGY: Buy Puts   PUT VLTY: 25.0
TG.PRICE: Range from 94 to 102   INTRST: 5.0%
  RANKING BASIS: 50% Exp.Ret. / 50% 1st St.Dev.Downside Exp.Ret.

Recommended Trade			Exp.Ret.	St. Dev.
1.	B	5 Apr 95p	@1 5/8	+606	404
2.	B	3 Feb 100p	@2 7/8	+216	414
3.	B	1 Feb 105p	@5 3/4	+106	197
4.	B	8 Apr 90p	@1 1/8	+145	'390
5.	B	1 Apr 105p	@7 1/8	+69	156
6.	B	8 Feb 95p	@1 1/8	+195	594
7.	B	2 Apr 100p	@4 3/4	+50	237

Source: Developed using OptionVue IV.

SPREADS AND STRADDLES

What Is a Spread?

Spreads and **straddles** (which are defined below) are combinations of option positions that are less risky than a single option position, but they also reduce the potential gain. In order to have less risk, the two (or more) option positions must be partially offsetting. The offsetting nature of the options also reduces the potential dollar profit when compared to a single option position. Thus, the different types of spreads generate payoff diagrams with varying return and risk characteristics. The most popular types of combination transactions are:

A calendar or time spread   the purchase of an option with one expiration month and the sale of another option with a different expiration month. This type of spread benefits from the faster decay in the time value for the nearby option.

A strike or price spread   the purchase of an option with one strike price and the sale of another option with a different strike price. The profit on this strategy relates to the forecast accuracy of the trader in predicting the direction in the market.

A straddle   the purchase (or sale) of both a call option and a put option.

FIGURE 5–7 Payoff Diagram at Expiration for Selling a Put Option

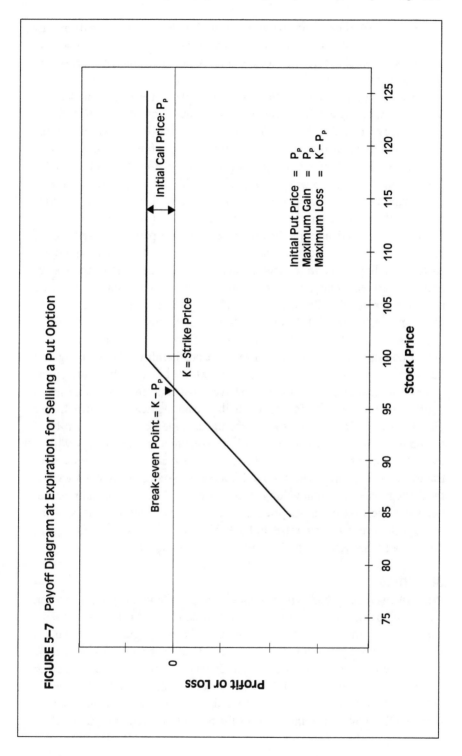

Purchasing a straddle is profitable if the stock *either* increases or decreases significantly in price. If the stock remains near the price that existed when the options were purchased, then a loss occurs. A sale of a straddle is profitable if the stock price is stable.

Many other types of combinations are possible. It has been estimated that strategies involving combinations of calls and puts, spreading over different strike prices, spreading over expiration months, and various combinations involving individual options, index options, and options on futures, total over one million different strategies! This diversity offers the trader a multitude of opportunities to generate a position with an acceptable risk-return combination, as well as opportunities to find combinations with superior returns if the relationships between the options are mispriced.[5]

Since the spread and straddle option positions are partially offsetting, the net profits from these transactions often are critically dependent on trading costs. If trading costs are a large percentage of the net cost of the spread transaction, then strategies that continually and solely use this strategy are usually unprofitable. Trading costs include commissions, bid-ask spread costs, and costs relating to poor executions. For example, the high commission costs of a full-service brokerage house for trading a small number of option contracts often adversely affect the profitability of the strategy. A trader can either use a discount broker and/or trade a large volume of options in order to reduce commissions. However, discount brokers often have a poorer execution record for trades at the desired price level, which also reduces the profitability of the spreading or straddle strategy. A rule of thumb to reduce commission effects is to execute a spread strategy with at least 10 contracts on each side of the spread or straddle. Bid-ask spreads for trades can also greatly affect the return of certain strategies, especially when the strategy is executed in volume. Care must be taken to issue an order that stipulates the maximum net price difference between the two sides of the strategy in order to minimize bid-ask effects and to lock in that price difference; otherwise, the trade could become very costly.[6]

Straddles

Purchasing a Straddle. The purchase of a straddle involves buying a call option and buying a put option, both with the same strike price and the same expiration month. Figure 5–8(a) illustrates the profit graph for buying a straddle. Figure 5–8(b) shows the components of the straddle, as well as the combination of the call and put. These graphs show that large increases *or* decreases in the price of the underlying stock result in a profit for the straddle purchase. However, if the stock price at the option expiration date changes *less* than the total cost of the call plus the put option, then the straddle loses

FIGURE 5–8(A)   Payoff Diagram at Expiration for the Purchase of a Straddle
(A) Payoff diagram

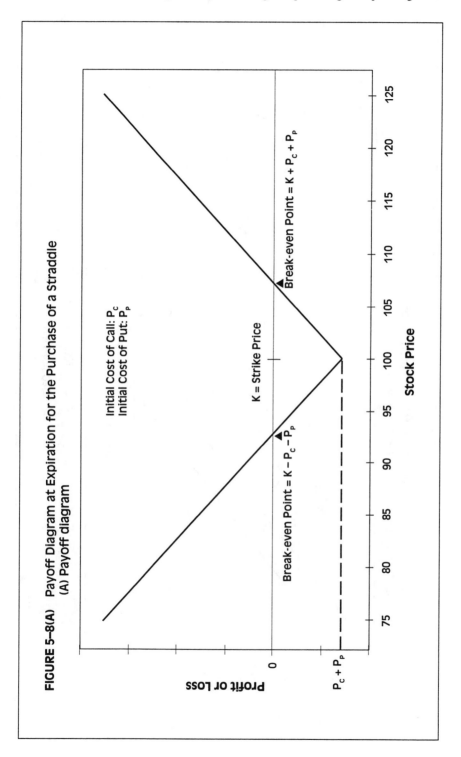

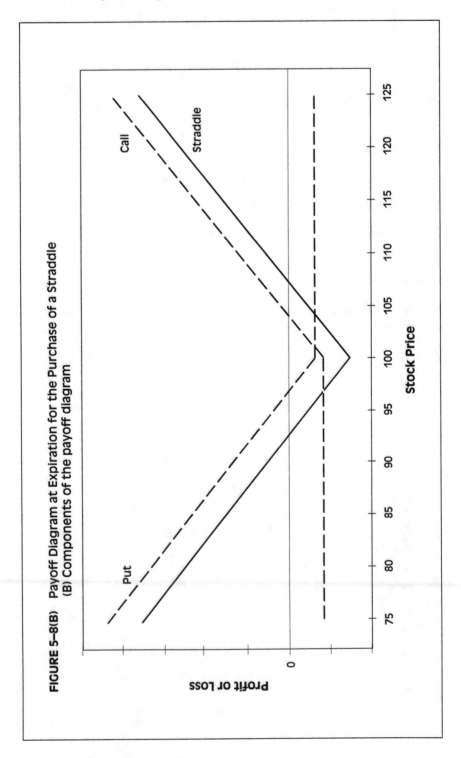

FIGURE 5–8(B) Payoff Diagram at Expiration for the Purchase of a Straddle
(B) Components of the payoff diagram

money. Thus, the upper and lower break-even points for a straddle are the strike price plus/minus the total cost of the two options.

$$BE_{STR} = K + P_C + P_P$$

$$and \ K - P_C - P_P \qquad (5-1)$$

where BE_{STR} = the break-even points for buying a straddle.

At expiration either the call or the put will be exercised, depending on which one is in-the-money at the time. Neither option is exercised when the ending stock price equals the strike price, which corresponds to the maximum loss for the straddle:

$$Max \ Loss_{STR} = P_C + P_P \qquad (5-2)$$

To determine the profit on a straddle one finds:

$$Profit_{STR} = |P_S - K| - P_C - P_P \qquad (5-3)$$

where $|P_S - K|$ is the absolute value of $P_S - K$

Example 5–1 illustrates these concepts.

Using Straddles. Traders purchase a straddle under one of two circumstances. The first circumstance exists when a large change in the stock price is expected, but the direction of the change is unknown. Examples include an upcoming announcement of earnings, uncertain takeover or merger speculation, a court case for damages, a new product announcement, or an uncertain economic announcement such as inflation figures or a change in the prime interest rate. Ideally, the trader should understand the importance of such an announcement better than the market, otherwise the option price should reflect the increase in the potential volatility of the stock/market. The second circumstance in which straddles are purchased occurs when the trader estimates that the true future volatility of the stock will be greater than the volatility that is currently impounded in the option price.

A conservative approach to trading a straddle *before* the expiration of the options is to sell one of the options *if* it creates a profit for the straddle. For example, if the stock price increases to the point where the straddle is above the break-even point, then the call option could be sold. In this case, a profit is assured *and* the trader would own a put option that is essentially costless. If the stock price subsequently declines sufficiently, the put option would add to the total profitability of the straddle without any risk to the trader. Of course, this approach forgoes any additional increases in the stock price after the call option is sold.[7]

EXAMPLE 5–1   Buying a Straddle

The following calculates the break-even, maximum loss, and profit on purchasing a straddle, given:

$P_c = {}^3/_4$ $P_p = 2\,{}^1/_2$ $K = 100$ P_s (at option expiration) $= 103$

Break-even:

$$BE_{STR} = K + P_c + P_p$$
$$\text{and } K - P_c - P_p \qquad (5\text{–}1)$$
$$= 100 + 3 + 2\,{}^1/_2 = 105\,{}^1/_2$$
$$\text{and } = 100 - 3 - 2\,{}^1/_2 = 94\,{}^1/_2$$

Maximum loss:

$$\text{Max Loss}_{STR} = P_c + P_p \qquad (5\text{–}2)$$
$$= 3 + 2\,{}^1/_2 = 5\,{}^1/_2$$

Profit:

$$\text{Profit}_{STR} = |P_s - K| - P_c - P_p \qquad (5\text{–}3)$$
$$= |103 - 100| - 3 - 2\,{}^1/_2 = -2\,{}^1/_2$$

Straddles and Pricing Sensitivities.   Buying a straddle with a call $\delta = .5$ and a put $\delta = -.5$ creates a delta neutral position. Either an immediate increase *or* decrease in the stock price creates a profit for the straddle, as shown in Figure 5–9. Thus, if the stock price increases, both the call and put deltas increase (the put delta becomes less negative), creating a $\delta > 0$. Positive deltas signify a profit for increasing stock prices. Similarly, if the stock price decreases, then both the call and put deltas decrease: $\delta < 0$ creates a profit for decreasing stock prices.[8] The disadvantage of buying the straddle is the negative theta due to the time decay: The option prices decline as time passes. Figure 5–9 also shows that a long straddle benefits from an increase in the volatility of the stock from the initial $\delta = 0.2$ (an increasing gamma), since *both* the call and put prices would increase without the need for a change in the stock price.

Selling a Straddle.   The sale of both a call option and a put option equals the sale of a straddle. The seller of the straddle keeps the total value of the call and put option prices, but is *obligated* to *sell* the stock (call) or *accept* the stock (put), depending on the value of the stock price at the expiration of the options. Figure 5–10 shows the payoff diagram for selling a straddle

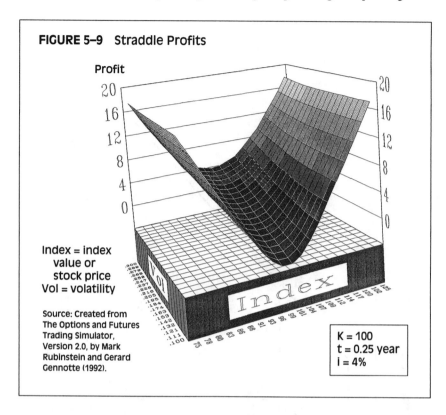

FIGURE 5–9   Straddle Profits

Profit

Index = index value or stock price
Vol = volatility

Source: Created from The Options and Futures Trading Simulator, Version 2.0, by Mark Rubinstein and Gerard Gennotte (1992).

K = 100
t = 0.25 year
i = 4%

naked—that is, when the seller of the straddle has no current long or short position in the underlying stock. The figure shows that a sale of a straddle is profitable as long as the difference between the stock price and the strike price at option expiration is less than the total of the call and put option prices received. Thus, the seller of the straddle must take care in evaluating the magnitude of the option prices before undertaking this strategy. Even so, this strategy is risky, since the potential loss can be substantial.

Selling a straddle is the *reverse* of buying a straddle. From Example 5-1 we find that a short straddle is profitable as long as the stock price is *between* the break-even points of 93 and 107. Thus, selling a straddle has the same break-even points as buying a straddle. The profit from selling a straddle is determined by finding:

$$\text{Profit}_{\text{SSTR}} = P_C + P_P - |P_S - K| \qquad (5\text{–}4)$$

where SSTR = selling a straddle

The maximum gain on selling a straddle is:

$$\text{Max Profit}_{\text{SSTR}} = P_C + P_P \qquad (5\text{–}5)$$

FIGURE 5–10   Payoff Diagram at Expiration for the Sale of a Straddle

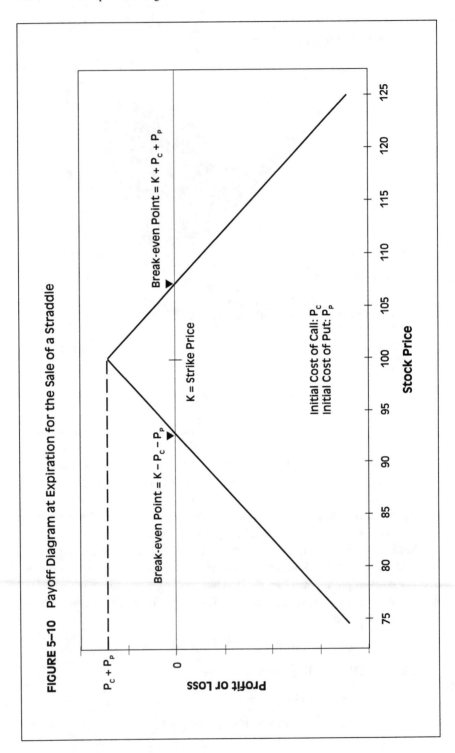

Selling a straddle is initiated under opposite conditions from purchasing a straddle. Thus, straddle sellers expect that a large price change will *not* occur, since no news is forthcoming. Also, straddles are sold when the spreader's estimate of the true future volatility of the stock is *less* than the volatility currently impounded in the option price.

CALENDAR AND STRIKE PRICE SPREADS

Calendar Spreads

Definitions and Concepts. A calendar spread exists when a call (or put) option with a deferred expiration is purchased while a nearby call (or put) option with the same strike price is sold. For example, one executes a calendar spread by buying a June 100 strike price and selling a March 100 strike price. Calendar spreads also are known as time spreads and horizontal spreads. The name "horizontal spread" is derived from the fact that different option expirations are represented horizontally in the newspaper. The objective of a calendar spread is to profit from the faster decay of the time value on the nearby option in comparison to the deferred option. Since both options have the same strike price, they will have the same intrinsic values at the expiration of the nearby option. Thus, the price difference between the options occurs because of their different expiration dates.

Profits and Losses. The call calendar spread shown in Figure 5–11 illustrates the payoff diagrams for three time periods prior to and at the expiration of the nearby option, with the thickest line representing the value of the spread when the nearby option expires. The figure shows that the spreader obtains the maximum profit when the stock price equals the strike price and the position is held until the nearby option expires. If the stock price moves away from the strike price, the profitability of this strategy decreases or even becomes a loss. This is because the time values for *both* option expirations decrease significantly as the options become deeper in-the-money or out-of-the-money. Thus, the maximum loss on a calendar spread position is the difference between the two option prices when purchased:

$$\text{Max loss}_{CS} = P_{C,D} - P_{C,N} \tag{5-6}$$

where Max loss$_{CS}$ = the maximum loss on a calendar spread
$P_{C,D}$ = the price of a deferred call option
$P_{C,N}$ = the price of a nearby call option

The break-even point for a calendar spread relates to the *relative* change in the time values. These changes are due to the effects of both the stock price

FIGURE 5–11   Payoff Diagram for a Calendar Spread

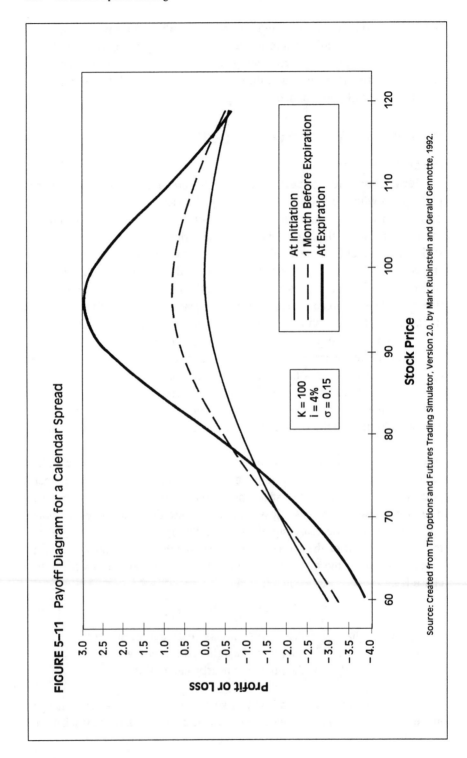

Source: Created from The Options and Futures Trading Simulator, Version 2.0, by Mark Rubinstein and Gerald Gennotte, 1992.

change *and* the time decay. Thus, no simple equation illustrates the break-even point. The profit for a calendar spread is the difference in the change in prices of the two positions:

$$\text{Profit}_{CS} = \Delta P_{C,D} - \Delta P_{C,N} \tag{5-7}$$

where $\Delta P = P_T - P_{T-1}$

Example 5–2 illustrates the maximum loss and profit for a call calendar spread.

Calendar Spreads, Time Decay, and Deltas. Figure 5–11 on page 182 shows that the profitability of the calendar spread changes with time. When the spread is initiated (the solid line in the figure), no profit is possible, but losses occur if the stock price changes. As time passes (the dashed and thick lines in the figure), a profit from the spread appears as a range around the strike price, which relates to the faster time value decay on the nearby option expiration. The effect of the differing decay rates of the time values of the options is shown more clearly in Figure 5–12. Here, the nearby short option is represented by the thick line on the lower part of the figure, while the deferred long option is represented by the thick line at the top of the figure. The thick line in the middle shows how the spread acts over time as the time

---

EXAMPLE 5–2 Trading a Calendar Spread

A trader executes a calendar spread to attempt to capture the time value. The current stock price is 100. A profit is obtained if the stock price stays near the strike price.

	When Initiated	At Nearby Expiration
P_s (March)		102
Nearby = March 100 (sell)	$P_{C,N} = 4$	2*
Deferred = June 100 (buy)	$P_{C,D} = 6\,1/2$	5

*$P_s - K$

Maximum loss:

$$\text{Max loss}_{CS} = P_{C,D} - P_{C,N} \tag{5-6}$$
$$= 6\,1/2 - 4 = 2\,1/2$$
$$\text{Profit}_{CS} = \Delta P_{C,D} - \Delta P_{C,N} \tag{5-7}$$
$$= -1\,1/2 - (-2) = 1/2$$

The profit is due to the greater reduction in the time value for the nearby option (which was sold) in comparison to the deferred option (which was purchased).

values of the two options change. Most important, notice that a major part of the spread change occurs near the expiration of the nearby option. Thus, a calendar spread has a positive theta. The rapid decline in theta near expiration shows how a calendar spread can be profitable: The positive theta from selling the nearby option increases faster than the negative theta from buying the deferred option decreases. However, the relationship shown in Figure 5–12 assumes that the stock price does not change. A change in the stock price alters these time value relationships.[9] Figure 5–13 shows the delta for a calendar spread for a constant time to option expiration. Figure 5–13 shows the effect of changing stock prices on the hedge ratio (sensitivity of the option price to changes in the stock price). The calendar spread is most sensitive to stock price changes near 95 for our example, and not sensitive when the options become deep-out-of- or deep-in-the-money. This is opposite a long call position, which has a large delta for deep-in-the-money positions. A negative delta for the spread occurs near 105, since this stock price creates losses for the calendar spread. Position delta is also relevant for spreads. Thus, if a spread has a $\delta = 0.2$, then each option spread has a $20 change in the spread position value for each $1 change in the stock price.

In summary, the profitability of a calendar spread depends on both the different decay times for the time values and the extent of the underlying stock price change. Before the spread is initiated, the spreader must analyze the effect of the potential change in the stock price by comparing the market's estimate of the future volatility of the stock with the spreader's estimate of the volatility. This comparison is a key factor in determining whether the calendar spread will be profitable.

Reverse Calendar Spread. A reverse calendar spread is achieved if the nearby expiration is *purchased* and the deferred option is *sold*. In this case, the spreader is forecasting that the stock *will* change significantly in price. A large change in price creates a profit, while small changes create losses (the spreader pays for the faster decaying time value on the nearby option). This strategy is used less frequently than the typical calendar spread, since a large price change is needed to obtain a limited profit while a loss is guaranteed if the stock price changes only to a small extent. Those who do implement this strategy cover the position several weeks before the nearby option expires so that they avoid the largest decay in the time value—that is, they resell the nearby option and buy back the deferred option.

Evidence. Gombola, Roenfeldt, and Cooley (1978) examine calendar spreads. They find average returns of 26.7% before commissions, although only 53% of the positions made money. After commissions the calendar spreads generated a –22.5% return. However, these results are based on the

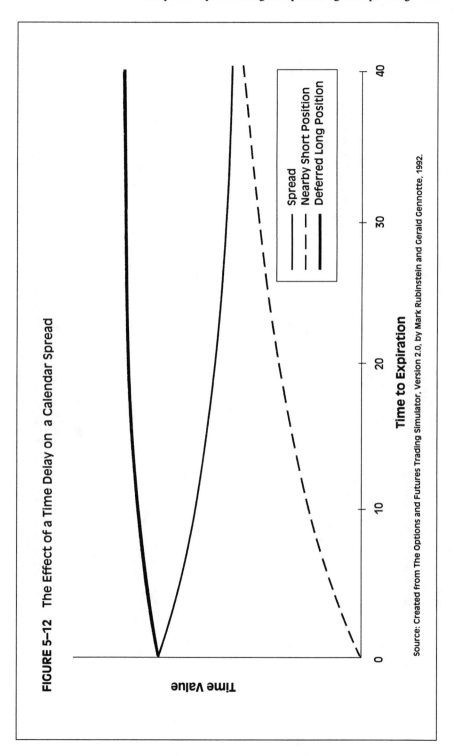

FIGURE 5–12   The Effect of a Time Delay on a Calendar Spread

Source: Created from The Options and Futures Trading Simulator, Version 2.0, by Mark Rubinstein and Gerald Gennotte, 1992.

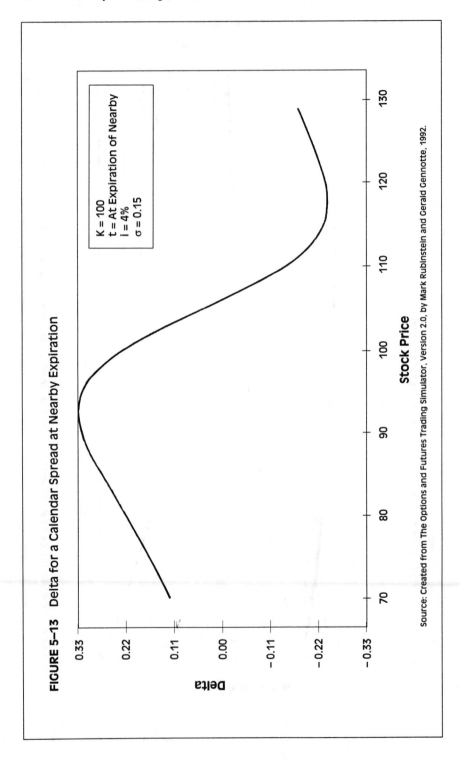

FIGURE 5–13 Delta for a Calendar Spread at Nearby Expiration

K = 100
t = At Expiration of Nearby
i = 4%
σ = 0.15

Stock Price

Delta

Source: Created from The Options and Futures Trading Simulator, Version 2.0, by Mark Rubinstein and Gerald Gennotte, 1992.

old fixed-commission schedule, which charged larger commissions than today's discount brokerage houses. In addition, the variability in the results was quite high, with a standard deviation of 89% for the after-commission results. The returns for the calendar spreads were inferior to simply buying call options, at least for the period covered by this study.[10]

Galai (1977) examines the profitable opportunities for calendar spreads. He finds that when the Black-Scholes model is used to determine an appropriate hedge ratio for the calendar spread, and this hedge ratio is kept for the length of the spread, then the shorter expiration options are *not* overpriced relative to the longer expiration options. However, when the hedge ratio is revised daily, the spreads are consistently profitable. These profits are cut in half when one day elapses between when the hedge ratios are calculated and when the trades are executed, although the results still show a significant level of profitability. Overall, the results for using the Black-Scholes model with option spreads are similar to using the same model with a hedge ratio between the option and the stock.

Strike Price Spreads

Bull Spread. A **bull spread** occurs when the strike price for the purchased option is *lower* than the strike price of the option sold. A bull spread is one type of strike price spread. Spreaders execute strike price spreads either with two call options or with two put options (in either case the trader buys the lower strike and sells the higher strike). The two options have the same expiration and the same underlying stock. An example of a bullish call spread is when a trader purchases a call option with a strike price of 100 and sells a call with a strike price of 110. Strike spreads also are known as money spreads or vertical spreads. The name "vertical spread" derives from the vertical placement of the different strike prices in the newspaper.

The shape of the payoff diagram for a bull spread in Figure 5–14 shows how it received the name bull spread: If the stock price increases, then the spread is profitable, while if the stock price decreases, the spread loses money. Typically, the purchased option is a near-the-money option. This provides the spreader with the opportunity to profit if the stock price increases sufficiently and reduces the loss (compared to an in-the-money option) if the stock price declines.

Figure 5–14 shows that if the stock price at option expiration is equal to or greater than the higher strike price—that is, when the higher strike price is at- or in-the-money—then the maximum profit of the spread is achieved. This maximum profit is due to an increase in the stock price. The size of the maximum profit for a bull spread is:

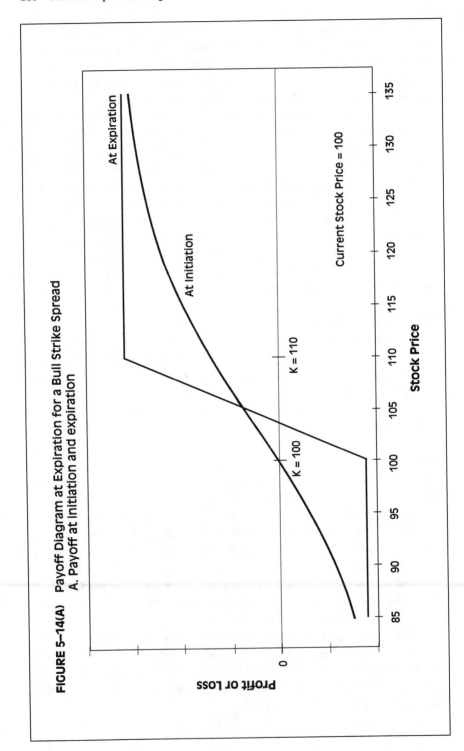

FIGURE 5–14(A)   Payoff Diagram at Expiration for a Bull Strike Spread
A. Payoff at Initiation and expiration

FIGURE 5–14(B)   Payoff Diagram at Expiration for a Bull Strike Spread
B. Components of a bull spread

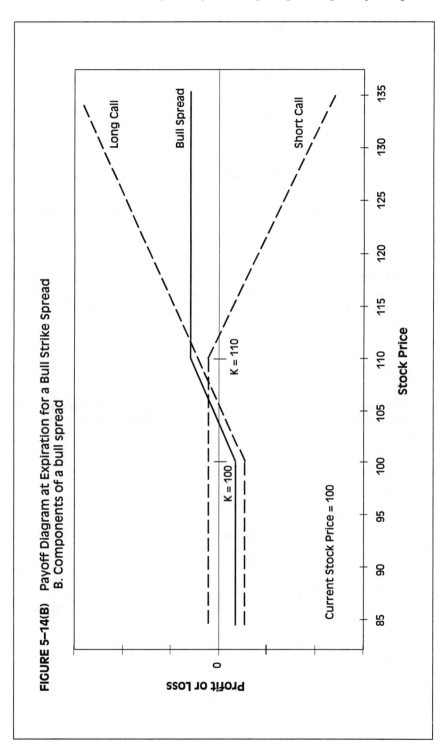

For calls: $\text{Max profit}_{BUS} = (K_H - K_L) - (P_{C,L} - P_{C,H})$ **(5–8)**

For puts: $= P_{P,H} - P_{P,L}$

where Max profit_{BUS} = the maximum profit of a bull spread

K_H = the higher strike price

K_L = the lower strike price

$P_{C,L}$ = the initial call price for the lower strike price option

$P_{C,H}$ = the initial call price for the higher strike price option

$P_{P,H}$ = the initial put price for the higher strike

$P_{P,L}$ = the initial put price for the lower strike

Example 5–3 illustrates a call bull spread.[11]

If the stock price at option expiration is equal to or less than the lower strike price (the lower strike being at- or out-of-the-money), then the bull spread generates the maximum loss possible. The equation that calculates the maximum loss is:

EXAMPLE 5–3   Call Bull Spread

The maximum profit, maximum loss, and profit for a bull spread using calls are found, given a current stock price of 100 and the following information:

For $K = 100$ $P_{C,L} = 5\,1/2$
       $K = 110$ $P_{C,H} = 2$

P_s (at option expiration) $= 107$

Maximum profit:

$$\text{Max profit}_{BUS} = (K_H - K_L) - (P_{C,L} - P_{C,H}) \qquad \textbf{(5–8)}$$

$$= (110 - 100) - (5\,1/2 - 2) = 6\,1/2$$

Maximum loss:

$$\text{Max loss}_{BUS} = P_{C,L} - P_{C,H} \qquad \textbf{(5–9)}$$

$$= 5\,1/2 - 2 = 3\,1/2$$

Profit:

$$\text{Profit}_{BUS} = (P_s - K_L) - (P_{C,L} - P_{C,H}) \qquad \textbf{(5–10)}$$

$$= (107 - 100) - (5\,1/2 - 2) = 3\,1/2$$

For calls: $\text{Max loss}_{\text{BUS}} = P_{C,L} - P_{C,H}$ (5–9)

For puts: $= (K_H - K_L) - (P_{P,H} - P_{P,L})$

Thus, for a call bull spread the maximum loss is the difference between the cost of the two options.

When the *stock price trades between the two strike prices* at option expiration, the spreader obtains either a gain or a loss, depending on the price of the stock.

For calls: $\text{Profit}_{\text{BUS}} = (P_S - K_L) - (P_{C,L} - P_{C,H})$ (5–10)

For puts: $= (P_{P,H} - P_{P,L}) - (K_H - P_S)$

Thus, the profit or loss for a call bull spread (when the ending $P_S > K_L$ and $P_S < K_H$) is equal to the stock price less the lower strike price less the difference between the option prices.

Exhibit 5–4 illustrates the type of information available from the OptionVue Selection function when spreads are chosen. Thus, the best spreads and expected profits are given based on the input criteria. The "Selection" function can also be used for the other strategies given in this chapter.

Bear Spread. A **bear spread** occurs when the strike price for the option purchased is higher than the strike price for the option sold. (This relationship holds for both calls and for puts.) Figure 5–15 shows that a bear spread is profitable when the stock price declines sufficiently, and creates a loss when the stock price increases. If the stock price at option expiration is less than or equal to the lower strike price (the lower strike price is out-of- or at-the-money), then the maximum profit is obtained. In other words, the bear spreader's maximum profits occur when both options expire out-of-the-money. The size of the maximum profit is:

For calls: $\text{Max profit}_{\text{BES}} = P_{C,L} - P_{C,H}$ (5–11)

For puts: $= (K_H - K_L) - (P_{P,H} - P_{P,L})$

where BES = bear spread.

The profit on a call bear spread occurs when the stock price declines sufficiently, because $P_{C,L} > P_{C,H}$ and $P_{C,L}$ is *sold* while $P_{C,H}$ is *purchased.* Comparing Equation (5–11) to Equation (5–9) shows that the maximum profit for a bear spread equals the maximum *loss* for a bull spread. Example 5–4 illustrates a bear put spread.

The maximum loss on a bear spread occurs when the stock price is greater than the higher strike price at option expiration. The size of this maximum loss is:

EXHIBIT 5–4 Selection Function from Optionvue for Bull Strike Price Spreads

SYMBOL: ABC TODAY'S DATE: JAN 01 VALUATION DATE: JAN 01
CAPITAL: $10,000 PRICE: 100 CALL VLTY: 23.0
STRATEGY: Vertical Debit Spreads PUT VLTY: 23.0
TARGET PRICE: Bell curve centered around 104 INTRST: 5.0%
RANKING BASIS: 70% Exp. Ret. / 30% 1st St.Dev.Downside Exp.Ret.

	Recommended Trade							Exp.Ret.	St. Dev.
1.	B	31	Feb100c	@ 3 1/2,	S	31	Feb110c @ 7/16	+3,061	0
2.	B	15	Feb95c	@ 6 5/8,	S	15	Feb110c @ 7/16	+2,981	0
3.	B	109	Feb105c	@ 1 1/4,	S	109	Feb110c @ 7/16	+2,589	0
4.	B	9	Feb90c	@10 7/8,	S	9	Feb110c @ 7/16	+2,295	0
5.	B	17	Feb95c	@ 6 5/8,	S	17	Feb105c @ 1	+1,572	0
6.	B	9	Apr90c	@12 1/4,	S	9	Apr110c @ 1 7/8	+1,507	0
7.	B	10	Feb90c	@10 7/8,	S	10	Feb105c @ 1	+1,425	0
8.	B	14	Apr95c	@ 8 3/4,	S	14	Apr110c @ 1 7/8	+1,295	0
9.	B	10	Apr90c	@12 1/4,	S	10	Apr105c @ 3 1/4	+925	0
10.	B	9	Jul90c	@14 3/4,	S	9	Jul110c @ 4	+607	0
11.	B	12	Feb90c	@10 7/8,	S	12	Feb100c @ 3 1/8	+510	0
12.	B	14	Apr90c	@12 1/4,	S	14	Apr100c @ 5 1/2	+420	0

Source: Developed from OptionVue IV.

FIGURE 5–15   Payoff Diagram at Expiration for a Bear Strike Price Spread

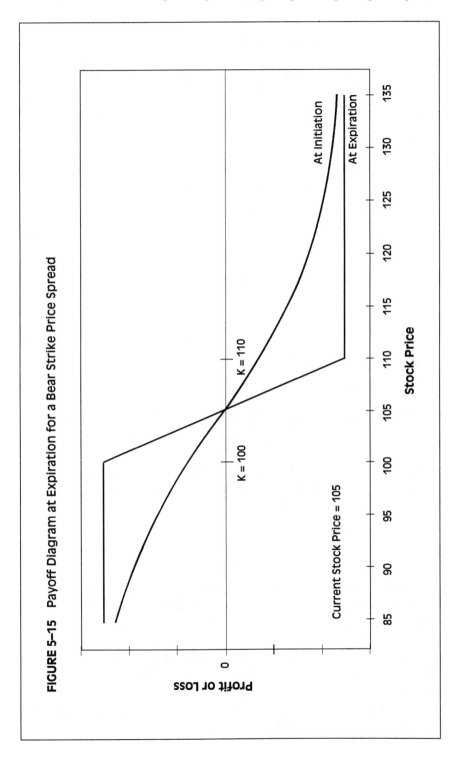

EXAMPLE 5–4 Bear Put Spread

The maximum profit, maximum loss, and profit for a bear spread using puts (when the current stock price is 105) are as follows, given:

For $\quad$ K = 100 $\quad$ $P_{P,L}$ = 3 1/2
$\qquad$ K = 110 $\quad$ $P_{P,H}$ = 8 1/2

P_S (at option expiration) = 108

Maximum profit:

$$\text{Maximum profit} = (K_H - K_L) - (P_{P,H} - P_{P,L}) \qquad \text{(5–11)}$$
$$= (110 - 100) - (8\,1/2 - 3\,1/2) = 5$$

Maximum loss:

$$\text{Maximum loss} = P_{P,H} - P_{P,L} \qquad \text{(5-12)}$$
$$= 8\,1/2 - 3\,1/2 = 5$$

Profit:

$$\text{Profit} = (K_H - P_S) - (P_{P,H} - P_{P,L}) \qquad \text{(5–13)}$$
$$= (110 - 108) - (8\,1/2 - 3\,1/2) = -3$$

For calls: $\qquad$ $\text{Max loss}_{BES} = (K_H - K_L) - (P_{C,L} - P_{C,H})$ $\qquad$ **(5–12)**

For puts: $\qquad\qquad\qquad = P_{P,H} - P_{P,L}$

This equation is equivalent to the maximum profit equation for a bull spread. The profit for a bear spread when the *stock price trades between the two strike prices* at option expiration is:

For calls: $\qquad$ $\text{Profit}_{BES} = (P_{C,L} - P_{C,H}) - (P_S - K_L)$ $\qquad$ **(5–13)**

For puts: $\qquad\qquad\qquad = (K_H - P_S) - (P_{P,H} - P_{P,L})$

Butterfly Spreads. A **butterfly spread** is a combination of a bull spread and a bear spread that involves three strike prices. To create a butterfly spread, a trader purchases an option with a low strike price and an option with a high strike price and sells two options with an intermediate strike prices. Equivalently, one creates a butterfly spread with a bull spread and a bear spread, and netting out the difference.[12] Figure 5–16 illustrates a butterfly spread. The shape of this graph is similar to the calendar spread shown in Figure 5–11. It is also similar to the shape of a straddle, except that a butterfly spread has a limited loss feature.[13]

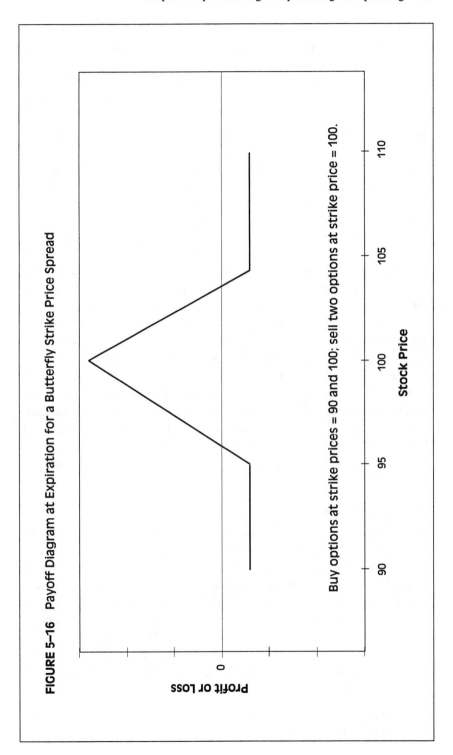

FIGURE 5–16   Payoff Diagram at Expiration for a Butterfly Strike Price Spread

Buy options at strike prices = 90 and 100; sell two options at strike price = 100.

Pricing Sensitivities of Strike Price Spreads. Figure 5–17 shows the delta for a bull strike price spread in relation to the stock price and volatility values. The greatest option price sensitivity occurs near the higher strike price, with delta moving toward zero for deep-in-the-money and deep-out-of-the-money options. Figure 5–18 illustrates the gamma of a strike price spread in relation to the stock price and volatility values. This figure shows that delta has the largest positive change near the lower strike price and the largest negative change near the higher strike price.

Evidence. Gombola, Roenfeldt, and Cooley (1978) find that bullish strike price spreads earned average rates of return of 6.5%, 22.5%, and 44% before commissions for three-, six-, and nine-month spread positions. In general, the percentage losses for the bull spreads during market declines were larger than the profits earned when the market increased, but a larger number of bull spread opportunities created the net positive profits. During market declines, 85 percent to 100 percent of the bull spreads lost money, while during market advances, only 23 percent to 28 percent of the spreads generated negative returns. After commissions, the returns from the bull spreads fell to –10.2 percent, 3.3 percent, and 23.5 percent for the three-, six- and nine-month strategies. The superior nine-month results in this study may be linked to the bull market during the time period in question.

Before commissions, the bull spread returns were significantly higher than the returns for simply buying calls, but the bull spreads no longer dominated buying call options after commissions. In addition, the bull spread strategy had large standard deviations—115 percent, 126 percent, and 108 percent after commissions. The bear spread results were much worse than the bull spreads because of the dominant upward market during the time period analyzed.

Pricing Spreads

Pricing spreads is an important topic for off-the-floor traders. Since spread profits are sensitive to relatively small mispricings of the relevant options, some spreaders decide on which option transactions to initiate based on mispricings alone. When examining potential mispricings of spreads, traders must take care to evaluate *both* sides of the spread. On many occasions, if one option is mispriced, other options on the same stock have similar "mispricings." In effect, these "mispricings" simply show that the implied volatility measures for these options differ from the estimate of the volatility used in the option model. In order to make a meaningful comparison of option prices using implied volatility, keep in mind that:

- Options with different *expirations* can have different annualized implied volatilities.

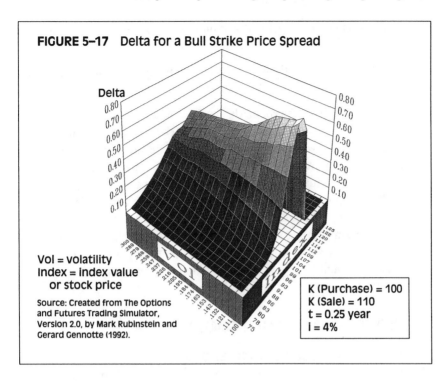

FIGURE 5–17   Delta for a Bull Strike Price Spread

Vol = volatility
Index = index value
   or stock price

Source: Created from The Options
and Futures Trading Simulator,
Version 2.0, by Mark Rubinstein and
Gerard Gennotte (1992).

K (Purchase) = 100
K (Sale) = 110
t = 0.25 year
i = 4%

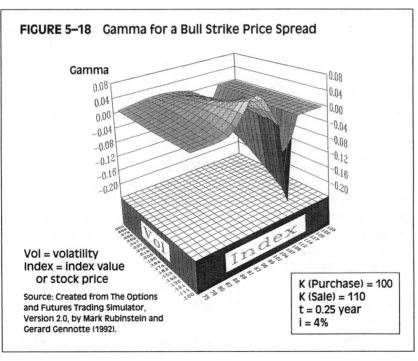

FIGURE 5–18   Gamma for a Bull Strike Price Spread

Vol = volatility
Index = index value
   or stock price

Source: Created from The Options
and Futures Trading Simulator,
Version 2.0, by Mark Rubinstein and
Gerard Gennotte (1992).

K (Purchase) = 100
K (Sale) = 110
t = 0.25 year
i = 4%

- The near-the-money, nearby option typically has the best estimate of the actual future stock volatility.

- Differences in the timing of the last trade for different options create different implied volatilities for the various options.

Calendar spreads are particularly sensitive to a mispricing of the nearby option. Unfortunately, in this case it is difficult to compare the implied volatilities of the two options, since they possess different expirations. Other option spread combinations can be profitable when the trader believes the market is using an inappropriate volatility value in the option pricing formula. Thus, inappropriate implied volatilities are also a possible cause of a mispriced option, although this type of mispricing is more difficult to determine with certainty. For example, a calendar spread is initiated when a trader believes the stock price will be stable over the time period of the spread, which is equivalent to saying that the option market is overestimating the volatility of the stock in pricing the option.

A SUMMARY AND OTHER COMBINATIONS

Summarizing Spread Combinations

Exhibit 5–5 summarizes the information on straddles and spreads discussed in this chapter. This exhibit shows which options are purchased/sold to create a given straddle/spread, and under what circumstances each position generates a profit or loss. This exhibit, in conjunction with the payoff diagrams for each spread combination, provides the basic information needed to understand the characteristics of the most widely used straddle and spread positions. Exhibit 5–6 summarizes the pricing sensitivities for these options transactions, with the sensitivities of a call and put given for comparison purposes.

Other Spreads and Option Combinations

Exhibit 5–7 provides summary information on spreads that are used less frequently by traders. These option positions are given in summary form because they are less popular than the other strategies and/or they provide payoff diagrams that are equivalent to the combinations discussed above.

Perhaps the most interesting strategies given in Exhibit 5–7 are the strap and the strip. These spread combinations provide greater leverage than other option positions, since more options are bought than sold, or vice versa. Figure 5–19 shows a strap before and at option expiration, and a straddle at expiration. The figure shows that the strap is similar to a straddle, except that the strap has greater upside leverage and loses more than a straddle if the

EXHIBIT 5–5   Summary of Spread Strategies

		Call		Put	
	Strike	**Jan**	**Feb**	**Jan**	**Feb**
Stock A (P = 100)	95	B	C	D	E
	100	F	G	H	I
	105	J	K	L	M

Name of Strategy	**Combination of Options Needed***	**Profit**	**Loss**
Straddle purchase	Buy F and H	Large increases or decreases in A	Small changes in A
Straddle sale	Sell F and H	Small changes in A	Large changes in A
Calendar spread	Sell F and buy G (or sell H and buy I)	Small changes in A, profit due to faster time decay for F	Large or moderate change in A
Reverse calendar spread	Buy F and sell G	Large change in A (profit limited)	Small change in A
Bull strike price spread	Buy F and sell J (or buy H and sell L)	A increases moderately	A decreases or remains same
Bear strike price spread	Buy F and sell B (or buy H and sell D)	A declines moderately	A increases or remains same
Butterfly spread	Buy B and J, sell 2 F	Small changes in A	Large changes in A (but limited loss)

* Often many different combinations are relevant. Only one combination is given here.

stock declines in price. Both of these features of a strap are due to the fact that the trader buys two call options and one put option. On the other hand, the strip combination involves buying one call option and two puts. Thus, a strip is more profitable than a straddle when stock prices decline, while the upside performance of a strip is inferior to a straddle.

Choosing a Strategy and Follow-Up Strategies

The initial option strategy employed by a speculator depends on the speculator's forecast of the direction of the market and any change in volatility. Exhibit 5–8 shows the appropriate strategies for each combination of market direction and volatility.

Once a strategy is implemented, a change in the forecast of market direction or volatility requires a change in the option position. For example,

EXHIBIT 5–6   The Relationship Between Pricing Sensitivities and Option Strategies

Strategy	At Initiation		
	Delta	Gamma	Theta
Buy a call	+	+	−
Buy a put	−	+	−
Straddle purchase: buy both a call and a put	0	+	−
Straddle sale: sell both a call and a put	0	−	+
Calendar spread: sell shorter expiration, buy longer expiration	0	−	+
Reverse calendar spread: buy shorter expiration, sell longer expiration	0	+	−
Bull strike price spread: buy higher strike, sell lower strike	+	0	0
Bear strike price spread: buy lower strike, sell higher strike	−	0	0
Butterfly spread: sell two near-the-money calls, buy one in-the-money call and one out-of-the-money call	0	−	+

if a call is originally purchased, Exhibit 5–9 shows how to change the position based on market direction and volatility. *Futures and Options Strategy Guide* by the CMEX provides such exhibits for the other speculative and spreading positions.

SUMMARY AND LOOKING AHEAD

This chapter discusses speculating and spreading with options. Buying options provides speculators with leverage, as well as limiting the loss on the position to the cost of the option. However, option speculators lose money the majority of the time. This chapter also discusses the strategies related to spreading. Spreading allows the trader to reduce the risk and net cost of the position by taking partially offsetting option positions, but it also limits the upside potential. In addition, spread results adversely suffer from large commission charges. The following chapter examines hedging with options.

EXHIBIT 5–7   Summary of Other Option Strategies

		Call		Put	
	Strike	Jan	Feb	Jan	Feb
Stock A (P = 100)	95	B	C	D	E
	100	F	G	H	I
	105	J	K	L	M

Name of Strategy	Combination of Options Needed*	Profit	Loss
Strap	Buy 2 F and 1 H	Greater upside leverage than straddle	Greater cost than a straddle (greater loss if A declines)
Strip	Buy 1 F and 2 H	Greater downside leverage than a straddle	Greater cost than a straddle (greater loss if A increases)
Diagonal bull spread	Buy G and sell J	If A increases moderately, preferably changing later	A declines or remains the same
Box spread	Buy F and sell J Buy L and sell H	When options are mispriced	If commissions are too high
Option hedge	Buy A, sell 2 F	Like selling a straddle	Large change in A
Reverse option hedge	Sell A, buy 2 F	Like buying a straddle	Small change in A

* Often many different combinations are relevant. Only one combination is given here.

END NOTES

[1] In fact, the large average positive returns during the up market period were influenced by some very large gains for the profitable trades, with 12% of the positions having a return in excess of 100%. Commissions reduced the average returns by 4% to 6%. The results from this study seem to be sensitive to the time period studied, since Roenfeldt, Cooley, and Gombola (1979) use the same procedure with six months' less data to determine an average return from buying options of −11%. The up and down market average returns were 50.1% and −67.6% before commissions and taxes. After commissions and taxes the average returns were −18.1%, 12.0%, and −45.6 percent for the overall, up, and down market periods.

Trennepohl and Dukes (1979) employ weekly prices for a similar time period, showing that purchasing call options with three months to expiration results in an average loss of 7% per week and 48% per option contract. In fact, Trennepohl and Dukes find that even in *bull* markets, three-month call options lose 20% of their annualized purchase

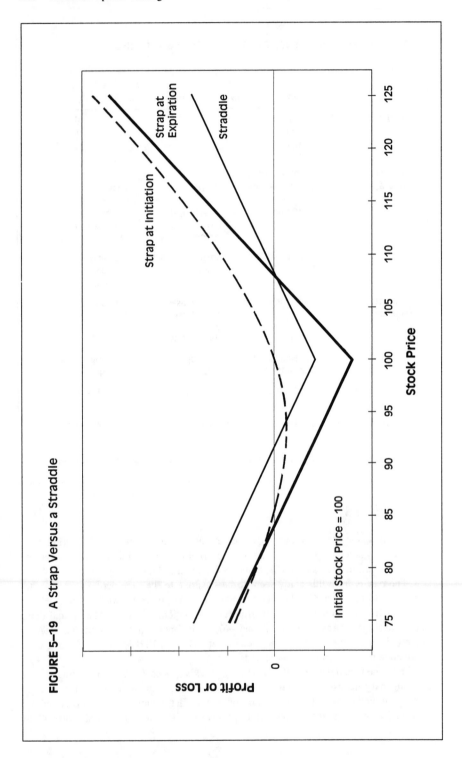

FIGURE 5–19   A Strap Versus a Straddle

EXHIBIT 5–8   Initiating a Market Position with Options

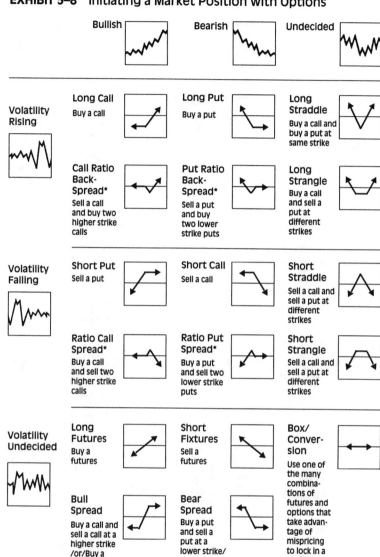

*All ratio spreads and ratio backspreads need more analysis. These strategies do not fit neatly into any of the nine market scenarios. Define your market expectation more closely and work out examples with different market scenarios before choosing these strategies. Also, ratio strategies are sometimes done at ratios other than one by two.

Source: Chicago Mercantile Exchange, *Futures and Options Strategy Guide*, p. 1.

EXHIBIT 5–9   Follow-up Strategies to Buying a Call Option

Bullish Bearish Undecided

Volatility Rising

Long Call
Hold on

Long Put
Sell a futures

Long Straddle
Buy a put at same strike

Long Strangle
Buy a put at a different strike

Volatility Falling

Short Put
Sell a put

Short Call
Sell two calls (one liquidates original call)

Short Straddle
Sell two calls (one liquidates original call) and sell a put at same strike

Ratio Call Spread*
Sell two higher strike calls

Short Strangle
Sell two calls (one liquidates original call) and sell a put at a different strike

Volatility Undecided

Bull Spread
Sell a higher strike call

Bear Spread
Sell a lower strikecall

Liquidate position

Long Futures
Sell a put at same strike

*All ratio spreads and ratio backspreads need more analysis. These strategies do not fit neatly into any of the nine market scenarios. Define your market expectation more closely and work out examples with different market scenarios before choosing these strategies. Also, ratio strategies are sometimes done at ratios other than one by two.

Source: Chicago Mercantile Exchange, *Futures and Options Strategy Guide*, p. 11.

value. Of course, such a loss occurs because the decay in the time value of the option is greater than the gain from any stock price increase.

[2] The volatility input to the option pricing model is determined by calculating the volatility over the previous six months.

[3] Gastineau (1979) and Gastineau and Madansky (1979) claim that other factors besides the time period cause these results, and state the following criticisms of the Merton et al. study:

- The option prices used in the study are 20% to 28% too low because of the model employed to calculate the price, which causes the returns for buying call options to be too high.

- The interest rates used in the model are too low, affecting the return by about two percentage points.

- The volatility value used in the model is too low. Since volatility increased over the period in question, this caused the option price to be too low, as the historical volatility would be less than the implied volatility.

- The method of creating the portfolios generates a bias toward higher-volatility stocks for in-the-money options and lower-volatility stocks for at-the-money and out-of-the-money options. This procedure significantly improves the performance of these strategies, since the time period and an increase in volatility are beneficial. Gastineau states that this criticism is the most important factor affecting the Merton et al. results.

[4] If the put seller wishes to execute a "covered" position to offset a potential price decline below the strike price, then the put seller must sell the stock short. The effect of generating a covered position becomes more evident when hedging with options is examined.

[5] The payoff diagrams for the strategies presented in this chapter show the resultant relationships between the stock price and the profit on the option spread position. Each spread is a combination of two option positions. Thus, one can develop the payoff diagram for any spread position simply by drawing the payoff diagram for the two separate option positions and combining these graphs. The individual option positions are not shown on these payoff diagrams in order to simplify the graphs and to concentrate on the characteristics of the spread transaction.

[6] Alternatively, a trader can "leg-in" or "leg-out" of a spread; this simply means a trader executes one side of a spread at one time and the other side at a later time. This procedure increases the risk of the spread. The spreader must also be aware of the potential early exercise of one side of the spread.

[7] A similar but alternative approach is to sell part of the total position when multiple contracts are held. This strategy reduces the potential total loss, while still allowing gains when a stock price either increases or decreases.

[8] Another way of describing this strategy is a positive gamma with a $\delta = 0$. *However, a strategy with a positive gamma and a non-zero delta would not be profitable for any stock price change.*

[9] Calendar spreads also are created with a combination of put options. In general, put calendar spreads are equivalent to call spreads, but differences can occur due to either a slight mispricing or early exercise of the puts.

[10] This study employed the pre-1975 fixed commission schedule to determine the commission rates. Current discount brokerage house commissions and/or reduced rates from volume transactions can be more beneficial to the spreader than the pre-1975 rates. On the other hand, option prices in the early years of the CBOE often were mispriced, and the use of end-of-day quotes often caused timing problems. These factors make the profitability of studies using such data biased upward. A more accurate method to determine potential profits would be to use bid-ask quotes.

[11] Alternatively, the maximum profit (if it exists) for a call bull spread is simply the difference between the two intrinsic values of the options at expiration minus the difference in the costs.

[12] In order to create a bull spread, one buys a call with the lower strike price and sells a call with a middle strike price. A bear spread is created by buying a call with a high strike price and selling a call with a middle strike price. One can now analyze the profit situation for the butterfly spread by examining each separate spread and combining the results.

[13] The terminology varies. Some authors call this option combination a sandwich spread. A butterfly spread then becomes the *sale* of the high and low strike price options and the *purchase* of the two options with intermediate strike prices. The payoff diagram for this latter description is the mirror image of Figure 5–14—the graph is "flipped over," with the point of the graph showing the maximum loss possible.

6

The purpose of hedging strategies is to reduce downside risk. In addition, using options to implement hedging strategies achieves risk-return characteristics that are not available when other hedging strategies are undertaken. Two basic option hedging strategies are selling a call option while buying/owning the stock, and buying a put option while owning the stock. Selling the call and buying stock is a popular institutional strategy called covered option writing. This strategy reduces the downside risk moderately, while providing the hedger with an income equal to the price of the option. However, covered call writing eliminates most of the upside potential of the stock. Evidence concerning this strategy shows that its risk-return characteristics are often superior to owning the stock or speculating in options. Another hedging strategy, buying a put while owning the stock, protects the hedger from a decline in the price of the stock while keeping the upside potential intact. This protection creates a cost to the hedger, this cost being the price of the put.

COVERED OPTION WRITING

The Concepts

Covered option writing involves the sale of a call option and the ownership of the underlying stock, with the covered writer receiving the option price from the buyer when the option is *sold*. Covered option writing is often referred to as a covered call. A simple example of a covered call is when a stock is purchased at 100 and an at-the-money call option is sold for a price of 4. If the stock price is above 100 at option expiration, then a profit of 4 is made on the transaction.

The payoff diagram shown in Figure 6–1 illustrates the basic characteristics, advantages, and disadvantages of this **hedging** procedure. The dashed line in Figure 6–1 represents the stock-only position, which is useful for comparison purposes. The solid line shows the payoff diagram for a covered call initiated with a strike price of K, with the stock being purchased at price K. Three important points are highlighted in the graph:

- The maximum profit for a covered call when the stock is purchased at the strike price is the price of the call option.

- The stock-only and covered call graphs cross when the option price equals the profit on the stock-only position. When the stock price is greater than this value, the stock-only position provides greater profits, and vice versa.

- The break-even of the covered call occurs at the stock price less the call option price. This break-even occurs at a price that is <u>less</u> than the corresponding break-even for the stock.

A covered call is like "selling insurance": The writer receives a premium to protect the call option buyer from a decline in price. Another way to think of covered calls is in terms of replicating the position with a dynamic stock position. In this case, the hedger would *decrease* the number of shares as stock prices rise, and increase the number of shares as prices decline. Figure 6–2 shows how the payoff diagrams for a long stock position and selling a call combine to make the payoff diagram of a covered call. Thus, if one adds the profits/losses of the two individual positions shown by the dashed lines in Figure 6–2, one obtains the covered call position shown by the solid line. The advantages and disadvantages of covered calls are explained in more detail below.

Advantages. The advantages of covered call writing are:

- Covered writing reduces the potential downside loss when compared to a stock-only position. For example, when the stock is bought at 100 and a call with a strike price of 100 is sold for 4, the covered call reduces the downside loss by 4 points. This protection occurs because the seller receives the call option price.

- Writing call options that are overpriced increases the option income received, although the writer must consider whether the higher time value is simply reflecting a higher volatility for the stock.

- The option writer keeps any dividends issued on the stock before the option is exercised.

Disadvantages. The disadvantages of covered call writing are:

- The option writer does *not* participate in any *stock price gains* above the strike price since the stock is called away at the strike price by the option buyer. Thus, covered option writing provides inferior profits to the stock-only position when the stock price rises to a point above the strike price plus the time value. In other words, a covered writer

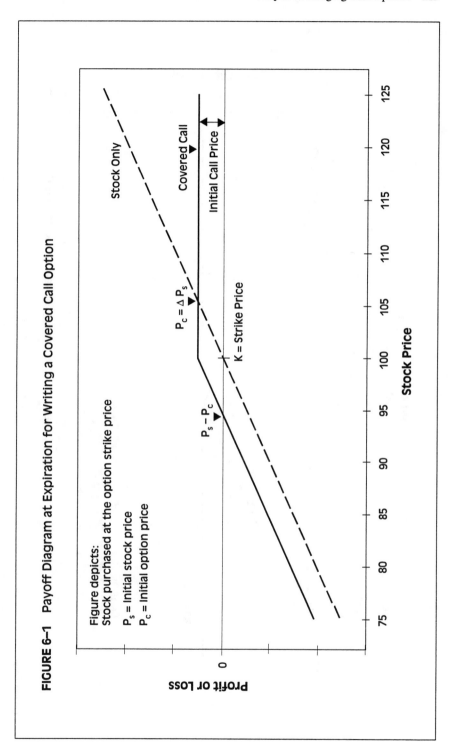

FIGURE 6–1 Payoff Diagram at Expiration for Writing a Covered Call Option

Figure depicts:
Stock purchased at the option strike price

P_s = Initial stock price
P_c = Initial option price

Stock Only

Covered Call

Initial Call Price

$P_c = \Delta P_s$

$P_s - P_c$

K = Strike Price

Stock Price

Profit or Loss

0

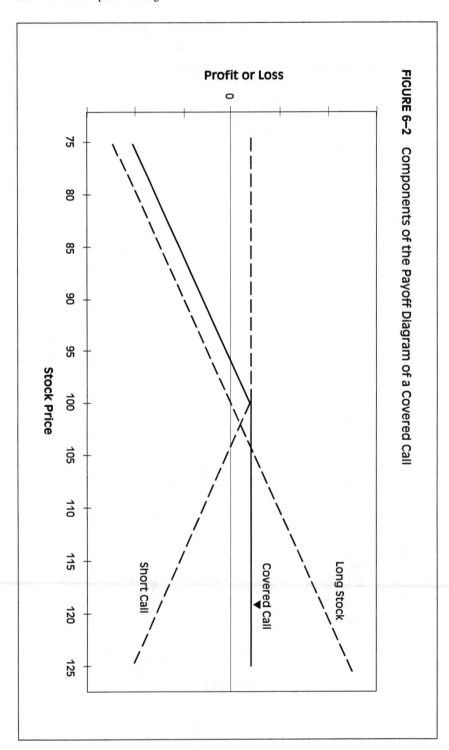

FIGURE 6–2   Components of the Payoff Diagram of a Covered Call

experiences an **opportunity loss** when the stock price increases significantly above the strike price. For our example, this occurs at any price above 104—that is, the strike price of 100 plus the time value of 4. Consequently, traders who can correctly forecast major upward moves for stocks on a consistent basis, while simultaneously avoiding losers, should not include call option writing as a strategy for their portfolios.

- Retail commissions eliminate most of the profits generated by covered writing positions executed by individuals.

An Example. Covered option writing reduces downside risk and provides income to the writer. Therefore, option writing is superior to a stock-only strategy if prices decline or if stocks trade in a relatively narrow price range. The disadvantage of option writing is that it is inferior to owning the stock when prices increase significantly, as occurred from 1982 to 1987 and during certain periods in the early 1990s. Example 6–1 shows the components of an in-the-money covered call transaction. Notice that the projected return for the example depends *only* on the stock price remaining above the strike price.

The Relationships for Covered Writing

The following discussions elaborate on the break-even point, profits, and losses for covered option writing in the more general case when the initial stock price does not equal the strike price:

- The break-even point for a covered call at option expiration exists at the point where the stock price is equal to the original stock price minus the original option price, as shown by Equation (6–1) (ignoring dividends):

$$BE_{CC} = P_S - P_C \qquad (6\text{--}1)$$

where BE_{CC} = the break-even point for the covered call
P_C = the price of the call option when it is originally sold— the proceeds from the sale of the call option
P_S = the price of the stock purchased when the call is sold

A profit for the covered call occurs whenever the stock price at option expiration is above this break-even point. Example 6–2 illustrates the break-even and other equations given in this section.

- The maximum profit for selling a covered call that was originally at-the-money occurs when the stock trades at or above the strike price at option expiration. The size of this maximum profit in this situation

EXAMPLE 6–1   An Example of Covered Call Writing

The following represents actual prices for an at-the-money covered call position:

Buy IBM stock 2/25	$51.75
Sell July 70 call (receive funds 2/25)	– 5.125
Net cost per share	$46.625

Since the writer receives the option price at the initiation of the trade, it is often considered a reduction in the net cost of the combined stock/option covered call position, as shown above. The break-even point on this position is 46 $5/8$, or a 9.9% downside protection from 51 $3/4$. The option expires in 141 days (4 $3/4$ months).

The maximum potential profit on the position is:

Stock sold via exercise of option	$50.00
Net cost of position	– 46.625
Gain from stock/option position	3.375
Dividend received (5/7)	+ .54
Total profit per share	3.915

The annualized rate of return on the covered call strategy is:

Return = (Profit/Net cost) (365/Number of days position held)
Return = (3.915/46.525) (365/141)
= 21.8%

equals the option price received. The writer of an *out-of-the-money* option benefits from any positive stock price change up to the strike price. In general, the maximum profit for a covered call is given in Equation (6–2):

$$\text{Max Profit}_{cc} = P_c - (P_s - K) \qquad (6\text{–}2)$$

where Max Profit$_{cc}$ = the maximum profit from a covered call position

Any dividends per share received while the covered position is held increase the maximum profit.

Equation (6–3) states the *net* profit (loss) from a covered call position:

$$\text{Profit}_{cc} = P_c + \text{Min}[\Delta P_s, K - P_s] \qquad (6\text{–}3)$$

where Profit$_{cc}$ = the profit on the covered call position
ΔP_s = the change in the price of the stock over the life of the option

EXAMPLE 6–2   Covered Call Break-even, Maximum Profits, and Profits

The following illustrates Equations (6–1) through (6–4) to calculate the break-even, maximum profits, and profits for a covered call position, given:

$P_s = 98$ P_s (at option expiration) $= 99$ $P_c = 1\,^1/_2$
$K = 100$ $t = 90$ days

Break-even:
$$BE_{cc} = P_s - P_c \tag{6–1}$$
$$= 98 - 1\,^1/_2 = 96\,^1/_2$$

Maximum profit:
$$\text{Max Profit}_{cc} = P_c - (P_s - K) \tag{6–2}$$
$$= 1\,^1/_2 - (98 - 100) = 3\,^1/_2$$

Profit:
$$\text{Profit}_{cc} = P_c + \text{Min}[\Delta P_s, K - P_s] \tag{6–3}$$
$$= 1\,^1/_2 + \text{Min}[+1, 100 - 98]$$
$$= 1\,^1/_2 + 1 = 2\,^1/_2$$

Annual return:
$$\text{Annual return} = [\text{Profit}_{cc}/(P_s - P_c)]\,(365/\text{Number of days position held}) \tag{6–4}$$
$$= [2\,^1/_2/(100 - 1\,^1/_2)]\,(365/90)$$
$$= 10.3\%$$

Again, dividends received increase the profits for a covered call. The annualized rate of return then can be obtained by Equation (6–4):

$$\text{Annual Return} = [\text{Profit}_{cc} / (P_s - P_c)]\,(365/\text{Number of Days Position Held}) \tag{6–4}$$

• In order to increase the likelihood of a profit (the stock trading above the covered call break-even point), analysis of the stock and/or market should eliminate potential "losers" from consideration. This strategy differs from typical security analysis, which attempts to pick winners.

• The option writer suffers a *net* loss if the stock price falls below the break-even point for the covered call—that is, a loss occurs if the stock falls below the original stock price by more than the price of the option. However, losses on the covered call position are less than losses on the stock-only position.

- Figure 6–3 illustrates an alternative way to conceptualize the payoffs of the covered call strategy by using a probability curve. This figure shows that covered calls truncate the upside return at the maximum return of the covered call—namely, 18% for this hypothetical example. However, it also shows that the probability of obtaining an 18% return is 70%.

Exhibit 6–1 shows the OptionVue Matrix when covered calls are employed. Here 300 shares of ABC stock are purchased and options on the 95, 100, and 105 strikes are sold. The deltas for the long stock (1.00) minus the short option (– 0.717, – 0.564, and – 0.408, respectively) show that covered writing using in-the-money options is a conservative strategy with a net delta of – 0.283, while an out-of-the-money covered call is more risky with a delta of – 0.592. The bottom summary of the OptionVue Matrix screen gives the delta, gamma, vega, and theta of the *combined* positions (in this case, long 300 shares and short 3 call options with different strike prices).

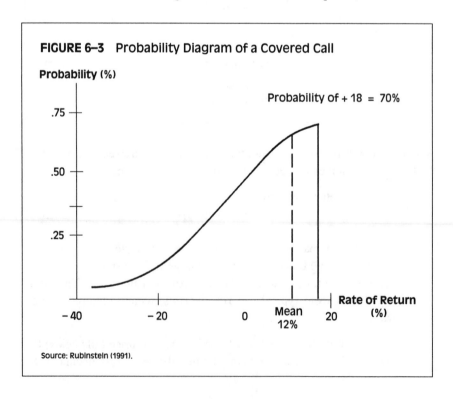

FIGURE 6–3 Probability Diagram of a Covered Call

Source: Rubinstein (1991).

Exhibit 6–1   OptionVue Matrix for Covered Calls

ACTUALS

├ ABC COM ┤
100   +300
1.00   300

OPTIONS

	├ FEB (31) ┤		├ APR (90) ┤		├ JUL (181) ┤		├ OCT (273) ┤	
CALLS	6 1/4	———	8 1/2	–1	11	———	13 1/4	———
95	.788		.717	– 71.7	.699		.698	
CALLS	3 1/8	———	5 5/8	–1	8 1/4	———	10 1/2	———
100	.538		.564	– 56.4	.591		.611	
CALLS	1 1/4	———	3 3/8	–1	6	———	8 1/8	———
105	.283		.408	– 40.8	.481		.522	

SUMMARY

Orig. Reqmt: $15,250   Commis: $0.00   Delta: +131.0 AvgMIV: 25.2%
Maint. Reqmt: $10,475   Gamma: – 9.03   Calls: 25.2%
      Cash Flow: –$30,000 Theta: +$9.87/day Vega: –56.1   Puts: ———

Format of numbers with each option/stock ABC:

    (1) price   (3) long/short position

    (2) delta   (4) position delta

Options are sold on the April 95, 100, and 105 calls (one each). Three hundred common shares ("Actuals") are purchased. The summary section shows the net position delta, position gamma, position vega, and the per-day theta.

Source: Developed using OptionVue IV.

Covered Option Writing: Strategies and Implementation

The Strategies. The strategies and types of participants for covered option writing differ, depending on whether the hedger sells an out-of-the-money or in-the-money call option. Figure 6–4 illustrates the payoff diagrams for in-the-money, at-the-money, and out-of-the-money covered calls—that is, the graphs show the effects of using differing strike prices. Out-of-the-money options are written by individuals and funds preferring to keep the stock and/or wishing to benefit from a stock price increase up to the strike price. Since the writer must pay a stock commission when the call option is exercised, writing out-of-the-money calls reduces the likelihood that such a commission will be required. Out-of-the-money covered writing also produces a larger overall profit than an in-the-money strategy when the stock price

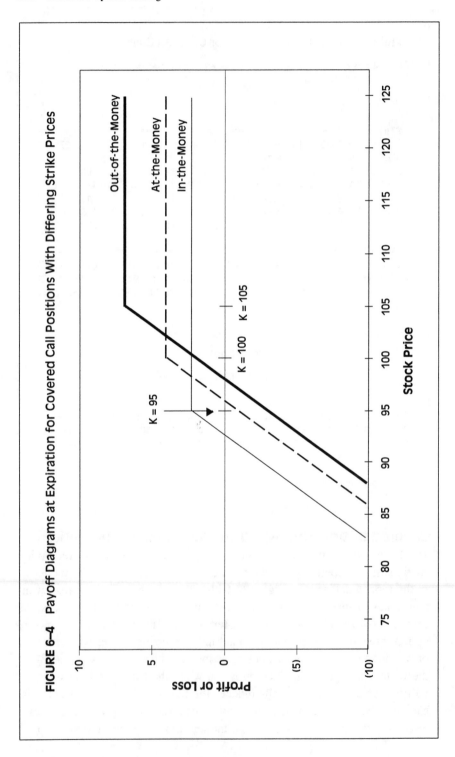

FIGURE 6–4 Payoff Diagrams at Expiration for Covered Call Positions With Differing Strike Prices

EXAMPLE 6–3   Comparing In-the-Money and Out-of-the-Money Covered Calls

To compare an in-the-money covered call to an out-of-the-money position, we continue our use of IBM calls. Here, the shorter-term April options with 50 days until expiration are employed to examine the various scenarios. The April 50 options sell for 3 3/4, while the April 55 calls sell for 1 1/2. No dividends are received before the April option expires.

Net cost of the options:	April 50	April 55	
Buy IBM stock 2/25	$51.75	$51.75	
Sell April call (receive funds 2/25)	– 3.75	– 1.50	
Net cost per share	$48.00	$50.25	

The maximum potential profit on the position is:

	April 50	April 55	April 55
	$P_s > 50$	no ΔP	$P_s > 55$
Stock sold via exercise of option	$50.00	—	– $55.00
Net cost of position	– 48.00	—	50.25
Gain from stock/option position	2.00	1.50	4.75
Return	30.4%	21.8%	69.0%

The benefits of using an out-of-the-money strategy are (1) the stock is not called away if the stock price remains below the strike price, saving on stock commissions, and (2) if the stock price does increase, the profit on the covered call increases.

increases sufficiently. This is because the out-of-the-money strategy profits both from the reception of the option price *and* from the stock price increase up to the strike price. The disadvantages of writing out-of-the-money calls are that a smaller downside protection exists in relation to an in-the-money strategy, the maximum potential profits are relatively small if the stock does not increase in price, and covered writing in general is inferior to a stock-only strategy for major stock price increases. Example 6–3 compares in-the-money and out-of-the-money covered calls.

An in-the-money covered call strategy is often executed by institutional funds that pay minimal commissions due to large block trading. These small commissions allow the funds to deliver the stock on a consistent basis without adversely affecting the net return from the strategy. In this case, the fund manager expects that the stock will be called away by the option buyer, with the return obtained from the time value plus dividends being larger than the return from a stock-only strategy when there is a stable or declining market. Since the option is in-the-money when initiated, the likelihood of option exercise is much greater than for an out-of-the-money covered call. This larger probability of exercise tends to stabilize the income from writing calls from one period to another. The principal disadvantage of writing in-the-money calls is the lower returns for this strategy in comparison to a stock-only position when a major price increase occurs.

Commissions. Commissions are a major factor affecting the potential profitability of covered option writing. Institutions trading 5000- or 10,000-share blocks of the stock and option typically pay a total of only 10 cents per share *round trip* for all stock and option commissions. Individuals who trade 100 shares at a time through a retail broker pay $1.50 or more per share round trip. Consequently, an annual rate of return of 24% generated by writing three-month in-the-money call options by an institution is reduced to 7% to 13% for an individual who pays retail commissions and only trades 100 shares at a time.

One method individual option writers use to reduce commissions is to use discount brokers, often in conjunction with trading several hundred shares at one time. However, one must take care to select a discount broker who provides executions at good market prices, since option writing returns are sensitive to small changes in the prices obtained for the stock and option transactions.[1] Another approach individuals employ to reduce stock commissions is to write out-of-the-money options, since a stock sale and commission are not required if the option is not exercised. Example 6–4 compares the effects of commissions for in-the-money and out-of-the-money covered calls for institutions and individuals.

A third approach is to leverage positions in order to increase the income from selling the options. In other words, the writer buys *twice* as many shares of the relevant stock by buying the stock on margin, while also selling twice as many call options. This procedure often is transacted in conjunction with selling out-of-the-money calls. In fact, if the stock price does increase, then the option writer receives the best of both worlds: additional option income *and* additional profits from the stock price increase. These profits are much greater than the interest paid on the money borrowed on margin. On the other hand, if the stock price *declines,* the option writer has both a loss on twice as many shares of stock *and* the cost of the margin funds, with only the option price and dividends as income. Consequently, this procedure generates leverage that subverts the lower risk characteristic of the typical covered option strategy.

Implementing Covered Writing. Covered call option writing has become the most popular option strategy for pension funds and specialized

EXAMPLE 6–4 The Effect of Commissions on Covered Calls

Using the information from Example 6–2, the following compares the effect of differing commissions for institutions and individuals on covered calls.

		Individuals	
	Institutions	Full-Service Broker	Discount Broker
For 100-share trades for individuals:			
Profits per share before commissions	$4.455	$4.455	$4.455
Commissions (buy/sell stock and options)	–0.10	–2.08	–0.98
Profits after commissions	4.355	2.365	3.475
Annualized return before commissions	24.8%	24.8%	24.8%
Annualized return after commissions	24.2%	13.2%	19.3%
For 1000-share trades for individuals:			
Profits per share before commissions	$4.455	$4.455	$4.455
Commissions (buy/sell stock and options)	–0.10	–1.43	–0.35
Profits after commissions	4.355	3.025	4.005
Annualized return after commissions	24.2%	16.8%	22.2%
Break-even protection:			
100-share individual trade	9.7%	5.8%	8.0%
1000-share individual trade	9.7%	7.1%	9.2%

Institutional returns are only marginally affected by commissions, since they pay only 10 cents per share round trip, stocks and options combined. However, the return for individuals trading 100 shares through full-service brokers is substantially reduced. Those who trade through discount brokers and/or who trade large numbers of shares have a smaller reduction in return. Commissions reduce out-of-the-money covered call returns to an even greater extent than they do for in-the-money strategies.

mutual funds. Pension funds use covered writing in an attempt to outperform the S&P 500 Index (especially during bear and fluctuating markets). Moreover, since pension funds have few alternatives to holding a major portion of their assets in common stocks, covered writing also provides some downside protection for their stock portfolio investment. However, since aggressive pension funds are oriented toward short-term performance, bull markets such as those in the 1980s discourage these aggressive funds from participating in covered writing. Mutual funds that are authorized to write covered options offer investors the lure of a consistent income higher than short-term interest rates plus downside protection on the stock portfolio. The public seems to have taken the lure, as 15 of the largest public funds that write options have combined assets of over $5.5 billion!

Our discussion of covered option writing implies that this strategy is a passive undertaking: one chooses an appropriate stock and then buys the stock and sells the associated option. However, monitoring and changing the position also can play an important part in increasing the returns for this strategy. For example, if the stock price declines significantly, such that the call option has a value near zero sometime during its life, then this particular option is repurchased and a new near-to-the-money option is sold. Such an action increases the total option income received during the year, although it can result in a net loss if the stock price rebounds and the stock is called away. Similarly, if the stock price increases significantly above the strike price (the time value is near zero), then the current option can be repurchased (at a loss) and another option at a higher strike price sold in order to receive additional option income. Consequently, the choices concerning which option strike price is optimal at a given time depend on forecasts of future stock prices and a tradeoff decision concerning risk versus return. These decisions, in conjunction with selecting the stocks that are the best candidates for option writing, make covered option writing an active strategy. Focus 6–1 discusses factors stated by institutional money managers that help provide above-average returns for their covered writing programs.

The Evidence Concerning Covered Option Writing

The Merton, Scholes, Gladstein Simulation. The evidence concerning covered option writing is mixed, reflecting the differing assumptions and methodologies employed in the studies on this subject. The Merton, Scholes, Gladstein (1978) research discussed in connection with buying call options also examines covered calls. One advantage of the Merton et al. analysis is that it involves an extensive time period, although this time span is available only because the authors employ simulated Black-Scholes option model prices rather than actual call option prices.[2]

Table 6–1 summarizes the Merton et al. results, showing that a simulated call writing program using 12 years of data provides inferior returns compared to a stock-only position. However, even though the option prices are most likely biased downward, the results do illustrate one important characteristic of covered option writing: This strategy is *less* risky than holding only stocks, with the risk decreasing as one goes from an out-of-the-money strategy to an in-the-money strategy. In fact, the risk/reward ratio calculated in this table shows that covered writing is at least as good as the stock-only position, if not better. (Smaller risk/return ratios are better, since they indi-

FOCUS 6–1   Factors Affecting the Returns for Institutional Covered Option Writing

Institutional option writers claim that the following factors allow them to obtain above-average returns when using an option writing strategy:

- Call options are overpriced (which is the general consensus on Wall Street), causing call option buyers to pay more for call options than they are worth. If call options are overpriced, then the option writers benefit by receiving larger time values. Overpriced calls may be due to supply and demand factors, or call buyers may simply be paying for potential jumps in the stock price. A one-quarter to three-eighths difference in the price on a three-month option is sufficient to make a 2 1/2% to 3% difference in the annual returns from covered writing.

- Short-term option expirations need to be sold in order to obtain higher per-day time values (longer-term options have smaller per-day time values due to a lesser demand from speculators).

- Trading in large blocks reduces per-share commissions significantly, allowing higher returns for this high-turnover strategy.

- Selecting high-quality stocks causes in-the-money options to be exercised 85% of the time. In other words, selecting high-quality stocks with an in-the-money strategy is almost equivalent to "pre-selling" the stock at a profit. Ignoring the quality of the stock creates "losers" in the portfolio, which reduces the overall portfolio return.

- Stipulating the net cost of the combined stock/option position when transactions are made increases the profitability. Thus, the money manager makes an agreement with a block trader to buy, say, 5000 shares of a stock *and* to sell 50 call options of a particular strike price, with the total net cost for *both* positions being agreed on before the transaction is finalized. Such an agreement eliminates price risk and provides the money manager with an opportunity to negotiate a favorable net cost in order to maximize profits. The block trader often agrees to these terms in order to unload large blocks of the stock with only a small price concession from the current market price.

- Receiving the cash dividend on the stock increases the return to the covered strategy by 2% to 5% per year. Thus, options are often written on stocks with moderate to large dividends. While early exercise can keep the fund from obtaining a given dividend, this effect is partially offset by the reinvestment of these funds at an earlier date than possible if the buyer waited until the expiration date of the option to exercise the right to buy the stock.

- A consistent and moderate rate of return policy via a covered writing program typically generates higher compound returns over a complete market cycle than an erratic strategy that has both large gains and large losses. The erratic strategy is often inferior, because the large losses create a lower base of investment funds.

TABLE 6–1 Simulated Covered Call Results

	10% in-the-money	At-the-money	10% out-of-the-money	20% out-of-the-money	Stock
136-stock portfolio:					
Average rate of return (%)	3.3	3.7	4.5	5.3	7.9
Standard deviation (%)	4.9	7.1	9.3	11.2	16.6
Standard deviation/return	1.48	1.92	2.07	2.11	2.10
Highest return (%)	14.6	19.3	24.7	30.4	54.6
Lowest return (%)	−9.9	−14.4	−17.4	−19.2	−21.0
Dow Jones stocks:					
Average rate of return (%)	2.9	2.9	3.2	3.5	4.1
Standard deviation (%)	3.7	6.2	8.6	10.4	13.7
Standard deviation/return	1.28	2.13	2.68	2.97	3.34
Highest return (%)	12.3	16.9	22.9	29.5	49.1
Lowest return (%)	−5.4	−9.2	−11.9	−13.8	−16.4

Source: Merton, Scholes, and Gladstein (1978), p. 207.

cate the risk per unit of return is smaller.) Table 6–1 shows the adverse effect of an upward trending market on the covered writing results during much of this time period—that is, the stock position has a 7.9% average return, and out-of-the-money covered calls provide better returns than at-the-money and in-the-money covered calls.[3]

Other Covered Call Results. Pounds (1978) also studies covered call writing by employing simulated Black-Scholes option prices. Pounds's study examines *three*-month covered positions for seven years for 43 active stocks by using out-of-the-money, at-the-money, and in-the-money covered option positions. All of the covered positions have higher returns than the stock-only position, with the out-of-the-money strategy registering the best results. In addition, all of the covered call results possess lower risk than the stock-only position, with the in-the-money strategy being the least risky. During specific subperiods either a stock-only, an out-of-the-money, or an in-the-money strategy generates superior returns, depending on the trend of the market. While commissions reduce the net returns, the covered strategies still outperform the stock-only position. Moreover, the commissions employed in this study were the pre-1975 rates, which reduced returns by 2% to 4% below those of the current commission structure. Overall, the out-of-the-money strategy is superior, because it participates in stock price increases and is affected least by the large commissions employed in the study. An

TABLE 6–2   Covered Option Writing: Actual Performance Results vs.
            the Indexes

Year	Covered Option Writing*	S&P 500 Stock Index	Solomon High Grade Bond Index
1975	25.2%	11.6%	9.4%
1976	30.9	23.9	18.6
1977	– 0.6	– 7.2	1.7
1978	8.7	6.3	0.0
1979	19.9	18.6	– 4.2
1980	25.7	32.4	– 2.8
1981	9.2	– 5.3	– 1.2
1982	15.6	21.4	42.5
1983	14.0	22.6	6.3
1984	5.0	6.2	16.9
1985	15.4	31.7	30.1
1986	13.6	18.6	19.9
1987	– 5 .8	5.3	0.0
1988	17.4	16.5	10.8
1989	27.8	31.7	16.2
1990	8.3	– 3.1	6.8
1991	24.3	30.5	19.9
1992	14.4	7.6	9.4
Compounded Annual Returns	14.94	14.98	11.11
Annual σ	9.85	12.91	12.33
Quarterly σ	5.03	7.83	6.24
Number of:			
Years < 8%	3	7	8
Quarters < 0%	16	21	20
Quarters > 9%	6	14	11

* Results from the covered writing program of Loomis, Sayles & Co. Results are quarterly returns
compounded to obtain annual returns; all returns include dividends or interest, as appropriate.
Number of quarters < 0% and > 9% are actual quarterly returns.
Source: Performance results from Loomis, Sayles & Co.

examination of the effect of the level of time values on the returns shows that
a *decrease* of 10% to 20% in the size of the time value would be critical in
determining whether the covered writing program is superior to a stock-only
strategy.[4]

Grube, Panton, and Terrell (1979) found that implementing a covered
call strategy reduces unsystematic risk more efficiently than a simple diversification policy of buying more stocks. Thus, a portfolio of 5 covered call
stock positions eliminates as much unsystematic risk as buying 12 to 15
stocks.

Institutional Results. Table 6–2 shows the performance for an actual
managed covered option writing program over the past 14 years by Loomis,

Sayles Inc. The Loomis, Sayles program for pension funds exceeds $400 million in asset value. The strategy includes writing three-month call options on individual stocks. The table compares these managed covered writing results to the S&P 500 and Dow Jones Industrial stock indexes and the Solomon bond index. The covered writing program was superior to the indexes from 1975 through 1981 for almost every year. From 1982 to 1987, the stock and bond indexes were superior to the covered writing results. Over the entire period, the covered writing results (after all costs) and the stock indexes had nearly equivalent returns, with the bond index lagging behind. The summary results for this table provide other interesting information: The covered writing strategy experienced fewer years below an 8% return than the indexes, and it had fewer losing quarters. But the covered writing approach also had only two quarters with returns above 9%, while the indexes experienced 10 to 14 such quarters.

The standard deviations for the results in Table 6–2 provide evidence concerning the variability of returns for the covered writing results versus the indexes: The annual and quarterly standard deviations show that covered writing is less risky than owning portfolios of stocks or bonds. Thus, these results support our general contentions concerning covered writing: Its return is more stable than a noncovered position and it has fewer losing periods, but it does not participate fully in a bull market.

Covered Writing with Options on Indexes. Covered writing with index options creates the difficulty of generating a portfolio of stocks with the same exact weights as the index option. Using a portfolio of fewer stocks or using different weights creates a crosshedge. Alderson and Zivney (1989) compare naive and optimal crosshedge portfolios for covered writing, finding that the optimal portfolios outperformed the naive portfolios. More important, they find that portfolios of 25 stocks can match the performance of a 100-stock portfolio for covered writing.

Ratio Writing

Ratio writing is the sale of call options in a multiple of the number of shares of stock owned. For example, when two call options (options on 200 shares of stock) are sold for each 100 shares of stock owned, one obtains a ratio writing position of 2 to 1. Figure 6–5 illustrates the payoff diagram at expiration of a ratio writing strategy, which shows how call ratio writing provides a larger profit to the call writer if stock prices remain stable, but also it causes significant losses if the stock price *either* increases or decreases sharply. Figure 6–5 shows that ratio writing has a payoff diagram similar to selling a straddle. Ratio writing is often initiated by individuals who want to capture additional option time values. However, this strategy also increases downside risk.

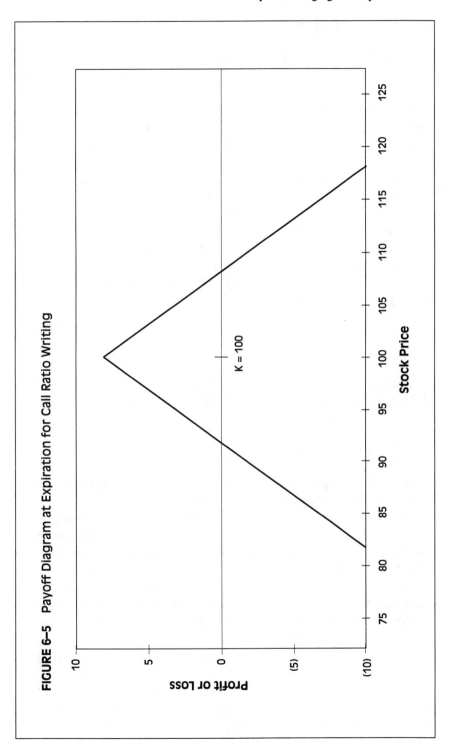

FIGURE 6–5 Payoff Diagram at Expiration for Call Ratio Writing

PROTECTIVE PUTS

The Concepts and Payoff Diagrams

A hedger who wants to eliminate the risk of a downward price movement in a currently held stock can purchase a put. Similarly, a market index put option is purchased to protect a portfolio of stocks. This strategy is called a **protective put**, because it protects the user against declines in the stock price below the strike price, while still allowing the hedger to participate in a major upward movement in prices.

Figure 6–6 illustrates the payoff diagram for a protective put. The protective put provides an advantage over a stock-only position if the stock price (at option expiration) is to the left of where the dashed and solid lines cross. Since the original stock price equals the strike price in this example, the maximum loss is simply the initial cost of the put. In general, the maximum *loss* on a protective put position is the put price less the intrinsic value for an in-the-money put, or the put price plus the amount the stock is above the strike price for an out-of-the-money put:

$$\text{Max loss}_{PP} = P_P + P_S - K \qquad (6\text{--}5)$$

where Max loss$_{PP}$ = the maximum loss on the protective put.

The break-even point of the protective put is the price of the stock at the initiation of the protective put plus the price of the put:

$$BE_{PP} = P_S + P_P \qquad (6\text{--}6)$$

where BE$_{PP}$ = the break-even point for the protective put

Example 6–5 compares the maximum loss and break-even points for in-the-money and out-of-the-money protective puts.

A protective put is *equivalent* to the figure for buying a call option: At the expiration date, there is a limited loss on the downside and unlimited gains on the upside.[5] However, a long call and a protective put are initiated by two different types of market participants. A long call option is purchased by a speculator who invests a limited amount of capital with the expectation of obtaining large gains within a short period of time. A protective put is purchased by a hedger who desires "insurance" against a drop in the price of a currently held asset.[6] The hedger purchasing a put may wish to be protected against a possible adverse court case announcement, a potential poor earnings report, or a failed merger. The hedger is willing to pay the insurance cost for this protection, that cost being the price of buying the put option. However, *continuously* purchasing puts for protection becomes costly, reducing the net return from the stock position significantly. Figure 6–7 shows

FIGURE 6–6   Payoff Diagram at Expiration for a Protective Put

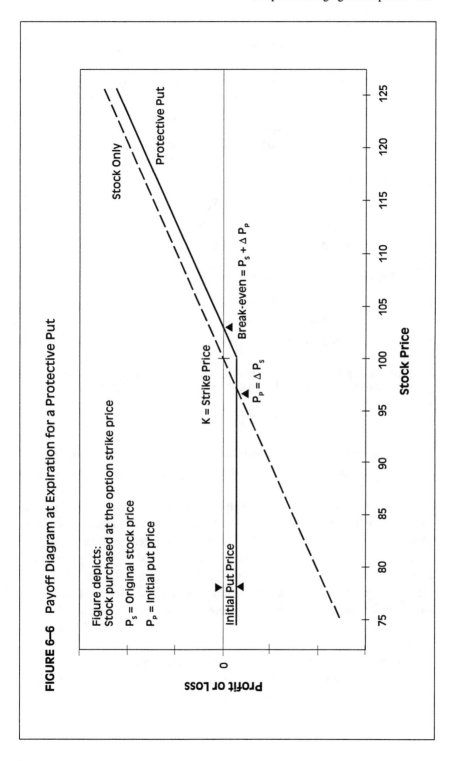

Figure depicts:
Stock purchased at the option strike price

P_s = Original stock price

P_p = Initial put price

Stock Only

Protective Put

K = Strike Price

Break-even = $P_s + \Delta P_p$

$P_p = \Delta P_s$

Initial Put Price

0

Profit or Loss

Stock Price

75   80   85   90   95   100   105   110   115   120   125

EXAMPLE 6–5   In-the-Money and Out-of-the-Money
                  Protective Puts

The maximum loss and break-even point for protective puts are affected by whether the put is in-the-money or out-of-the-money.

In-the-Money	Out-of-the-Money
$P_s = 97$	$P_s = 97$
$K = 100$	$K = 95$
$P_p = 5\,^3/_4$	$P_p = 3$

Maximum loss:

$$\text{Max loss}_{pp} = P_p + P_s - K \qquad (6\text{--}5)$$

In-the-money: $= 5\,^3/_4 + 97 - 100 = 2\,^3/_4$

Out-of-the-money: $= 3 + 97 - 95 = 5$

Break-even:

$$BE_{pp} = P_s + P_p \qquad (6\text{--}6)$$

In-the-money: $= 97 + 5\,^3/_4 = 102\,^3/_4$

Out-of-the-money: $= 97 + 3 = 100$

Thus, the maximum loss is smaller for an in-the-money protective put, but the break-even is less for an out-of-the-money protective put.

---

the components of a protective put—that is, how the profits/losses on the long stock and long put positions combine to equal the payoff of a protective put position.

The figure for a protective put illustrates its advantages. When prices increase, the hedger owns a position with a beta risk that is equivalent to the stock. When prices decrease substantially, the hedger ends up holding a position with a beta equal to 0. The disadvantage is that buying a put creates a cost. Another way of viewing a protective put is in terms of a dynamic replicating portfolio of stock and cash. In this case, the number of shares of stock are increased as stock prices increase, and stock shares are sold as prices decrease. This concept is the basis of the strategy called "portfolio insurance."

As with a call option (the protective put has the same payoff diagram as a long call), the profit/loss on a protective put depends on the ending stock price. The equation for the profit on a protective put is:

FIGURE 6–7 Components of the Payoff Diagram of a Protective Put

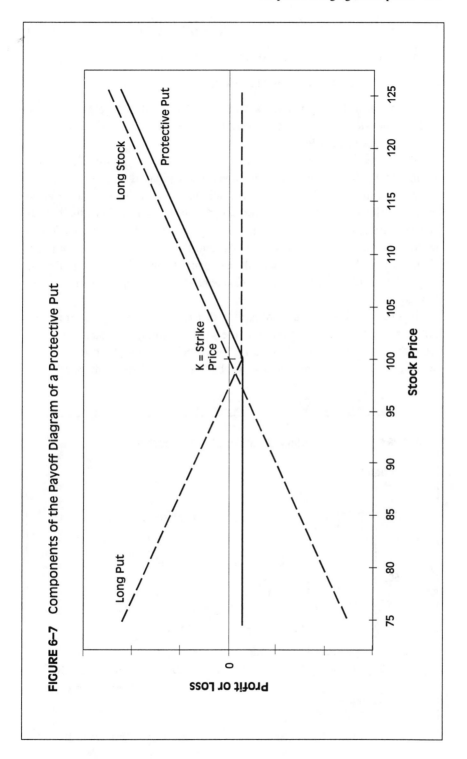

$$\text{Profit}_{PP} = -P_p + \text{Max} \, [\Delta P_S, K - P_S] \qquad (6\text{--}7)$$

where Profit_{PP} = the profit on the protective put position

P_S = the original stock price

For example, if the original stock price is 103 when the strike price is 100, and the put price is 2, then the profit of the protective put is –5 (a loss) when the final stock price is 99.

The protective put strategy provides a guaranteed minimum selling price for the stock, although this guaranteed price is purchased for a cost. The cost of the guarantee and the level of the selling price are determined by the exercise price of the put and the current price of the stock. Thus, the hedger can choose an in-the-money, near-the-money, or out-of-the-money put. These options provide a tradeoff between cost and the minimum price guarantee. Equivalently, the strike price acts like a deductible on an insurance policy: A larger deductible (lower strike price) means that the hedger has more risk, but the cost of the insurance is lower.[7]

Figure 6–8 illustrates the probability distribution for buying a protective put. A protective put (long put plus the stock position) truncates the losses from the stock portfolio, eliminating losses below the strike price. This is achieved at a cost: There is a large probability that a loss of about 5% will

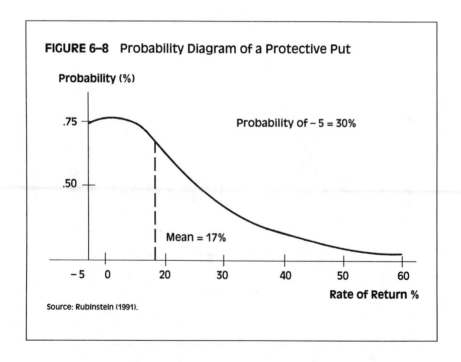

FIGURE 6–8 Probability Diagram of a Protective Put

Probability (%)

Probability of – 5 = 30%

Mean = 17%

Rate of Return %

Source: Rubinstein (1991).

Exhibit 6–2   OptionVue Matrix for Protective Puts

ACTUALS
```
        ├ ABC COM ┤
        100      +300
          1.00    300
```

OPTIONS

	├ FEB (31) ┤		├ APR (90) ┤	├ JUL (181) ┤	├ OCT (273) ┤
PUTS 90	3/16 ——		1 1/8 ——	2 1/4 ——	3 1/8 ——
	− .061		− .156	− .204	− .221
PUTS 95	15/16		+1 2 3/8 ——	3 3/4 ——	4 3/4 ——
	− .212 − 21.2		−.283	−.301	−.302
PUTS 100	2 3/4 +1		4 3/8 ——	5 3/4 ——	6 3/4 ——
	− .462 − 46.2		−.436	−.410	−.389
PUTS 105	5 3/4 +1		7 1/8 ——	8 3/8 ——	9 1/4 ——
	− .717 − 71.7		−.592	−.519	−.478
PUTS 110	10 ——		10 5/8 ——	11 1/2 ——	12 1/4 ——
	− 1.00		−.728	−.623	−.564

SUMMARY

Orig. Reqmt: $15,937	Commis: $0.00	Delta: +160.8	AvgMIV: 24.7%
Maint. Reqmt: $11,412		Gamma: +14.1	Calls: 25.2%
Cash Flow: −$30,937	Theta: − $10.11/day	Vega: +30.0	Puts: 24.5%

Format of numbers with each option/stock ABC:

    (1) price   (3) long/short position

    (2) delta   (4) position delta

Put options are purchased on the February 95, 100, and 105 calls (one each). Three hundred common shares ("Actuals") are purchased. The summary section shows the net position delta, position gamma, position vega, and the per-day theta.

Source: Developed using OptionVue IV.

occur when the protective put strategy is employed (the 5% loss shown in the figure varies according to the situation).

Exhibit 6–2 shows the OptionVue Matrix for protective puts. The net deltas for the long stock in combination with the 95, 100, and 105 put strike prices are .782 (1 − .212), .538 (1 − .462), and .283 (1 − .717). Thus, an in-the-money 105 protective put is the most conservative strategy, while an out-of-the-money protective put will react most to stock price increases. The combined portfolio delta, gamma, vega, and theta appear under the summary part of the screen.

Using Index Puts

Using index put options with a portfolio provides additional benefits in comparison to a protective put strategy for individual stocks. If the fund or individual believes that the market will experience a short-term decline, then buying a put provides downside protection for the systematic risk component of the portfolio. The alternative—selling all of the stocks in the portfolio when a market decline is anticipated—is not usually feasible, given the transactions costs involved, the loss of dividends, potential liquidity problems, and the tax consequences. The put option strategy works well if the forecast is correct *and* if the portfolio is highly correlated with the market index. The number of index puts purchased generally should have a total stock value equal to the total value of the portfolio. However, if the portfolio has a significantly different degree of risk than the market (the portfolio beta differs significantly), then the index value is multiplied by the portfolio beta in order to determine the number of puts to buy.

Protective Puts Versus Covered Calls

Figure 6–9 compares the payoff diagrams of a protective put to a covered call at option expiration. Both strategies involve hedge positions, but this diagram shows that their characteristics vary significantly. The covered call reduces the downside loss when compared to a stock-only position, because the option price is received by the writer. On the other hand, a protective put eliminates *any* loss below the strike price less the cost of the put, as well as allowing the protective put hedger to participate in gains on the stock. Thus, for large stock price gains or losses, the protective put outperforms the covered call. For moderate changes in the stock price, the covered call is superior. Consequently, the type of hedge position to undertake depends on the forecast of the *volatility* of the underlying stock price.

The Evidence

Merton, Scholes, and Gladstein (1982) examine the historical performance of protective puts by using simulated option prices for a 14-year period. The methodology of this study is essentially equivalent to their companion study on buying call options and covered call writing discussed earlier. Merton, Scholes, and Gladstein find that protective puts provide an inferior return to a stock-only strategy over the entire time period for the 136-stock portfolio. In-the-money, at-the-money, and out-of-the-money strategies earn 5.9%, 6.7%, and 7.3%, respectively, during this time period, as compared to a 7.7% return for a stock-only position. However, the risk for a protective put is significantly less than the risk for the stock position: The standard deviations

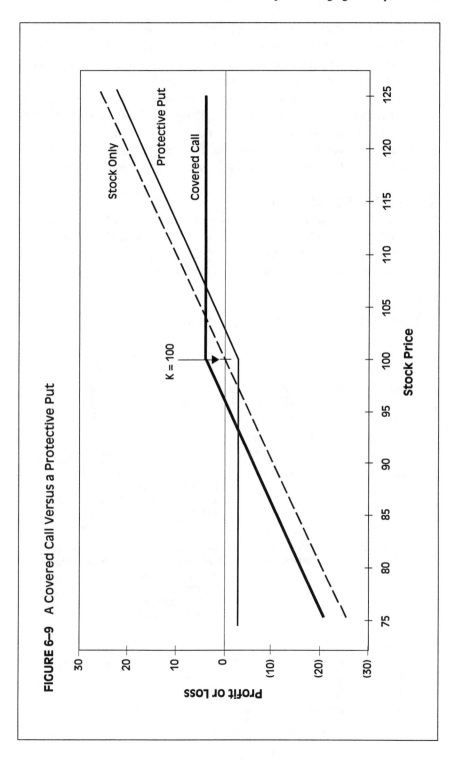

FIGURE 6–9   A Covered Call Versus a Protective Put

for the in-the-money, at-the-money, and out-of-the-money positions are 7.1%, 9.5%, and 12.0%, respectively, as compared to a standard deviation of 16.1% for the stock position. The same results for the Dow Jones stock sample show that the returns for the protective put strategies are essentially equivalent to the stock-only portfolio, but the protective puts are significantly less risky. Thus, the ending values for the Dow Jones portfolios hedged with protective puts are larger than the value for the stock-only portfolio. Moreover, the upward trend in the market for the majority of the period of the study biases the results against a protective put strategy.

Other Hedging Strategies

Exhibit 6–3 lists several other option strategies used in conjunction with stocks. These strategies are similar to the strategies discussed above and/or are used less frequently than the more popular strategies examined previously. The important characteristics of these strategies are given in the exhibit.

EXHIBIT 6–3 Summary of Other Stock-Option Hedging Strategies

		Call		Put	
	Strike	Jan	Feb	Jan	Feb
Stock A (P = 100)	95	B	C	D	E
	100	F	G	H	I
	105	J	K	L	M

Strategy	Combination of Positions Needed*	Advantage	Disadvantage
Buy stock, sell put	Buy A and sell H	If A increases, then profit from A as well as keep put price	If A declines moderately, then do worse than A (downside leverage)
Buy stock, sell call, sell put	Buy A, sell F and H	Similar to covered call in shape, but keep both call *and* put time values; profit larger than A only for moderate changes in A	Inferior to A only for *large* changes in A
Sell stock short, buy call (covered short-sale)	Sell A, buy F	Graph same as buying put: profit when A declines *moderately*	If A increases or stays the same

* Often many different combinations are relevant; only one combination is given here.

One conservative strategy involving options is called "dividend capture." Corporations buy stock in other companies paying large dividends in order to exclude 85% of these dividends from income taxes. In order to avoid the risk associated with a drop in the stock price over the required 15-day holding period of the stock, the corporation sells a deep-in-the-money call option to execute a hedge.

SUMMARY AND LOOKING AHEAD

This chapter discusses hedging with options. Covered option writing is one type of hedging strategy. Covered writing reduces the downside loss as compared to owning the stock, but it also limits the upside gain. Option writers benefit from receiving the price of the option. The protective put strategy eliminates the majority of the downside risk from holding a stock position, with the hedger paying the cost of the put to receive the required protection. Chapters 7 to 9 involve options applications, such as options on futures, currency options, and over-the-counter options.

END NOTES

[1] A major criticism of discount brokers by traders is that executions are poor—that is, transaction prices are away from the market by one-eighth to one-quarter of a point (or more), and the trade is not made quickly after it is received by the broker.

[2] Gastineau's (1979) and Gastineau and Madansky's (1979) criticisms of the Merton et al. approach are covered in Chapter 5. These criticisms suggest that the Merton et. al. results are biased against covered option writing, as well as reflecting the upward trend of the market during the period in question. In addition, the use of six-month options in the Merton et al. study negates the possibility of generating additional time values after three months if the stock price increases or decreases significantly.

[3] Merton, Scholes, and Gladstein estimate that each 10% error in the estimate of the option price affects the covered writing returns by 1% for the 136 stock sample and .8% for the Dow Jones sample. Thus, the simulated option prices would need to be 40% too low for an at-the-money covered strategy to beat the stock-only strategy for the 139-stock portfolio, and 15% too low for the Dow Jones sample to beat the stock-only strategy. Gastineau (1979) suggests that errors in the input factors for the Merton et. al. simulation could account for errors of this magnitude in the Merton et al. option prices. Such errors would then adversely affect the covered writing results. Moreover, the covered call strategy is handicapped by the bull market that occurred during a major part of the time period in question.

[4] Pounds also examines the profitability of using a "roll-up/roll-down" strategy of changing the strike price of the option employed when the time value substantially declines due to stock price movements. This "active portfolio strategy" for six-month options is inferior to a "passive strategy" of no readjustments, since the former strategy generates additional commissions. Trennepohl and Dukes (1979) examine the performance of three-, six-, and nine-month near-the-money covered calls by using actual

market prices for a four-year period of time. These strategies earn 12.5% to 15.5% before commissions, compared to a stock-only return of 0.1%. However, market trends affect these results in a manner similar to other studies. After commissions, these returns decline to 6.0%, 4.5%, and 10.0% for the three-, six-, and nine-month strategies, respectively. However, pre-1975 commissions are employed in the study, which adversely affects the results for anyone dealing in multiple contracts. In addition to obtaining superior returns, the covered call positions are less risky than the stock position. Similarly, Roenfeldt, Cooley, and Gombola (1979) find covered writing to be superior to buying stocks on both a return and risk basis. However, these covered writing returns are only 8% to 10% on an annualized basis, and the stock-only strategy is slightly superior during bull market periods.

[5] Puts tend to be exercised before the expiration date more often than calls; thus the return distribution differs slightly between a protective put and a long call position.

[6] This "insurance" is similar to other types of insurance. For example, an owner of a house pays an insurance premium to protect the value of the house against a loss due to fire, flood, or accidents. Similarly, purchasing a put protects against a loss due to a declining stock price.

[7] The insurance aspect of a protective put strategy also can be implemented by "dynamic portfolio insurance." A well-publicized concept, dynamic portfolio insurance advocates emphasize the downward protection and upward potential offered by such a strategy. The differences between a dynamic put strategy and the protective put concept discussed here are twofold. First, in order to reduce the costs associated with buying puts, the dynamic put strategy is implemented only when the stock/market is forecasted to decline (or is implemented gradually as the market starts to decline). Second, due to the cost of buying puts, and since put options often are not liquid enough to implement such a strategy, stock index futures often are employed to simulate a dynamic portfolio insurance strategy.

Options on Futures | 7

Options on futures provide the buyer the right to buy (call option) or sell (put option) a futures contract at a specific strike price for a specific period of time. Options on stock index futures, T-bond and T-note futures, Eurodollar futures, energy futures, and certain agricultural futures are active contracts, with each contract having its own characteristics. Each option on futures has a specific futures contract as the underlying security, with a call option buyer receiving a long position in the futures and the put buyer receiving a short futures position at option expiration (if the option is exercised).

The pricing of options on futures typically is based on the Black model, which adapts the Black-Scholes model to options on futures. However, the early exercise provision of American options on futures creates pricing problems for the Black European pricing model. In particular, traders often exercise in-the-money options on futures early in order to invest the proceeds at the risk-free interest rate. Put-call parity is also useful for pricing options on futures. Moreover, put-call parity in combination with the Black model for call options creates a model for pricing put options on futures. The basic speculative and hedging applications of options on futures parallel those of options on stocks, including covered option writing and using protective puts.

A BACKGROUND TO OPTIONS ON FUTURES

What Are Options on Futures?

An option on an asset, such as a stock, provides the right to buy the asset (a call option) or the right to sell the asset (a put option) at the strike price until the option expires. If the option is exercised, the asset changes hands at the strike price.[1] **Options on futures** (or, equivalently, futures options) are contracts in which *futures* are the underlying asset and that change hands at the time of delivery. As with other options, the option buyer has the right (but not the obligation) to execute the option. Thus, the call buyer can choose to exercise the option to buy the futures contract at the strike price (take a long position in the futures at the strike price), while the put buyer can choose to sell the futures contract at the strike price (take a short position in the futures at the strike price). All of the typical option concepts apply. For example, the owner of a call option will exercise the right to buy the futures contract only if doing so produces a profit or reduces a loss.

Options on futures were banned from exchange trading in 1936. During the late 1970s and early 1980s, before options on futures trading were allowed on organized exchanges in the United States, over-the-counter options houses sold options on international commodities such as sugar. While commodity options trading in London was a respectable enterprise, many of the U.S. options houses doubled or tripled the London price of these options, used hard-sell telephone pitches to unsophisticated customers, and abruptly closed offices when their customers' options became profitable, subsequently reopening under a new name. In response to these illegal over-the-counter practices, the Commodity Futures Trading Commission allowed each exchange to trade one option on futures contract, starting in 1982. The success of this program caused permanent authorization for options on futures in 1987. Currently, options on futures are traded on futures exchanges for many types of futures contracts, including stock index futures, interest rate futures, currency futures, and agricultural and commodity futures. Options on financial futures constitute over 40% of the entire futures options volume, with currency options on futures contributing around 20% and agricultural futures options less than 20%. Energy futures options have a volume of about 15%.

What Are the Advantages of Options on Futures?

Options on futures have the following benefits over futures contracts:

- Options have a limited loss feature that futures do not possess.

- A long call and a short put position create a synthetic long futures position (as discussed later).[2]

- Although both futures options and futures have equivalent price limits that restrict the maximum price change for a given day, a number of the futures options continue to trade after futures hit their price limits, since near-the-money option prices move less than the underlying futures contracts. For example, during the October 1987 market crash, T-bond futures hit their daily price limit, but options on T-bond futures continued to trade. However, stock index options stop trading when the intraday circuit breakers become effective.

- Options on futures allow producers of commodities to hedge quantity risk as well as price risk, while futures only allow one to hedge price risk. Since agricultural producers do not know the size of the harvest, futures options provide a less risky method for hedging.

However, futures options need futures contracts to exist, since futures are the delivery and pricing instrument needed for the futures options to trade.

Options on futures also provide these benefits that typically do not exist for an option on the underlying cash asset:

- Futures contracts are liquid and trade continuously when the futures exchange is open, allowing option traders access to the prices of an actively traded underlying asset. This characteristic is beneficial for the pricing of the options contract.[3]

- Implementing option strategies involving the underlying security, such as covered call and protective put hedges, are often easier with futures options. This is because options on the cash asset could require a complicated portfolio of stocks, an illiquid bond, or options on many different grades of wheat.

- Delivery of the futures contract when the option is exercised is a simple wire transfer of a standardized futures contract with no quality variations. Moreover, exercise of a futures option results in a futures position with limited margin requirements, while exercise of a cash option requires purchase of the cash asset.

- The regulations of the exchanges provide safeguards for the option trader that do not exist for the over-the-counter version of these options.

- The ability to exercise options on futures contracts early allows the trader to invest accumulated profits in a risk-free asset without needing cash to buy the asset. (This characteristic of options on futures is discussed below.)

Despite the advantages of options on futures over options on cash assets, cash options have a high volume for certain securities, such as the S&P 100 Index and foreign currencies.

CHARACTERISTICS AND QUOTATIONS OF OPTIONS ON FUTURES

The characteristics and quotation procedures for options on futures are stated below. Currency options on futures are discussed in conjunction with cash currency options in Chapter 8. Exhibit 7–1 provides an example of the quotations of options on futures contracts.

EXHIBIT 7–1   Options on Futures Quotations

INDEX

S & P 500 STOCK INDEX (CME)
$500 times premium

Strike Price	Calls–Settle			Puts–Settle		
	May	Jun	Jly	May	Jun	Jly
425	...	16.70	...	2.40	4.75	6.40
430	10.50	13.10	...	3.50	6.15	...
4.35	7.10	9.80	...	5.10	7.80	9.60
440	4.35	7.00	...	7.35	10.00	11.75
445	2.35	4.70	...	10.30	12.65	14.30
450	1.10	3.05	4.95	14.05	15.95	17.35

Est. vol. 7,374;
Thur vol. 4,104 calls; 6,925 puts
Op. Int. Thur 28,968 calls; 92,068 puts

INTEREST RATE

T-BONDS (CBT)
$100,000; points and 64ths of 100%

Strike Price	Calls–Settle			Puts–Settle		
	May	Jun	Sep	May	Jun	Sep
108	4-04	3-55	3-42	...	0-10	1-15
110	2-04	2-14	2-30	...	0-32	2-01
112	0-07	1-00	1-36	0-05	1-18	3-07
114	...	0-23	0-59	2-08	2-41	4-29
116	...	0-05	0-33	...	4-22	7-39
118	...	0-01	0-17	...	6-18	...

Est. vol. 115,000;
Thur vol. 57,061 calls; 41,220 puts
Op. Int. Thur 321,142 calls; 330,023 puts

T-NOTES (CBT)
$100,000; points and 64ths of 100%

	May	Jun	Sep	May	Jun	Sep
110	3-01	2-59	2-41	0-01	0-13	1-04
111	2-00	2-02	2-02	0-01	0-28	1-29
112	1-01	1-18	1-33	0-01	0-55	1-59
113	0-05	0-45	1-06	0-05	1-31	2-30
114	0-01	0-21	0-50	...	2-17	3-09
115	0-01	0-08	0-34	...	...	3-56

Est. vol. 25,000;
Thurs vol. 10,256 calls; 10,810 puts
Op. Int. Thur 99,041 calls; 135,972 puts

EURODOLLAR (CME)
$ million; pts. of 100%

Strike Price	Calls–Settle			Puts–Settle		
	Jun	Sep	Dec	Jun	Sep	Dec
9625	0.54	0.46	0.27	.0004	0.03	0.18
9650	0.30	0.25	0.14	0.10	0.07	0.30
9675	0.08	0.09	0.06	0.04	0.16	0.46
9700	0.01	0.02	0.03	0.22	0.34	0.68
9725	.0004	.0004	0.01	0.46	0.57	0.91
9750	.0004	.0004	.0004	0.71	...	...

Est. vol. 51,488;
Thur vol. 34,089 calls; 59,702 puts
Op. Int. Thur 526,390 calls; 561,143 puts

METALS

GOLD (CMX)
100 troy ounces; $ per troy ounce

Strike Price	Calls–Settle			Puts–Settle		
	Jun	Jly	Aug	Jun	Jly	Aug
330	17.70	19.60	20.30	.30	1.00	1.50
340	9.00	11.50	12.50	1.50	2.60	3.60
350	3.30	5.50	6.80	5.80	6.60	7.80
360	1.30	2.30	3.70	12.60	13.50	14.60
370	.70	1.30	2.00	22.50	22.70	22.70
380	.30	.80	1.40	32.50	31.70	31.50

Est. vol. 12,000;
Thur vol. 2,400 calls; 1,464 puts
Op. Int. Thur 101,355 calls; 29,260 puts

SILVER (CMX)
5,000 troy ounces; cts per troy ounce

Strike Price	Calls–Settle			Puts–Settle		
	Jun	Jly	Sep	Jun	Jly	Sep
350	48.3	48.9	52.0	0.1	0.7	1.5
375	24.5	26.4	32.0	1.3	3.2	6.2
400	7.5	12.0	17.8	9.3	13.8	17.0
425	2.2	5.6	10.8	29.0	32.4	35.0
450	0.7	2.8	6.3	52.5	54.6	55.0
475	0.4	2.0	4.5	77.2	78.8	78.0

Est. vol. 5,000;
Thur vol. 3,037 calls; 901 puts
Op. Int. Thur 65,249 calls; 14,723 puts

OIL

CRUDE OIL (NYM)
1,000 bbls; $ per bbl.

Strike Price	Calls–Settle			Puts–Settle		
	Jun	Jly	Aug	Jun	Jly	Aug
18	2.35	2.54	2.67	.01	.04	.06
19	1.37	1.61	1.78	.03	.11	.16
20	.51	.79	.98	.17	.28	.35
21	.08	.25	.45	.74	.74	.82
22	.01	.09	.17	1.67	1.57	...
23	.01	.03	.05	2.67	2.51	...

Est. vol. 15,184;
Thur vol. 11,166 calls; 17,083 puts
Op. Int. Thur 374,312 calls; 189,800 puts

HEATING OIL No. 2 (NYM)
42,000 gals.; $ per gal.

Strike Price	Calls–Settle			Puts–Settle		
	May	Jun	Jly	May	Jun	Jly
52	.0382	.0384	.0432	.0001	.0007	.0018
54	.0182	.0209	.0266	.0001	.0032	.0051
56	.0001	.0085	.0139	.0018	.0107	.0123
58	.0001	.0029	.0065	.0218	.0250	.0248
60	.0001	.0010	.0025	.0418	.0431	.0407
62	.0001	.0003	.0010	......	......	......

Est. vol. 2,343;
Thur vol. 422 calls; 834 puts
Op. Int. Thur 26,143 calls; 21,963 puts

GASOLINE–Unlead (NYM)
42,000 gals.; $ per gal.

Strike Price	Calls–Settle			Puts–Settle		
	May	Jun	Jly	May	Jun	Jly
56	.0435	.0454	.0469	.0001	.0009	.0022
58	.0241	.0275	.0301	.0001	.0030	.0053
60	.0001	.0135	.0180	.0006	.0089	.0123
62	.0001	.0051	.0095	.0206	.0205	.0245
64	.0001	.0019	.0044	......	......	......
66	.0001	.0009	.0020	.0006	......	......

Est. vol. 4,968;
Thurs vol. 3,207 calls; 1,730 puts
Op. Int. Thur 38,797 calls; 27,383 puts

AGRICULTURAL

CORN (CBT)
5,000 bu.; cents per bu.

Strike Price	Calls–Settle			Puts–Settle		
	May	Jly	Sep	May	Jly	Sep
200	25	29¾	35	...	⅛	¼
210	15¼	20½	26¼	...	¼	1¾
220	5¼	11¾	19½	...	2¼	4¾
230	...	6⅝	13¾	4¾	6¾	9
240	...	3⅜	10	14½	13¾	15½
250	...	1⅞	7½	24½	21½	22½

Est. vol. 10,000;
Thur vol. 7,306 calls; 3,284 puts
Op. Int. Thur 109,472 calls; 56,255 puts

SOYBEANS (CBT)
5,000 bu.; cents per bu.

Strike Price	Calls–Settle			Puts–Settle		
	May	Jly	Aug	May	Jly	Aug
550	42	45¼	48¾	...	1	3½
575	16¾	25	32	...	5¾	11½
600	...	12¾	21¼	8¼	18¼	25¾
625	...	6⅞	15¼	33	37½	44¾
650	...	4	12	...	59¾	65¾
675	...	2½	8¾	...	83	...

Est. vol. 5,000;
Thur vol. 5,528 calls; 1,631 puts
Op. Int. Thur 113,307 calls; 49,179 puts

WHEAT (CBT)
5,000 bu.; cents per bu.

Strike Price	Calls–Settle			Puts–Settle		
	May	Jly	Sep	May	Jly	Sep
330	22	2¾	6½	½	27½	28¾
340	12	1½	4¾	⅛	36½	...
350	1½	1	3½	⅜	45½	...
360	⅛	⅝	2½	9	55¼	...
370	⅛	⅜	1¾	19½	65	...
380	⅛	⅛	1¼	29	...	...

Est. vol. 4,000;
Thur vol. 1,707 calls; 2,024 puts
Op. Int. Thur 31,107 calls; 19,532 puts

SUGAR—WORLD (CSCE)
112,000 lbs.; cents per lb.

Strike Price	Calls–Settle			Puts–Settle		
	Jun	Jly	Oct	Jun	Jly	Oct
11.50	1.00	1.32	1.26	0.15	0.44	0.90
12.00	0.71	0.95	1.09	0.33	0.60	1.23
12.50	0.50	0.74	0.90	0.62	0.89	1.54
13.00	0.33	0.57	0.76	0.95	1.19	1.90
14.00	0.10	0.35	0.55	1.72	1.97	2.69
15.00	0.08	0.20	0.39	2.70	2.82	3.53

Est. vol. 9,244;
Thur vol. 3,686 calls; 2,463 puts
Op. Int. Thur 41,616 calls; 30,467 puts

Source: Futures Exchanges, April 23.

Stock Index Options

The most active stock index option on futures is the S&P 500 contract. This contract has strike prices differing by 5 points and active options for the first three expirations. Expirations exist for the current and next month and two additional expirations in the financial cycle of March, June, September, and December. The total cost of the option is 500 times the quoted option price. Thus, each 0.05 price change (the minimum tick size) results in a change of $25 for the option. For example, the 440 call for the May S&P 500 futures options in Exhibit 7–1 cost 4.35, or $500 X 4.35 = $2175 per option. Options also exist on the Major Market Index futures, the NYSE Composite Index futures, and the Nikkei 225 Stock Average futures; however, their option volumes are 200 or fewer contracts per day.

Each option expires in the last half of the expiration month. The S&P 500 options on futures that expire during a financial futures cycle month stop trading on the Thursday prior to the third Friday of the expiration month. Options that expire during other months stop trading on the third Friday of the month. When an option on a stock index futures contract is exercised, then call option buyer receives a long position (the put buyer takes a short position) in the *next* futures expiration. Thus, if a January S&P 500 options futures is exercised, a call buyer receives the March S&P 500 futures contract.[4]

Interest Rate Options

Active options on futures trade for the following contracts: T-bonds, Ten-year T-notes, Five-year T-notes, Eurodollars, and the British Long Gilt bond. Low-volume options on futures trade for the Municipal Bond Index, the one-month LIBOR contract, T-bills, and Two-year T-notes. The T-bond and Eurodollar futures options have open interest that exceeds 400,000 and 600,000 option contracts, respectively, making these options the most successful contracts traded.

The T-bond and T-note interest rate futures options have expirations within 30 days (the nearby option) plus options for the following two months in the financial cycle. The Municipal bond, Eurodollar, T-bill, and Long Gilt contracts trade options that expire only for the financial cycle. T-bond and T-note options on futures expire during the month *previous* to the futures expiration (specifically, on the Friday at least five business days before the first notice day for the futures delivery). Hence, a September option on T-bond futures actually expires in August. Similarly, the nearby option month actually expires during the month previous to the month quoted in the paper (an August option expires in July, etc.).

The prices of long-term interest rate options on futures (T-bonds, T-notes, Municipal bonds, and the Gilt contract) are quoted in 1/64ths of a point. Thus, a quoted price of 1-10 represents 1 and 10/64ths points. Each point is 1% of the par value of the $100,000 futures contract, or $1000. For example, the June 110 T-bond futures options in Exhibit 7–1 are quoted at 2 and 14/64, or $2218.75 per option. The strike prices for T-bonds are in units of two points. Ten-year T-notes and the Municipal bond contract have strike price intervals of one point. The Five-year T-note options on futures have strike price intervals of one-half point. The short-term interest rate options on futures have strike price intervals of one-quarter to one-half percentage point, depending on the contract and the level of interest rates. The par value for the Eurodollar, LIBOR, and T-bill contracts is $1,000,000. Therefore, options on futures par values are based on the par values of the underlying futures contracts. Exhibit 7–2 provides the contract specifications for the options on financial futures contracts.

One major advantage of active interest rate futures options as compared to over-the-counter debt options is the liquidity of the exchange-traded contracts. Hence, those wishing to trade a large volume or those who want to offset a current position quickly and at a fair price are more likely to achieve their aims if an active interest rate futures option contract exists. In addition, futures options can be exercised at any time, while over-the-counter options are European-style options that can be exercised only on the expiration date.

Agricultural and Commodity Options

Options on futures for agricultural items, oil, livestock, and metals exist for a number of different commodities, but many of these options on futures contracts have volume below 1000 contracts per day. The most active agricultural options on futures are for corn, soybeans, wheat, coffee, and sugar, with 2000 to 12,000 options contracts traded per day for these con-tracts. Live cattle options are the only active livestock options on futures contract. Each option has its own quotation procedures, size of contract, expiration months, and strike price intervals. Newspapers such as *The Wall Street Journal* specify these characteristics (or see Exhibit 7–1).

The crude oil options on futures is a very active market, with option volume of 30,000 to 50,000 contracts per day. Heating oil and gasoline options on futures trade 3000 to 4000 contracts per day. The strike price interval for crude oil options is $1.

Gold and silver options on futures are active, with copper and platinum options being less active. The price of the gold options is in dollars times 100 troy ounces per contract. Gold has strike price intervals of $10.00. Silver options are in cents times 5000 troy ounces per contract. Silver has strike intervals of 25 cents.

EXHIBIT 7–2   Contract Specifications for Major Financial Options on Futures

Option Contract on:	Price Interval	Strike Interval	Daily Price Limit	Contract Months*	Last Trading Day	Automatic Exercise
S&P 500 futures	.05 = $25	5 points	Close when S&P 500 futures close	(1)	(2)	(5)
T-bond futures	$^1/_{64}$ = $15.625	2 points (1 point nearby)	3 points	(3)	(4)	(5)
10-year T-note futures	$^1/_{64}$ = $15.625	1 point	3 points	(3)	(4)	(5)
5-year T-note futures	$^1/_{64}$ = $15.625	$^1/_2$ point	3 points	(3)	(4)	(5)
Eurodollar futures	.01 = $25	.25 of an index point (7)	None	FC*	(6)	(5)
Gold	$.10 = $10	$10 (below $500)	$75 monthly		(8)	(5)

(1) The current month and the next calendar month plus the financial cycle.
(2) During a futures expiration month, trading stops on the Thursday before the third Friday of the month. For a nonfutures expiration month, trading stops on the third Friday of the month.
(3) A contract with less than 30 days until expiration plus the financial cycle.
(4) Noon on the Friday preceded by at least five business days before the first notice day of delivery of the futures contract.
(5) All in-the-money options at expiration are automatically exercised (as of late 1993).
(6) The last day and time as the underlying futures expire.
(7) The strike interval is .50 when the index is below 91.00 (the interest rate is above 9%).
(8) Second Friday of month before futures expiration.

* FC = the financial cycle of March, June, September, and December.
Source: Exchange booklets.

General Characteristics

The underlying security for an option on futures contract is a futures contract. Hence, the size of the option contract is equivalent to the underlying futures contract. A long position in a call option on futures gives the buyer the right to take a long position in the underlying futures contract at the strike price. A long position in a put gives the buyer the right to take a short position in the underlying futures contract. Conversely, the seller (writer) of a call assumes the obligation to take a short position in the futures (if the buyer exercises the option), while the seller of a put has the obligation to take a long futures position. Futures options are American options; therefore, they can be exercised on any day that the exchange is open. When an option is exercised, the clearinghouse randomly chooses the seller to take the futures position opposite the option buyer.

Options on futures buyers do not require a margin payment, since the most they can lose is the cost of the option. However, the seller of an option on futures must put up margin on the option account, because a loss can occur for the seller (the seller must be ready to take a futures position at a price that immediately creates a loss). The margin needed in the account for the seller is calculated daily. When an option on futures is exercised, the previous owner of the option receives the profit (the difference between the futures price and the strike price), while the previous short on the option must pay this amount. For example, if the strike price of an S&P 500 futures option is 430 and the futures contract trades at 437 when the call option on the futures is exercised, then the call buyer receives a payment of $3500 (7 points X 500) from the seller; in addition, the call buyer receives a long futures position and the seller takes a short futures position. Since a futures position is undertaken, both the new long and new short for the futures must put up futures margins (unless the futures contract is covered immediately). Exhibit 7–3 summarizes the positions and cash flows when futures options are exercised.

The option position is created with the clearinghouse of the exchange (but there must be both a buyer and a seller of the option to create the position). The clearinghouse *automatically* exercises expiring in-the-money futures options if the option is sufficiently in-the-money and if the corresponding futures are also expiring, unless specific instructions are given not to exercise the contract. Such automatic exercises are executed because the in-the-money options have value. For example, in-the-money options on S&P 500 futures during the expiration month are automatically exercised. Options on T-bond and T-note futures must be at least two points in-the-money to be automatically exercised.

Trading Options on the Exchange

Futures options are traded on the futures exchanges next to the associated futures contracts. While most of the futures traders are scalpers—that is, they buy at the bid and sell at the ask price—only about 10% of the options on futures traders are scalpers. Most of the option floor traders are spreaders between different strike prices or generate a synthetic position by an appro-

EXHIBIT 7–3   Positions and Cash Flows When Futures Options Are Exercised

Option	Futures Position	Cash Flows
Call		
Owner	Receives long futures position	Receives $P_F - K$
Seller	Takes short futures position	Pays $P_F - K$
Put		
Owner	Takes short futures position	Receives $K - P_F$
Seller	Receives long futures position	Pays $K - P_F$

P_F = the futures price when option is exercised
K = the option exercise price

priate combination of the options and the futures contracts. Such trades reduce the risk for the option floor traders, since typically there is insufficient liquidity in any one option for many traders to operate as scalpers.

Since the floor traders use spreads and synthetic trades, finding the fair option price and the option deltas and thetas become important trading tools. These sensitivities allow the floor trader to limit risk and to determine whether options are mispriced. Implied volatilities also provide important information concerning whether certain options are mispriced and the market attitude about future changes in the underlying futures contract.

THE PRICING OF OPTIONS ON FUTURES CONTRACTS

In general, the pricing relationships explained for options on stocks are also valid for options on futures. In fact, at expiration a European call on a futures contract provides a price that is equivalent to a European call on the cash asset, if both can be exercised at the same time and at option expiration. This equivalent price occurs because the exercise of the call provides a futures contract that expires immediately.[5] However, several exceptions do exist for an American option on futures, which is the type of contract traded in the United States. For example, if the futures option is sufficiently in-the-money, it can be more profitable to exercise the option early than to wait until option expiration. Thus, in this case, an American option on the futures is worth more than an American option on the cash asset (when the latter has no cash flows). The effect of early exercise and other differences in pricing between options on futures and options on the cash asset are explored in conjunction with the pricing equations discussed below.

The Black Model for Calls

Fisher Black (1976) developed a model to price options on futures. The model is based on the Black-Scholes model for options on cash assets without intermediate cash flows. When the option and corresponding futures contracts expire simultaneously, Equation (7–1) determines the fair value of a call option on futures:

$$P_C = e^{-rt} [P_F N(d_1) - K N(d_2)] \qquad (7\text{-}1)$$

where

$$d_1 = \frac{\ln(P_F/K) + (0.5\ \sigma^2)t}{\sigma\sqrt{t}} \qquad (7\text{-}2)$$

$$d_2 = d_1 - \sigma\sqrt{t} \qquad (7\text{-}3)$$

The equation for d_1 above does not contain the risk-free rate, as it does in the Black-Scholes option equation for stocks: For stocks one must consider the opportunity cost of funds invested in the stock, while for futures no investment funds are needed.[6] Normal distribution and natural logarithm tables are found in Appendices A and B at the back of the book. Example 7–1 illustrates the usage of the Black model.

The prices obtained from the Black model can be slightly smaller than the actual option market prices. The reason for this is that futures contracts involve a daily resettlement on the profits/losses of the contract. This is equivalent to a continuous dividend for a stock option. Since the Black model is based on a European model, which assumes that intermediate cash flows such as dividends and marking-to-market do not exist and early exercise is not possible (i.e., a forward contract), the Black model is not completely accurate.[7] Figure 7–1 shows the implied and historical volatility of the S&P 500 futures options. Here the implied volatility is consistently higher than the historical volatility.

Early Exercise of Options on Futures Contracts

The discussion of options on stocks determined that call options are typically "worth more alive than dead"—that is, it is more profitable to trade a call option than to exercise it, due to the existence of the option time value. In particular, using the Black-Scholes model for European options to value stock options provides an accurate value for an American option as long as the stock does not pay dividends. When a stock pays dividends, the call option buyer might exercise the American option early to obtain the dividend. This early exercise characteristic affects the option value. Put options

EXAMPLE 7–1 The Black Model and S&P 500 Options on Futures

The Black model for finding the fair value of a call option on futures is:

$$P_C = e^{-rt} [P_F N(d_1) - K N(d_2)] \qquad (7-1)$$

where

$$d_1 = \frac{\ln(P_F/K) + (0.5 \, \sigma^2)t}{\sigma \sqrt{t}} \qquad (7-2)$$

$$d_2 = d_1 - \sigma\sqrt{t} \qquad (7-3)$$

The inputs for an option on the S&P 500 futures are as follows:

$P_F = 442.15$ $K = 445$ $\sigma_s = 0.21$ $r = 3.3\%$ $t = 82/365 = .22466$

$$d_1 = \frac{\ln(442.15/445) + 0.5 \, (0.21)^2 \, (0.22466)}{0.21 \sqrt{0.2247}}$$

$$= \frac{\ln(0.9935955) + 0.5 \, (0.0441) \, (0.22466)}{0.21 \, (0.474025)}$$

$$= \frac{-0.00643 + 0.00495375}{0.0995453}$$

$$= -0.01483$$

$$d_2 = -0.01483 - 0.21\sqrt{0.2247}$$
$$= -0.01483 - 0.0995463$$
$$= -0.11438$$

$N(d_1) = 0.4941$
$N(d_2) = 0.4544$

$$P_C = e^{-.033(.2247)} [442.15(0.4941) - 445(0.4544)]$$
$$= e^{-.007415} [218.466 - 202.208]$$
$$= 0.99261 \, (16.258)$$
$$= \$16.14$$

on stocks also are exercised early, if the option is sufficiently in-the-money, in order to invest the proceeds at the risk-free interest rate.

Both call and put options on futures are exercised early if the option is sufficiently in-the-money. A deep-in-the-money option has a minimal option time value and changes point-for-point with the underlying futures contract. If the option is exercised, the resulting futures position will behave equivalently to the option, but the value of the option when exercised can be

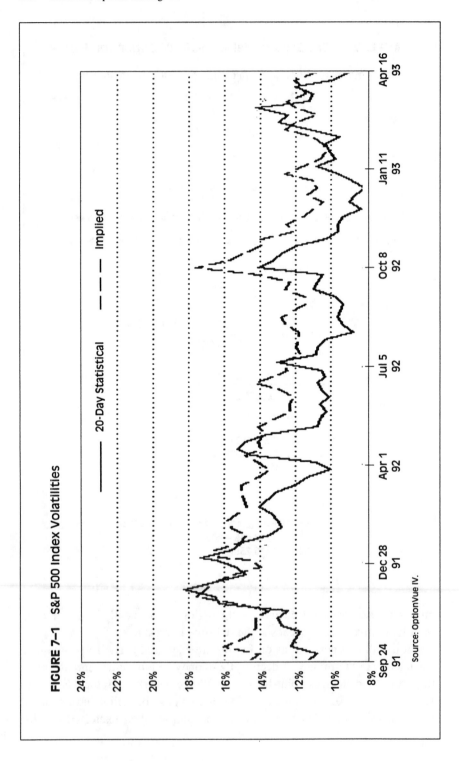

FIGURE 7–1   S&P 500 Index Volatilities

Source: OptionVue IV.

invested in a risk-free instrument to earn extra income. This is not possible with a stock option, since the purchase of the underlying stock requires funds. In fact, Gay, Kolb, and Yung (1989) show that over 55% of all futures options exercised are early exercises.[8]

One aspect of the early exercise question is whether options on futures are priced differently from options on cash, and if so, by how much. This is important for certain situations in which both types of options exist, such as for stock indexes, currencies, and debt. This question arises because of the benefit of exercising an option on futures contract early to invest the profits from the option. The following relationships exist between the two types of options:

- If the cash asset does not have a cash flow (e.g., a dividend), the call futures option is worth more than the cash option.

- If the rate of return on any cash flow is less than the risk-free interest rate for investing funds, then the call futures option is worth more than the cash option.

- If the return on the cash flow equals the risk-free rate, the two options have equivalent values.

- If the rate of return on cash flow is more than the risk-free rate, the call futures option is worth less than the cash option.

Put futures options have the opposite relationships to put cash options. Table 7–1 shows the size of the difference between call futures options and call cash options when no intermediate cash flows exist.

Comparing Options on Futures Prices

The early exercise provision of an American option provides a benefit over the European option that should be reflected in the option's price. However, the Black model prices the European (no early exercise) version of options on futures. Table 7–2 uses the results from Barone-Adesi and Whaley (1987) to compare hypothetical European and approximate American options on futures values for a six-month option with a strike price equal to 100.[9] This table shows that European out-of-the-money model values are approximately the same as their American counterparts. However, in-the-money option values reflect the benefit of exercising the American option early.

Another aspect of the futures option pricing process is to compare actual market prices to model prices. Table 7–3 uses results from Whaley (1986) to provide a summary of the market/model comparison for options on S&P 500 futures. This table shows that differences between market and model prices are not large. However, out-of-the-money and near-the-money options do have market prices that are generally less than the model price, while in-the-

TABLE 7–1 Percentage Differences Between Call Options on Futures and Call Cash Options

| | Days Until Option Expiration | | | | |
P_s/K	30	60	90	180	270
0.80	0.00	0.00	0.00	1.20	2.20
0.90	0.00	0.00	0.47	1.58	3.15
1.00	0.29	0.56	1.02	2.48	4.51
1.10	0.61	1.15	1.72	3.79	6.34
1.20	1.22	2.13	2.89	5.52	8.70

Note: Cash asset has no intermediate cash flows; interest rate = 15%; standard deviation = 0.25

Source: Brenner, Courtadon, and Subrahmanyam (1985).

TABLE 7–2 Call Values for European and American Options on Futures

Futures Price	European Call	Approximate American Call
80	$ 0.30	$ 0.30
90	1.70	1.72
100	5.42	5.48
110	11.73	11.90
120	19.91	20.34

strike price = 100 standard deviation = 0.20
interest rate = 0.08 time to expiration = 1/2 year

Source: Barone-Adesi and Whaley (1987).

money options have market prices that are above model prices. Studies on more recent data, such as those by Jordan, Seale, McCabe, and Kenyon (1987) on soybean futures options and Bailey (1987) on gold futures options, find even smaller differences between market and model prices. Moreover, one difficulty in interpreting differences in market versus model prices based on empirical studies is whether the differences occur because the market is mispricing the options or because the model is incorrect.

TABLE 7-3 Market Less Model Prices for Options on S&P 500 Futures

	Calls				Puts			
	t < 6	6 < t < 12	t > 12	All t	t < 6	6 < t < 12	t > 12	All t
$P_F/K < 0.98$	−0.063	−0.137	−0.087	−0.103	−0.106	−0.091	−0.106	−0.101
$0.98 \leq P_F/K \leq 1.02$	−0.123	−0.076	0.007	−0.092	−0.082	−0.020	0.134	−0.041
$P_F/K > 1.02$	0.058	0.118	0.070	0.081	0.129	0.191	0.306	0.193
All strikes	−0.076	−0.056	−0.012	−0.061	−0.019	0.081	0.229	0.053

Table depicts the average pricing difference for the market price less the American model price. P_F/K is the ratio of the futures price to the option strike price—that is, the extent to which it is out-of-the-money ($P_F/K < 1$) or in-the-money ($P_F/K > 1$); t is the number of weeks until option expiration.

Source: Whaley (1986).

Pricing Options on T-Bond Futures

In addition to the early exercise problem, the Black model has difficulty in pricing options on T-bond futures. This problem results from two characteristics of this contract: First, options on T-bond futures expire more than one month prior to the futures expiration. Second, this contract prices an interest-sensitive asset. The Black model assumes a constant interest rate, while T-bond prices directly reflect changing interest rates. Merville and Overdahl (1986) illustrate the pricing problems associated with applying the Black model to options on T-bond futures. Investment houses in New York are actively attempting to solve this pricing problem.

Put-Call Parity

The concept of put-call parity for options on futures is equivalent to put-call parity for stocks. Exhibit 7-4 shows how the payoffs from a long futures, long put, short call, and risk-free bond position with a face value of $P_F − K$ generate a payoff of zero, whether the futures are above or below the strike price at option expiration.[10] Since the entire portfolio has a payoff of zero at option expiration, the initial value of the portfolio must also be zero. Consequently,

$$P_P - P_C + (P_F - K) e^{-rt} = 0 \qquad (7\text{-}4)$$

where P_F = the original futures price

Solving for the put price:[11]

$$P_P = P_C - (P_F - K) e^{-rt} \qquad (7\text{-}5)$$

Since traded options on futures are American options, the European model in Equation (7–5) can give answers slightly different from actual exchange prices. However, Jordan and Seale (1986) and Blomeyer and Boyd (1988) find that deviations for actual options on futures prices from Equation (7–5) are unusual, and most deviations are not large enough to obtain a profit.

Figure 7–2 shows the implied and historical volatility for Eurodollar futures options. Notice the large increase in volatility in October, and the relationship between the implied and historical volatility during this time period.

The Black Model for Puts

Employing put-call parity from Equation (7–5) and the Black model for call options on futures from Equations (7–1) to (7–3) results in the Black equation for put options on futures with continuously compounded interest rates:

$$P_P = K e^{-rt} [1 - N(d_2)] - P_F e^{-rt} [1 - N(d_1)] \qquad (7\text{-}6)$$

where d_1 and d_2 are defined as Equations (7–2) and (7–3).

The Delta and Theta Sensitivities

As with stock options, the pricing model for options on futures creates option sensitivities. The sensitivity values for options on cash and options on futures are almost identical when one employs the same underlying price and

---

EXHIBIT 7–4 Put-Call Parity Payoffs for Options on Futures

Instrument	Current Value	Payoffs at Option Expiration $P_{F,E} < K$	Payoffs at Option Expiration $P_{F,E} > K$
Long futures	0	$P_{F,E} - P_F$	$P_{F,E} - P_F$
Long put	P_P	$K - P_{F,E}$	0
Short call	$-P_C$	0	$-(P_{F,E} - K)$
Bonds	$(P_F - K)e^{-rt}$	$P_F - K$	$P_F - K$
Portfolio		0	0

P_F = original futures price
$P_{F,E}$ = futures price at option expiration
Bond face value = $P_F - K$

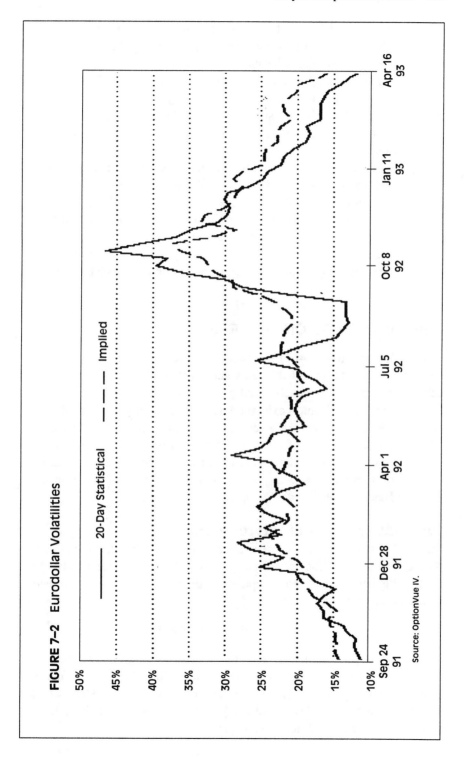

FIGURE 7–2   Eurodollar Volatilities

Source: OptionVue IV.

option strike price.[12] Recall that delta represents the hedge ratio and the extent to which the option price changes for a given change in the underlying futures price. For example, call delta values for a S&P 500 options on futures contract state the change in the option price for a one-point change in the futures price. The deltas for an out-of-the-money option such as the 445 strike price in Exhibit 7–1 are smaller in value than in-the-money options, since an in-the-money strike price changes almost point-for-point with the futures price change.

Options are a wasting asset over time, as measured by theta. Shorter-term options have less time value, and this time value decreases faster for shorter-term options. Many options on futures contracts, especially options on financial futures, possess expirations within one month of the current date as well as for the financial cycle. The shorter-term options are useful for traders with short-term expectations concerning volatility. Such traders buy options when they expect the volatility to increase and sell options when they expect volatility to decrease.

USES OF OPTIONS ON FUTURES

In general, the strategies used for options on futures parallel those for options on cash assets. The payoff diagrams and basic pricing relationships discussed in Chapters 1 to 4 apply equally well to options on futures contracts. However, options on futures exist for a number of underlying assets that do not trade options on the cash asset, at least on an organized exchange. In addition, the motivations of the users of options on futures contracts can differ from the users of options on cash because of the application needed. Moreover, the model used to price options on futures differs from the standard Black-Scholes model for cash assets.

Synthetic Options and Futures Positions

Since futures contracts do not generate dividends or interest, a trader does not need to consider the cost of carrying a cash asset. Consequently, the relationship between call and put options on futures and the futures contracts themselves is straightforward:

$$\text{Long call} + \text{short put} \ = \ \text{long futures} \tag{7-7}$$

Various combinations of this relationship exist, as given in Exhibit 7–5. Exhibit 7–5 shows that if a trader buys a call option when a short futures position is already held, a synthetic put option is created. The relationships shown in Exhibit 7–5 allow a trader to generate numerous combinations of securities for various risk-return strategies.

EXHIBIT 7–5   Synthetic Options-Futures Combinations

Synthetic long futures	= call – put
Synthetic call	= put + futures
Synthetic put	= call – futures
Synthetic short futures	= put – call
Synthetic short call	= – put – futures
Synthetic short put	= – call + futures

Note: A minus sign indicates a short position in the security. The synthetic instrument created here has the same profit and loss characteristics as the actual instrument.

Speculation

Options on the S&P 500 futures provide the trader with a means to speculate on the broad market by using the limited loss feature of options. While S&P 100 cash options exist, the S&P 500 options on futures follow a broader market of 500 stocks. Speculators can use options on futures to foretell increased volatility in the underlying cash market. In fact, Bates (1991) shows that the time value on options on S&P 500 futures showed evidence of the 1987 market crash *prior* to October 1987. In particular, out-of-the-money puts became unusually expensive the year before the crash.

The options on debt futures, agricultural futures, and commodity futures provide speculative opportunities that are not available with cash options, at least on organized exchanges. These options on futures provide the advantages of a limited loss, a small cost, and leverage. Trading in the futures themselves involves the possibility of unlimited losses and margin calls.

Hedging

Hedgers, like speculators, can use options on futures in the same manner as options on cash assets. Therefore, strategies such as covered option writing and purchasing a put provide downside protection for an existing asset position.[13]

Covered option writing for stock index options on futures is similar to covered option writing for stocks, except that the hedger often does not have a portfolio of stocks that exactly matches the stock index. In this case, the number of calls sold is adjusted for the beta of the portfolio of stocks and for the size of the portfolio holdings. In addition, if the portfolio is not well diversified, then basis risk exists between the stock portfolio and the stock index. However, the motivation for the writer of the cash option is equivalent to that of the writer of an option on futures position. Thus, option writing can provide additional income if the hedger believes that the market will be

---

EXHIBIT 7–6   Strategies with Interest Rate Options on Futures

Situation:	Objective:	Strategy:
An institutional bond portfolio contains bonds scheduled to mature in three months and the money will be available for reinvestment at that time.	To achieve protection against a possible decline in interest rates and higher bond prices without forgoing the opportunity to benefit from lower bond prices if interest rates should rise.	Buy call options on T-bond futures.
An institution has a substantial portion of its funds in Treasury bills and other money market investments—perhaps to maintain a high level of liquidity and to avoid the risks associated with long-term investments.	To participate in any significant increase in the value of long-term bonds without forgoing the advantages of short-term investments.	Buy call options on T-bond futures.
The management of a bond portfolio is considering an immunization strategy to protect against rising interest rates and declining bond prices.	To protect the market value of the portfolio while retaining the opportunity to profit if bond prices should increase.	Buy put options on T-bond futures.
An investment portfolio includes a substantial number of Treasury bonds. The outlook is for relatively stable interest rates and bond prices.	To increase current portfolio return.	Write call options on T-bond futures against bonds held in the portfolio.
An institution plans, in about three months, to sell bonds that it currently holds in its portfolio. It anticipates that bond prices at that time will be approximately the same as they are now.	To obtain an above-the-market net price when bonds are sold.	Write call options on futures.

Source: "Options on U.S. Treasury Bond Futures for Institutional Investors," Chicago Board of Trade, pp. 9–13. This source has examples of each of the above strategies.

---

relatively flat over the life of the option.[14] Brooks (1991) uses a risk-return evaluation tool called stochastic dominance to show that implementing covered call writing with futures options provides larger returns than using cash index options. Similarly, Brooks finds that using futures put options is superior to using cash put options.

Options on interest rate futures provide opportunities for hedging strategies not explored in previous chapters, since exchange-traded options on cash debt are not active contracts. Exhibit 7–6 lists examples of the more important strategies using interest rate options on futures and the objective of such strategies. One of the examples listed in Exhibit 7–6 is covered option writing on a fixed-income portfolio. Such a strategy is beneficial when interest rate volatility is minimal. Moreover, the portfolio manager can write the covered options on cash bonds, even though a T-bond futures contract is the delivery instrument for the options contract, since the cash T-bond can be delivered into the futures contract. Alternatively, the option position can be closed before the typical exercise time to avoid delivery of the futures.[15] DeRonne (1985) illustrates how to use futures options for hedging interest rate instruments for specific market scenarios. Brophy (1984) discusses some aspects of commercial hedging uses of options on agricultural futures.

SUMMARY AND LOOKING AHEAD

Options on futures contracts extend the benefits of options contracts to an entirely new range of securities. The Black model is often used to price futures options. However, the early exercise opportunities for options on futures create unique pricing problems for these contracts. The lack of a closed-form model to price options contracts provides uncertainties and opportunities for those using these contracts. The following chapter examines currency options on both the cash currency and the futures contract.

END NOTES

[1] Index options settle by means of a cash transfer of the difference in price between the final asset price and the strike price since delivering a portfolio of assets is too cumbersome.

[2] Similarly, a long put and a short call create a synthetic short futures position. However, futures can create option positions only if a dynamic hedging program with futures is initiated. A dynamic hedge involves constantly revising the hedge position. Moreover, this strategy assumes that large jumps in the underlying futures price do not occur, since such jumps negate the ability to revise the hedge position quickly.

[3] One reason futures options can provide more accurate pricing than exchange-traded options on cash assets is because the futures options trade alongside the futures contracts on the exchanges. Hence, the floor traders know the current price of the underlying futures contracts.

[4] If an option that expires in March, June, September, or December is exercised on the last trading day, then the option is settled via cash since the futures contract is no longer trading. The cash settlement is based on the S&P 500 Index value on the open of the next day, the third Friday of the contract month. This is the same procedure used to settle the futures contract.

[5] The value of a European option on futures calculated via a model could differ from the option on the cash asset, since the futures contract typically is more volatile than the cash asset.

[6] Margin on the futures can be posted in T-bills rather than cash so that no immediate cash investment is needed. The Black-Scholes and the Black models can be shown to be equivalent if $P_F e^{-rt}$ is substituted for P_S in the Black-Scholes model. Thus, the two models will give equivalent results *if* the volatilities of the cash and futures instruments are equivalent *and* intermediate cash flows such as marking—to-market of the futures are ignored. Moreover, note that if no uncertainty existed—that is, $N(d_1)$ and $N(d_2)$ equal 1.0 —then the Black model is $P_C = e^{-rt} [P_F - K]$, which means that the value of the call option when certainty exists equals the present value of the proceeds when the option is exercised.

[7] American options on futures are equivalent to a series of European options. In other words, the early exercise of an option on futures contract obtains the intrinsic value of the option, but forfeits the remaining daily opportunities to exercise the option at a later time. Because it is difficult to value a series of European options in a simple manner, there is no closed-form solution for the value of an American option on futures contract. Only an approximate solution exists.

[8] To avoid arbitrage for a European call on futures, $P_C \geq Max[0, P_F(1 + i)^{-t} -K(1 + i)^{-t}]$. The exercisable value for an American call on futures is Max $[0, P_F - K]$. Since $(1 + i)^{-t} \leq 1$, we have: Max $[0, (1 + i)^{-t} (P_F - K)] \geq$ Max $[0, P_F - K]$. Therefore, it *may* be beneficial to exercise an in-the-money American call at any time. A similar argument holds for puts on futures.

[9] Adesi and Whaley use several approximation methods to value options on futures. The method they propose is superior on a computational basis for obtaining these values.

[10] If the exercise price is greater than the futures price, one issues rather than buys bonds.

[11] Since $P_F = P_C (1 + i)^t$ when no intermediate cash flows are relevant, substituting P_C for $P_F (1 + i)^{-t}$ results in the put-call parity equation for stocks without dividends.

[12] For example, the equation for the delta for options on futures is $e^{-rt} N(d_1)$, which is equivalent to the delta equation for options on cash.

[13] Covered option writers for stocks have the advantage of receiving the cash dividends on the stocks held. Covered option writers for options on futures do not receive any cash inflows, since futures do not pay dividends or interest.

[14] Short options on futures require that margin be deposited to avoid potential losses. While any such losses on the short call option are offset by gains in the stock portfolio position, margins do require interim cash payments.

[15] While options can be written on over-the-counter cash options on specific T-bonds, it is important to make sure that liquidity exists for the specific T-bond and that the option price does not include a large premium related to its over-the-counter nature. Over-the-counter options on specific T-bonds do avoid the basis risk that is possible with options on T-bond futures. Thus, if futures options are employed and the cash bond used does not correspond to the cheapest-to-deliver bond priced by the T-bond futures contract, then basis risk exists.

Currency | **8**
Options |

Options on currency take two forms: options on cash and options on futures. A currency call option on cash provides the right to buy the foreign exchange at a specific strike price in the domestic currency for a specified period of time. A put option on a foreign currency provides the right to sell the foreign exchange at a specific strike price in the domestic currency for a specified period of time. Options on currency futures provide the right to take a long position in a currency futures contract at a specific strike price (call) or a short position in a currency futures (put).

The pricing equation for cash currency options parallels the stock Black-Scholes model, except that both U.S. and foreign interest rates must be considered. Consequently, the values of the cash options and any possible mispricings are affected by these relative interest rates. The Black model is employed for options on futures pricing. Strategies with currency options parallel those used for stock options, except that one is speculating or hedging the relative value of a foreign currency in relation to the dollar.

TYPES AND CHARACTERISTICS OF CURRENCY OPTIONS

Both **currency options** on cash and **options on currency futures** are actively traded in the United States. Currency options on cash trade over 10 million contracts per year, while options on currency futures trade more than 6 million contracts. Currency options are treated separately from other options because of their specialized nature, the need to understand the quotation procedure of the underlying cash asset, and the pricing formula for each option. However, the basic pricing relationships for currency options are equivalent to the pricing relationships for stock options.

Cash currency quotations and currency forwards are covered in Appendix 8A. One must know how the underlying cash currencies are quoted in order to understand the meaning of the quotations of currency options.

Options on Currency

A call option on a foreign currency provides the right to buy the foreign exchange at a specific strike price in the domestic currency for a specific period of time. For example, a call on British pounds provides the right (but not the obligation) to buy pounds at the dollar strike price of the option until the option expires (American option) or at option expiration (European option). Similarly, a put option on a foreign currency provides the right to sell the foreign exchange at a specific strike price in the domestic currency for a specific period of time.

American options dominate the trading of exchange-traded options since these options provide the benefit of allowing exercise on any day that the exchange is open. The Philadelphia and London exchanges actively trade American options on cash foreign currency. European options are traded on the Philadelphia Exchange and are issued by over-the-counter dealers; exchange-traded European options have substantially less liquidity than the American options. Options on cash currencies expire on the Friday prior to the third Wednesday in the option expiration month (as of October 1993), except for the options designated "EOM" (which expire on the last Friday of the month). Expiration months are the next two calendar months plus the financial cycle of March, June, September, and December. (Long-term options with expirations of 18 and 24 months also exist, but have minimal volume.) The Philadelphia Exchange trades currency options from 7:00 P.M. to 2:30 P.M. the next day (6:00 P.M. during daylight saving time)—20 ½ hours

EXHIBIT 8–1   Currency Option Characteristics

Contract	Contract Size*	Strike Price Increment	Minimum Price Change*		Opening Price Limit**
Australian dollar	50,000AD	$0.01	$0.0001	= $5.00	$.02
British pound	31,250BP	$0.025	$0.0001	= $3.125	$.02
Canadian dollar	50,000CD	$0.005	$0.0001	= $5.00	$.02
German mark	62,500DM	$0.005***	$0.0001	= $6.25	$.02
Japanese yen	6,250,000JY	$0.0005***	$0.000001	= $6.25	$.0002
Swiss franc	62,500SF	$0.005***	$0.0001	= $6.25	$.02

* Futures options are twice these sizes.
** For futures options *only.*
*** These strike intervals are called "half-strikes." They exist only for the three nearest months. Half-strikes futures options exist for the first four expiration months and for the five nearest-to-the-money options including the Australian dollar. Otherwise full strike prices exist, which are twice the size of the half-strikes. The creation of new strikes as currency prices change depends on the decision of the specialist. European options can have fewer strike prices.

total. This extensive time period provides access to the Japanese market. Exhibit 8–1 provides contract size, strike price increments, and minimum price changes for the active currency option contracts.

Exhibit 8–2 shows the quotations for cash currency options traded on the Philadelphia Exchange. Options on foreign currencies exist for those countries that have an important international trading activity. These options on foreign currencies include the Australian dollar, British pound, Canadian dollar, French franc, German mark, Japanese yen, and Swiss franc. Cross-rate options exist between the German mark and Japanese yen (as well as for the British pound and mark), but they have minimal volume. The "r" designation in the quotes means that the option in question did not trade during the day; an "s" means that particular option has never traded. The size of the cash option contracts is one-half the size of both the corresponding futures contracts and the options on futures contracts. Thus, cash currency options are less expensive than the equivalent currency options on futures contracts.

As an example of how to interpret these quotations, let us use the British pound call option with a strike price of 160 ($1.60). Since the pound trades at 157.48 ($1.5748) in the cash market, this is a near-the-money (or technically an out-of-the-money) option. The June call for this option sells for 2.20. Since the British pound trades in U.S. cents per unit of the foreign currency, the quote of 2.20 represents 2.20 cents per pound, or equivalently $0.0220 per pound. Multiplying this cost by the 31,250 pounds per option contract provides the total cost of $687.55 for one cash option on British pounds. Similarly, the 155 British pound call option is an in-the-money option, since the current value for the pound is 157.48 and the strike price of this option is only 155. The June 155 call sells for 4.15 cents per pound. Multiplying by 31,250 pounds provides the $1296.87 cost of this option.

In the foreign exchange market, British pounds are quoted in terms of the number of U.S. dollars per one pound. This is the same convention used by the options market—that is, options are quoted as the cost of *one unit* of the foreign exchange in U.S. currency (often in terms of one U.S. cent). However, other foreign currencies, such as the German mark and Japanese yen, are quoted in the cash market in terms of the number of foreign currency units (mark or yen) per one U.S. dollar. Thus, a yen quote would be 110 yen/ $. The options market, to maintain consistency across all options and to reduce confusion, quotes all currency options as the cost in U.S. currency for one unit of the foreign currency. In other words, an option on the mark is quoted as a cost in U.S. cents per one mark (to obtain the total cost, one multiplies by the 62,500 marks for one option contract). Similarly, an option on the yen is quoted in 1/100ths of a U.S. cent per yen (due to the large number of yen per one U.S. dollar); the total cost of a yen option contract is

EXHIBIT 8–2 Options on Currency Quotations

OPTIONS

PHILADELPHIA EXCHANGE

Option & Underlying	Strike Price	Calls–Last May	Jun	Sep	Puts–Last May	Jun	Sep
50,000 Australian Dollars-cent per unit							
A Dollr ...	68	r	r	r	r	0.15	r
71.43 ...	71	r	r	r	r	0.97	r
31,250 British Pound-German Mark cross.							
BPd-GMk	240	r	9.50	r	r	r	r
249.29 ...	242	r	8.00	r	r	r	r
249.29 ...	252	1.00	r	r	r	r	r
31,250 British Pound-European Style.							
BPound	150	r	r	r	r	r	2.97
157.48 ...	152½	r	4.66	r	r	r	r
157.48 ...	155	r	r	r	1.93	r	r
157.48 ...	170	r	0.30	r	r	14.85	r
157.48 ...	145	r	r	r	r	r	1.88
31,250 British Pounds-cents per unit.							
BPound ...							
157.48 ...	150	r	r	r	0.23	0.95	2.80
157.48 ...	152½	5.33	r	r	0.62	1.60	r
157.48 ...	155	3.60	4.15	r	1.20	r	5.03
157.48 ...	157½	2.00	2.84	r	3.36	3.65	r
157.48 ...	160	1.10	2.20	r	r	r	r
157.48 ...	162½	0.38	1.04	r	r	r	r
50,00 Canadian Dollars-cents per unit.							
CDollar.....	78½	r	0.89	r	r	r	r
79.26 ...	79½	r	0.40	r	r	r	r
79.26 ...	80	0.13	r	r	r	r	r
79.26 ...	81½	r	r	r	r	2.45	r
62,500 European Currency Units-cents per unit.							
ECU.....	120	r	r	r	0.53	r	r
123.40 ...	124	1.05	r	r	r	r	r
250,000 French Francs-European Style.							
FFranc.....							
187.11 ...	17¼	r	r	r	r	0.32	r
187.11 ...	18	r	7.20	r	r	r	r
187.11 ...	19	r	1.50	r	r	r	r
187.11 ...	19¼	s	1.10	r	s	r	r
62,500 German Marks-Japanese Yen cross.							
GMk-Jyn...	68½	r	r	s	0.48	r	s
62,500 German Marks-European Style.							
DMark...							
63.19 ...	61½	1.62	1.90	s	r	r	s
63.19 ...	62	1.40	1.52	r	0.56	r	r
63.19 ...	62½	1.04	r	s	0.60	r	s
63.19 ...	63	r	1.10	r	r	r	r
63.19 ...	64½	r	r	s	r	2.30	s
63.19 ...	66	0.08	r	r	r	r	r
62,500 German Marks-cents per unit.							
DMark...							
63.19 ...	61	2.23	r	r	0.20	0.55	1.46
63.19 ...	61½	r	r	s	0.31	0.72	s
63.19 ...	62	1.43	1.64	r	0.44	0.88	1.97
63.19 ...	62½	1.09	r	s	0.61	1.11	s
63.19 ...	63	0.81	1.11	1.48	0.86	r	r
63.19 ...	63½	0.61	0.75	s	r	r	s
63.19 ...	64	0.43	r	r	1.32	r	r
63.19 ...	64½	0.32	0.62	s	1.80	r	s
63.19 ...	66	r	0.27	r	r	r	r
63.19 ...	67	r	0.16	r	r	r	r
6,250.00 Japanese Yen-100ths of a cent per unit.							
JYen...							
90.51 ...	88	2.50	2.80	r	0.23	0.59	1.40
90.51 ...	89	r	r	r	0.46	0.86	r
90.51 ...	90	1.22	r	r	0.89	1.25	2.20
90.51 ...	90½	1.06	r	s	1.00	r	s
90.51 ...	91	r	r	2.10	1.23	r	r
90.51 ...	91½	r	1.01	s	r	r	s
90.51 ...	92	0.41	0.80	r	r	r	r
90.51 ...	93	r	r	1.32	r	r	r
6,250,00 Japanese Yen-European Style.							
JYen...	87	r	r	r	r	r	0.95
90.51 ...	93	r	0.60	r	r	r	r
90.51 ...	94	r	r	0.96	r	r	r
62,500 Swiss Francs-European Style.							
SFranc....	65	r	r	r	r	0.14	r
70.04 ...	67	r	r	r	r	0.43	r
70.04 ...	68	1.55	r	r	0.31	r	r
70.04 ...	69	1.49	1.91	r	0.63	r	r
70.04 ...	71	0.49	r	r	r	r	r
62,500 Swiss Francs-cents per unit.							
SFranc....							
70.04 ...	68	r	2.53	r	r	1.00	r
70.04 ...	68½	1.40	s	s	r	0.95	s
70.04 ...	69	r	1.85	r	0.65	1.11	2.06
70.04 ...	69½	1.06	r	s	r	r	s
70.04 ...	70	r	0.70	r	r	r	r
70.04 ...	70½	0.73	r	s	r	r	s
70.04 ...	71	0.46	r	r	r	r	r
70.04 ...	72	r	0.60	1.45	r	r	r

	Strike Price	Apr	May	Jun	Apr	May	Jun
31,250 British Pound-German mark EOM.							
Bpd-GMk	250	0.88	2.68	r	r	r	r
31,250 British Pound EOM-cents per unit.							
BPound ...	147½	r	r	r	0.04	r	r
157.48 ...	150	r	r	r	0.06	r	r
157.48 ...	152½	r	r	r	0.28	r	r
157.48 ...	155	r	r	r	0.48	r	r
157.48 ...	157½	0.64	r	r	r	r	r
50,000 Canadian Dollars EOM-cents per unit.							
CDollr ...	79½	0.08	r	r	r	r	r
250,000 French Francs EOM-10ths of a unit per unit.							
FFranc ...	18¾	r	r	r	r	3.80	r
62,500 German Marks EOM-cents per unit.							
DMark ...	61	r	r	r	0.08	r	r
63.19 ...	62	1.05	r	r	0.17	r	r
63.19 ...	63	0.52	0.94	r	0.60	1.16	r
63.19 ...	64	0.19	r	r	r	r	r
63.19 ...	60½	r	r	r	0.03	0.33	r
63.19 ...	61½	r	r	r	0.07	0.52	r
63.19 ...	62½	0.90	r	r	0.28	r	r
63.19 ...	63½	0.30	0.60	r	r	r	r
63.19 ...	64½	0.10	r	r	r	r	r
6,250,000 Japanese Yen EOM-100ths of a cent per unit.							
JYen ...	85	5.35	r	r	r	r	r
90.51 ...	88	2.30	r	r	r	r	r
90.51 ...	89	r	r	r	0.20	r	r
90.51 ...	90	r	1.34	r	0.50	1.14	r
90.51 ...	88½	1.95	r	r	0.11	r	r
90.51 ...	91½	r	r	r	r	r	r
62,500 Swiss Franc EOM-cents per unit.							
SFranc ...	68	r	r	r	0.11	r	r
70.04 ...	70	r	r	r	0.62	r	r
70.04 ...	67½	r	r	r	0.06	r	r
70.04 ...	68½	1.44	r	r	0.15	r	r

Total Call Vol. 48,562   Call Open Int. 604,938
Total Put Vol. 73,759   Put Open Int. 505,326

r = Option not traded on this day.
s = Option does not exit.

Source: Option Exchange, April 23.

EXHIBIT 8–3   Relationships Between U.S. and Foreign Currency Values

Option Position	Value of U.S. $*	Value of Foreign Currency*	Direction of $/FC Quote (and Futures Price)	Direction of FC/$ Quote	Direction of Option Position	Profit or Loss on Option Position
Long Call	↑	↓	↓	↑	↓	Loss
	↓	↑	↑	↓	↑	Profit
Short Call	↑	↓	↓	↑	↓	Profit
	↓	↑	↑	↓	↑	Loss
Long Put	↑	↓	↓	↑	↑	Profit
	↓	↑	↑	↓	↓	Loss
Short Put	↑	↓	↓	↑	↑	Loss
	↓	↑	↑	↓	↓	Profit

* ↑ strengthens ↓ weakens

found by multiplying this cost by the 6,250,000 yen for one option contract. Exhibit 8–3 illustrates the various currency option positions, the possible changes in currency values, and the resultant profit/loss on the option.[1]

Options on Currency Futures

Call options on currency futures provide the right to take a long position in a currency futures contract at a specific strike price for a specific period of time. Put options on currency futures provide the right to take a short position in a currency futures contract at a specific strike price for a specific period of time. Active futures options on currency trade for the Japanese yen, German mark, British pound, and Swiss franc. Less active futures options exist for the Canadian dollar, Australian dollar, mark/yen cross-rate, and the U.S. dollar index. Each futures option has a size in foreign currency units that is equivalent to the underlying futures contract size. All futures options are American options. Expiration months are the next two calendar months and the financial cycle. Strike price intervals depend on the currency. The British pound has intervals of one-quarter cent, the mark has intervals of one-half cent, and the yen has intervals of one-half of 1/100th of a cent. Other currency futures options strike price intervals are evident from the quotations given.

Exhibit 8–4 shows the quotes for the currency futures options. The quotation procedures are equivalent to the quotes for cash currency options, except that the appropriate decimal for the strike price is omitted. Thus, the

EXHIBIT 8–4 Options on Currency Futures Quotations

CURRENCY

JAPANESE YEN (CME)
12,500,000 Yen; cents per 100 yen

Strike	Calls–Settle			Puts–Settle		
Price	May	Jun	Jly	May	Jun	Jly
8950	1.41	1.88	...	0.40	0.87	...
9000	1.09	1.59	1.99	0.58	1.08	...
9050	0.82	1.33	1.74	0.81	1.32	...
9100	0.61	1.11	...	1.10	1.60	...
9150	0.44	0.92	...	1.43	...	...
9200	0.32	0.75	1.13	1.81	2.23	...

Est. vol. 5,840;
Thur vol. 4,947 calls; 5,492 puts
Op. Int. Thur 37,335 calls; 36,982 puts

DEUTSCHEMARK (CME)
125,000 marks; cents per mark

Strike	Calls–Settle			Puts–Settle		
Price	May	Jun	Jly	May	Jun	Jly
6200	1.14	1.56	1.56	0.35	0.77	1.40
6250	0.83	1.29	1.33	0.54	1.00	...
6300	0.57	1.03	1.13	0.78	1.24	...
6350	0.40	0.82	0.95	1.11	1.53	...
6400	0.26	0.66	0.80	1.47	1.86	...
6450	0.16	0.50	...	...	...	...

Est. vol. 28,000;
Thur vol. 7,659 calls; 6,141 puts
Op. Int. Thur 178,294 calls; 132,712 puts

CANADIAN DOLLARS (CME)
100,000 Can. $, cents per Can. $

Strike	Calls–Settle			Puts–Settle		
Price	May	Jun	Jly	May	Jun	Jly
7800	...	1.28	...	0.07	0.23	...
7850	0.72	0.93	...	0.16	0.37	...
7900	0.40	0.63	...	0.34	0.57	...
7950	0.18	0.41	...	0.62	0.85	...
8000	0.07	0.25	...	1.01	1.19	...
8050	0.02	0.15	...	...	1.58	...

Est. vol. 502;
Thurs vol. 91 calls; 111 puts
Op. Int. Thur 3,580 calls; 4,496 puts

BRITISH POUND (CME)
62,500 pounds; cents per pound

Strike	Calls–Settle			Puts–Settle		
Price	May	Jun	Jly	May	Jun	Jly
1525	4.90	5.72	5.92	0.44	1.28	2.58
1550	3.02	4.12	4.46	1.06	2.16	3.60
1575	1.54	2.78	3.30	2.08	3.30	...
1600	0.76	1.78	2.38	...	4.80	...
1625	0.34	1.10	1.68	...	6.62	...
1650	0.14	0.64	...	...	8.64	...

Est. vol. 4,349;
Thur vol. 197 calls; 1,040 puts
Op. Int. Thur 15,970 calls; 11,521 puts

SWISS FRANC (CME)
125,00 francs; cents per franc

Strike	Calls–Settle			Puts–Settle		
Price	May	Jun	Jly	May	Jun	Jly
6900	1.34	1.83	2.12	0.42	0.91	...
6950	1.02	1.54	...	0.60	1.12	...
7000	0.76	1.29	1.61	0.84	1.37	...
7050	0.54	1.06	...	...	...	...
7100	0.38	0.87	1.21	...	1.95	...
7150	...	0.57	...	...	2.64	...

Est. vol. 3,914;
Thur vol. 687 calls; 660 puts
Op. Int. Thur 11,701 calls; 15,315 puts

U.S. DOLLAR INDEX (FINEX)
1,000 time index

Strike	Calls–Settle			Puts–Settle		
Price	May	Jun	Jly	May	Jun	Jly
88	...	...	...	0.18	0.57	...
89	...	...	...	0.43	0.91	...
90	...	1.28	...	0.85	1.37	...
91	0.38	0.86	...	1.47	1.94	...
92	0.16	0.55	...	2.25	2.63	...
93	0.06	0.33	...	3.14	3.41	...

Est. vol. 660;
Thur vol. 118 calls; 104 puts
Op. Int. Thur 1,230 calls; 2,421 puts

... means not traded.

Source: Futures Exchanges, April 23.

strike price for the British pound futures option is listed as 1600 rather than 160.0 cents (or $1.60). Similarly, the yen strike price of 9000 is actually 90.00 cents per 100 yen (or 0.9000 cent per yen). The correct placement of the decimal can be determined by looking at the equivalent cash currency option quotation.

Let us use the July yen futures option for an example of how to interpret the quotes for options on currency futures contracts. The quote for the July 9000 in-the-money yen futures option is 1.99. This quote is cents per 100 yen or, equivalently, 0.0199 cents per yen. Converting to dollars, we have $0.000199 per yen, or a total option cost of $2487.50 when we multiply by the contract size of 12,500,000 yen.

Taking Positions in Currency Options

Currency options, unlike most other markets, have an active over-the-counter (OTC) market. OTC options allow the option trader to customize the strike price, expiration date, and amount of the option. OTC currency options also exist on currencies not traded on the exchanges. However, the cost of these options will include a premium to the writer for the extra risk undertaken, since the option cannot be hedged with traded options. In addition, OTC options typically are written for amounts of $1 million or more. OTC

currency options also allow the creation of unique options to meet specialized needs. These options and their uses are discussed in Chapter 9.[2]

One interesting aspect of exchange-traded currency options is that different
option positions provide equivalent positions once the option is exercised. Thus,
for cash currency options the following obtain equivalent positions:

- Both the long call and short put positions obtain a long position in the
  foreign currency if the options are exercised (this position is paid for
  using the domestic currency—in our case, U.S. dollars). However,
  the long call holder decides if and when to exercise, while the short
  put trader does *not* determine when to exercise.

- Both the short call and long put obtain the domestic (U.S.) currency
  and pay out the foreign currency. The long put has the exercise
  option, while the short call does not.[3]

For currency options on futures, the following obtain equivalent positions:

- Both a long call and a short put take a long position in the associated
  futures contract.

- Both a short call and a long put take a short position in the associated
  futures contract.

THE PRICING OF CURRENCY OPTIONS

The pricing relationships discussed in Chapter 2 are relevant for currency
options and currency futures options (except for the early exercise issues for
futures options discussed in Chapter 7). Cash currency options can be priced
with a modified Black-Scholes model. Currency options on futures are
priced with the Black model discussed in Chapter 7.

The Modified Black-Scholes Model

Garman and Kohlhagen (1983) and Grabbe (1983) develop modified Black-
Scholes models for currency options. The important modification is to
consider the risk-free interest rate in both the foreign country and the
domestic (U.S.) country. The resultant interest rates can be stated either in
terms of the rates themselves or (more commonly) in terms of the value of a
discount bond that earns the risk-free rate over the life of the option. Thus,
the value of the U.S. (domestic) discount bond is defined as:

$$B = 1 / [1 + i (T/360)] \qquad (8\text{-}1)$$

where B = the domestic discount bond, which has a value of one
               unit of the domestic currency at maturity

i = the domestic risk-free interest rate

T = the number of days until the bond matures

Correspondingly, the value of the foreign bond is:

$$B^* = 1 / [1 + i^* (T/360)] \qquad \text{(8-2)}$$

where B* = the foreign discount bond, which has a value of one unit of the foreign currency at maturity

i* = the foreign risk-free interest rate

The above simplification allows us to state the modified Black-Scholes model for currency call options in terms of the discrete values of B and B*, as follows:[4]

$$P_C = P_S B^* N(d_1) - K B N(d_2) \qquad \text{(8-3)}$$

where

$$d_1 = \frac{\ln(P_S B^* / K B) + 0.5 \sigma_S^2 t}{\sigma_S \sqrt{t}} \qquad \text{(8-4)}$$

$$d_2 = d_1 - \sigma_S \sqrt{t} \qquad \text{(8-5)}$$

P_S = the currency exchange rate in terms of cost in domestic (U.S.) currency for one unit of the foreign currency

σ_S = the annualized standard deviation of the continuously compounded return on the cash exchange rate.[5]

Example 8-1 shows how to find the value of a call option on foreign exchange.

The principal difference between the option model in Equation (8-3) and the Black-Scholes model for stock options is in the use of the interest rates in *both* countries of the currency quotation. Consequently, Table 8-1 shows simulated values for a call option on British pounds showing the effect of differing interest rates on the call option value. In addition, in-the-money, near-the-money, and out-of-the-money options are shown. Examination of this table shows the following:

- If i = i*, then *higher* rates of interest are associated with *lower* call option prices.

- Call values increase as the domestic U.S. interest rate increases (for a constant foreign interest rate).

EXAMPLE 8–1   Finding the Call Value on Foreign Exchange

The modified Black-Scholes equation for finding the fair value of a call option on currency is as follows:

$$P_c = P_s B^* N(d_1) - K B N(d_2) \qquad (8\text{-}3)$$

where

$$d_1 = \frac{\ln(P_s B^* / K B) + 0.5\, \sigma_s^2\, t}{\sigma_s \sqrt{t}} \qquad (8\text{-}4)$$

$$d_2 = d_1 - \sigma_s \sqrt{t} \qquad (8\text{-}5)$$

Given the input information, we can find the fair value of an option on German marks.

P_s = $0.6131 (the current cost of one mark in U.S. dollars—that is, the $/DM quote)

K = $0.61 (the strike price of the option in $/DM)

Time to expiration = 80 days (t = 80/365 = 0.21918; T = 80/360 = 0.22222)

σ_s = 0.25 (the standard deviation of the $/DM value)

i = 3.5% (the domestic U.S. annual interest rate)

i* = 6.5% (the foreign annual interest rate)

To employ Equation (8-3), we need the discount bond values for B and B*:

$$B = 1 / [1 + i\, (T/360)] \qquad (8\text{-}1)$$

$$B^* = 1 / [1 + i^*\, (T/360)] \qquad (8\text{-}2)$$

For this example:

$$B = 1 / [1 + 0.035\, (0.22222)] = 1 / 1.00777 = 0.992290$$

$$B^* = 1 / [1 + 0.065\, (0.22222)] = 1 / 1.014444 = 0.985762$$

Therefore,

$$d_1 = \frac{\ln[(.6131)\,(.985762) / (.61)\,(.992290)] + .5\,(.25)^2\,(.21918)}{(0.25)\,(\sqrt{0.21918})}$$

$$= \frac{\ln(0.9984698) + .006849}{0.1170417}$$

$$= (-.00153 + .006849) / 0.1170417$$

$$= +.0454$$

$$d_2 = -.04543 - 0.25\,\sqrt{0.21918}$$

$$= +.04543 - 0.11704$$

$$= -.0716$$

From normal distribution tables (after interpolating)

$N(d_1)$ = 0.5181 $N(d_2)$ = 0.4722

The call fair value is: P_c = $.6131 (0.985762) (0.5181) – $0.61 (0.992290) (0.4722)

$$= \$0.31312 - \$0.28582$$

$$= \$.0273, \text{ or } 2.73 \text{ cents}$$

TABLE 8–1 The Effect on Relative Interest Rates on Foreign Exchange Calls Options

Inputs: $\sigma = 0.20$ $P_c = \$1.50/£$ $t = 90$ days

K = 145	i* (British interest rate)			
i (U.S. interest rate)	3%	5%	7%	9%
3%	8.62	8.15	7.69	7.24
5%	9.06	8.58	8.11	7.65
7%	9.52	9.02	8.54	8.06
9%	9.98	9.47	8.98	9.49

K = 150	i* (British interest rate)			
i (U.S. interest rate)	3%	5%	7%	9%
3%	5.90	5.53	5.17	4.82
5%	6.26	5.88	5.50	5.14
7%	6.64	6.23	5.85	5.47
9%	7.02	6.61	6.21	5.82

K = 155	i* (British interest rate)			
i (U.S. interest rate)	3%	5%	7%	9%
3%	3.84	3.56	3.30	3.04
5%	4.12	3.82	3.55	3.28
7%	4.41	4.10	3.81	3.53
9%	4.71	4.39	4.08	3.79

Source: Developed using OptionVue IV.

As with the option pricing models for other assets, the above modified Black-Scholes equation is for European call options. American options, which can be exercised any time before option expiration, do not have a closed-form solution to their value. The key pricing relationships for American versus European currency options are as follows:

- The greater the differential of the foreign interest rate over the domestic interest rate, the greater the value of the American call option in comparison to the European call option.

- The greater the differential of the foreign interest rate over the domestic interest rate, the smaller the difference in value between the American put option and the European put option (an American option is worth at least as much as a European option).

- If the domestic interest rate is above the foreign interest rate, the above relationships are reversed.

Tests of the currency option model by Tucker (1985) find a large number of pricing errors that could be exploited by floor traders, but not by others. Shastri and Tandon (1986) compare the European currency option model with an American version. They find that a high foreign interest rate causes the European-modified Black-Scholes model to misprice currency options because of the probability of early exercise.

The concepts of the pricing sensitivities for currency options are equivalent to those examined in earlier chapters. However, the foreign and domestic interest rates do affect the equations specifying these sensitivities.[6]

Pricing Options on Currency Futures

Currency futures options are priced in the same manner as other futures options (see Chapter 7). Since the underlying security is a futures contract, we do not need to worry about the relative interest rates in the two countries (although this factor does affect the futures price). Other characteristics of options on futures apply to currency futures options, including the effect of early exercise of the American options on the pricing process of these options. Figure 8–1 shows the implied and historical volatility of the British pound call option on futures. This figure illustrates the significant change in volatility for the pound that can occur and the relationship between the historical and implied volatility associated with such changes.

Interest Rate Parity

The values of currency options are affected by the relative interest rates for the two currencies relevant for the option. These same interest rates are the key factors used to develop interest rate parity (Daigler, 1993) develops this relationship). Interest rate parity provides the pricing relationship for currency forward and futures contracts. Interest rate parity also is used in the pricing of currency options. The equation describing the price of a forward/futures value in terms of the current currency exchange rate and the interest rates in the two countries (interest rate parity) is:

$$P_F = \frac{P_S \, [1 + i(T/360)]}{1 + i^*(T/360)} \qquad (8\text{-}6)$$

FOCUS 8–1 Option Tables and the Simulator

The Option Simulator allows the user to examine relationships among different options in a number of ways. One method is to create a table of option values (or sensitivities) as the input variables change. As shown in the table below, an Option Simulator table allows four variables to change: the strike price and time to expiration (see the two left vertical columns) and the exchange rate and volatility (see the top two rows). Note that the domestic and foreign interest rates are described by DIntRate and FIntRate, respectively. The user chooses from the list of input variables provided. Once the table is created, all the user has to do to create a table of delta, gamma, and so on, sensitivities is to move the arrow key to the desired output. In the table below, the option values are given in dollars—that is, an option worth 8 cents is shown as 0.08 rather than the typical representation of 8.00 shown in other tables in this chapter and in the newspaper.

FOREIGN-EXCHANGE EUROPEAN OPTIONS (LOGNORMAL)

Call
Domestic Interest Rate = .040   Foreign Interest Rate = .060

Value		ExchRate = 1.45			ExchRate = 1.50			ExchRate = 1.55		
Yrs		Volatility								
Strike	To Exp	.150	.200	.250	.150	.200	.250	.150	.200	.250
	.10	.03	.04	.04	.06	.07	.07	.10	.10	.11
1.45	.20	.04	.05	.06	.06	.08	.09	.10	.11	.12
	.30	.04	.06	.07	.07	.09	.10	.11	.12	.13
	.10	.01	.02	.02	.03	.04	.05	.06	.07	.07
1.50	.20	.02	.03	.04	.04	.05	.06	.07	.08	.09
	.30	.02	.04	.05	.04	.06	.08	.07	.09	.10
	.10	.00	.01	.01	.01	.02	.03	.03	.04	.05
1.55	.20	.01	.02	.03	.02	.03	.04	.04	.05	.07
	.30	.01	.02	.04	.03	.04	.06	.05	.06	.08

Source: Created from The Options and Futures Trading Simulator, Version 2.0, by Hark Rubinstein and Gerald Gennotte (1992).

Equation (8–6) shows that the relative interest rates i (the domestic or U.S. rate) and i* (the foreign rate) affect the futures/forward rate. Thus, when funds are invested in a foreign currency, i* can be earned, while i is forgone. This difference in interest earned can be viewed as the cost of carry, and is similar to the dividend yield for stock index positions. This relationship is used in one form of the put-call parity relationship discussed below.

FIGURE 8–1   British Pound Volatilities

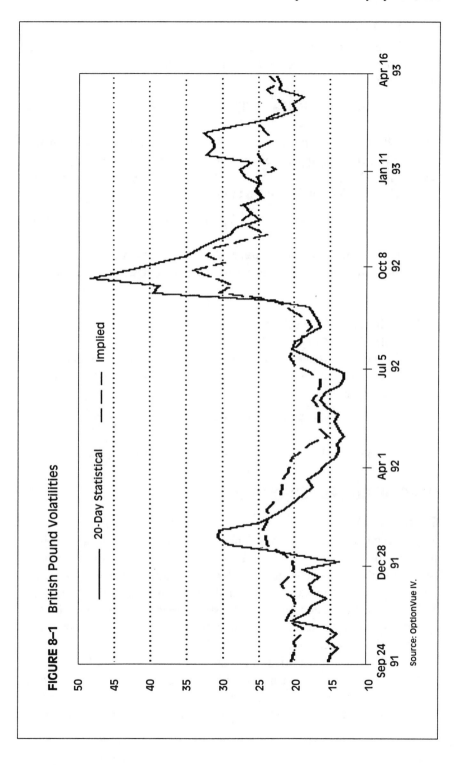

Source: OptionVue IV.

Put-Call Parity

Put-call parity for currency options can be developed by employing two equivalent strategies, as shown in Exhibit 8–5. The resultant put-call parity equation is:

$$P_P = P_C - P_S [1 + i* (T/360)]^{-1} + K [1 + i (T/360)]^{-1} \qquad (8\text{-}7)$$

An equivalent put-call parity relationship can be developed by using the interest rate parity theorem in conjunction with Equation (8–7). Thus, substituting P_S from Equation (8–6) into (8–7) results in the following put-call parity relationship in terms of the futures rate:

$$P_P = P_C + [K - P_F] [1 + i (T/360)]^{-1} \qquad (8\text{-}8)$$

In other words, the put and call prices differ by the exercise price less the futures price discounted to the present time by the domestic risk-free interest rate.

The Modified Black-Scholes
Put Equation for Currency Options

Using the modified Black-Scholes equation for a call option on currencies and the put-call parity equation results in the following modified Black-Scholes put equation:

$$P_P = K B [1 - N(d_2)] - P_S B* [1 - N(d_1)] \qquad (8\text{-}9)$$

This equation is calculated in the same manner as the call option for currencies.

USES OF CURRENCY OPTIONS

Speculation

Speculating in currency options requires care in order to understand when a profit or loss will occur. Buying a call option means that the speculator receives the foreign exchange—say, British pounds. The trader wants the pounds to increase in value. Thus, if the pound increases from $1.55 to $1.70, then a call option with a $1.55 strike price becomes valuable (the speculator can use the call to buy pounds at the strike of $1.55 and then sell the pounds in the open market for $1.70). Therefore, the value of the foreign currency *increases* if the price in dollars (per one unit of the foreign currency) increases. The equivalent benefit occurs for any other currency call option—that is, if the quotation of the U.S. currency (cents) per one unit of the foreign currency (FC) *increases,* then the value of the call position increases.[7]

EXHIBIT 8–5 Developing Put-Call Parity for Currency Options

Let us examine strategies (A) and (B) concerning foreign currencies:
A) Buy a put on one unit of a foreign currency (priced in terms of the domestic currency) with a strike price of K, resulting in a put price of P_p.
B) Initiate each of the following three trades:

- Sell (that is, issue or sell short) a discount bond denominated in the foreign currency, which pays interest at i*, with the bond maturing at the end of the period, with a value of one unit of the foreign currency. The foreign currency proceeds received from selling the bond are converted into the domestic (U.S.) currency at the exchange rate P_s. Thus, the total amount of domestic currency received is $P_s [1 + i*(T/360)]^{-1}$.

- Buy K domestic (U.S.) discount bonds at a price of $1/[1 + i(T/360)]$ each for a total price of $K [1 + i(T/360)]^{-1}$.

- Buy a currency call option at the domestic (U.S.) price of P_c for one unit of the foreign currency with strike price K.

The total investment for strategy (B) in terms of the domestic currency is:

$$P_c - P_s [1 + i*(T/360)]^{-1} + K [1 + i(T/360)]^{-1}$$

The following table shows that at the expiration of the options (which corresponds to the maturity of the discount bond), both strategies (A) and (B) provide the same profits—that is, they are equivalent strategies.

Strategy	$P_s < K$	$P_s \geq K$
A: buying put	$K - P_s$	0
B: selling foreign bonds	$-P_s$	$-P_s$
buying domestic bonds	K	K
buying a call	0	$P_s - K$
Total for strategy B	$K - P_s$	0

Since the two strategies provide equivalent payoffs at option expiration, we can equate the investments to define put-call parity as:

$$P_p = P_c - P_s [1 + i* (T/360)]^{-1} + K [1 + i (T/360)]^{-1} \qquad (8\text{-}7)$$

Puts are the opposite. Owning a currency put provides the right to *sell* the foreign currency. Thus, one benefits if the value of the foreign currency declines. Consequently, if the $/FC declines, then owning a put is worth more money, since it takes fewer dollars to buy one unit of the foreign currency.

Hedging

Buying a protective put as insurance is one method for hedging against declines in the foreign currency value when one owns the foreign currency. Thus, if the foreign exchange falls below the put strike price, the buyer of the put is protected below the strike price of the option. Such a position is useful if the put buyer has (or will have) *foreign exchange to sell*. On the other hand, if one has to *buy foreign exchange in the future,* buying a call option provides protection against the value of that foreign exchange increasing above the option strike price. An example of buying a call option as a hedge is when goods are imported from another country to sell in the United States, but the goods must be paid for in the foreign currency at some time in the future. Without protection from an increase in the value of the foreign currency, the importer could profit from the sale of the goods but lose money on the foreign exchange transaction. Hence, while buying a call option and creating a protective put have the same profit diagram, a long call is useful as a hedge when the foreign currency is needed in the future, while a protective put is needed for a hedge if one currently owns the foreign currency.

A covered call provides another strategy for hedging a foreign currency position. Unlike a protective put, a covered call *receives* the option time value instead of paying it. However, as discussed in Chapter 7, a covered call has a maximum upside gain but potentially large downside losses (although smaller downside losses than owning the foreign exchange without selling a call). A covered call is used for protection when the trader already has the foreign currency (or an asset denominated in the foreign currency) and will sell the foreign currency in the future. Buying a call option is employed for protection when one must *pay* for a security or asset in the future *in terms of the foreign currency.*

SUMMARY AND LOOKING AHEAD

Options on currencies and options on currency futures are distinguished from other options because of the unique characteristics of the underlying cash asset: the foreign currency value relative to the dollar. Thus, the quotation, uses, and pricing of these options are based on the relative value of the foreign currency, which in turn is affected by the foreign and domestic interest rates. Chapter 9 examines financial engineering concepts, including debt and other over-the-counter options, exotic options, and swaps.

END NOTES

[1] One note of caution is needed when one reads cash option currency quotes from older versions of *The Wall Street Journal*. The value given in older *Journals* for the underlying cash currency value did *not* correspond to the end-of-day quote for the currency. In fact, the currency quote given with the option more closely corresponded to the *previous* day's currency value. This timing difference between the currency's quotation and the option's quote led to difficulties, such as the apparent violations of the pricing relationships given in Chapters 1 and 2. Thus, one often found a currency option that was apparently selling for less than its intrinsic value, *if* one employed the underlying cash currency value provided with the option quotes. Currently, the cash currency quotes more accurately reflect true cash prices.

[2] Another type of option contract involving currencies is futures-style options. Futures-style options used to trade in London and differ from typical options in that they are marked-to-market daily. Thus, the futures-style call buyer pays the call writer daily any amount equal to the decrease in the market value of the call, while the call writer pays the buyer daily any amount equal to the increase in the market value of the call. In addition, the call buyer has the right to purchase one currency at the strike price stated in terms of a second currency. A futures-style put is similar in nature, except that it gives the owner the right to sell the currency.

[3] Equivalent positions are also possible between options traded in the United States and those traded in other countries. For example, exercising a long call on British pounds with strike price K in the United States generates the same long position in British pounds as does either a long put with strike price 1/K on U.S. dollars obtained in London *or* a short call on U.S. dollars obtained in London (if exercised). Moreover, these type of options also can be obtained over-the-counter in the United States.

[4] Interest rates for the option equations in this chapter are treated as simple discount rates. The equivalent continuously compounded interest rate formula according to Garman and Kohlhagen (1983), which is a more direct adaptation of the Black-Scholes approach, is:

where

$$P_C = P_s \, e^{-r^*t} \, N(d_1) - K \, e^{-rt} \, N(d_2)$$

$$d_1 = \frac{\ln(P_s \, e^{-r^*t} / K) + [r + 0.5 \, \sigma_s^2]t}{\sigma_s \sqrt{t}}$$

$$d_2 = d_1 - \sigma_s \sqrt{t}$$

and r = the domestic risk-free continuously compounded interest rate

r^* = the foreign risk-free continuously compounded interest rate

In this continuous model, the foreign interest rate acts like a continuously compounded dividend yield for stocks. Thus, the only difference between this formula and the Black-Scholes formula for a non-dividend-paying stock is the substitution of $P_s \, e^{-r^*t}$ for P_s.

[5] As with stock options, the continuously compounded standard deviation is calculated by employing the logarithmic percentage change of each observation and then finding the standard deviation of this series.

[6] In particular, the delta for a call on a currency when continuous discounting is employed is $e^{-i^* t} N(d_1)$.

[7] Recall that foreign currency other than the British pound is quoted as the number of units of FC per one U.S. dollar, the *inverse* of how currency options are quoted. Thus, care must be taken when determining the strength or weakness of a foreign currency. If the $/FC increases, then the value of the FC increases; however, if the FC/$ increases, then the value of the FC *weakens* (since one must pay more units of the FC for one U.S. dollar).

APPENDIX 8A
Foreign Exchange Markets and Their Futures Contracts

Foreign Exchange Markets

Foreign currency exchange is traded for most countries in the Western block that have active import/export dealings in the world market. Currencies are traded via telephone with major money center banks in large cities. The largest markets are in New York, London, and Tokyo; other major currency trades are located in Chicago, Los Angeles, San Francisco, and Singapore. These banks typically deal in transactions of $1 million or more, although smaller orders are taken during quiet trading periods. Some regional banks take orders for less than $1 million and provide specialized services to their customers. Currently more than $650 billion of foreign exchange is traded *daily,* making the currency markets the largest markets in the world. Most of this trading occurs in a few currencies such as the U.S. dollar, Japanese yen, German mark (Deutschemark), and British pound sterling. However, 90% of the currency trading takes place *with respect to* the U.S. dollar, causing the dollar to be what is known as a "vehicle currency." Thus, even cross-trades between two other currencies (say, the yen and mark) are quoted as a combination of two separate trades with the dollar (yen/$ and mark/$). This more complex method is done to reduce the number of quotations dealers need to make and to eliminate arbitrage possibilities if *pairs* of rates became mispriced in relation to one another.

Uses of Foreign Exchange

Banks initially provide foreign exchange trading as a service to corporations to obtain the corporation's international financing business. This service includes advise on market timing for forex trading, easy accessibility to traders, advice on the economies of the various countries, competitive currency rates, and an ability to handle a large volume of trading. Moreover, banks also employ foreign currency trading in order to achieve international branch banking asset-liability management, to limit the inventories of currencies in their trading departments, to provide liquidity for currencies traded, and to obtain international trade financing agreements. Trading by bank dealers to achieve currency balance can require dealing in a third currency to obtain the desired liquidity and risk exposure.

Finally, once dealer trading departments in banks are active, they also attempt to achieve profits by trading the foreign currencies for their own accounts. The purpose of such trading is to increase the overall return of the currency operations. These trading returns are generated from arbitrage with exchange rate differentials, commissions and fees (including the bid-ask spread), and trading profits from taking positions in a currency.

Foreign Exchange Quotations

A currency quotation represents an exchange rate between the domestic currency and the designated foreign currency. Exhibit 8A–1 shows the foreign exchange quotations with respect to the U.S. dollar for all major countries. These quotations are labeled "Exchange Rates" in *The Wall Street Journal.* The quotations provide both the number of U.S. dollars needed to purchase one unit of the foreign currency (U.S. dollar equivalent or direct quotation) and the number of foreign currency units needed to purchase one U.S. dollar (Currency per U.S. dollar or indirect quotation). Traders typically quote only the number of foreign currency units per U.S. dollar. For example, the value of the Japanese yen is stated in Exhibit 8A–1 as 126.85 which means that 126.85 yen are needed to obtain one U.S. dollar or that one dollar would buy 126.85 yen. One exception to the indirect quoting of currency values by traders is the British pound, which is quoted in terms of the number of dollars needed to purchase one pound. Specifically, Exhibit 8A–1 quotes the British pound as $1.781. When a trade is executed for a currency there is also a bid-ask spread between the sale price and the purchase price. The size of this bid-ask spread depends on the size of the market, the stability of the currency, and the desirability of the specific currency on the world currency markets.

The major currencies also have forward contracts. The 30-, 90-, and 180-day forward exchange rates listed in Exhibit 8A–1 refer to the number of days from the date of the transaction when the currency exchange will take place. Grabbe (1991) explains the intricacies of the cash and forward markets for currencies.

Figures 8A–1 and 8A–2 show the historical Japanese yen per dollar and German DM per dollar exchange rates from the mid-1970s to the early 1990s. The value of the dollar has declined from 295 yen to the dollar in January 1977 to 133 yen in late 1991. More dramatically, there was a significant drop in the yen/dollar exchange rate from 295 to 180 in 1977 and 1978, and then a decline from 260 to 120 from March 1985 to December 1987. The German mark shows an even greater tendency for trends, declining from 2.60 DM/$ in 1976 to 1.70 DM/$ in 1979, then rising to 3.40 DM/$ in February 1985, before plunging to 1.60 DM/$ in December 1987. These extreme price moves provide opportunities for speculators in foreign exchange and currency futures, as well as illustrating periods where hedging is crucial for those dealing in foreign exchange markets.

EXHIBIT 8A–1   Foreign Currency Rates and Currency
Futures Quotations

	Open	High	Low	Settle	Change	Lifetime High	Low	Open Interest

JAPANESE YEN (IMM) 12.5 million yen; $ per yen (.00)

	Open	High	Low	Settle	Change	Lifetime High	Low	Open Interest
Mar	.7905	.7926	.7856	.7887	+.0013	.8114	.7000	53,749
June	.7889	.7912	.7844	.7853	+.0016	.8097	.7015	4,125
Sept	...	...	.7846	+.0019	.8055	.7265	1,649
Dec	...	...	.7848	+.0019	.8005	.7512	1,623
Mar93	...	...	.7860	+.0028	.8005	.7960	1,112

Est vol 25,243; vol Mon 16,588; open int 62,258, +685.

DEUTSCHEMARK (IMM) 125,000 marks; $ per mark

	Open	High	Low	Settle	Change	Lifetime High	Low	Open Interest
Mar	.6310	.6329	.6200	.6211	–.0068	.6575	.5353	54,832
June	.5227	.6244	.6120	.6134	–.0064	.6490	.5322	2,540
Sept	.6155	.6162	.6060	.6069	–.0060	.6400	.5685	454

Est vol 63,440; vol Mon 39,923; open int 57,886 –340.

CANADIAN DOLLAR (IMM) 100,000 dlrs.: $ per Can $

	Open	High	Low	Settle	Change	Lifetime High	Low	Open Interest
Mar	.8668	.8682	.8636	.8646	–.0007	.8857	.8253	15,719
June	.8826	.8626	.8584	.8591	–.0007	.8820	.8330	1,864
Sept	...	...	.8540	–.0007	.8774	.8348	120

Est vol 5,437; vol Mon 3,766; open int 17,797, –599.

BRITISH POUND (IMM) 62,500 Pds; $ per pound

	Open	High	Low	Settle	Change	Lifetime High	Low	Open Interest
Mar	1.7876	1.7930	1.7600	1.7620	–.0158	1.8646	1.5560	19,885
June	1.7580	1.7850	1.7320	1.7358	–.0146	1.8346	1.6410	1,095

Est vol 18,116; vol Mon 11,193; open int 21,078, –85.

SWISS FRANC (IMM) 125,000 francs; $ per franc

	Open	High	Low	Settle	Change	Lifetime High	Low	Open Interest
Mar	.7119	.7137	.7006	.7022	–.0049	.7398	.6225	23,626
June	.7065	.7075	.6945	.6963	–.0045	.7328	.6546	689

Est vol 24,438: vol Mon 17,152; open int 24,354, –2,607.

AUSTRALIAN DOLLAR (IMM) 100,00 dlrs.; $ per A.$

	Open	High	Low	Settle	Change	Lifetime High	Low	Open Interest
Mar	.7428	.7432	.7373	.7374	+.0011	.7880	.7307	1,390

Est vol 386; vol Mon 434; open int 1,398, +16.

Source: Quotes from bank currency dealers and exchange rates.

Currency Futures

The International Monetary Market (IMM) of the Chicago Mercantile Exchange (CMEX) trade currency futures. Currency trading began on the IMM in 1972 and therefore have the distinction of being the first financial futures contracts.

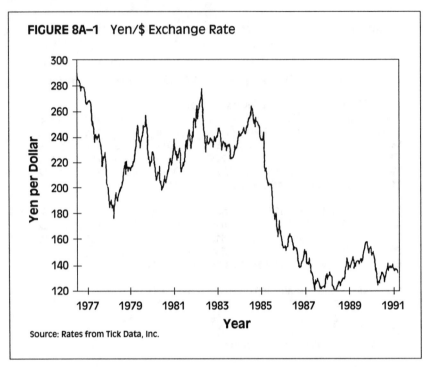

FIGURE 8A–1 Yen/$ Exchange Rate

Source: Rates from Tick Data, Inc.

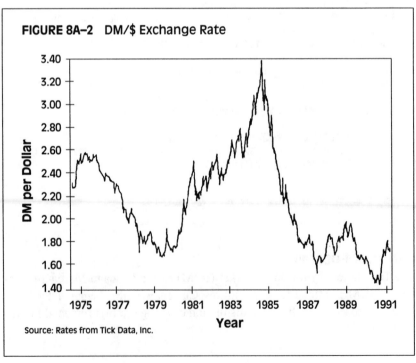

FIGURE 8A–2 DM/$ Exchange Rate

Source: Rates from Tick Data, Inc.

The IMM of the CMEX actively trades currency futures contracts on the British pound, Canadian dollar, Japanese yen, Swiss franc, and German mark. The Australian dollar currently has minimal volume on the IMM, while the French franc and Mexican peso contracts are inactive. Each currency contract trades a specified number of units of the foreign currency. For example, the futures quotations in Exhibit 8A–1 show that the British pound contract is based on 62,500 pounds, whereas the Japanese yen futures contracts are for 12.5 million yen. The number of units of the other foreign currencies used as the basis of the futures contract is listed with the futures quotations. When the seller of thse futures delivers the foreign exchange, then the buyer of the futures contract receives the number of units of the foreign currency at the futures exchange rate existing at that time.

The quotes for the foreign currency futures contracts are all in dollars per foreign currency. For example, the March expiration of the Japanese yen contract has a settle price of .007867 dollars per yen, as shown in Exhibit 8A–1. Multiplying by 12.5 million yen for one contract results in a value of $108,375. Similarly, one can determine that a change of 0.000001 in the value of the contract is worth $12.50. The currency futures typically trade the next four expirations in the quarterly financial cycle, although the nearby expiration month is most active.

Financial Engineering: 9
Synthetic Instruments
and Exotic Options

Financial engineering uses futures, options, and other financial instruments to control risk and maximize the value of financial strategies. Financial engineering includes developing new financial products to meet a need, as well as combining existing products to meet a specific goal.

Swaps have become an important tool in the interest rate market. An interest rate swap is a financial agreement to exchange interest payments on a fixed-rate loan with those of a variable-rate loan. The *net* difference in interest payments exchanges hands for each payment period. Parties use swaps for risk management, for example, to exchange fixed interest rates for floating rates, and to obtain a better interest rate. "Swaptions" are options on swaps.

Over-the-counter options are created and traded by major financial institutions to meet the specific needs of firms that are not met by conventional options. Popular over-the-counter options involve interest rates and energy. Caps, floors, and collars are interest rate options that provide a *series* of call and/or put options on interest rates over a period of time that lock in interest rate costs. Sycurves are options on the slope of the yield curve.

Exotic options are options with unusual characteristics. Range forwards are combinations of options that involve a zero initial cost. Average rate options provide a payoff on an average asset price. Other exotic options include compound options (call on a call), lookback options, down-and-out options, and two-color rainbow options.

WHAT IS FINANCIAL ENGINEERING?

The Concepts
Financial engineering involves the development and creative application of products to solve financial problems and to maximize the value of financial techniques. A financial engineer uses financial models, statistics, mathematics, accounting, and tax knowledge to determine how to reduce risk exposure, enhance portfolio management, and solve liquidity, funding, and other

problems of the firm. A number of securities are used by the financial engineer. Futures, options, swaps, bonds, stocks, and hybrids of these securities are relevant to the problems encountered by those managing risk and solving corporate problems. The applications of these instruments to financial engineering problems are broad-based and far-reaching, requiring a concrete knowledge of financial models and related areas, plus an ability to create new solutions for new problems. The subject matter of financial engineering is diverse and cannot be adequately described here. The interested reader should see one of the books in this area, such as *Financial Engineering* by Marshall and Bansal (1993). Here, we outline financial engineering in relation to its basic uses with futures, options, and related securities.

Uses of financial engineering include implementing and enhancing arbitrage strategies, developing new products, and managing the risk of new products sold to customers (new products are called financial innovations). A financial innovation can be a major new product that solves a problem not addressed by current products (such as the introduction of financial futures or index options) or a novel twist on an existing product (such as making stock index arbitrage operational by reducing risk through instantaneous purchase of all stocks in a cash index). Three types of financial engineering applications are:

- **Deal making (marketing):** structuring a solution with a currently existing product to solve a particular need of a client.

- **New product generation:** developing a new product or procedure to solve existing problems for a number of firms.

- **Finding loopholes:** finding accounting, tax, or regulatory loopholes to create a benefit to the firm.

Futures, Options, and Financial Engineering

A number of the applications of options contracts discussed in previous chapters are examples of financial engineering:

- Appendix 2A showed how the proper combination of options contracts is equivalent to a futures contract.

- Chapter 3 examined the creation of synthetic calls and puts by floor traders for conversions and reverse conversions.

- Combinations of options (such as straddles, spreads, and strangles) discussed in Chapter 6.

- Chapter 7 showed how synthetic futures, calls, or puts could be generated using futures and options on futures.

In addition, futures applications related to financial engineering are (see Daigler (1993) for a discussion of these topics):

- Creating synthetic instruments with futures that enhance the return of the position above the equivalent cash return.

- Portfolio insurance is a dynamic futures trading strategy that creates payoffs equivalent to an option contract (if price changes are continuous).

In general, most applications of futures and options to risk management could be considered financial engineering. However, the financial engineering phrase typically is reserved for newer or more creative applications of financial instruments. For example, a major source of profits on Wall Street during the past few years has been the development of new risk management instruments that are sold over-the-counter. Many of these instruments are options: options on products that do not have an exchange-traded equivalent, options that have unusual characteristics, or options with a longer life than exists for exchange-traded options. These over-the-counter options are examined later in this chapter.

SWAPS AND SWAPTIONS

Swap Concepts

Swaps are financial instruments that are typically associated with financial engineering. An **interest rate swap** is a financial agreement to exchange interest payments of a fixed-rate loan with a variable-rate loan. The *net* difference in interest payments exchanges hands for each payment period. Principal amounts are *not* swapped. Swaps often are arranged between financial institutions in the United States and Europe, since U.S. institutions prefer fixed-rate loans but the demand is for variable-rate loans; however, the opposite situation exists in Europe. The purpose of these basic "vanilla" swaps is to change the interest rate risk of the institution. For example, a savings and loan often is forced to issue fixed-rate mortgages, especially during low interest rate environments, because of consumer demand. In order to control its interest rate risk, the savings and loan converts the fixed-rate mortgage to a variable-rate loan via a swap.

An interest rate swap also can create interest savings compared to alternative agreements. To create such a benefit, both parties must be creditworthy, since the net interest payments are transferred only when the interest is due. Example 9–1 shows how an exchange of payments can benefit the two parties in a swap when a relative credit risk premium exists between the parties.

EXAMPLE 9–1 An Interest Rate Swap

	Firm A	Firm B	Differential
Fixed-rate loans	8.5%	9.1%	60 bp
Variable-rate loans	LIBOR + 15 bp	LIBOR + 35 bp	20 bp
Net differential			40 bp

where bp stands for basis points.

Firm A has a better credit rating than firm B; therefore, its cost of funds is lower for both fixed- and variable-rate loans. However, the differential between firms A and B for the fixed-rate loan is 60 basis points, whereas it is only 20 basis points for a variable-rate loan. The initiation of a swap can generate total savings of 40 basis points for the two firms and any broker who acts as an intermediary. Thus, let us assume that the following loans are initiated, including an agreement between the two firms on how to split the benefits:

	Firm A	Firm B
Fixed-rate loans	Obtains loan at 8.5%	Pays swap rate of 8.9% fixed to Firm A
Variable-rate loans	Pays swap rate of LIBOR + 30 bp to Firm B	Obtains loan at LIBOR + 35 bp
Net payment	LIBOR + 30 bp + (8.5 − 8.9) = LIBOR − 10 bp	8.9 + [LIBOR + 35 bp − (LIBOR + 30 bp)] = 8.95
Savings	LIBOR + 15 bp − (LIBOR − 10 bp) = 25 bp	9.1 − 8.950 = 15 bp

The swap saves Firm A 25 basis points as compared with a variable-rate loan taken directly by the firm, and it saves Firm B 15 basis points on a fixed-rate loan. If a broker is involved, then a fee of 5 to 10 basis points is paid to the broker.

Originally, the motivation for swap agreements was to obtain a *lower* interest rate than that available without a swap, as shown in Example 9–1. Since fixed and floating rates were priced differently, such benefits were available in the swap market. However, the swap market is more efficient now, eliminating many of the benefits from simple swaps. The motivation for current swaps is to achieve risk management goals, such as matching floating to floating interest rates of assets to liabilities and obtaining tax or institutional benefits. An example of a tax swap occurs when zero coupon bonds are taxed differently in different countries. Institutional factors include financial institutions that are required to have a specified asset-liability structure.

Swaps directly relate to futures markets, since it can be shown that swaps are equivalent to a portfolio of forward contracts. Thus, swaps are essentially equivalent to futures, if the time period is equivalent. The liquidity of these markets and the usefulness of changing the risk factors of a loan show the importance of swaps to firms and financial institutions. In fact, market makers who take on one side of a swap temporarily until they find the other side of the swap will hedge their positions with futures, typically with the Eurodollar futures market. Three-year and five-year swap futures were started by the Chicago Board of Trade, but were not successful.

The size of the over-the-counter swap market has grown from zero in 1981 to more than $3 trillion in outstanding swaps by the early 1990s. Currently, over 300 different *types* of swaps are offered by financial institutions. While interest rate swaps are the most used swap instrument, currency swaps are also an active market, with over $800 million of such swaps in force by the early 1990s. One use for currency swaps is dual currency bonds. A dual currency bond pays interest in one currency and the principal in a second currency. Swaps can create the equivalent of a dual currency bond. More recently, equity swaps have been popular. Macroeconomic swaps are predicted as the next major innovation in the swap market. An example of a macroeconomic swap is a swap that pays a floating rate that is pegged to GNP while receiving a fixed rate. Such a swap would be beneficial to firms such as General Motors, whose profits are related to the business cycle.

Swap Risk and Pricing Swaps

Risk exists for interest rate swap contracts, because funds are transferred only when an interest payment is due. Since the swap contract is a good faith agreement, with no principal amount changing hands, the potential default by one of the parties creates swap risk. Swap risk is actually a compound risk. The initial risk is whether the counterparty to the swap agreement will default. Second, if a default occurs, the cost of creating a replacement swap generates a market risk for the swap. Those who enter into swap agreements need to check the credit risk of the counterparty carefully in order to minimize swap risk.

To price swaps, one needs a model of forward rates (the term structure). Term-structure models used on Wall Street are proprietary, sophisticated applications of financial theory. However, swap models also must consider the potential default risk of the parties. The more sophisticated swap contracts are very difficult to price.[1]

Swaptions

A **swaption** is an option on a swap. A call buyer has the right to enter into a swap agreement to receive fixed payments based on a fixed interest rate and pay floating interest rates.[2] A put buyer has the right to pay the fixed interest rate and receive the floating interest rate. Thus, a swaption buyer is buying insurance (at a cost) to enter into a swap if the interest rate changes in an unfavorable direction.

OVER-THE-COUNTER OPTIONS

Reasons for the Existence of Over-the-Counter Options

Corporations have specific needs to control their risk posture. Therefore, corporations approach investment houses and major financial institutions to inquire about what type of specialized instruments can be devised so that the corporation can hedge its risks. The investment house investigates how it can devise a synthetic instrument, such as an option to meet client needs; how it can hedge its own risk; the appropriate pricing of the instrument; and how much interest the instrument will create in the financial community. If all of these factors indicate a feasible financial instrument, then a new option (or other instrument) is born. This process is one application of financial engineering.

Many types of over-the-counter options exist. Interest rate options are an important type of over-the-counter option, since exchange-traded options on debt are not liquid (although futures options on certain debt options are actively traded), and interest rate options are linked to the movement of rates rather than to prices in order to better hedge against changes in loan interest rates. Options on specific commodities, such as energy products, also are issued over-the-counter. Finally, certain so-called **exotic options** trade over-the-counter. Exotic options have unusual characteristics, such as when the option is valuable only if the asset changes significantly in price.

Pricing of Specialized Options

Options on new products are created because of customer demand to control risk. Wall Street firms determine how they can hedge their risks of creating such an option, often by dynamically trading an existing futures contract, and then add an appropriate premium for risk and profit to the fair price of the option. The fair option price is determined by creating an option pricing model based on the characteristics of the option. Such models are often binomial models. These products typically carry a large premium.

Most over-the-counter options are European in nature—that is, they can be exercised only at option expiration. This characteristic helps limit the risk of the investment house that issues the option. Given the specialized nature of these contracts, and how they are hedged by the investment house, it is typically difficult to trade over-the-counter options before they expire.

INTEREST RATE OPTIONS

An **interest rate option** is an option that has a payoff based on the underlying interest rate. Thus, an interest rate option differs from an option on debt, with the latter having a payoff based on the *price* of the underlying debt instrument. Interest rate options are useful for hedging variable-rate loans by both the debtholder and the issuer of the loan. Other interest rate options are based on the spread between long- and short-term interest rates. Exchange-traded interest rate options trade only a few options a day, while their over-the-counter equivalents have an active new issue market.

Caps, Floors, and Collars

Corporations and financial institutions often wish to limit their risk of changing interest rates. If a corporation has a loan at a variable interest rate (such as LIBOR), then the risk of higher interest rates is an important consideration. The corporation therefore wants to limit the maximum interest rate it will pay over the life of the loan. A financial institution that lends funds at a variable interest rate has a risk of lower interest rates. The financial institution wants to limit the minimum interest rate it will receive for the loan.

A **cap** is a series of call options on an interest rate, typically LIBOR. If interest rates increase, the seller of the cap pays the cap buyer the difference between the interest rate and the strike price at *each payment date* of the option. Thus, the strike price is the cap on the interest rate. The strike price is often the interest rate at the time the option is issued. The buyer of the cap pays for the interest rate option when the cap is initiated. The payment of an in-the-money option is usually made at the payment date of the interest on the underlying cash instrument rather than at the expiration of the option. Thus, an option expiring in 30 days that is based on the 90-day LIBOR rate pays off in 120 days, after the LIBOR instrument matures. The payoff amount of the cap at any specific payment date is determined as follows:

$$\text{payoff} = F \; \frac{t}{360} \; \frac{\text{Max}(0, \text{LIBOR} - K)}{100} \tag{9-1}$$

where F = the face value of the underlying instrument
t = the length of time of the interest period
K = the interest rate strike price

Thus, if LIBOR rises to 8% and a corporation buys a cap with K = 6% for a 90-day interest rate period, then the payoff per $1 million is:

$$\text{payoff} = \$1,000,000 \ (90 \ / \ 360) \ \text{Max} \ (0, 8 - 6) \ / \ 100$$

$$= \$1,000,000 \ (0.25) \ (0.02) \ = \ \$5,000$$

A **floor** option is a series of put options on the interest rate. If the interest rate decreases after the puts are obtained, then the seller of the floor pays the floor buyer the difference between the strike price and the interest rate. The strike price is the floor. A floor is useful to a bank that lends money at LIBOR and wishes to protect itself against interest rates falling below the strike price.[3]

A **collar** is a combination of a cap and a floor.[4] Buying both a cap and a floor would give the buyer protection against both an increase and a decrease in the interest rate. However, since most firms only need protection against a change in rates in one direction, buying a cap and *selling* a floor at different interest rates (or vice versa) provides the necessary protection *and* reduces the cost of the option. Of course, in this situation the option hedger reduces the benefits from an advantageous interest rate change because of the sale of one side of the collar.[5]

Options on the Slope of the Yield Curve

Sycurve options are options on the slope of the yield curve. Sycurve options have generated interest in the financial community for hedging mismatches in short-term versus long-term interest rates. For example, a bond portfolio manager who attempts to have a portfolio of interest-sensitive securities to match the behavior of the yield curve can use a sycurve option to overcome mismatches between the portfolio and the current yield curve. Alternatively, an extreme example of a mismatch is a portfolio in which the bonds are mostly of one maturity, while the performance of the portfolio is measured against a bond benchmark made up of only long-term and short-term bonds (a "barbell" portfolio). In addition, a financial institution whose asset and liability structure differs from the yield curve can use a sycurve option to change the effective composition of the balance sheet.

An example of a sycurve option is a 2/10 sycurve call. This call option represents the right to "buy" the curve—that is, to buy the two-year end of the yield curve and sell the 10-year end of curve—at a specified yield spread. Since yields are the inverse of prices, a sycurve call option profits when the difference between the 10-year and 2-year yields *increases in value*. The payoff to the 2/10 sycurve becomes:

$$\text{Max} \ \{[(Y_{10} - Y_2) - K], 0\} \qquad \qquad \textbf{(9-2)}$$

where Y_{10} and Y_2 are the 10-year and 2-year yields from the term structure

If the strike price (in basis points) is 20, then a six-month price for a 2/10 sycurve could be 10 basis points (or $\$100,000 = 10$ b.p. $\times$ .01 $\times$ $1 million face value). If the spread widens to 40 basis points at option expiration, then the payoff is (40 – 20) b.p. × .01 × $1,000,000, or $200,000, with a net profit of $100,000.

Payoff diagrams of interest rate options and sycurve options show the interesting payoffs that can be obtained. Buying a sycurve call produces the typical call option payoff diagram: As the *spread* between the long-term and short-term yields increases above the strike price, the profit of the call increases. However, combining a sycurve with other interest rate options creates complex profit graphs. Figure 9–1 shows a call on a simple 2-year interest rate option in relation to both the 2-year and 10-year yields. This simple call profits as yields increase on the 2-year call; changes in the 10-year yield have no effect on the option. Figure 9–2 shows a put on a 10-year yield. Here, changes in the 10-year yield affect the put value. Figure 9–3 shows how a *combination* of the 2-year call and 10-year put creates a more complex payoff structure. This combination profits if *either* the 2-year yield falls below the 9% strike *or* the 10-year yield rises above 9%; if both situations exist, then both parts of the option are in-the-money (the upper-right portion of the graph). Finally, Figure 9–4 adds a *short* position in a sycurve 2/10 call to the long 2-year call and 10-year put positions. This combination is in-the-money for the following combinations:

- Low 2-year yields and low 10-year yields

- High 10-year yields and high 2-year yields.

When 10-year yields are high and 2-year yields are low (when both the 2-year call and 10-year put are in-the-money), the short 2/10 sycurve loses the exact amount of money gained by the other options. Of course, the benefit of this combined position is a lower cost, since one is short the sycurve option.

Pricing Interest Rate Options

One cannot use the Black-Scholes model to price interest rate options because of its assumption that interest rates are constant. Often, the binomial model is used for these types of options. Investment houses are attempting to find a closed-form equation to accurately price these types of options.

COMPOUND AND EXOTIC OPTIONS

Exotic options have unusual characteristics; for example, when they become in-the-money, combining several simple options into one complex option, or forming an option on an option. The interest rate options defined above as caps, floors, and collars are technically exotic options, but their widespread

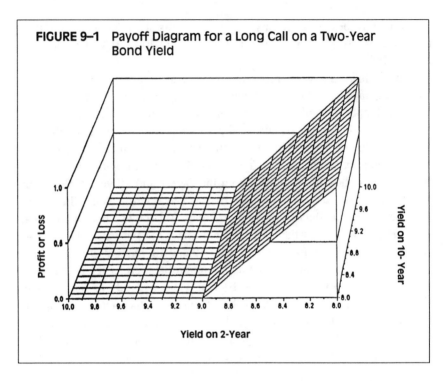

FIGURE 9–1 Payoff Diagram for a Long Call on a Two-Year Bond Yield

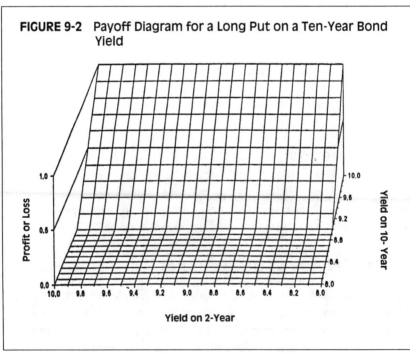

FIGURE 9-2 Payoff Diagram for a Long Put on a Ten-Year Bond Yield

FIGURE 9–3 Payoff Diagram for a Long Two-Year Call and Long Ten-Year Put

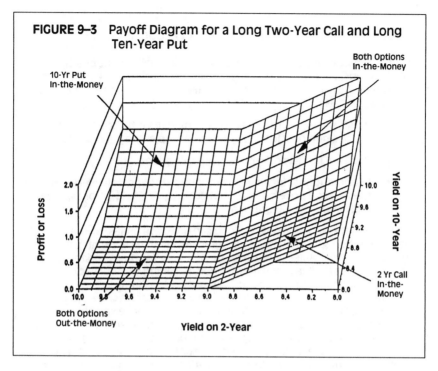

FIGURE 9–4 Payoff Diagram for a Long Two-Year Call, Long Ten-Year Put, Short a Sycurve 2/10 Call.

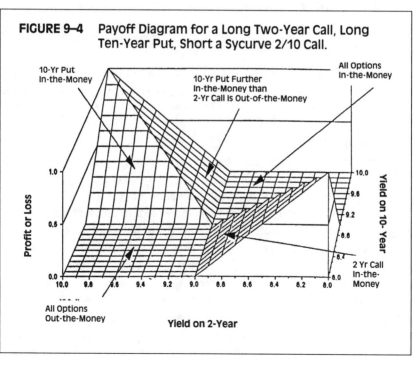

FOCUS 9–1   The Options Simulator and Exotic Options

One of the most unique and interesting aspects of the Options Simulator is its inclusion of exotic options and the choices to examine the characteristics of these options. The Simulator includes 34 different options, such as:

- Various versions of the European model, with choices as to the distribution of price changes (for example, the jump process)
- Binomial models of various types of options
- Exotic options, including compound options, four versions of the average price options, lookback, barrier, two-color rainbow, and all-or-nothing options.

For each of the available options, one can generate tables for the values and the option sensitivities. The program lets you decide what variables to include in the tables and the range of inputs for these variables. The tables of option values used in this book, including the lookback option table in this chapter, are created from the Option Simulator.

The Simulator also allows the user to view and print two- and three-dimensional graphs based on these options. Thus, once you choose the variables and data ranges to use, the program calculates and displays the relationships in graphical format. The orientation of the graph and the colors for the three-dimensional curves can even be changed. Finally, the Simulator runs option replication strategies for several types of options, as well as graphing the results of these strategies.

---

use makes them no longer "exotic" in nature. Similarly, some of the options discussed below have extensive use in some markets, but are not yet widespread in all markets.

Range Forwards

A **range forward** for an asset (often foreign exchange) is the purchase of a call option with a strike price of K_1 and the sale of a put option with a strike price of K_2 ($K_1 > K_2$), such that the total initial cost of the transaction is zero. The purpose of a range forward is to have the cost of an asset fall within a designated range, without adding an extra cost to the transaction. Thus, the strike prices are chosen such that the forward price of the asset is between K_1 and K_2 and the cost of the call is equal to the cost of the put. These characteristics cause the total cost of the range option to be zero for the buyer at option initiation. The first three columns of Exhibit 9–1 show the option payoffs at option exercise for a range forward.

Figure 9–5(a) illustrates buying a call with a K_1 strike price and selling a put with a K_2 strike, which creates a range forward. Figure 9–5(b) shows the

EXHIBIT 9–1   Payoff Table for a Range Forward

Price of FC	Value of a Long Call	Value of a Short Put	Option Payoffs at Expiration	Total Cost of the Asset
$P_{FC} \geq K_1$	$P_{FC} - K_1$	0	$P_{FC} - K_1$	K_1
$K_1 > P_{FC} > K_2$	0	0	0	P_{FC}
$K_2 \geq P_{FC}$	0	$-[K_2 - P_{FC}]$	$P_{FC} - K_2$	K_2

P_{FC} = value of the foreign currency

FIGURE 9-5   Range Forward Payoff and Cost Diagrams

A. The Range Forward Components

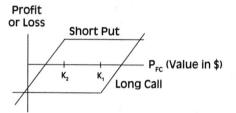

B. The Net Range Forward Diagram

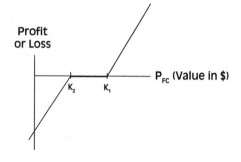

C. The Cost of Purchasing the Asset with a Range Forward

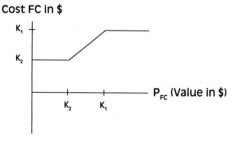

resultant effect of combining the two positions: A profit occurs when $P_{FC} >$ K_1 and a loss occurs if $P_{FC} < K_2$. Figure 9–5(c) shows the effect when the range forward is exercised (the asset is purchased via the exercise of the call or the asset is received when the put is exercised by the buyer), or when the asset is purchased if the range option is not exercised. Thus, Figure 9–5(c) is a *total cost* diagram of the asset at option expiration; this payoff diagram is equivalent to a bull spread diagram. The last column of Exhibit 9–1 shows the total cost of the asset for the three possible states of nature given for the final asset price.[6]

Solomon Brothers started to issue range forwards on foreign currency in 1985. The range forward is useful for corporations wanting to guarantee that the cost of the future foreign exchange will be between K_1 and K_2, without having to pay for the protection afforded by the range forward. For a range forward, the buyer chooses one of the strikes and the seller calculates the other strike such that the total cost of the range forward is zero. Range forwards can also be applied to other assets. When K_1 and K_2 are chosen so that the call price does not equal the put price, this combination is called a **cylinder option**. For a cylinder option, the buyer chooses both strike prices and then pays or receives the net value of the options. Citicorp and other investment houses sell cylinder options.

Average-Rate Options

An **average rate option** pays at option expiration the difference between the strike price and the *average* rate or price, A, of the asset over the life of the option. Thus, an average rate call option pays the Max[0, A – K], while an average rate put option pays the Max[0, K – A], where A is the average price of the asset. The average A can be either an arithmetic average or a geometric average of the asset price over the life of the option. Average-rate options are most common for foreign exchange and interest rate assets. They are used by corporations that have daily (or periodic) responsibilities for foreign exchange or interest rates. For example, if a firm wishes to convert 10 million marks to dollars per day and avoid the adverse effect of exchange-rate risk, then average rate options can be used for this periodic exchange. Similarly, if a financial institution has sold certificates of deposit that will mature weekly for the next six months (the institution will then resell CDs at the going interest rate), and it believes interest rates will increase steadily over the period, then an average rate option can control the future interest rate cost. These average rate options provide similar protection to obtaining separate hedging instruments each day or week of the time period over which the option is active.

Compound Options

A **compound option** is an option on an option. A **cacall** is a call on a call option—that is, it is a call that pays the value of *another* call option at expiration. A **caput** is a call on a put—that is, it is a call that pays the value of a put at option expiration. The cost of an option on an option is lower than a simple call or put *if* the option holder does *not* receive the underlying option at expiration of the cacall or caput. The cost of an option on an option is higher if the underlying option is received. The value of a call compound option at the expiration of the compound option on either a call or a put is:

cacall: $$\text{Max}\{0, PV_t[\text{Max}(0, P_S{}^* - K|T)] - k\} \qquad \textbf{(9-3)}$$

caput: $$\text{Max}\{0, PV_t[\text{Max}(0, K - P_S|T] - k\} \qquad \textbf{(9-4)}$$

where the compound option has a strike price k and time to expiration t and the underlying option has a strike price K and time to expiration $T > t$. $P_S{}^*$ is the value of the underlying asset at time t and PV_t is the present value at time t of the quantity in brackets.

Lookback and Barrier Options

A **lookback call** is identical to a standard European call except that the strike price is equal to the *minimum* price of the underlying asset during the life of the option. A **lookback put** is identical to a European put except that the strike price is equal to the *maximum* price of the asset during the life of the option. Thus, lookback options are always exercised at option expiration, since they are always in the money. The only question concerning a lookback option is the final strike price, which will determine the payoff of the option.[7] The payoff at option expiration of a lookback call is:

$$\text{Max}\,[0, P_{S,n} - \text{Min}\,(P_{S,1}, P_{S,2},...,P_{S,n})] = P_{S,n} - \text{Min}\,(P_{S,1}, P_{S,2},...,P_{S,n}) \quad \textbf{(9-5)}$$

where $P_{S,t} = P_S$ at time t

Lookback options have become an active over-the-counter option, with several billion dollars being traded. Table 9–1 shows the values of lookback call options as time, volatility, dividends, interest rate, and strike prices change. Comparing these values to option values of typical call options (such as in Table 2–2) shows that lookback calls have values approximately twice that of regular calls. Figure 9–6 illustrates the value in a three-dimensional graph as the underlying asset value and the time to expiration change. The benefit of such a graph is to show the relevant relationships when an intuitive understanding is difficult to obtain without such a figure. This is even more relevant for the option sensitivities for exotic options; for example, Figure 9-7 provides the gamma for a lookback option.

TABLE 9–1 Lookback Call Values

σ	M	Div = .03 European i = .10				Div = .10 European i = .03							
		1	3	6	12	1	3	6	12	1	3	6	12
.2	70	30.31	30.91	31.81	33.66	30.72	32.09	33.96	37.12				
	75	25.35	26.04	27.12	29.46	25.83	27.41	29.60	33.38				
	80	20.39	21.20	22.62	25.60	20.94	22.75	25.34	29.80				
	85	15.43	16.54	18.53	22.27	16.05	18.20	21.31	26.52				
	90	10.58	12.45	15.18	19.68	11.24	14.04	17.81	23.75				
	95	6.50	9.53	12.95	18.02	7.06	10.88	15.27	21.80				
	100	4.78	8.46	12.15	17.44	5.19	9.61	14.28	21.05				
.3	70	30.31	30.96	32.24	35.19	30.72	32.12	34.20	37.89				
	75	25.35	26.23	28.06	31.84	25.83	27.54	30.18	34.72				
	80	20.41	21.77	24.33	28.99	20.95	23.16	26.50	31.92				
	85	15.59	17.84	21.23	26.72	16.17	19.20	23.33	29.57				
	90	11.25	14.73	18.91	25.06	11.81	15.98	20.86	27.78				
	95	8.12	12.75	17.48	24.06	8.57	13.83	19.26	26.65				
	100	6.97	12.07	17.01	23.73	7.34	13.06	18.70	26.26				
.4	70	30.31	31.31	33.53	38.02	30.73	32.38	35.14	39.81				
	75	25.38	26.97	30.02	35.44	25.86	28.12	31.69	37.32				
	80	20.57	23.11	27.05	33.33	21.09	24.27	28.70	35.21				
	85	16.11	19.90	24.69	31.70	16.64	21.01	26.27	33.53				
	90	12.41	17.52	22.99	30.55	12.89	18.53	24.48	32.31				
	95	9.96	16.06	21.98	29.88	10.36	16.97	23.38	31.58				
	100	9.11	15.58	21.65	29.66	9.46	16.44	23.00	31.33				

$P_s = 100$

payoff: max $[0, S_n - \min(S_n, S_{n'}, \ldots, S_n)]$

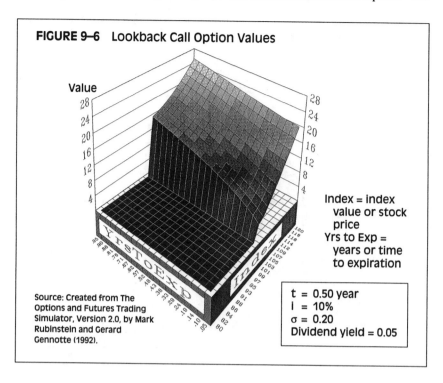

FIGURE 9–6 Lookback Call Option Values

Index = index value or stock price
Yrs to Exp = years or time to expiration

t = 0.50 year
i = 10%
σ = 0.20
Dividend yield = 0.05

Source: Created from The Options and Futures Trading Simulator, Version 2.0, by Mark Rubinstein and Gerard Gennotte (1992).

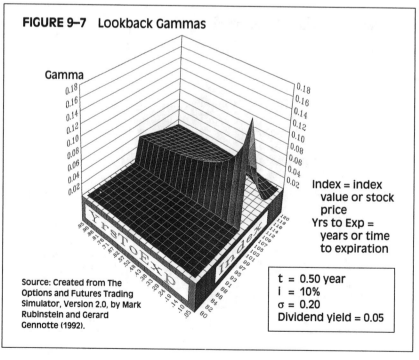

FIGURE 9–7 Lookback Gammas

Index = index value or stock price
Yrs to Exp = years or time to expiration

t = 0.50 year
i = 10%
σ = 0.20
Dividend yield = 0.05

Source: Created from The Options and Futures Trading Simulator, Version 2.0, by Mark Rubinstein and Gerard Gennotte (1992).

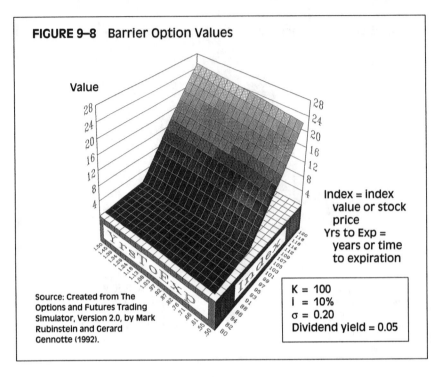

FIGURE 9–8   Barrier Option Values

Value

Index = index value or stock price
Yrs to Exp = years or time to expiration

Source: Created from The Options and Futures Trading Simulator, Version 2.0, by Mark Rubinstein and Gerard Gennotte (1992).

K = 100
i = 10%
σ = 0.20
Dividend yield = 0.05

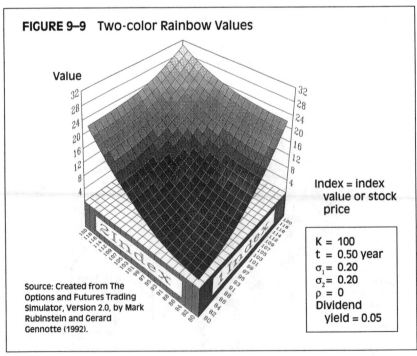

FIGURE 9–9   Two-color Rainbow Values

Value

Index = index value or stock price

Source: Created from The Options and Futures Trading Simulator, Version 2.0, by Mark Rubinstein and Gerard Gennotte (1992).

K = 100
t = 0.50 year
σ₁ = 0.20
σ₂ = 0.20
ρ = 0
Dividend yield = 0.05

A **down-and-out call option** is an option that becomes worthless if the cash asset price reaches or falls below a threshold price, often called a **barrier**; thus, the alternative name barrier option. A **down-and-in call option** is an option that becomes active only if the cash asset price reaches or crosses the threshold. An **up-and-out put option** is an option that becomes worthless if the cash asset price reaches or goes above a threshold price. An **up-and-in put option** activates only if the cash price reaches or crosses the threshold. Figure 9–8 illustrates the value of a barrier call option in relation to the time to expiration and the asset value.

Rainbow Options

Two-color rainbow options are options in which the payoff is based on two underlying asset prices. For example, one type of a two-color rainbow option is based on the product of two underlying asset prices. Thus, this call rainbow option payoff is:

$$\text{Max } [0, (P_{S1} P_{S2}) - K] \qquad \text{(9-6)}$$

where P_{S1} and P_{S2} equal the prices of the two underlying cash assets at option expiration

A guaranteed exchange rate call on a foreign stock index is a rainbow option in which the payoff from the normal option on the foreign stock index is converted into the domestic currency using a prespecified exchange rate. Other rainbow options include the option to exchange one risky asset for another, options to deliver the worse (or better) of two risky assets, and options on the minimum (or maximum) of two risky assets. Figure 9–9 shows how the value of a two-color rainbow option changes in relation to the values of the two underlying assets. The graph clearly shows how the *interrelationship* between the asset values are important to the option value.

SUMMARY

Financial engineering provides solutions for risk management situations that cannot be handled by exchange-traded securities. Swaps are one type of financial product that can effectively control interest rate (and other types of) risk without the use of futures or options contracts. Over-the-counter options meet needs not adequately met by options traded on the exchanges. Interest rate over-the-counter options include caps, collars, and floors. Exotic options are options with unusual characteristics, such as a call on a call or a down-and-out option.

END NOTES

[1] A good source for additional information on swaps is *The Swaps Market* by Marshall and Kapner (1993).

[2] This is called the right to go short a swap, since the call buyer receives the fixed interest rate.

[3] A long swap contract at a fixed rate K is simply a long cap at K and a short floor at K. Similarly, a short swap at a fixed rate K is a short cap at K and a long floor at K.

[4] If one is long a cap and short a floor, this is equivalent to a series of range forward contracts if the strike prices differ (range forwards are discussed shortly).

[5] A collar also is defined as buying a call at a lower strike price K_1, selling a call at a higher strike price K_2, and lending the present value of K_1. The value of the collar at option expiration is defined as:

$$\text{Min } [\text{Max}(P_{S,E}, K_1), K_2]$$

where $0 < K_1 < K_2$

or alternatively:

$$K_1 + \text{Max } [0, P_{S,E} - K_1] - \text{Max } [0, P_{S,E} - K_2]$$

such that the payoffs become:

Price of S	Payoff
$P_{S,E} < K_1$	K_1
$K_1 \leq P_{S,E} \leq K_2$	$P_{S,E}$
$K_2 < P_{S,E}$	K_2

[6] Another definition of a range forward is buying a forward contract, buying a put with strike K_2, and selling a call with strike K_1.

[7] A forward-start call has its strike price determined at a prespecified time in the future, called the grant date. At this date, the strike price is set equal to a prespecified percentage of the market price of the underlying asset.

APPENDIX A
Values for the Probabilities from the Normal Distribution

This table presents the values for the normal distribution N(d). The value for N(d) is needed to solve option pricing models. N(d) represents the probability associated with a specific value of "d". The values for "d" in statistics books are often labeled as the "z-statistic." Values for N(– d) are found by taking 1.0 – N(d) from this table.

z	0.00	0.01	0.02	0.03	0.04	0.05	0.06	0.07	0.08	0.09
0.0	.5000	.5040	.5080	.5120	.5160	.5199	.5239	.5279	.5319	.5359
0.1	.5398	.5438	.5478	.5517	.5557	.5596	.5636	.5675	.5714	.5753
0.2	.5793	.5832	.5871	.5910	.5948	.5987	.6026	.6064	.6103	.6141
0.3	.6179	.6217	.6255	.6293	.6331	.6368	.6406	.6443	.6480	.6517
0.4	.6554	.6591	.6628	.6664	.6700	.6736	.6772	.6808	.6844	.6879
0.5	.6915	.6950	.6985	.7019	.7054	.7088	.7123	.7157	.7190	.7224
0.6	.7257	.7291	.7324	.7357	.7380	.7422	.7454	.7486	.7517	.7549
0.7	.7580	.7611	.7642	.7673	.7704	.7734	.7764	.7794	.7823	.7852
0.8	.7881	.7910	.7939	.7967	.7995	.8023	.8051	.8078	.8106	.8133
0.9	.8159	.8186	.8212	.8238	.8264	.8289	.8315	.8340	.8365	.8389
1.0	.8413	.8438	.8461	.8485	.8508	.8531	.8554	.8577	.8599	.8621
1.1	.8643	.8665	.8686	.8708	.8729	.8749	.8770	.8790	.8810	.8830
1.2	.8849	.8860	.8888	.8907	.8925	.8943	.8962	.8980	.8997	.9015
1.3	.9032	.9049	.9066	.9082	.9099	.9115	.9131	.9147	.9162	.9177
1.4	.9192	.9207	.9222	.9236	.9251	.9265	.9279	.9292	.9306	.9319
1.5	.9332	.9345	.9357	.9370	.9382	.9394	.9406	.9418	.9429	.9441
1.6	.9452	.9463	.9474	.9484	.9495	.9505	.9515	.9525	.9535	.9545
1.7	.9554	.9564	.9573	.9582	.9591	.9599	.9608	.9616	.9625	.9633
1.8	.9641	.9649	.9656	.9664	.9671	.9678	.9686	.9693	.9699	.9706
1.9	.9713	.9719	.9726	.9732	.9738	.9744	.9750	.9756	.9761	.9767
2.0	.9772	.9778	.9783	.9788	.9793	.9798	.9803	.9808	.9812	.9817
2.1	.9821	.9826	.9830	.9834	.9838	.9842	.9846	.9850	.9854	.9857
2.2	.9861	.9864	.9868	.9871	.9875	.9878	.9881	.9884	.9887	.9890
2.3	.9893	.9896	.9898	.9901	.9904	.9906	.9909	.9911	.9913	.9916
2.4	.9918	.9920	.9922	.9925	.9927	.9929	.9931	.9932	.9934	.9936
2.5	.9938	.9940	.9941	.9943	.9945	.9946	.9948	.9949	.9951	.9952
2.6	.9953	.9955	.9956	.9957	.9959	.9960	.9961	.9962	.9963	.9964
2.7	.9965	.9966	.9967	.9968	.9969	.9970	.9971	.9972	.9973	.9974
2.8	.9974	.9975	.9976	.9977	.9977	.9978	.9979	.9979	.9980	.9981
2.9	.9981	.9982	.9982	.9983	.9984	.9984	.9985	.9985	.9986	.9986
3.0	.9987	.9987	.9987	.9988	.9988	.9989	.9989	.9989	.9990	.9990

APPENDIX B
Natural Logorithms

x	ln x	x	ln x	x	ln x	x	ln x
		0.50	− 0.69315	1.00	0.00000	1.5	0.40547
.01	− 4.60517	.51	.67334	1.01	.00995	1.6	7000
.02	− 3.91202	.52	.65393	1.02	.01980	1.7	0.53063
.03	.50656	.53	.63488	1.03	.02956	1.8	8779
.04	.21888	.54	.61619	1.04	.03922	1.9	0.64185
.05	− 2.99573	.55	.59784	1.05	.04879	2.0	9315
.06	.81341	.56	.57982	1.06	.05827	2.1	0.74194
.07	.65926	.57	.56212	1.07	.06766	2.2	8846
.08	.52573	.58	.54473	1.08	.07696	2.3	0.83291
.09	.40795	.59	.52763	1.09	.08618	2.4	7547
0.10	− 2.30259	0.60	− 0.51083	1.10	.09531	2.5	0.91629
.11	.20727	.61	.49430	1.11	.10436	2.6	5551
.12	.12026	.62	.47804	1.12	.11333	2.7	9325
.13	.04022	.63	.46024	1.13	.12222	2.8	1.02962
.14	− 1.96611	.64	.44629	1.14	.13103	2.9	6471
.15	.89712	.65	.43708	1.15	.13976	3.0	9861
.16	.83258	.66	.41552	1.16	.14842	4.0	1.38629
.17	.77196	.67	.40048	1.17	.15700	5.0	1.60944
.18	.71480	.68	.38566	1.18	.16551	10.0	2.30258
.19	.66073	.69	.37106	1.19	.17395		
0.20	− 1.60944	0.70	− 0.35667	1.20	.18232		
.21	.56065	.71	.34249	1.21	.19062		
.22	.51413	.72	.32850	1.22	.19885		
.23	.46968	.73	.31471	1.23	.20701		
.24	.42712	.74	.30111	1.24	.21511		
.25	.38629	.75	.28768	1.25	.22314		
.26	.34707	.76	.27444	1.26	.23111		
.27	.30933	.77	.26136	1.27	.23902		
.28	.27297	.78	.24846	1.28	.24686		
.29	.23787	.79	.23572	1.29	.25464		
0.30	− 1.20397	0.80	− 0.22314	1.30	.26236		
.31	.17118	.81	.21072	1.31	.27003		
.32	.13943	.82	.19845	1.32	.27763		
.33	.10866	.83	.18633	1.33	.28518		
.34	.07881	.84	.17435	1.34	.29267		
.35	− 1.04982	.85	− 0.16252	1.35	.20010		
.36	.02165	.86	.15032	1.36	.30748		
.37	− 0.99425	.87	.13926	1.37	.31481		
.38	.96758	.88	.12783	1.38	.32208		
.39	.94161	.89	.11653	1.39	.32930		
0.40	− 0.91629	0.90	− 0.10536	1.40	.33647		
.41	.89160	.91	.09431	1.41	.34359		
.42	.86750	.92	.08338	1.42	.35066		
.43	.84397	.93	.07257	1.43	.35767		
.44	.82098	.94	.06188	1.44	.36464		
.45	.79851	.95	.05129	1.45	.37156		
.46	.77653	.96	.04082	1.46	.37844		
.47	.75502	.97	.03046	1.47	.38526		
.48	.73397	.98	.02020	1.48	.39204		
.49	.71335	.99	.01005	1.49	.39878		

Terminology

* Identifies more important terms.

*__Arbitrage__ Otaining risk-free profits by simultaneously buying and selling identical or similar instruments in different markets.

*__At-the-money__ An option that has its stock price equal to the strike price.

*__Average rate option__ An option that pays the difference between the strike price and the *average* rate (or price) of the asset over the life of the option.

__Barrier option__ An option that becomes either active or inactive when the cash asset crosses a threshold.

*__Bear spread__ A strike price spread in which the lower strike price option is sold and the higher strike price option is purchased. A significant decrease in the stock price creates a profit for this type of spread.

*__Binomial option pricing model__ A model that determines the fair value for an option based on a limited number of discrete changes for the stock price.

*__Black-Scholes option model__ An equation that determines the fair value for a call option in terms of the current stock price, the option exercise price, the time to expiration of the option, the volatility of the stock, and the current risk-free interest rate.

__Box spread__ A combination of two calls with different strike prices and two puts with strike prices equivalent to the calls. All options have the same expiration date.

*__Bull spread__ A strike price spread in which the trader purchases the lower strike price option and sells the higher strike price option. A significant increase in the stock price creates a profit for this type of spread.

__Butterfly spread__ A combination of a bull and a bear spread—that is, the trader buys the low and high strike price options and sells two of the intermediate strike prices. This spread is similar to a straddle, but it possesses a limited loss.

__Cacall__ A call on a call option that pays the value of *another* call option at expiration.

*__Calendar (time) spread__ The sale of a nearby option and the purchase of a deferred option. The objective of this strategy is to profit from the faster decay of the time value for the nearby option. The profitability of this strategy also depends on a relatively small change in the stock price, since large price changes create losses.

*__Call option__ Gives the buyer the right to purchase the stock (or asset) at a fixed price for a specific period of time. The "fixed price" is called the strike price. Since the buyer has the right, *but not the obligation* to purchase the asset, the buyer exercises this right only if the stock price is greater than the strike price at option expiration.

*__Cap__ A series of call options on the interest rate that locks in a maximum interest rate.

__Caput__ A call on a put option that pays the value of a put at option expiration.

*__Cash settlement__ The buyer receives from the seller the difference between the index value and the strike price of the option. Index options settle in cash at option expiration.

*__Collar__ A combination of a cap and a floor.

Compound option   An option on an option (see cacall and caput).

*__Conversion__   Buying an underpriced put and selling an overpriced synthetic put, with the synthetic put being a short call and long stock position.

*__Covered option writing (covered call)__   The sale of a call option in conjunction with the purchase or ownership of the underlying stock. The time value received from the sale of the call option enhances the total portfolio return, while the option price received provides partial downside protection against a decline in the value of the stock. However, this strategy does not fully participate in stock price increases.

*__Currency option__   Owning an option on a foreign currency provides the right to buy (call) or the right to sell (put) the foreign exchange at a specific strike price in the domestic currency for a specific period of time.

Cylinder option   A range option in which the call price does not equal the put price.

Deferred options   Options that expire after the nearby option.

*__Delta__   The change in the option price for each $1 change in the stock price. Delta is an instantaneous hedge ratio.

Derivative   A procedure from calculus that determines the change in one variable given a very small change in the other variable.

Derivative asset   A contract whose payoff at expiration is determined by the price of the underlying asset.

Down-and-in call option   An option that activates only if the cash asset price reaches or crosses a threshold.

Down-and-out call option   An option that becomes worthless if the cash asset price reaches or crosses a threshold.

Elasticity   *See* lambda.

Exercise price   *See* "strike price."

*__Exotic option__   An option with unusual characteristics concerning exercise or the underlying security.

*__Expiration (date)__   When the option stops trading. After this date the option is worthless, since it cannot be exercised.

*__Fair value__   A fair value for an option occurs when the option price provides an *expected* profit of zero to both the buyer and seller of the option.

*__Financial engineering__   The development and creative application of products to solve financial problems and to maximize the value of financial techniques.

*__Floor__   A series of put options on the interest rate that locks in a minimum interest rate.

*__Gamma__   The change in the delta (hedge ratio) for a given change in the stock price; relates to the volatility of the stock.

*__Hedge ratio__   The number of shares of the asset (for example, stock) as a proportion of the number of shares of the option such that a risk-free combination is produced for a (small) change in the asset price.

*__Hedging (with options)__   Taking a position in options which reduces the potential downside loss of the combined asset/option portfolio in comparison to the asset-only position.

*__Implied volatility__   The estimated future volatility of the underlying stock, determined by solving the Black-Scholes option model by using the current call option price.

*__In-the-money__   A call option having its stock price greater than the strike price; or a put option having its stock price less than the strike price.

*__Index option__   An option on a stock index, with the index representing a portfolio of individual stocks.

Instantaneous   A change that occurs immediately. Such a change is a "very small change" when associated with a derivative.

Interest rate option   An option that has a payoff based on the underlying interest rate.

*__Interest rate swap__   A financial agreement to exchange interest payments of a fixed-rate loan with those of a variable-rate loan.

*__Intrinsic value__   The difference between the stock price and the strike price, or zero, whichever is greater. A call option has a positive intrinsic value if the stock price is greater than the strike price. A put option has a positive intrinsic value if the stock price is less than the strike price.

*__Lambda__   The percentage change in the option price for a given percentage change in the stock price. Also known as leverage.

LEAPS   Long-term options expiring up to three years in the future. LEAPS stands for "Long-term Equity Anticipation Securities."

Leverage   The percentage change for the option price is greater than the percentage change for the underlying stock price. Thus, leverage magnifies the rate of return (or loss) on the option in comparison to the return on the stock.

Liquidity   The trader's ability to buy or sell an instrument quickly, without significantly affecting the instrument's price.

Lookback call   An option that is identical to a standard European call except that the strike price is equal to the *minimum* price of the underlying asset during the life of the option.

Lookback put   An option that is identical to a European put except that the strike price is equal to the *maximum* price of the asset during the life of the option.

Market microstructure   The study of price behavior within the day and the structure of the market trading system affecting this price behavior.

Naked call (selling a)   The sale of a call option *without* owning the underlying stock. A naked call creates large losses for the seller if the stock price increases. If the stock price trades above the strike price at option expiration, then the naked seller must purchase the stock in the open market at that time in order to deliver the stock into the call option. Consequently, this strategy is considered very risky.

*__Near-the-money__   The stock price is approximately the same as the strike price of the option.

Nearby option   The next option expiration month.

*__Open interest__   The number of contracts that have both a long and a short position.

Opportunity loss   Forgoing a gain (or reducing a loss) by not taking a specific action.

Option class   The designation for all of the options on the same stock.

Option cycle   The expiration months for options on a particular stock depend upon its "cycle." All stock options have expirations in the current and next month. In addition, the January cycle trades the next two option months with expirations in January, April, July, and October; similarly, the February and March cycles are separated by three-month intervals.

*__Option on currency futures__   Owning an option on currency futures provides the right to take a long position (call) or the right to take a short position (put) in a currency futures contract at a specific strike price for a specific period of time.

*__Option on futures__   An option contract having a futures contract as the underlying asset; thus, the futures contract changes hands at delivery.

Option series   An option with a specific strike price and expiration date.

*__Out-of-the-money__   A call option having its stock price less than the strike price of the option; or a put option having its stock price greater than the strike price of the option.

Pricing sensitivities The important relationships between the characteristics of the option and the option price. The pricing sensitivities are designated as delta, lambda, gamma, theta, vega, and rho.

***Protective put** An option hedging strategy where a put is purchased in order to provide protection against a decline in the value of the currently held stock position.

***Put-call parity** The relationship between a call option, a put option, the underlying stock, and the cost of financing that equates the value of a call plus risk-free instrument to the value of a put plus the underlying stock.

***Put option** Gives the buyer the right to *sell* the stock (or asset) at a fixed price for a specific period of time. A large decline in the price of the stock is profitable for a put buyer.

***Range forward** The purchase of a call with a strike price of K_1 and the sale of a put with a strike price of K_2 (with $K_1 > K_2$) such that the total initial cost of the forward contract is zero.

Ratio spread Buying one option and selling another option on the same stock, where the number of shares traded for each option is based on an option pricing model hedge ratio. The purpose of this spread is to benefit from the relative mispricings of the two options.

Ratio writing The sale of call options such that the number of options sold is a multiple of the number of stock shares owned.

***Reverse conversion** Buying an underpriced call and selling an overpriced synthetic call, with the synthetic call being a short put and a short stock position.

Reverse hedge When the stock is sold short and the option purchased.

***Rho** The change in the option price for a given change in the risk-free interest rate.

Scalper A floor trader who buys at the bid and sells at the ask price.

Short sale Selling a stock now, with the promise to buy the stock back later. A short sale profits from a decline in the stock price.

***Spread** A combination of option trades that reduces risk in comparison to a purely speculative position, but also reduces the potential gain. Examples of a spread are: buying both a call and a put option (also known as a straddle); buying one strike price and selling a different strike price; and buying one expiration month and selling a different expiration month.

***Straddle** The purchase (or sale) of both a call and a put option. Buying a straddle is profitable when the stock price changes significantly.

***Strike price** The "fixed price" at which the option buyer can execute the option. The buyer of the option can purchase the stock (call option) or sell the stock (put option) at this fixed price, *regardless* of the current price of the stock in the market.

***Strike (price) spread** The purchase of an option with one strike price and the sale of a different strike price. Which option is purchased/sold depends on whether the spreader is bullish or bearish.

Stock split/dividend An increase in the number of shares issued to each shareholder by the corporation. A 2–1 stock split means that an owner of 100 shares of a particular stock will have 200 shares after the split, with the stock price being cut in half. A stock dividend occurs when the additional stock received is less than a 25% increase in the number of shares currently owned.

Swaption An option on a swap.

***Sycurve option** An option on the slope of the yield curve.

Synthetic call A combination of instruments that acts like a call option.

Synthetic put   A combination of instruments that acts like a put option.

Systematic risk   The risk associated with market movements. This risk cannot be reduced by diversification.

*****Theta**   The change in the option price for a given change in the time until expiration of the option.

Time to expiration factor   As the time until the expiration of the option becomes shorter, the price and time value of the option become smaller (everything else held constant); this relationship is called "time decay."

*****Time value**   The difference between the option price and the intrinsic value. The size of this difference depends on the time until option expiration, the difference between the stock price and the strike price, and the volatility of the stock.

Two-color rainbow option   An option in which the payoff is based on two underlying asset prices.

Unsystematic risk   The risk associated with the individual stock and industry factors. This risk is reduced substantially by diversifying the portfolio with the purchase of additional stocks of other companies.

Up-and-out put option   An option that becomes worthless if the cash asset price reaches or goes above a threshold price.

Up-and-in put option   An option that activates only if the cash price reaches or crosses a threshold.

*****Vega**   The change in the option price for a given change in the volatility of the stock (also known as kappa).

*****Volatility factor**   The greater the volatility of the underlying stock, the larger the time value and, therefore, the greater the option price.

*****Writer**   The seller of an option.

Bibliography

Alderson, Michael J., and Terry L. Zivney (1989). "Optimal Cross-Hedge Portfolios for Hedging Stock Index Options," *Journal of Futures Markets,* Vol. 9, No. 1, February, pp. 67-76.

Bailey, W. (1987). "An Empirical Investigation of the Market for Comex Gold Futures Options," *Journal of Finance,* Vol. 42, No. 5, December, pp. 1187-1194.

Barone-Adesi, G., and Robert Whaley (1987). "Efficient Analytic Approximation of American Option Values," *Journal of Finance,* Vol. 42, No. 2, June, pp. 301-320.

Bates, David (1991). "The Crash of '87: Was It Expected? The Evidence from Options Markets," *Journal of Finance,* Vol. 46, No. 3, July, pp. 1009-1044.

Beckers, S. (1981). "Standard Deviations Implied in Option Prices as Predictors of Future Stock Price Variability," *Journal of Banking and Finance,* Vol. 5, No. 3, September, pp. 363-382.

Bhattacharya, Mihir (1983). "Transactions Data Tests of Efficiency of the Chicago Board Options Exchange," *Journal of Financial Economics,* Vol. 12, No. 2, August, pp. 161-185.

Black, Fischer (1975). "Fact and Fantasy in the Use of Options," *Financial Analysts Journal,* Vol. 31, No. 4, July-August 1975, pp. 36-41 and 61-72.

Black, Fischer (1989). "How We Came Up With the Option Formula," *Journal of Portfolio Management,* Vol. 15, No. 2, Winter, pp. 4-8.

Black, Fischer (1976). "The Pricing of Commodity Contracts," *Journal of Financial Economics,* Vol. 3, No. 1-2, January-March, pp. 167-179.

Black, Fischer, and Myron Scholes (1972). "The Valuation of Option Contracts and a Test of Market Efficiency," *Journal of Finance,* Vol. 27, No. 2, May, pp. 399-418.

Black, Fisher, and Myron Scholes (1973). "The Pricing of Options and Corporate Liabilities," *Journal of Political Economy,* Vol. 81, No. 3, May/June, pp. 637-654.

Black, Fisher, and Myron Scholes (1972). "The Valuation of Option Contracts and a Test of Market Efficiency," *Journal of Finance,* Vol. 27, No. 2, May, pp. 399-418.

Blomeyer, Edward C., and James C. Boyd (1988). "Empirical Tests of Boundary Conditions for Options on Treasury Bond Futures," *The Journal of Futures Markets,* Vol. 8, No. 2, April, pp. 185-198.

Blomeyer, Edward C., and Herb Johnson (1988). "An Empirical Examination of the Pricing of American Put Options," *Journal of Financial and Quantitative Analysis,* Vol. 23, No. 1, March, pp. 13-22.

Blomeyer, Edward C., and Robert C. Klemkosky (1983). "Tests of Market Efficiency of American Call Options," in *Option Pricing,* ed. Menachem Brenner. Lexington Ma.: Heath.

Brennan, Michael J., and Eduardo S. Schwartz (1977). "The Valuation of American Put Options," *Journal of Finance,* Vol. 32, No. 2, May, pp. 449-462.

Brenner, M., G. Courtadon, and M. Subrahmanyam (1985). "Options on the Spot and Options on Futures," *Journal of Finance,* Vol 40, No. 5, December, pp. 1303-1317.

Brenner, Menachem, and Marti G. Subrahmanyam (1988). "A Simple Formula to Compute the Implied Volatility," *Financial Analysts Journal,* Vol. 45, No. 5, September-October, pp. 80-83.

Brooks, Robert (1991). "Analyzing Portfolios with Derivative Assets: A Stochastic Dominance Approach Using Numerical Integration," *Journal of Futures Markets,* Vol. 11, No. 4, August, pp. 411-440.

Brophy, Daniel F. (1984). "Commercial Use of Options," *Review of Futures Markets,* Vol. 3, No. 2, pp. 174-180.

Chiras, Donald P., and Steven Manaster (1978). "The Information Content of Option Prices and a Test of Market Efficiency," *Journal of Financial Economics,* Vol. 6, No. 2/3, June-September, pp. 213-234.

Cootner, John S., and James F. Horrell (1989). "An Analysis of Index Option Pricing," *Journal of Futures Markets,* Vol. 9, No. 5, October, pp. 449-459.

Cox, John (1975). "Notes on Option Pricing I: Constant Elasticity of Variance Diffusions." Working Paper, Stanford University.

Cox, John C,. and Stephen A. Ross (1976). "The Valuation of Options for Alternative Stochastic Processes," *Journal of Financial Economics,* Vol. 3, No. 1/2, January-March, pp. 145-166.

Cox, John C., Stephen A. Ross, and Mark Rubinstein (1979). "Options Pricing: A Simplified Approach," *Journal of Financial Economics,* Vol. 7, No. 3, September, pp. 229-264.

Cox, John C., and Mark Rubinstein (1985). *Options Markets.* Englewood Cliffs, N.J.: Prentice-Hall, Inc.

Daigler, Robert T. (1993). *Managing Risk with Financial Futures: Pricing, Hedging and Arbitrage.* Chicago: Probus Publishing.

Dawson, Paul, and Gordon Gemmill (1990). "Returns to Market Making on the London Traded Options Market," *Review of Futures Markets,* Vol. 9, No. 3, pp. 666-680.

DeRonne, William A. (1985). "Pension Funds and Futures Markets: Option Hedging of Fixed-Rate Assets," *Review of Futures Markets,* Vol. 4, No. 2, pp. 232-241.

Evnine, Jeremy, and Andrew Rudd (1985). "Index Options: The Early Evidence," *Journal of Finance,* Vol. 40, No. 3, July, pp. 743-756.

Fedenia, Mark, and Theoharry Grammatikos (1992). "Options Trading and the Bid-Ask Spread of the Underlying Stocks," *Journal of Business,* Vol. 65, No. 3, July, pp. 335-351.

French, Dan W., and Edwin D. Maberly (1992). "Early Exercise of American Index Options," *Journal of Financial Research,* Vol. 15, No. 2, Summer, pp. 127-137.

Galai, Dan (1977). "Tests of Market Efficiency on the Chicago Board Options Exchange," *The Journal of Business,* Vol. 50, No. 2, April, pp. 167-195.

Garman, Mark B., and Michael J. Klass (1980). "On the Estimation of Security Price Volatilities from Historical Data," *Journal of Business,* Vol. 53, No. 1, January, pp. 67-78.

Garman, Mark B., and Steven W. Kohlhagen (1983). "Foreign Currency Option Values," *Journal of International Money and Finance,* Vol. 2, No. 3, December, pp. 231-237.

Gastineau, Gary L. (1979). *The Stock Options Manual,* 2d Ed. New York: McGraw-Hill.

Gastineau, Gary L., and Albert Madansky (1979). "Why Simulations Are an Unreliable Test of Option Strategies," *Financial Analysts Journal,* Vol. 35, No. 5, September-October 1979, pp. 61-76.

Gay, Gerald D., Robert W. Kolb, and Kenneth Yung (1989). "Trader Rationality in the Exercise of Futures Option Positions," *Journal of Financial Economics,* Vol. 23, No.2, August, pp. 339-362.

Geske, Robert (1979). "A Note on an Analytic Formula for Unprotected American Call Options on Stocks with Known Dividends," *Journal of Financial Economics,* Vol. 7, No. 4, December, pp. 375-380.

Geske, Robert, and Herb Johnson (1984). "The American Put Option Valued Analytically," *Journal of Finance,* Vol. 39, No. 5, December, pp. 1511-1524.

Gombola, Michael J., Rodney L. Roenfeldt, and Philip L. Cooley (1978). "Spreading Strategies in CBOE Options: Evidence on Market Performance," *Journal of Financial Research,* Vol. 1, No. 1, Winter, pp. 35-44.

Grabbe, J. Orlin (1983). "The Pricing of Call and Put Options on Foreign Exchange," *Journal of International Money and Finance,* Vol. 2, No. 3, December, pp. 239-253.

Grabbe, J. Orlin (1991). *International Financial Markets,* 2d ed. New York: Elsevier.

Grube, R. Corwin, Don B. Panton, and J. Michael Terrell (1979). "Risks and Rewards in Covered Call Positions," *Journal of Portfolio Management,* Vol. 5, No. 2, Winter 1979, pp. 64-68.

Harvey, Campbell R., and Robert E. Whaley (1992). "Dividends and S&P 100 Index Option Valuation," *Journal of Futures Markets,* Vol. 12, No. 2, April, pp. 123-137.

Harvey, Campbell R., and Robert E. Whaley (1992). "Market Volatility Prediction and the Efficiency of the S&P 100 Index Option Market," *Journal of Financial Economics,* Vol. 31, No. 1, February, pp. 43-74.

Huang, Espen Gaarder (1993). "Opportunities and Perils of Using Option Sensitivities," *Journal of Financial Engineering,* Vol. 2, No. 2, September.

Jameson, Mel, and William Wilhelm (1992). "Market Making in the Options Markets and the Costs of Discrete Hedge Rebalancing," *Journal of Finance,* Vol. 47, No. 2, June, pp. 765-779.

Jarrow, Robert A., and Andrew Rudd (1983). *Option Pricing.* Homewood, Il: Irwin.

Jordan, James V., W. Seale, N. McCabe, and D. Kenyon (1987). "Transactions Data Tests of the Black Model for Soybean Futures Options," *The Journal of Futures Markets,* Vol. 7, No. 5, October, pp. 535-554.

Jordan, James V., and William E. Seale (1986). "Transactions Data Tests of Minimum Prices and Put-Call Parity for Treasury Bond Futures Options," *Advances in Futures and Options Research,* Vol. 1, Part A, pp. 63-87.

Klemkosky, Robert C., and Bruce G. Resnick (1980). "An Ex-Ante Analysis of Put-Call Parity," *Journal of Financial Economics,* Vol. 8, No. 4, December, pp. 363-378.

Klemkosky, Robert C., and Bruce G. Resnick (1979). "Put-Call Parity and Market Efficiency," *Journal of Finance,* Vol. 34, No. 5, December, pp. 1141-1156.

Kumar, Ramon, Atulya Sarin, and Kuldeep Shastri (1992). "The Behavior of Option Price Around Large Block Transactions in the Underlying Security," *Journal of Finance,* Vol. 47, No. 3, July, pp. 879-889.

Kutner, George W. (1988) "Black-Scholes Revisited: Some Important Details," *Financial Review,* Vol. 23, No. 1, February, pp. 95-104.

Latane, Henry, and Richard Rendleman (1976). "Standard Deviations of Stock Price Ratios Implied in Option Prices," *Journal of Finance,* Vol. 31, No. 2, May, pp. 369-381.

Marshall, John, and Vipul Bansal (1993). *Financial Engineering,* 2d ed. Miami: Kolb Publishing.

Marshall, John F., and Kenneth R. Kapner (1993). *The Swaps Market,* 2d ed. Miami: Kolb Publishing.

MacBeth, James D., and Larry J. Merville (1979). "An Empirical Examination of the Black-Scholes Call Option Pricing Model," *Journal of Finance,* Vol. 34, No. 5, December, pp. 1173-1186.

MacBeth, James D., and Larry J. Merville (1980). "Tests of the Black-Scholes and Cox Call Option Valuation Models," *Journal of Finance,* Vol. 35, No. 2, May, pp. 285-300.

Merton, Robert (1976). "Option Pricing When Underlying Stock Returns are Discontinuous," *Journal of Financial Economics,* Vol. 3, No. 1/2, January-March, pp. 125-144.

Merton, Robert C. (1973). "The Theory of Rational Option Pricing," *Bell Journal of Economics and Management Science,* Spring, Vol. 4, No. 1, pp. 141-183.

Merton, Robert C., Myron S. Scholes, and Mathew L. Gladstein (1978). "The Returns and Risk of Alternative Call Option Portfolio Investment Strategies," *Journal of Business,* Vol. 51, No. 2, April, pp. 183-242.

Merton, Robert C., Myron S. Scholes, and Mathew L. Gladstein (1982). "The Returns and Risk of Alternative Put Option Portfolio Investment Strategies," *Journal of Business,* Vol. 55, No. 1, January, pp. 1-56.

Merville, Larry J., and James A. Overdahl (1986). "An Empirical Examination of the T-bond Futures (Call) Options Markets under Conditions of Constant and Changing Variance Rates," *Advances in Futures and Options Research,* Vol. 1, Part A, pp. 898-918.

"Options on U.S. Treasury Bond Futures for Institutional Investors," Chicago Board of Trade, booklet, no date.

Parkinson, Michael (1977). "Option Pricing: The American Put," *Journal of Business,* Vol. 50, No. 1, January, pp. 21-36.

Pounds, Henry M. (1978). "Covered Call Option Writing: Strategies and Results," *The Journal of Portfolio Management,* Vol. 4, No. 2, Winter, pp. 31-42.

Ritchken, Peter (1987). *Options: Theory, Strategy, and Applications.* Glenview, Il: Scott, Foresman.

Roenfeldt, Rodney L., Philip L. Cooley, and Michael J. Gombola (1979). "Market Performance of Options on the Chicago Board Options Exchange," *Journal of Business Research,* Vol. 7, pp. 95-107.

Roll, Richard (1977). "An Analytic Valuation Formula for Unprotected American Call Options on Stocks with Known Dividends," *Journal of Financial Economics,* Vol. 5, No. 2, November, pp. 251-258.

Rubinstein, Mark (1991). "Classnotes," The University of California at Berkeley.

Rubinstein, Mark (1985). "Nonparametric Tests of Alternative Option Pricing Models Using All Reported Trades and Quotes on the 30 Most Active CBOE Option Classes from August 23, 1976 Through August 31, 1978," *Journal of Finance,* Vol. 40, No. 2, June, pp. 455-480.

Rubinstein, Mark, and Gerard Gennotte (1992). *Options and Futures Trading Simulator,* Version 2.0.

Rutz, Roger (1988). "Clearance, Payment and Settlement Systems in the Futures, Options, and Stock Markets," *Review of Futures Markets,* Vol. 7, No. 3, pp. 346-370.

Shastri, Kuldeep, and Kishore Tandon (1986). "On the Use of European Models to Price American Options on Foreign Currency," *Journal of Financial Research,* Vol. 8, No. 4, Winter, pp. 275-285.

Sheikh, Aamir M. (1991). "Transaction Data Tests of S&P 100 Call Option Pricing," *Journal of Financial and Quantitative Analysis,* Vol. 26, No. 4, December, pp. 459-475.

Stephan, Jens A., and Robert E. Whaley (1990). "Intraday Price Change and Trading Volume Relations in the Stock and Options Markets," *Journal of Finance,* Vol. 45, No. 1, March, pp. 191-220.

Sterk, William (1983a). "Comparative Performance of the Black-Scholes and Roll-Geske-Whaley Option Pricing Models," *Journal of Financial and Quantitative Analysis,* Vol. 18, No. 3, September, pp. 345-354.

Sterk, William (1983b). "Option Pricing and the In- and Out-of-the-Money Bias," *Financial Management,* Vol. 12, No. 4, Winter, pp. 47-53.

Sterk, William (1982). "Tests of Two Models for Valuing Call Options on Stocks with Dividends," *Journal of Finance,* Vol. 37, No. 5, December, pp. 88-99.

Szala, Ginger (1988). "Fischer Black, Myron Scholes," *Futures,* pp. 8-9.

Trennepohl, Gary L., and William P. Dukes (1979). "Return and Risk from Listed Option Investments," *Journal of Financial Research,* Spring, Vol. 2, No. 1, pp. 37-49.

"Using S&P 500 Stock Index Options and Futures," (1987). Chicago Mercantile Exchange, booklet.

Whaley, Robert E. (1981). "On the Valuation of American Call Options on Stocks with Known Dividends," *Journal of Financial Economics,* Vol. 9, No. 2, June, pp. 207-211.

Whaley, Robert E. (1982). "Valuation of American Call Options on Dividend Paying Stocks: Empirical Tests," *Journal of Financial Economics,* Vol. 10, No. 1, March, pp. 29-58.

Whaley, Robert E. (1986). "Valuation of American Futures Options: Theory and Empirical Tests," *Journal of Finance,* Vol. 41, No. 1, March, pp. 127-150.

CREDITS

Examples, Exhibits, and Tables

Chapter 2

Table 2-2 and Exhibits 2A-1 and 2B-1, Copied by permission of Mark Rubinstein from "Classnotes, University of California, Berkeley," 1991.

Chapter 3

Tables 3-1, 3-2, 3A-1, and 3A-2 and Exhibits 3-2 and 3-3, Copied by permission of Mark Rubinstein from "Classnotes, University of California, Berkeley," 1991./ Focus 3-1, Created by permission of Mark Rubinstein from The Options and Futures Trading Simulator, Version 2.0, by Mark Rubinstein and Gerald Gennotte, copyright 1992. / Table 3-3 and Focus 3-2, Created by permission of OptionVue Systems International from OptionVue IV.

Chapter 4

Tables 4-1, 4-2, 4-3, 4-4, 4-5, 4-6, and 4-7 and Focus 4-2, Created by permission of OptionVue Systems International from OptionVue IV.

Chapter 5

Exhibit 5-1, Created by permission of Mark Rubinstein from The Options and Futures Trading Simulator, Version 2.0, by Mark Rubinstein and Gerald Gennotte, copyright 1992./ Exhibits 5-2, 5-3, and 5-4, Created by permission of OptionVue Systems International from OptionVue IV./ Table 5-1, Robert C. Merton, Myron S. Scholes, and Mathew L. Gladstein, "The Returns and Risk of Alternative Call Option Portfolio Investment Strategies," *The Journal of Business*, Vol. 51, No. 2, April 1978, p. 219. Reprinted by permission of The University of Chicago Press./ Exhibits 5-8 and 5-9, *Futures and Options Strategy Guide*, p. 1, 11. The Chicago Mercantile Exchange.

Chapter 6

Exhibits 6-1 and 6-2, Created by permission of OptionVue Systems International from OptionVue IV./ Table 6-1, Robert C. Merton, Myron S. Scholes, and Mathew L. Gladstein, "The Returns and Risk of Alternative Call Option Portfolio Investment Strategies," *The Journal of Business*, Vol. 51, No. 2, April 1978, p. 207. Reprinted by permission of The University of Chicago Press./ Table 6-2, Used by permission of William T. Mullen, Loomis, Sayles & Co.

Chapter 7

Table 7-1, M. Brenner, G. Courtadon, and M. Subrahmanyam, "Options on the Spot and Options on Futures," *The Journal of Finance*, Vol 40, No. 5, December 1985, pp. 1303-1317. Reprinted by permission of *The Journal of Finance*./ Table 7-2, G. Barone-Adesi and Robert Whaley, "Efficient Analytic Approximation of American Option Values," *The Journal of Finance*, Vol. 42, No. 2, June 1987, pp. 301-320. Reprinted by permission of *The Journal of Finance*./ Table 7-3, Robert Whaley, "Valuation of American Futures Options: Theory and Empirical Tests," *The Journal of Finance*, Vol. 41, No. 1, March 1986, pp. 127-150. Reprinted by permission of *The Journal of Finance*./ Exhibit 7-6, "Options on U.S. Treasury Bond Futures for Institutional Investors," pp. 9-13. Copyright © Board of Trade of the City of Chicago.

Chapter 8

Table 8-1, Created by permission of OptionVue Systems International from OptionVue IV./ Focus 8-1, Created by permission of Mark Rubinstein from The Options and Futures Trading Simulator, Version 2.0, by Mark Rubinstein and Gerald Gennotte, copyright 1992.

Chapter 9

Table 9-1, Copied by permission of Mark Rubinstein from "Classnotes, University of California, Berkeley," 1991.

Figures

Chapter 2
Figure 2-3, Created by permission of Mark Rubinstein from The Options and Futures Trading Simulator, Version 2.0, by Mark Rubinstein and Gerald Gennotte, copyright 1992./ Figure 2-4, Copied by permission of Mark Rubinstein from "Classnotes, University of California, Berkeley," 1991.

Chapter 3
Figures 3-3 and 3-4, Created by permission of OptionVue Systems International from OptionVue IV.

Chapter 4
Figures 4-1, 4-2, 4-3, 4-4, 4-5, 4-6, 4-7, 4-8, 4-9, 4-10, 4-11, 4-12, 4-14, 4-15, Created by permission of Mark Rubinstein from The Options and Futures Trading Simulator, Version 2.0, by Mark Rubinstein and Gerald Gennotte, copyright 1992./ Figure 4-13, Espen Gaardner Haug, "Opportunities and Perils of Using Option Sensitivities," *The Journal of Financial Engineering,* Vol.2 No. 2, September 1993.

Chapter 5
Figure 5-1, Copied by permission of Mark Rubinstein from "Classnotes, University of California, Berkeley," 1991./ Figures 5-2, 5-3, 5-4, 5-5, 5-9, 5-11, 5-13, 5-17, 5-18, Created by permission of Mark Rubinstein from The Options and Futures Trading Simulator, Version 2.0, by Mark Rubinstein and Gerald Gennotte, copyright 1992.

Chapter 6
Figures 6-3 and 6-8, Copied by permission of Mark Rubinstein from "Classnotes, University of California, Berkeley," 1991.

Chapter 7
Figures 7-1 and 7-2, Created by permission of OptionVue Systems International from the background database of OptionVue IV.

Chapter 8
Figure 8-1, Created by permission of OptionVue Systems International from the background database of OptionVue IV.

Chapter 9
Figures 9-6, 9-7, 9-8, and 9-9, Created by permission of Mark Rubinstein from The Options and Futures Trading Simulator, Version 2.0, by Mark Rubinstein and Gerald Gennotte, copyright 1992.

Index

PERSONAL COMPUTER MODELS FOR OPTIONS AND FUTURES

PC models for options are available from the author that provide the following:

- Determine the fair price of stock options, currency options, and options on futures

- Determine the option sensitivities

- Show the payoff diagrams for most of the option strategies discussed in this book

- Shows a three period binomial approach to option pricing

- Determines the put-call parity relationship

The user inputs the relevant information about the option into the model and the PC program provides the results. Therefore, these PC models are very useful to help the user understand the mechanics and uses of options markets, as well as provide the desired results. Those wishing a real time computer trading program, or a program which provides an analysis of alternative option choices, should examine the OptionVue IV program discussed in the text (costing approximately $900).

Estimated cost of the package of PC programs is $75. Those interested in additional information should contact the author at:

Dr. Robert T. Daigler
Department of Finance
College of Business
Florida International University
Miami, Florida 33199

or Fax 305-348-4245

Please allow one to two weeks for delivery.

PC models now are also available for futures markets (see the companion book *Managing Risk with Financial Futures*). Contact the author at the above address/fax number for additional information.